The Oracle8i™ DBA: SQL and PL/SQL Cram Sheet

This Cram Sheet contains the distilled, key facts about Oracle8i in the area of SQL and PL/SQL. Review this information last thing before you enter the test room, paying special attention to those areas where you feel you need the most review. You can transfer any of these facts from memory onto a blank sheet of paper before beginning the exam.

SQL COMMANDS

1. SQL consists of DDL, DCL, and DML statements.

2. DDL (Data Definition Language) consists of commands used to define or alter database internal structures such as tables, views, indexes, and so on. DDL commands include **CREATE**, **ALTER**, **DROP**, and **TRUNCATE**.

3. DCL (Data Control Language) consists of commands used to control data access, such as the several forms of the **GRANT** command. This can also refer to database control language elements such as **STARTUP**, **SHUTDOWN**, **ALTER SYSTEM**, etc.

4. DML (Data Manipulation Language) consists of commands used to populate or alter database data contents. DML commands include **INSERT**, **UPDATE**, **DELETE**, and **SELECT**.

5. SQL has intrinsic functions that allow for data type conversion and data manipulation.

6. SQL has operators that define operations between values and expressions.

7. **SELECT** statements make use of joins, which can be one of the following types:

   - *Equijoins*—State equality or inequality operations

   - *Outer joins*—Used when one of the tables is deficient in data to complete the specified relationship

   - *Self-joins*—Used when a table is joined to itself by use of table aliases

8. SQL supports **SORT**, **COLLECTION**, and **SET** operations.

PRECEDENCE OF OPERATORS

9. The precedence of operators is as follows:

   - *(+) and (–)*—Unary operators (positive and negative number indicators) and the **PRIOR** operators

   - *(*) and (/)*—Multiplication and division operators

   - *Binary (=)*—Arithmetic operators (such as addition "+" and subtraction "–") and the concatenation operator (‖)

   - *All comparison operators*—Includes the **NOT**, **AND**, and **OR** logical operators.

10. Parentheses always override precedence. Operators inside parentheses are always evaluated first.

FUNCTIONS

11. Functions are either scalar (single row) or aggregate (group) in nature. A single-row function returns a single result row for each

40. Roles are used to group a collection of privileges, roles, and grants that can then be granted en masse to a user or another role.

41. Grants and privileges are given at the system, table, or column level.

42. Special roles such as **OSOPER**, **OSDBA**, **CONNECT**, **RESOURCE**, and **DBA** are automatically created:

- **OSOPER**—Grants all rights except the ability to create a database.
- **OSDBA**—Grants **OSOPER** and the right to create databases.
- **CONNECT**—Grants a basic set of privileges.
- **RESOURCE**—Grants a set of privileges that specifically apply to a developer.
- **DBA**—Grants almost unlimited rights that a DBA would use.

DATABASE DESIGN

3. The five-step system development cycle consists of the following:

1. *Strategy and analysis*—Users are interviewed and requirements are generated. Design documents are written. Entities, attributes, and relationships are identified as well as relationships.

2. *Design*—The actual system is designed in detail. Entity relationship diagrams (ERDs), function decompositions, and data flow diagrams are created. In object-oriented design, Universal Modeling Language (UML) diagrams may be used instead of ERDs.

3. *Build and document*—The system is built mapping the ERD to tables and columns (or objects) and relationships to primary key and foreign key relationships (or **REF** values). The function decompositions and data flows are used to create forms, reports, and other application modules.

4. *Transition*—The system is moved from development into production. During this period, user acceptance testing is performed, and final documentation is generated.

5. *Production*—The system is placed into production, code is locked down, and a firm change control process is implemented. This is the final stage.

44. Entities (or objects) can be either parent, child, dependent, or independent. An entity (or object) is a thing of importance.

45. Relationships (or **REF**s) are named associations between things of significance and have cardinality and optionality. Relationships can be one-to-one, one-to-many, or even many-to-many, although most should be either required or optional one-to-manys. A **REF** can be only a one-one relationship from child back to parent record.

46. Normalization is the process where repeating values (attributes) are removed from an entity until all attributes in the entity relate only to the entity's unique identifier. The most common form of normalization is third normal form.

18. The things you can't do with the **ALTER TABLE** command include the following:
    - Modify a column that has values to be shorter or to be a different data type than it already is.
    - Add a **NOT NULL** column to a table that has rows in a single step operation with only the **ALTER TABLE** command.
    - Alter a column to **NOT NULL** if it has rows with null values in that column.
    - Rename a column.
    - Change a column's data type to an incompatible data type.

DATA DICTIONARY

19. At its lowest level, the data dictionary consists of **X$** and **K$** C structs, not normally viewable or used by DBA.

20. The data dictionary has **V$** virtual views or tables, which contain variable data such as statistics.

21. The data dictionary has dollar ($) tables, which actually contain database metadata about tables, views, indexes, and other database structures.

22. At the uppermost layer, the data dictionary has **DBA_** views about all objects, **ALL_** views about all objects a user can access, and **USER_** views about all objects a user owns.

PL/SQL

23. PL/SQL consists of the PL/SQL engine, which can be incorporated in the forms, SQL*Plus, or reports executables. The PL/SQL engine processes procedural statements and passes the SQL statements to the SQL processor.

24. A PL/SQL procedure may return one or more values. It is used to perform many functions, such as table input, table output, and value processing.

25. A PL/SQL function must return one and only one value and cannot be used to perform input and output. A function should be used only to manipulate existing data; this ties in with the concept of function purity.

26. A procedure consists of header, declarative, and executable (which may contain an exception handling block) sections.

27. An anonymous PL/SQL block is an externally stored PL/SQL block that is not named and contains at a minimum an executable block. It may, however, contain a declarative and executable (with or without exception handling block) section. An anonymous PL/SQL block can be called from any Oracle environment. An anonymous PL/SQL block is used to form the heart of table triggers.

28. To process **SELECT** commands, PL/SQL uses either an explicit cursor (which usually returns more than one row) or an implicit cursor (which can return only one row or an exception will be raised). Explicit cursors must be defined, **OPEN**ed, **FETCH**ed from, and **CLOSE**d unless they are used in a **CURSOR FOR LOOP**.

29. Flow control in PL/SQL uses loops, which can be counted **FOR** loops, conditional **WHILE** loops, or conditional infinite loops.

30. Conditional flow control uses the **IF...THEN...ELSE** construct in PL/SQL.

31. Multiple **IF** constructs can be nested using the **IF...ELSIF** construct.

32. The **GOTO** is used for unconditional branching in PL/SQL.

33. The **NULL** command is a special command in PL/SQL used to fulfill the requirement for a flow control command to be followed by an executable command. Although **NULL** is an executable command, it does nothing.

34. SQL in the form of DML can be used in PL/SQL. Generally speaking, without using specially provided procedure packages, DDL cannot be used in PL/SQL.

35. **COMMIT** is used in PL/SQL to commit changed data explicitly.

36. **ROLLBACK** is used in PL/SQL to return altered data to its previous state.

USERS AND GRANTS

37. Users can be created, altered, and dropped using the **CREATE**, **ALTER**, and **DROP** commands.

38. Users are granted profiles, roles, and privileges

39. Profiles are used to limit resource usage and can be used to enforce password limitations.

row of a queried table or view, whereas an aggregate function returns a single value for a group of rows.

12. A single-value function can appear in a **SELECT** if the **SELECT** doesn't contain a **GROUP BY** clause. Single-value functions can also appear in **WHERE**, **START WITH**, and **CONNECT BY** clauses. Single-row functions can also be nested.

LIMITS ON A VIEW

13. A view can't be updated if:
   - It has a join.
   - It uses a **SET** operator.
   - It contains a **GROUP BY** clause.
   - It uses any group function.
   - It uses a **DISTINCT** operator.
   - It has flattened subqueries.
   - It uses nested table columns.
   - It uses **CAST** and **MULTISET** expressions.

DELETE AND TRUNCATE COMMANDS

14. The **DELETE** command is used to remove some or all rows from a table allowing **ROLLBACK** of the command if no **COMMIT** is executed.

15. The **TRUNCATE** command is used to remove all rows from a table, and no **ROLLBACK** is allowed.

OUTER JOINS

16. The restrictions on outer joins are as follows:
   - The (+) operator can appear only in the **WHERE** clause and can apply only to a table or view.
   - If there are multiple join conditions, the (+) operator must be used in all of these conditions.
   - The (+) operator can be applied to a column only, not to an expression. However, it can be applied to a column inside an arbitrary expression.
   - A condition containing a column with a (+) cannot be **OR** related to another condition; neither can it be used in an **IN** condition.

- A column marked with the (+) operator cannot be compared to a subquery.
- Only one table in a multitable join can have the (+) operator applied to its joins to one other table.

THE ALTER TABLE COMMAND

17. The following are things you can do with the **ALTER TABLE** command:
   - Use the **ADD** clause to add columns that have null values to any table.
   - Use the **MODIFY** clause to increase the size of columns or to change the precision of numeric columns.
   - Use the **MODIFY** clause to change columns with all null values so that the columns are shorter or have a different data type.
   - Alter the **PCTFREE**, **PCTUSED**, **INITRANS**, or **MAXTRANS** values for any table.
   - Use the **STORAGE** clause to alter the storage parameters for any table.
   - Use the **PARALLEL** clause to change or remove the parallelism of a table.
   - Use **CACHE** or **NOCACHE** to specify whether a table is to be cached or not.
   - Use the **DROP** clause to remove a constraint or a column.
   - Use the **DEFAULT** value clause to add a default value to any column.
   - Use the **DISABLE** clause to disable a constraint. (This is the only way to disable a constraint.) When the **CASCADE** option is specified with **DISABLE**, it also disables all dependent integrity constraints.
   - Use the **DEALLOCATE UNUSED** clause to deallocate space that is not being used. (You can use the **KEEP** option to specify a safety margin above the high-water mark.)
   - Use the **ENABLE** clause to enable a constraint that was created as disabled. (The **ENABLE** clause can be used only in **CREATE** and **ALTER TABLE** commands.)
   - Use the **ADD CONSTRAINT** clause to add a primary, not null, check, or foreign key constraint to an existing table.
   - Use the **SET** command to mark a column as unused.

Oracle8i™ DBA: SQL and PL/SQL

Michael R. Ault

Oracle8i™ DBA: SQL and PL/SQL Exam Cram

Limits of Liability and Disclaimer of Warranty

Trademarks

The Coriolis Group, LLC
14455 N. Hayden Road
Suite 220
Scottsdale, Arizona 85260

(480)483-0192
FAX (480)483-0193
www.coriolis.com

Library of Congress Cataloging-in-Publication Data
Ault, Michael R
     Oracle 8i DBA : SQL and PL/SQL exam cram / Michael R. Ault.
         p. cm. -- (Exam Cram)
     Includes bibliographical references and index.
     ISBN 1-57610-037-7
     1. Electronic data processing personnel--Certification. 2. Database management--Examinations--Study guides. 3. SQL (Computer program language) 4. Oracle (Computer file) I. Title. II. Series.
QA76.3 .A96   2001
005.75'85--dc21
                                                  2001032385
                                                  CIP

Publisher
Steve Sayre

Acquisitions Editor
Sharon Linsenbach

Product Marketing Manager
Susan Hughes

Project Editor
Marcus Huff

Technical Reviewer
Charles Pack

Production Coordinator
Todd Halvorsen

Cover Designer
Laura Wellander

Layout Designer
April Nielsen

Printed in the United States of America
10 9 8 7 6 5 4 3 2 1

⑨ CORIOLIS™

The Coriolis Group, LLC • 14455 North Hayden Road, Suite 220 • Scottsdale, Arizona 85260

A Note from Coriolis

Our goal has always been to provide you with the best study tools on the planet to help you achieve your certification in record time. Time is so valuable these days that none of us can afford to waste a second of it, especially when it comes to exam preparation.

Over the past few years, we've created an extensive line of *Exam Cram* and *Exam Prep* study guides, practice exams, and interactive training. To help you study even better, we have now created an e-learning and certification destination called **ExamCram.com**. (You can access the site at **www.examcram.com**.) Now, with every study product you purchase from us, you'll be connected to a large community of people like yourself who are actively studying for their certifications, developing their careers, seeking advice, and sharing their insights and stories.

We believe that the future is all about collaborative learning. Our **ExamCram.com** destination is our approach to creating a highly interactive, easily accessible collaborative environment, where you can take practice exams and discuss your experiences with others, sign up for features like "Questions of the Day," plan your certifications using our interactive planners, create your own personal study pages, and keep up with all of the latest study tips and techniques.

We hope that whatever study products you purchase from us—*Exam Cram* or *Exam Prep* study guides, *Personal Trainers, Personal Test Centers,* or one of our interactive Web courses—will make your studying fun and productive. Our commitment is to build the kind of learning tools that will allow you to study the way you want to, whenever you want to.

Visit ExamCram.com now to enhance your study program.

Help us continue to provide the very best certification study materials possible. Write us or email us at **learn@examcram.com** and let us know how our study products have helped you study. Tell us about new features that you'd like us to add. Send us a story about how we've helped you. We're listening!

Good luck with your certification exam and your career. Thank you for allowing us to help you achieve your goals.

ExamCram.com Connects You to the Ultimate Study Center!

Look for these other products from The Coriolis Group:

Oracle8i DBA: Backup and Recovery Exam Cram
by Debbie Wong

Oracle8i DBA: Performance and Tuning Exam Cram
by Zulfiqer Habeeb

Oracle8i DBA: Network Administration Exam Cram
by Barbara Ann Pascavage

Oracle8i DBA: Architecture and Administration Exam Cram
by Peter Sharman

Java 2 Exam Cram, Second Edition
by Bill Brogden

MCSE SQL 2000 Administration Exam Cram
by Kalani Kirk Hausman

This third revision I dedicate primarily to the love of my life, Susan.
I would also like to dedicate this to my daughters
and to my future son-in-law, Mike Bojczuk.
As with my other works, this is also dedicated to God,
who gave me the abilities that allowed the creation of this book.

About the Author

Mikhael R. Ault has spent the last 22 years working at least part time with computers and the last sixteen years working with relational database management systems (RDBMSs). Prior to that, he spent six years in the U.S. Navy on nuclear submarines. He started his work with RDBMSs on Informix in 1985 and then worked with INGRES for four years and with Oracle for the last twelve years.

Mike has a BS in Computer Science and five Oracle Master Certificates, including the performance–based Oracle Version 6 Database Administrator Master Certificate. Mike has been certified in all levels of the OCP program for DBAs through Oracle8i. In all, Mike has over 450 hours of classroom training in Oracle to go with his twelve years of hands-on experience.

Mike is the author of *ORACLE7.0 Administration and Management, Oracle8.0 Administration and Management, ORACLE8i Administration and Management,* and *UNIX System Administrator's Companion* from John Wiley and Sons, and *Oracle8 Black Book, Oracle7 DBA Exam Cram: Test 1 and Test 2, Oracle7 DBA Exam Cram: Test 3 and Test 4* (with B. Pascavage, M. Bearard, and P. Collins), *Oracle8 DBA: SQL and PL/SQL Exam Cram* and *Oracle8 DBA: Performance and Tuning Exam Cram* (with J. Brinson), from The Coriolis Group. He is also sole author of the *Oracle8i Database Administration Workshop* for ElementK (formally Ziff-Davis Education).

Mike is a frequent contributor to *ORACLE, Oracle Internals,* and *DBMS* magazines and is a frequently top-rated presenter at Oracle Open World conferences and at IOUG-A conferences, as well as ECO, SEOUG, SCOUG, and EOUG. He has worked in the nuclear, aerospace, pharmaceutical, and telecom industries, and has a reputation for customer satisfaction.

Mike currently resides in Alpharetta, Georgia, with his wife of twenty-eight years, Susan, and a slightly neurotic dog, Pepper. Mike works for TUSC (The Ultimate Software Consultants) as a Senior Technical Management Consultant. He can be reached by email at **mikerault@earthlink.net.**

Acknowledgments

I would like to thank Charles Peck and Darren Meiss for their help with getting this book to print. I would also like to thank the rest of the Coriolis team, including Marcus Huff, Sharon Linsenbach, and Todd Halvorsen for their help. Finally, as with the other books I have published, thanks to all those unsung heroes that do the proofing, printing, conversions, artwork, and all the other complex jobs required to convert a book from bits and bytes to the printed page.

Contents at a Glance

Table of Contents

Introduction

Welcome to *Oracle8i: DBA SQL and PL/SQL Exam Cram*. This book will help you get ready to take—and pass—the first of the five-part series of exams for Oracle Certified Professional-Oracle8i Certified Database Administrator (OCP-DBA) certification. In this Introduction, I talk about Oracle's certification programs in general and how the *Exam Cram* series can help you prepare for Oracle8i's certification exams.

Exam Cram books help you understand and appreciate the subjects and materials you need to pass Oracle certification exams. The books are aimed strictly at test preparation and review. They do not teach you everything you need to know about a topic. Instead, they present and dissect the questions and problems that you're likely to encounter on a test.

Nevertheless, to completely prepare yourself for any Oracle test, I recommend that you begin by taking the Self-Assessment included in this book, immediately following this Introduction. This tool will help you evaluate your knowledge base against the requirements for an OCP-DBA under both ideal and real circumstances.

Based on what you learn from that exercise, you might decide to begin your studies with some classroom training or by reading one of the many DBA guides available from Oracle and third-party vendors. I also strongly recommend that you install, configure, and fool around with the software or environment that you'll be tested on, because nothing beats hands-on experience and familiarity when it comes to understanding the questions you're likely to encounter on a certification test. Book learning is essential, but hands-on experience is the best teacher of all!

The Oracle Certified Professional (OCP) Program

The OCP program for DBA certification currently includes five separate tests. A brief description of each test follows, and Table 1 shows the required exams for the OCP-DBA certification:

Table 1   Oracle8i OCP-DBA Requirements

Oracle8i

All 5 of these tests are required	
Exam 1Z0-001	Introduction to Oracle: SQL and PL/SQL
Exam 1Z0-023	Oracle8i: Architecture and Administration
Exam 1Z0-024	Oracle8i: Performance and Tuning
Exam 1Z0-025	Oracle8i: Backup and Recovery
Exam 1Z0-026	Oracle8i: Network Administration

If you are currently an OCP certified in Oracle8, you need take only the upgrade exam (Oracle8i: New Features for Administrators, Exam 1Z0-020) to be certified in Oracle8i. If you have passed Introduction to Oracle: SQL and PL/SQL during your pursuit of Oracle8 certification, you do not need to retake it for Oracle8i certification.

➤ *Introduction to Oracle: SQL And PL/SQL (Exam 1Z0-001)*—Test 1 is the base test for the series. Knowledge tested in Test 1 will also be used in all other tests in the DBA series. Besides testing knowledge of SQL and PL/SQL language constructs, syntax, and usage, Test 1 covers Data Definition Language (DDL), Data Manipulation Language (DML), and Data Control Language (DCL). Also covered in Test 1 are basic data modeling and database design.

➤ *Oracle8i: Database Administration (Exam 1Z0-023)*—Test 2 deals with all levels of database administration in Oracle8i (primarily version 8.1.5 and above). Topics include architecture, startup and shutdown, database creation, management of database internal and external constructs (such as redo logs, rollback segments, and tablespaces), and all other Oracle structures. Database auditing, use of National Language Support (NLS) features, and use of SQL*Loader and other utilities are also covered.

➤ *Oracle8i: Backup And Recovery (Exam 1Z0-025)*—Test 3 covers one of the most important parts of the Oracle DBA's job: database backup and recovery operations. Test 3 tests knowledge in backup and recovery motives, architecture as it relates to backup and recovery, backup methods, failure scenarios, recovery methodologies, archive logging, supporting 24x7 shops, troubleshooting, and use of Oracle8i's standby database features. The test also covers the use of the Recovery Manager (RMAN) product from Oracle.

➤ *Oracle8i: Performance Tuning (Exam 1Z0-024)*—Test 4 covers all aspects of tuning an Oracle8i database. Topics in both application and database tuning are covered. The exam tests knowledge in diagnosis of tuning problems, database optimal configuration, shared pool tuning, buffer cache tuning, Oracle block usage, tuning rollback segments and redo mechanisms, monitoring and detecting lock contention, tuning sorts, load optimization, and tuning in OLTP, DSS, and mixed environments.

➤ *Oracle8i: Network Administration (Exam 1Z0-026)*—Test 5 covers all parts of the Net8 product: NET8, Oracle Names Server, the listener process, lsnrctl (the listener control utility), and the NET8 configuration files sqlnet.ora, tnsnames.ora, and listener.ora.

To obtain an OCP certificate in database administration, an individual must pass all five exams. You do not have to take the tests in any particular order. However, you're usually better off taking the examinations in order because the knowledge tested builds from each exam. The core exams require individuals to demonstrate competence with all phases of Oracle8i database lifetime activities. If you already have your Oracle8 certification, you need to take only one exam—Oracle8i: New Features for Administrators (Exam 1Z0-020)—to upgrade your status.

The entire process commonly can take a year or so, and many individuals find that they must take a test more than once to pass. The primary goal of the *Exam Cram* series is to make it possible, given proper study and preparation, to pass all of the OCP-DBA tests on the first try.

Finally, certification is an ongoing activity. After an Oracle version becomes obsolete, OCP-DBAs (and other OCPs) typically have a six-month time frame in which they can become recertified on current product versions. (If an individual does not get recertified within the specified time period, his certification becomes invalid.) Because technology keeps changing, and new products continually supplant old ones, this should come as no surprise.

The best place to keep tabs on the OCP program and its various certifications is on the Oracle Web site. The current root URL for the OCP program is at **www.oracle.com/education/index.html?content.html**. Oracle's certification Web site changes frequently, so if this URL doesn't work, try using the Search tool on Oracle's site (**www.oracle.com**) with either "OCP" or the quoted phrase "Oracle Certified Professional Program" as the search string. This will help you find the latest and most accurate information about the company's certification programs.

Taking a Certification Exam

Alas, testing is not free. You'll be charged $125 for each test you take, whether you pass or fail. In the United States and Canada, Sylvan Prometric administers tests. Sylvan Prometric can be reached at 1-800-891-3926, any time from 7:00 A.M. to 6:00 P.M., Central Time, Monday through Friday. If you can't get through at this number, try 1-612-896-7000 or 1-612-820-5707.

To schedule an exam, call at least one day in advance. To cancel or reschedule an exam, you must call at least one day before the scheduled test time (or you may be charged the $125 fee). When calling Sylvan Prometric, please have the following information ready for the telesales staffer who handles your call:

➤ Your name, organization, and mailing address.

➤ The name of the exam you want to take.

➤ A method of payment. (The most convenient approach is to supply a valid credit card number with sufficient available credit. Otherwise, payments by check, money order, or purchase order must be received before a test can be scheduled. If the latter methods are required, ask your order-taker for more details.)

An appointment confirmation will be sent to you by mail if you register more than five days before an exam, or it will be sent by fax if less than five days before the exam. A Candidate Agreement letter, which you must sign to take the examination, will also be provided.

On the day of the test, try to arrive at least 15 minutes before the scheduled time slot. You must supply two forms of identification, one of which must be a photo ID.

All exams are completely closed book. In fact, you will not be permitted to take anything with you into the testing area. I suggest that you review the most critical information about the test you're taking just before the test. (*Exam Cram* books provide a brief reference—The Cram Sheet, located inside the front of this book—that lists the essential information from the book in distilled form.) You will have some time to compose yourself, to mentally review this critical information, and even to take a sample orientation exam before you begin the real thing. I suggest that you take the orientation test before taking your first exam; they're all more or less identical in layout, behavior, and controls, so you probably won't need to do this more than once.

When you complete an Oracle8i certification exam, the testing software will tell you whether you've passed or failed. Results are broken into several topical areas. Whether you pass or fail, I suggest you ask for—and keep—the detailed report that the test administrator prints for you. You can use the report to help you prepare for another go-round, if necessary, and even if you pass, the report shows areas you may need to review to keep your edge. If you need to retake an exam, you'll have to call Sylvan Prometric, schedule a new test date, and pay another $125.

Tracking OCP Status

Oracle generates transcripts that indicate the exams you have passed and your corresponding test scores. After you pass the necessary set of five exams, you'll be certified as an Oracle8i DBA. Official certification normally takes anywhere from four to six weeks (generally within 30 days), so don't expect to get your credentials overnight. Once certified, you will receive a package with a Welcome Kit that contains a number of elements:

➤ An OCP-DBA certificate, suitable for framing.

➤ A license agreement to use the OCP logo. After it is sent into Oracle, and your packet of logo information is received, the license agreement allows you to use the logo for advertisements, promotions, documents, letterhead, business cards, and so on. An OCP logo sheet, which includes camera-ready artwork, comes with the license.

Many people believe that the benefits of OCP certification go well beyond the perks that Oracle provides to newly anointed members of this elite group. I am starting to see more job listings that request or require applicants to have an OCP-DBA certification, and many individuals who complete the program can qualify for increases in pay and/or responsibility. As an official recognition of hard work and broad knowledge, OCP certification is a badge of honor in many IT organizations.

How to Prepare for an Exam

At a minimum, preparing for OCP-DBA exams requires that you obtain and study the following materials:

➤ The Oracle8 Server version 8.1.5 Documentation Set on CD-ROM.

➤ The exam preparation materials, practice tests, and self-assessment exams on the Oracle certification page (**www.oracle.com/education/index.html? content.html**). Find the materials, download them, and use them!

➤ This *Exam Cram* book. It's the first and last thing you should read before taking the exam.

In addition, you'll probably find any or all of the following materials useful in your quest for Oracle8i DBA expertise:

➤ *OCP resource kits*—Oracle Corporation has a CD-ROM with example questions and materials to help with the exam; generally, requesting them from your Oracle representative provides these free. They have also been offered free for the taking at most Oracle conventions, such as IOUGA-Alive! and Oracle Open World.

➤ *Classroom training*—Oracle, TUSC, LearningTree, and many others offer classroom and computer-based training-type material that you will find useful to help you prepare for the exam. But a word of warning: These classes are fairly expensive (in the range of $300 per day of training). However, they do offer a condensed form of learning to help you brush up on your Oracle knowledge. The tests are closely tied to the classroom training provided by Oracle, so I would suggest taking at least the introductory classes to get the Oracle-specific (and classroom-specific) terminology under your belt.

➤ *Other publications*—You'll find direct references to other publications and resources in this book, and there's no shortage of materials available about Oracle8i DBA topics. To help you sift through some of the publications out there, I end each chapter with a "Need to Know More?" section that provides pointers to more complete and exhaustive resources covering the chapter's subject matter. This section tells you where to look for further details.

➤ *The Oracle Support CD-ROM*—Oracle provides a Support CD-ROM on a quarterly basis. This CD-ROM contains useful white papers, bug reports, technical bulletins, and information about release-specific bugs, fixes, and new features. Contact your Oracle representative for a copy.

➤ *The Oracle Administrator and PL/SQL Developer*—These are online references from RevealNet, Inc., an Oracle and database online reference provider. These online references provide instant lookup on thousands of database and developmental topics and are an invaluable resource for study and learning about Oracle. Demo copies can be downloaded from **www.revealnet.com**. Also available at the RevealNet Web site are the DBA and PL/SQL Pipelines, online discussion groups where you can obtain expert information from Oracle DBAs worldwide. The costs of these applications run about $400 each (current pricing is available on the Web site) and are worth every cent.

These required and recommended materials represent a nonpareil collection of sources and resources for Oracle8i DBA topics and software. In the section that follows, I explain how this book works and give you some good reasons why this book should also be on your required and recommended materials list.

About This Book

Each topical *Exam Cram* chapter follows a regular structure, along with graphical cues about especially important or useful material. Here's the structure of a typical chapter:

➤ *Opening hotlists*—Each chapter begins with lists of the terms, tools, and techniques that you must learn and understand before you can be fully conversant with the chapter's subject matter. I follow the hotlists with one or two introductory paragraphs to set the stage for the rest of the chapter.

➤ *Topical coverage*—After the opening hotlists, each chapter covers a series of topics related to the chapter's subject. Throughout this section, I highlight material most likely to appear on a test using a special Exam Alert layout, like this:

This is what an Exam Alert looks like. Normally, an Exam Alert stresses concepts, terms, software, or activities that will most likely appear in one or more certification test questions. For that reason, any information found offset in Exam Alert format is worthy of unusual attentiveness on your part. Indeed, most of the facts appearing in The Cram Sheet appear as Exam Alerts within the text.

Occasionally in *Exam Crams*, you'll see tables called "Vital Statistics." The contents of Vital Statistics tables are worthy of an extra once-over. These tables contain informational tidbits that might show up in a test question.

Even if material isn't flagged as an Exam Alert or included in a Vital Statistics table, *all* the contents of this book are associated, at least tangentially, to something test-related. This book is tightly focused for quick test preparation, so you'll find that what appears in the meat of each chapter is critical knowledge.

I have also provided tips that will help build a better foundation of data administration knowledge. Although the information may not be on the exam, it is highly relevant and will help you become a better test-taker.

 This is how tips are formatted. Keep your eyes open for these, and you'll become a test guru in no time!

➤ *Practice questions*—A section at the end of each chapter presents a series of mock test questions and explanations of both correct and incorrect answers. I also try to point out especially tricky questions by using a special icon, like this:

Ordinarily, this icon flags the presence of an especially devious question, if not an outright trick question. Trick questions are calculated to "trap" you if you don't read them carefully, and more than once at that. Although they're not ubiquitous, such questions make regular appearances in the Oracle8i exams. That's why exam questions are as much about reading comprehension as they are about knowing DBA material inside out and backward.

➤ *Details and resources*—Every chapter ends with a section titled "Need to Know More?". This section provides direct pointers to Oracle and third-party resources that offer further details on the chapter's subject matter. In addition, this section tries to rate the quality and thoroughness of each topic's coverage. If you find a resource you like in this collection, use it, but don't feel compelled to use all these resources. On the other hand, I recommend only resources I use on a regular basis, so none of my recommendations will be a waste of your time or money.

The bulk of the book follows this chapter structure slavishly, but I'd like to point out a few other elements. Chapter 14 includes a sample test that provides a good review of the material presented throughout the book to ensure that you're ready for the exam. Chapter 15 provides an answer key to the sample test. In addition, you'll find a handy glossary and an index.

Finally, look for The Cram Sheet, which appears inside the front of this *Exam Cram* book. It is a valuable tool that represents a condensed and compiled collection of facts, figures, and tips that I think you should memorize before taking the test. Because you can dump this information out of your head onto a piece of paper before answering any exam questions, you can master this information by brute force—you need to remember it only long enough to write it down when you walk into the test room. You might even want to look at it in the car or in the lobby of the testing center just before you walk in to take the test.

How to Use This Book

If you're prepping for a first-time test, I've structured the topics in this book to build on one another. Therefore, some topics in later chapters make more sense after you've read earlier chapters. That's why I suggest that you read this book from front to back for your initial test preparation.

If you need to brush up on a topic, or you have to bone up for a second try, use the index or table of contents to go straight to the topics and questions that you need to study. Beyond the tests, I think that you'll find this book useful as a tightly focused reference to some of the most important aspects of topics associated with being a DBA, as implemented under Oracle8i.

Given all the book's elements and its specialized focus, I've tried to create a tool that you can use to prepare for—and pass—the Oracle OCP-DBA set of examinations. Please share your feedback on the book with me, especially if you have ideas about how I can improve it for future test-takers. I'll consider everything you say carefully, and I try to respond to all suggestions. You can reach me via email at **aultm@tusc.com**. Or you can send your questions or comments to **learn@examcram.com**. Please remember to include the title of the book in your message; otherwise, I'll be forced to guess which book of mine you're making a suggestion about. Also, be sure to check out the Web pages at **www.examcram.com**, where you'll find information updates, commentary, and certification information.

Thanks, and enjoy the book!

Self-Assessment

I've included a Self-Assessment in this *Exam Cram* to help you evaluate your readiness to tackle Oracle Certified Professional-Oracle8i Certified Database Administrator (OCP-DBA) certification. It should also help you understand what you need to master the topic of this book—namely, Exam 1Z0-001 (Test 1), "Introduction to Oracle: SQL and PL/SQL." But before you tackle this Self-Assessment, let's talk about the concerns you may face when pursuing an Oracle8i OCP-DBA certification, and what an ideal Oracle8i OCP-DBA candidate might look like.

Oracle8i OCP-DBAs in the Real World

In the next section, I describe an ideal Oracle8i OCP-DBA candidate, knowing full well that only a few actual candidates meet this ideal. In fact, my description of that ideal candidate might seem downright scary. But take heart; although the requirements to obtain an Oracle8i OCP-DBA may seem pretty formidable, they are by no means impossible to meet. However, you should be keenly aware that it does take time, requires some expense, and consumes a substantial effort.

You can get all the real-world motivation you need from knowing that many others have gone before you. You can follow in their footsteps. If you're willing to tackle the process seriously and do what it takes to obtain the necessary experience and knowledge, you can take—and pass—the certification tests. In fact, the *Exam Crams* and the companion *Exam Preps* are designed to make it as easy as possible for you to prepare for these exams. But prepare you must!

The same, of course, is true for other Oracle certifications, including the following:

➤ Oracle8 OCP-DBA, which is similar to the Oracle8i OCP-DBA certification.

➤ Application Developer, Oracle Developer Rel 1 OCP, which is aimed at software developers and requires five exams.

➤ Application Developer, Oracle Developer Rel 2 OCP, which is aimed at software developers and requires five exams.

➤ Oracle Database Operators OCP, which is aimed at database operators and requires only one exam.

➤ Oracle Java Technology Certification OCP, which is aimed at Java developers and requires five exams.

The Ideal Oracle8i OCP-DBA Candidate

Just to give you some idea of what an ideal Oracle8i OCP-DBA candidate is like, here are some relevant statistics about the background and experience such an individual might have. Don't worry if you don't meet these qualifications (or if you don't even come close), because this world is far from ideal, and where you fall short is simply where you'll have more work to do. The ideal candidate will have the following:

➤ Academic or professional training in relational databases, Structured Query Language (SQL), performance tuning, backup and recovery, and Net8 administration.

➤ Three-plus years of professional database administration experience, including experience installing and upgrading Oracle executables, creating and tuning databases, troubleshooting connection problems, creating users, and managing backup and recovery scenarios.

I believe that well under half of all certification candidates meet these requirements. In fact, most probably meet less than half of these requirements (that is, at least when they begin the certification process). But, because all those who have their certifications already survived this ordeal, you can survive it, too—especially if you heed what this Self-Assessment can tell you about what you already know and what you need to learn.

Put Yourself to the Test

The following series of questions and observations is designed to help you figure out how much work you'll face in pursuing Oracle certification and what kinds of resources you may consult on your quest. Be absolutely honest in your answers, or you'll end up wasting money on exams you're not ready to take. There are no right or wrong answers, only steps along the path to certification. Only you can decide where you really belong in the broad spectrum of aspiring candidates.

Two things should be clear from the outset, however:

➤ Even a modest background in computer science will be helpful.

➤ Hands-on experience with Oracle products and technologies is an essential ingredient to certification success.

Educational Background

1. Have you ever taken any computer-related classes? [Yes or No]

   If Yes, proceed to question 2; if No, proceed to question 4.

2. Have you taken any classes on relational databases? [Yes or No]

   If Yes, you will probably be able to handle Oracle's architecture and network administration discussions. If you're rusty, brush up on the basic concepts of databases and networks. If the answer is No, consider some basic reading in this area. I strongly recommend a good Oracle database administration book such as *Oracle8i Administration and Management* by Michael Ault (Wiley, 2000). Or, if this title doesn't appeal to you, check out reviews for other, similar titles at your favorite online bookstore.

3. Have you taken any networking concepts or technologies classes? [Yes or No]

   If Yes, you will probably be able to handle Oracle's networking terminology, concepts, and technologies (but brace yourself for frequent departures from normal usage). If you're rusty, brush up on basic networking concepts and terminology. If your answer is No, you might want to check out the Oracle technet Web site (**http://technet.oracle.com**) and read some of the white papers on Net8. If you have access to the Oracle MetaLink Web site or the Technet Web site, download the Oracle Net8 Administration manual.

4. Have you done any reading on relational databases or networks? [Yes or No]

   If Yes, review the requirements from questions 2 and 3. If you meet those, move to the next section, "Hands-On Experience." If you answered No, consult the recommended reading for both topics. This kind of strong background will be of great help in preparing you for the Oracle exams.

Hands-On Experience

Another important key to success on all of the Oracle tests is hands-on experience, especially with Net8 Assistant. If I leave you with only one realization after taking this Self-Assessment, it should be that there's no substitute for time spent installing, configuring, and using the various Oracle products upon which you'll be tested repeatedly and in depth.

5. Have you installed, configured, and worked with Net8? [Yes or No]

   If Yes, make sure that you understand basic concepts as covered in Exam 1Z0-013, "Oracle8i: Database Administrator" (Test 2) and advanced concepts as covered in Exam 1Z0-014, "Oracle8i: Performance Tuning" (Test 4).

You should also study the Net8 configuration and administration for Exam 1Z0-001 (Test 1), "Introduction to Oracle: SQL and PL/SQL."

 You can download the candidate certification guide, objectives, practice exams, and other information about Oracle exams from the company's Training and Certification page on the Web at **www.oracle. com/education/index.html?content.html**.

If you haven't worked with Oracle, you must obtain a copy of Oracle8i or Personal Oracle8i. Then, learn about the database and Net8.

 For any and all of these Oracle exams, the candidate guides for the topics involved are a good study resource. You can download them free from the Oracle Web site (**www.oracle.com/education/index.html? content.html**). You can also download information on purchasing additional practice tests ($99 per exam).

If you have the funds, or your employer will pay your way, consider taking a class at an Oracle training and education center.

Before you even think about taking any Oracle exam, make sure you've spent enough time with Net8 to understand how it may be installed and configured, how to maintain such an installation, and how to troubleshoot that software when things go wrong. This will help you in the exam—as well as in real life.

Testing Your Exam-Readiness

Whether you attend a formal class on a specific topic to get ready for an exam or use written materials to study on your own, some preparation for the Oracle certification exams is essential. At $125 a try, pass or fail, you want to do everything you can to pass on your first try. That's where studying comes in.

I have included in this book several practice exam questions for each chapter and a sample test, so if you don't score well on the chapter questions, you can study more and then tackle the sample test at the end of the book. If you don't earn a score of at least 70 percent after this test, you'll want to investigate the other practice test resources I mention in this section.

For any given subject, consider taking a class if you've tackled self-study materials, taken the test, and failed anyway. If you can afford the privilege, the opportunity to interact with an instructor and fellow students can make all the difference in the world. For information about Oracle classes, visit the Training and Certification page at **www.oracle.com/education/index.html?content.html**.

If you can't afford to take a class, visit the Training and Certification page anyway, because it also includes free practice exams that you can download. Even if you can't afford to spend much, you should still invest in some low-cost practice exams from commercial vendors, because they can help you assess your readiness to pass a test better than any other tool.

6. Have you taken a practice exam on your chosen test subject? [Yes or No]

If Yes—and you scored 70 percent or better—you're probably ready to tackle the real thing. If your score isn't above that crucial threshold, keep at it until you break that barrier. If you answered No, obtain all the free and low-budget practice tests you can find (or afford) and get to work. Keep at it until you can comfortably break the passing threshold.

 There is no better way to assess your test readiness than to take a good-quality practice exam and pass with a score of 70 percent or better. When I'm preparing, I shoot for 80-plus percent, just to leave room for the "weirdness factor" that sometimes shows up on Oracle exams.

Assessing Your Readiness for Exam 1Z0-001 (Test 1)

In addition to the general exam-readiness information in the previous section, other resources are available to help you prepare for the Introduction to Oracle: SQL and PL/SQL exam. For starters, visit the RevealNet pipeline (**www.revealnet.com**) or **http://technet.oracle.com**. These are great places to ask questions and get good answers, or simply to observe the questions that others ask (along with the answers, of course).

Oracle exam mavens also recommend checking the Oracle Knowledge Base from RevealNet. You can get information on purchasing the RevealNet software at **www.revealnet.com**.

For Introduction to Oracle: SQL and PL/SQL preparation in particular, I'd also like to recommend that you check out one or more of these books as you prepare to take the exam:

➤ Ault, Michael. *Oracle8i Administration and Management.* Wiley, 2000.

➤ Loney, Kevin. *Oracle8i DBA Handbook.* Oracle Press, 2000.

➤ Kreines, David C., and Laskey, Brian. *Oracle Database Administration.* O'Reilly, 1999.

➤ Toledo, Hugo. *Oracle Networking.* Oracle Press, 1996.

Stop by your favorite bookstore or online bookseller to check out one or more of these books. In my opinion, the first two are the best general all-around references on Oracle8i available, and the third complements the contents of this *Exam Cram* very nicely. The fourth book provides excellent basic information on networking.

One last note: Hopefully, it makes sense to stress the importance of hands-on experience in the context of the Introduction to Oracle: SQL and PL/SQL exam. As you review the material for this exam, you'll realize that hands-on experience with Oracle8i commands, tools, and utilities is invaluable.

Onward, through the Fog!

After you've assessed your readiness, undertaken the right background studies, obtained the hands-on experience that will help you understand the products and technologies at work, and reviewed the many sources of information to help you prepare for a test, you'll be ready to take a round of practice tests. When your scores come back positive enough to get you through the exam, you're ready to go after the real thing. If you follow my assessment regime, you'll not only know what you need to study, but when you're ready to make a test date at Sylvan. Good luck!

Oracle OCP
Certification Exams

Terms you'll need to understand:

✓ Radio button

✓ Checkbox

✓ Exhibit

✓ Multiple-choice question formats

✓ Careful reading

✓ Process of elimination

Techniques you'll need to master:

✓ Assessing your exam-readiness

✓ Preparing to take a certification exam

✓ Practicing (to make perfect)

✓ Making the best use of the testing software

✓ Budgeting your time

✓ Saving the hardest questions until last

✓ Guessing (as a last resort)

As experiences go, test-taking is not something that most people anticipate eagerly, no matter how well they're prepared. In most cases, familiarity helps ameliorate test anxiety. In plain English, this means you probably won't be as nervous when you take your fourth or fifth Oracle certification exam as you will be when you take your first one.

But no matter whether it's your first test or your tenth, understanding the exam-taking particulars (how much time to spend on questions, the setting you'll be in, and so on) and the testing software will help you concentrate on the material rather than on the environment. Likewise, mastering a few basic test-taking skills should help you recognize—and perhaps even outfox—some of the tricks and gotchas you're bound to find in some of the Oracle test questions.

In this chapter, I explain the testing environment and software, as well as describe some proven test-taking strategies you should be able to use to your advantage.

Assessing Exam-Readiness

Before you take any Oracle exam, I strongly recommend that you read through and take the Self-Assessment included with this book (it appears just before this chapter, in fact). This will help you compare your knowledge base to the requirements for obtaining an Oracle Certified Professional (OCP), and it will also help you identify parts of your background or experience that may be in need of improvement, enhancement, or further learning. If you get the right set of basics under your belt, obtaining Oracle certification will be that much easier.

After you've gone through the Self-Assessment, you can remedy those topical areas where your background or experience may not measure up to an ideal certification candidate. But you can also tackle subject matter for individual tests at the same time, so you can continue making progress while you're catching up in some areas.

After you've worked through an Exam Cram, have read the supplementary materials, and have taken the practice test at the end of the book, you'll have a pretty clear idea of when you should be ready to take the real exam. Although I strongly recommend that you keep practicing until your scores top the 70 percent mark, 75 percent would be a good goal to give yourself some margin for error in a real exam situation (where stress will play more of a role than when you practice). After you hit that point, you should be ready to go. But if you get through the practice exam in this book without attaining that score, you should keep taking practice tests and studying the materials until you get there. You'll find more information about other practice test vendors in the Self-Assessment, along with even more pointers on how to study and prepare. But now, on to the exam itself!

The Testing Situation

When you arrive at the Sylvan Prometric Testing Center where you scheduled your test, you'll need to sign in with a test coordinator. He will ask you to produce two forms of identification, one of which must be a photo ID. After you've signed in and your time slot arrives, you'll be asked to leave any books, bags, or other items you brought with you, and you'll be escorted into a closed room. Typically, that room will be furnished with anywhere from one to half a dozen computers, and each workstation is separated from the others by dividers designed to keep you from seeing what's happening on someone else's computer.

You'll be furnished with a pen or pencil and a blank sheet of paper, or in some cases, an erasable plastic sheet and an erasable felt-tip pen. You're allowed to write down any information you want on this sheet, and you can write stuff on both sides of the page. I suggest that you memorize as much as possible of the material that appears on The Cram Sheet (inside the front of this book), and then write that information down on the blank sheet as soon as you sit down in front of the test machine. You can refer to the sheet any time you like during the test, but you'll have to surrender it when you leave the room.

Most test rooms feature a wall with a large window. This allows the test coordinator to monitor the room, to prevent test-takers from talking to one another, and to observe anything out of the ordinary that might go on. The test coordinator will have preloaded the Oracle certification test you've signed up for, and you'll be permitted to start as soon as you're seated in front of the machine.

All Oracle certification exams permit you to take up to a certain maximum amount of time (usually 90 minutes) to complete the test (the test itself will tell you, and it maintains an on-screen counter/clock so that you can check the time remaining any time you like). Each exam consists of between 60 and 70 questions, randomly selected from a pool of questions.

The passing score varies per exam and the questions selected. For Exam 1Z0-001, the passing score is 68 percent for USA with the latest test update, 72 percent in locations where the test has not been updated.

All Oracle certification exams are computer-generated and use a multiple-choice format. Although this might sound easy, the questions are constructed not just to check your mastery of basic facts and figures about Oracle8i DBA topics, but they also require you to evaluate one or more sets of circumstances or requirements. Often, you'll be asked to give more than one answer to a question; likewise, you may be asked to select the best or most effective solution to a problem from a range of choices, all of which technically are correct. The tests are quite an adventure, and they involve real thinking. This book shows you what to expect and how to deal with the problems, puzzles, and predicaments you're likely to find on the tests—in particular, Exam 1Z0-001, "Introduction to Oracle: SQL and PL/SQL."

Test Layout And Design

A typical test question is depicted in Question 1. It's a multiple-choice question that requires you to select a single correct answer. Following the question is a brief summary of each potential answer and why it was either right or wrong.

Question 1

The file my_file.sql was loaded using the GET command. You issue this SQL*Plus command:

```
SAVE my_file REPLACE
```

What task has been accomplished?

- O a. A new file was created.
- O b. The existing file was replaced.
- O c. The command was continued to the next line of the SQL prompt.
- O d. No task was accomplished because a file extension was not designated.

The "most" correct answer is b. The **SAVE** command has only one option: **REPLACE**. **SAVE** without **REPLACE** requires that the file not exist; **SAVE** with **REPLACE** replaces an existing file or creates one if the file doesn't exist. No file extension is required; the default is ".sql." Answer a is incorrect because the **REPLACE** option is specified. With just a **SAVE**, a new file is created; with a **SAVE...REPLACE**, an existing file is replaced. Answer c is incorrect because the continuation of a line is done automatically when you press Return. Answer d is incorrect because if a suffix isn't specified, a default one is added.

This sample question corresponds closely to those you'll see on Oracle certification tests. To select the correct answer during the test, you would position the cursor over the radio button next to answer b and click the mouse to select that particular choice. The only difference between the certification test and this question is that the real questions are not immediately followed by the answers. In fact, in the actual exam, you won't be able to see the correct answers at all. This is the format for the practice questions you will see throughout the book.

Next, examine this question where one or more answers are possible. This type of question provides checkboxes, rather than radio buttons, for marking all appropriate selections.

Question 2

> Which three ways can the SQL buffer be terminated?
>
> ❏ a. Enter a slash (/).
>
> ❏ b. Press Return (or Enter) once.
>
> ❏ c. Enter an asterisk (*).
>
> ❏ d. Enter a semicolon (;).
>
> ❏ e. Press Return (or Enter) twice.
>
> ❏ f. Press Esc twice.

The correct answers for this question are a, d, and e. A slash (/) is usually used for termination of PL/SQL blocks, procedures, and functions, but it can also be used for SQL commands. A semicolon (;) is generally used for terminating SQL commands. Pressing the Return key (or the Enter key on many keyboards) twice in succession will also tell the buffer your command is complete, but will not execute it. Most of the time, the slash or semicolon will also result in execution of the previous command (except within a PL/SQL block); a subsequent entry of the slash, the semicolon, or an "r" (short for run) will be required to execute the command(s) terminated with a double Return.

For this type of question, one or more answers must be selected to answer the question correctly. For Question 2, you would have to position the cursor over the checkboxes and click on the appropriate checkbox next to items a, d, and e to obtain credit for a correct answer.

These two basic types of questions can appear in many forms. They constitute the foundation on which all the Oracle certification exam questions rest. More complex questions may include so-called "exhibits," which are usually tables or data-content layouts of one form or another. You'll be expected to use the information displayed in the exhibit to guide your answer to the question.

Other questions involving exhibits may use charts or diagrams to help document a workplace scenario that you'll be asked to troubleshoot or configure. Paying careful attention to such exhibits is the key to success—be prepared to toggle between the picture and the question as you work. Often, both are complex enough that you might not be able to remember all of either one.

Using Oracle's Test Software Effectively

A well-known test-taking principle is to read over the entire test from start to finish first, but to answer only those questions that you feel absolutely sure of on the first pass. On subsequent passes, you can dive into more complex questions, knowing how many such questions you have to deal with.

Fortunately, Oracle test software makes this approach easy to implement. At the bottom of each question, you'll find a checkbox that permits you to mark that question for a later visit. (Note that marking questions makes review easier, but you can return to any question by clicking the Forward and Back buttons repeatedly until you get to the question.) As you read e`'h question, if you answer only those you're sure of and mark for review those that you're not, you can keep going through a decreasing list of open questions as you knock the trickier ones off in order.

There's at least one potential benefit to reading the test over completely before answering the trickier questions: Sometimes, you find information in later questions that sheds more light on earlier ones. Other times, information you read in later questions might jog your memory about Oracle8 DBA facts, figures, or behavior that also will help with earlier questions. Either way, you'll come out ahead if you defer those questions about which you're not absolutely sure of the answer(s).

Keep working on the questions until you are absolutely sure of all your answers or until you know you'll run out of time. If you still have unanswered questions, you'll want to zip through them and guess. No answer guarantees zero credit for a question, but a guess has at least a chance of being correct. (Oracle scores blank answers and incorrect answers as equally wrong.)

At the very end of your test period, you're better off guessing than leaving questions blank or unanswered.

Taking Testing Seriously

The most important advice I can give you about taking any Oracle test is this: Read each question carefully. Some questions are deliberately ambiguous; some use double negatives; others use terminology in incredibly precise ways. I've taken numerous practice tests and real tests myself, and in nearly every test I've missed at least one question because I didn't read it closely or carefully enough.

Here are some suggestions on how to deal with the tendency to jump to an answer too quickly:

➤ Make sure you read every word in the question. If you find yourself jumping ahead impatiently, go back and start over.

➤ As you read, try to restate the question in your own terms. If you can do this, you should be able to pick the correct answer(s) much more easily.

➤ When returning to a question after your initial read-through, reread every word again—otherwise, the mind falls quickly into a rut. Sometimes seeing a question afresh after turning your attention elsewhere lets you see something you missed before, but the strong tendency is to see what you've seen before. Try to avoid that tendency at all costs.

➤ If you return to a question more than twice, try to articulate to yourself what you don't understand about the question, why the answers don't appear to make sense, or what appears to be missing. If you chew on the subject for a while, your subconscious might provide the details that are lacking, or you may notice a "trick" that will point to the right answer.

Above all, try to deal with each question by thinking through what you know about being an Oracle8i DBA—utilities, characteristics, behaviors, facts, and figures involved. By reviewing what you know (and what you've written down on your information sheet), you'll often recall or understand things sufficiently to determine the answer to the question.

Question-Handling Strategies

Based on the tests I've taken, a couple of interesting trends in the answers have become apparent. For those questions that take only a single answer, usually two or three of the answers will be obviously incorrect, and two of the answers will be plausible. But, of course, only one can be correct. Unless the answer leaps out at you (and if it does, reread the question to look for a trick; sometimes those are the ones you're most likely to get wrong), begin the process of answering by eliminating those answers that are obviously wrong.

Things to look for in the "obviously wrong" category include spurious command choices or table or view names, nonexistent software or command options, and terminology you've never seen before. If you've done your homework for a test, no valid information should be completely new to you. In that case, unfamiliar or bizarre terminology probably indicates a totally bogus answer. As long as you're sure what's right, it's easy to eliminate what's wrong.

Numerous questions assume that the default behavior of a particular Oracle utility (such as SQL*Plus or SQL*Loader) is in effect. It's essential, therefore, to know and understand the default settings for SQL*Plus, SQL*Loader, and Server Manager utilities. If you know the defaults and understand what they mean, this knowledge will help you cut through many Gordian knots.

Likewise, when dealing with questions that require multiple answers, you must know and select all of the correct options to get credit. This, too, qualifies as an example of why careful reading is so important.

As you work your way through the test, another counter that Oracle thankfully provides will come in handy—the number of questions completed and questions outstanding. Budget your time by making sure that you've completed one-fourth of the questions one-quarter of the way through the test period (between 13 and 17 questions in the first 22 or 23 minutes). Check again three-quarters of the way through (between 39 and 51 questions in the first 66 to 69 minutes).

If you're not through after 85 minutes, use the last five minutes to guess your way through the remaining questions. Remember, guesses are potentially more valuable than blank answers, because blanks are always wrong, but a guess might turn out to be right. If you haven't a clue with any of the remaining questions, pick answers at random, or choose all a's, b's, and so on. The important thing is to submit a test for scoring that has an answer for every question.

Mastering The Inner Game

In the final analysis, knowledge breeds confidence, and confidence breeds success. If you study the materials in this book carefully and review all of the questions at the end of each chapter, you should be aware of those areas where additional studying is required.

Next, follow up by reading some or all of the materials recommended in the "Need To Know More?" section at the end of each chapter. The idea is to become familiar enough with the concepts and situations that you find in the sample questions to be able to reason your way through similar situations on a real test. If you know the material, you have every right to be confident that you can pass the test.

After you've worked your way through the book, take the practice test in Chapter 14. The test provides a reality check and helps you identify areas you need to study further. Make sure you follow up and review materials related to the questions you miss before scheduling a real test. Only when you've covered all the ground and feel comfortable with the whole scope of the practice test should you take a real test.

If you take the practice test (Chapter 14) and don't score at least 75 percent correct, you'll want to practice further. At a minimum, download the practice tests and the self-assessment tests from the Oracle Education Web site's download page (its location appears in the next section). If you're more ambitious or better funded, you might want to purchase a practice test from one of the third-party vendors that offer them.

Armed with the information in this book and with the determination to augment your knowledge, you should be able to pass the certification exam. But if you don't work at it, you'll spend the test fee more than once before you finally do pass. If you prepare seriously, the execution should go flawlessly. Good luck!

Additional Resources

By far, the best source of information about Oracle certification tests comes from Oracle itself. Because its products and technologies—and the tests that go with them—change frequently, the best place to go for exam-related information is online.

If you haven't already visited the Oracle certification pages, do so right now. As I'm writing this chapter, the certification home page resides at **www.oracle.com/ education/certification/** (see Figure 1.1).

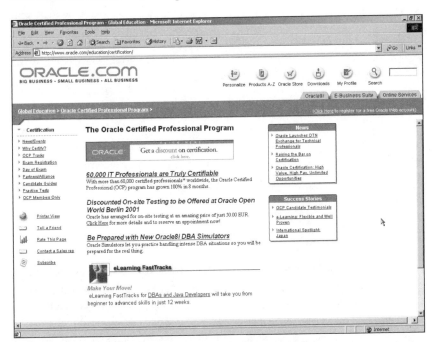

Figure 1.1   The Oracle certification page should be your starting point for further investigation of the most current exam and preparation information.

Note: This page might not be there by the time you read this, or it may have been replaced by something new and different, because things change regularly on the Oracle site. Should this happen, please read the section titled "Coping With Change on the Web," later in this chapter.

The menu options in the left column of the page point to the most important sources of information in the certification pages. Here's what to check out:

➤ *News/Events*—Any new tests will be described here.

➤ *Why Certify?*—Your question may get answered here.

➤ *OCP Tracks*—This is a detailed section that provides many jump points to detailed test descriptions for the several OCP certifications.

➤ *Exam Registration*—This section provides information for phone registration and a link to the Prometric Web page for online registration. Also, this section provides a list of testing sites outside of the USA.

➤ *Day of Exam*—This section provides an explanation of what will happen on the day of your exam.

➤ *Partners/Alliances*—This link provides information about test discounts and other offers for Oracle Partner companies.

➤ *Candidate Guides*—This link provides detailed study guides for all Oracle OCP examinations.

➤ *Practice Tests*—This section provides a download of the latest copy of the assessment test after you fill out an online questionnaire.

➤ *OCP Members Only*—After you are certified, you will be issued a username and password for this area.

Of course, these are just the high points of what's available in the Oracle certification pages. As you browse through them—and I strongly recommend that you do—you'll probably find other things I didn't mention here that are every bit as interesting and compelling.

Coping With Change on the Web

Sooner or later, all the specifics I've shared with you about the Oracle certification pages, and all the other Web-based resources I mention throughout the rest of this book, will go stale or be replaced by newer information. In some cases, the URLs you find here might lead you to their replacements; in other cases, the URLs will go nowhere, leaving you with the dreaded "404 File not found" error message.

When that happens, please don't give up. You can always discover a way to find what you want on the Web—if you're willing to invest some time and energy. To begin with, most large or complex Web sites—and Oracle's qualifies on both counts—offer a search engine. As long as you can get to Oracle's home page (and I'm sure that it will stay at www.oracle.com for a long while yet), you can use this tool to help you find what you need.

The more particular or focused you can make a search request, the more likely it is that the results will include information you can use. For instance, you can search the string "training and certification" to produce a lot of data about the subject in general, but if you're looking for the Preparation Guide for the Oracle DBA tests, you'll be more likely to get there quickly if you use a search string such as this:

```
"DBA" AND "preparation guide"
```

Likewise, if you want to find the training and certification downloads, try a search string such as this one:

```
"training and certification" AND "download page"
```

Finally, don't be afraid to use general search tools such as **www.yahoo.com**, **www.hotbot.com**, or **www.excite.com** to search for related information. Even though Oracle offers the best information about its certification exams online, there are plenty of third-party sources of information, training, and assistance in this area that do not have to follow a party line like Oracle does. The bottom line is this: If you can't find something where the book says it lives, start looking around. If worse comes to worst, you can always email me! I just might have a clue. My email address is **mikerault@earthlink.net**.

Writing Basic SQL Statements, Including the Restricting and Sorting of Values

2

Terms you'll need to understand:

✓ **SELECT**

✓ Equijoin

✓ Self-Join

✓ Outer-Join

✓ Cartesian product

✓ **SORT**

✓ **GROUP BY**

✓ Subquery

Techniques you'll need to master:

✓ Using the **SELECT** command to retrieve data from tables

✓ Using the equijoin to relate multiple tables to each other

✓ Using the self-join to flatten hierarchical data

✓ Using the outer-join to return data from a second table even if the join value is not present

✓ Structuring **SELECT** statements to avoid Cartesian products

✓ Sort and Grouping methods

✓ Using subqueries and inline views

In this chapter, we discuss the **SELECT** command. The **SELECT** command allows you to retrieve values from a table or set of tables, optionally performing conversions using functions. The **SELECT** command will be the major command most users execute against the database and will be your biggest source of headaches in the realm of tuning and maintaining performance in the database environment. Because the **SELECT** command is the most-used command, we cover it first.

The SELECT Command

The **SELECT** command is used to retrieve values that have been stored in a table or set of tables; the retrieval is usually based on some selection criteria. An unrestricted **SELECT** retrieves all values from the specified table, view, or snapshot. A restricted **SELECT** contains a **WHERE** clause with some restricting clauses. The **SELECT** command is also the basis for all subqueries in all other commands.

In order to **SELECT** from a table, you must have the **SELECT** privilege on the table or have the **SELECT ANY TABLE** system privilege. To **SELECT** from the base table(s) of a view, the owning schema of the view must have the **SELECT** privilege on the table or have the **SELECT ANY TABLE** system privilege.

Unless forced by the **DESC** qualifier into descending order or retrieved by way of an indexed-column lookup, all **SELECT** query results using an **ORDER BY** are returned in ascending (**ASC**) order. In the case of an indexed column, the rows will be returned in the order of the indexed column in the index. If no **ORDER BY** is specified or no index is used to retrieve the values, then the rows returned by a query will be in the same order as they are in the table.

At the absolute minimum, a **SELECT** statement consists of a **SELECT** command with an expression (expressions are fully covered in Chapter 3) and a **FROM** clause that specifies from where the data is to be selected. This is why the **DUAL** table is required with nondirected **SELECT** statements, such as **FROM** sequences or non-table-related, single-value functions such as **SYSDATE**. The dual table is a single row, single value table used for **SELECT** commands that otherwise wouldn't have a table to use in a **FROM** clause.

Figure 2.1 shows the complete syntax of the **SELECT** command.

The parameters have the following definitions:

➤ DISTINCT—Returns only one copy of any duplicate rows or of specific columns, as determined by the position of the **DISTINCT** parameter and returned by the **SELECT** statement. If the **DISTINCT** parameter is placed

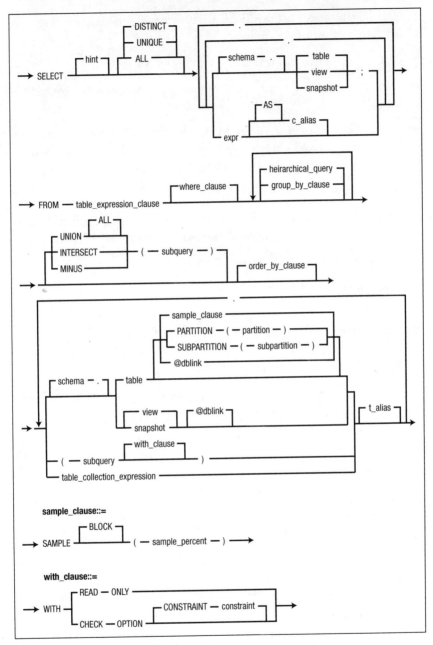

Figure 2.1   Syntax of the **SELECT** command.

immediately following the **SELECT** statement, all combinations of the columns that follow will be distinct.

➤ ALL—Returns all rows with duplicates (default value).

➤ * (an asterisk)—Used to return all columns from the specified table, view, or snapshot.

➤ PARTITION(*partition_name*), SUBPARTITION(*subpartition_name*)— Used when you know that the data is located in a particular partition or subpartition of a base table (such as monthly or quarterly data).

➤ expr—Selects an expression.

➤ c_alias—Column alias, used in subsequent statements in the **SELECT** command to refer to its column. A column alias cannot exceed 30 characters.

➤ schema—Owner of the table, view, or snapshot.

➤ table_name, view_name, view, snap—Name of the object from which values are selected.

➤ dblink—The database link to the remote instance where the object of the **SELECT** command is located. If a link is not specified, the object must be local or the **dblink** be masked by a synonym.

➤ subquery—Subquery that's specified identically to a view query definition.

➤ WITH—Uses the **CHECK ONLY** or **READ ONLY** options to restrict how a subquery handles data insertion (in the case of a subquery used in an UPDATE). With **READ ONLY**, the subquery columns cannot be updated. With **CHECK ONLY**, Oracle prohibits any changes to that table that would produce rows that are not included in the subquery.

➤ TABLE—Tells Oracle that a column is actually a nested object, such as a nested table or **VARRAY**, and instructs Oracle to flatten the return set.

➤ t_alias—Table alias, used in subsequent subqueries or in **WHERE** conditions. After a table alias is specified, the table name can no longer be used, or an error will be generated. A table alias cannot exceed 30 characters.

➤ SAMPLE—The **SAMPLE** clause is used to tell Oracle to perform a percentage of rows or percentage of blocks sample instead of a complete table scan. Used for some statistical analysis.

WARNING: The use of statistically incorrect assumptions when using this feature can lead to incorrect or undesirable results.

➤ **WHERE**—Used to restrict the returned rows to a designated subset. Only **WHERE** clauses result in the use of indexes.. A **SELECT** command without a **WHERE** clause will return all rows of the specified tables, joined in a Cartesian product. A Cartesian product is wasteful of resources and is generally not the desired result. In rare cases, a non-restricted **SELECT** can result in the use of an index if all of the columns selected are in the index. You may also force the use of an index using a **HINT**.

➤ **ORDER BY**—Forces order of the returned rows to either ascending (**ASC**): from least to most, which is the default order; or descending: from highest to lowest, with the descending (**DESC**) operator. The **ORDER BY** clause doesn't restrict rows, it only orders the returned data set. The **ORDER BY** clause can use the column name, column-order specifier, or column alias to identify the columns to be used in the sort. The columns specified for a sort are sorted in left-to-right order, so the values returned are sorted first by the leftmost column, then by the next, and so forth, until all columns have been sorted.

➤ **START WITH...CONNECT BY**—Returns rows in a hierarchical order.

➤ **GROUP BY**—Groups the rows based on the specified column's values. The *expr* for the statement must include at least one grouping function, such as **COUNT()**. All columns not participating in the grouping functions must be included in the **GROUP BY** column list. **GROUP BY** does not restrict values; it merely groups them. A **GROUP BY** clause, unless overridden with the **ORDER BY** sort option **DESC**, always returns values sorted in ascending order. A **GROUP BY** clause can use the column name but not the column-position specification or the column alias. The **CUBE** and **ROLLUP** allow pseudo-crosstab reporting by doing summations based on the **GROUP BY** and **DECODE** values. **CUBE** performs cross-tabulation while **ROLLUP** performs automatic subtotaling.

➤ **HAVING**—Restricts the **GROUP BY** clause to those groups for which the **HAVING** clause is **TRUE**. You can't have a **HAVING** clause without a **GROUP BY** clause.

➤ **UNION, UNION ALL, INTERSECT, MINUS**—Specify the set operation for the **SELECT** commands specified.

➤ **ASC, DESC**—Determine the ordering of the returned set of values.

➤ **FOR UPDATE**—Locks the selected rows.

➤ **OF**—Locks the rows of only the specified table or table columns.

➤ **NOWAIT**—Returns control to you if the **SELECT** command attempts to lock a row that is locked by another user. Otherwise, the **SELECT** command waits for any locked rows to be free and returns the results when they are free.

If two or more tables have the same column names in a **SELECT** statement, the table name or table alias must be used to differentiate them.

Column aliases can be used in **ORDER BY** but in no other clauses.

If **DISTINCT** is used, the total number of bytes selected in all select list expressions is limited to the size of a data block minus some overhead.

Hints can be used to tell the Oracle optimizer how to optimize the query, thus forcing query behavior to what you want, instead of what the optimizer thinks it should be.

If all you could do with a **SELECT** command was look at data from one table, it would be pretty useless. We take a look at joins and subqueries in the following subsections.

Any common named columns in joined tables must be prefixed by table names, view names, snapshot names, or a specified alias.

Hierarchical Queries

Hierarchical joins occur when one column in the join relates to another, such as in a plan_table created by execution of the UTLXPLAN.SQL script and used by the **EXPLAIN PLAN** command. Hierarchical queries are usually resolved using self-joins. An example of a hierarchical query is the classic bill-of-materials table. In tables that may have hierarchical joins, the **START WITH...CONNECT BY...WHERE** combination allows you to break out this relationship:

➤ The **START WITH** clause specifies the root row of the hierarchy.

➤ The **CONNECT BY** clause specifies the relationship between the parent and child rows. This clause must contain a **PRIOR** operator to refer to the parent row.

➤ The **WHERE** clause is used to restrict the rows returned by the query without affecting other rows of the hierarchy.

The **LEVEL** clause creates a level pseudo-column that returns an integer corresponding to the row's level within the hierarchy.

Hierarchical queries are restricted in that the same **SELECT** command that performs a hierarchical query cannot perform a join, nor can it contain an **ORDER BY** clause. Listing 2.1 shows a hierarchical query against the **PLAN_TABLE**. In this example, the explain plan generated by the **EXPLAIN PLAN** command against a **SQL** statement is returned indented based on the level of the plan step within the plan hierarchy.

Listing 2.1   Example hierarchical query.

```
SELECT LPAD( ' ' , 2*LEVEL) || OPERATION || ' ' || OBJECT_NAME
QUERY_PLAN
FROM PLAN_TABLE
CONNECT BY PRIOR ID = PARENT_ID
START WITH ID=1;
```

Joins

Joins are **SELECT** commands that retrieve data from two or more tables. Remember that a table can be joined to itself by the use of table aliases. The **WHERE** clause in a **SELECT** statement provides join conditions. Join conditions determine how data is selected from each table in the join to fill in the specified columns in the select list. Listing 2.2 shows a simple equijoin between two tables.

Listing 2.2   Example simple join.

```
select
    d.deptno,
    d.dname,
    e.empno,
    e.sal,
    e.comm
from
    dept d,
    emp e
where
    d.deptno=e.deptno;
```

Note: The minimum number of joins required to relate a set of tables is the number of tables in the join minus one (so, for three tables, two joins at a minimum will be required). If you use fewer than n–1 joins, the properly joined tables will have their results Cartesian-joined to the table or tables that are left out.

In a test of a join of the **DBA_TABLES, DBA_TAB_COLUMNS, DBA_TAB_PRIVS,** and **DBA_OBJECTS** views—using a join between the **TABLE_NAME** columns and leaving the join to the **OBJECT_NAME** column out of the conditions—a count of 607,662 was returned. When the proper joins between **TABLE_NAME** and **OBJECT_NAME** and between **DBA_TABLES** and **DBA_OBJECTS** were added, the result count dropped to 210.

An *equijoin* uses any of the equality operators (=, !=, <, >, <>, >=, <=). Depending on the optimizer algorithm chosen, the total size of the columns in the equijoin of a single table may be limited to **db_block_size** bytes minus overhead. An equijoin is generally used to display data from two (or more) tables that have common values residing in corresponding columns. Listing 2.3 is an equijoin using the = operator.

A *self-join* joins a table to itself. Employing this option requires that table aliases be used. Listing 2.3 shows a self-join.

Listing 2.3   Example of a self-join.

```
select avg(b.good/(b.good+a.garbage))*100 good_percent
from sql_garbage a, sql_garbage b
where a.users=b.users
and a.garbage is not null and b.good is not null;
(Notice the use of table aliases)
```

A *Cartesian product* results if two tables are specified in a **SELECT** statement without a qualifying **WHERE** clause and join condition. This statement generates a result set with all possible combinations of the rows in the tables, such that the number of rows returned is equal to the product of the number of rows in each table. (That is, if table A has 10 rows, and table B has 20 rows, 200 rows will be returned. Obviously, if we extrapolate this concept to a couple of million row tables, you can see that a Cartesian product is not a desirable outcome the majority of the time.)

An *outer join* extends the results of a simple query. It returns all rows that satisfy the join condition and those rows from one of the tables for which no rows from the other table satisfy the join condition. The outer-join operator is (+)—the plus sign surrounded by parentheses. The operator is placed on the side of the join statement deficient in information. The outer-join operator can appear only in the **WHERE** clause applied to a column name. If the specified tables have multiple join conditions, the operator must be present in all of the specified conditions. The outer join can't be used in an **OR** expression, and the outer-join operator can't be applied to a column compared using an **IN** condition or subquery.

The basic format for an outer join is shown in Figure 2.2.

The restrictions on outer joins are as follows:

➤ The (+) operator can appear only in the **WHERE** clause and can apply only to a table or view.

➤ If there are multiple join conditions, the (+) operator must be used in all of these conditions.

➤ The (+) operator can be applied only to a column, not to an expression. But it can be applied to a column inside an arbitrary expression and to the **TABLE** clause for a nested table or **VARRAY**.

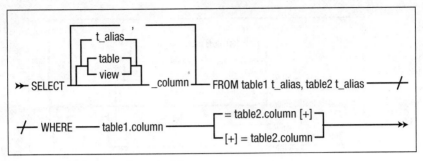

Figure 2.2   Basic syntax of an outer join.

➤ A condition containing a column with a **(+)** operator cannot be **OR**-related to another condition; neither can it be used in an **IN** condition.

➤ A column marked with the **(+)** operator cannot be compared to a subquery.

➤ Only one table in a multitable join can have the **(+)** operator applied to its joins to one other table.

Subqueries

Subqueries are used to return one or more values or sets of values to be used for comparison purposes. A subquery using a single-row comparison operator can return only a single value. A subquery can't use ordering clauses, such as **OR-DER BY** or **GROUP BY**, and it cannot contain a **FOR UPDATE** clause. The subquery must return a single value if it's used in an equality comparison, but if it's used with **IN**, a subquery can return multiple values. Other than the restriction on the use of **ORDER BY, GROUP BY,** and **FOR UPDATE**, the syntax of the subquery is nearly identical to a standard **SELECT** statement.

One caveat to the limitation on **GROUP BY** and **ORDER BY** in a subquery is in the special case of an inline view subquery. An inline view can use a **GROUP BY** or an **ORDER BY** clause. An inline view is a subquery that is placed in the **FROM** section of the **SELECT** and is treated identically to a view.

To allow subqueries against nested tables, a **TABLE** clause has been added to the **FROM** clause, as shown in Figure 2.3.

NULL Operations

Oracle supports **NULL** operations. Any operation that involves a one-sided **NULL** (multiply by **NULL**, divide by **NULL**, add **NULL**, or subtract **NULL**) will result in a **NULL**. Almost all functions, if called with a **NULL** operand, will return a **NULL** (with the exception of **NVL** and **DECODE**, which can be used

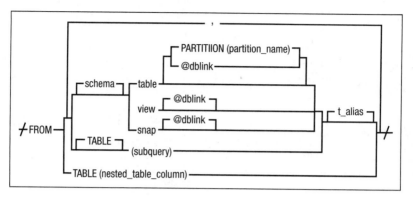

Figure 2.3 Addition of **TABLE** to **FROM** in subselect.

to convert **NULL** values). The special clauses **IS NULL** and **IS NOT NULL** must be used when **NULL**s are expected.

If a column contains a **NULL** value, it is ignored for most mathematical operations, such as **SUM, AVG, MIN, MAX,** and **COUNT.** The comparison operators—such as =, !=, <, >, and <>—will not work against **NULL** values. An example would be the following:

```
SELECT COUNT(*) FROM restrictions WHERE use_restrict!='ADMIN';
```

The return from the above **SELECT** statement will be only columns that have values that don't match **"ADMIN"**, *excluding* **NULL** values. For the **SELECT** statement to include **NULL** values, it will have to be rewritten as:

```
SELECT COUNT(*) FROM restrictions WHERE use_restrict!='ADMIN'
OR  use_restrict IS NULL;
```

Top-N Queries

Another special form of query that uses a subquery that has been optimized for Oracle8i is the Top-n query. This query was very difficult in previous versions but by using the form of query shown in Listing 2.4 the query becomes if not simple, at least doable in Oracle8i.

Listing 2.4   Example Top-n query.

```
SELECT displayed_column_list FROM
   (SELECT inner_column_list FROM table
   WHERE condition_list
   ORDER BY Top-N_column ASC|DESC)
WHERE  ROWNUM <=  N;
```

Tables 2.1 and 2.2 shows the various **NULL** and **TRUTH** logic used by Oracle.

Table 2.1	NULL test logic table.	
	NULL	**NOT NULL**
NULL	TRUE	FALSE
NOT NULL	FALSE	TRUE

Table 2.2	TRUTH logic table.		
	TRUE	**FALSE**	**UNKNOWN**
OR operator			
TRUE	TRUE	TRUE	TRUE
FALSE	TRUE	FALSE	UNKNOWN
UNKNOWN	TRUE	UNKNOWN	UNKNOWN
NOT operator			
	FALSE	TRUE	UNKNOWN
AND operator			
TRUE	TRUE	FALSE	UNKNOWN
FALSE	FALSE	FALSE	FALSE
UNKNOWN	UNKNOWN	FALSE	UNKNOWN

SELECT Examples

Because the **SELECT** command is the prevalent command in the test questions, let's show some more detailed examples using **SELECT**. Generally speaking, the exam covers the following **SELECT** command topics:

➤ Selecting rows

➤ Limiting selected rows

➤ Using single row functions

➤ Displaying data from multiple tables

➤ Group functions

➤ Subqueries

➤ Sorting

In this chapter, we examine each of these exam topics and show examples using data dictionary views and tables for each type of query.

SELECTing Rows

The command used for selecting rows is of course the **SELECT** command. Probably the simplest form of the **SELECT** is the totally unrestricted, select everything:

```
SELECT * FROM dba_objects;
```

The problem with a simple **SELECT** of everything in a table comes when the table has the following :

➤ Very long rows or data items such as **LOBs**, **REFs**, or **LONG** datatypes

➤ A large number of rows

In either case, you must restrict either the number of columns or the number of rows returned. Table 2.3 shows the structure of the **DBA_OBJECTS** data dictionary view. Notice the number of columns and the total length possible for a single row.

The total length of a single row could exceed 251 bytes if we did an unrestricted query from the **DBA_OBJECTS** view. In many cases, the maximum row length that can be viewed without wrapping is 132 bytes. The **DBA_OBJECTS** view may have several thousand rows, so again we will want to restrict the number of rows returned as well as the number—and perhaps size—of columns.

Table 2.3 Structure of the DBA_OBJECTS View.		
Name	**Null?**	**Type**
OWNER	Y	VARCHAR2(30)
OBJECT_NAME	Y	VARCHAR2(128)
SUBOBJECT_NAME	Y	VARCHAR2(30)
OBJECT_ID	Y	NUMBER
DATA_OBJECT_ID	Y	NUMBER
OBJECT_TYPE	Y	VARCHAR2(15)
CREATED	Y	DATE
LAST_DDL_TIME	Y	DATE
TIMESTAMP	Y	VARCHAR2(19)
STATUS	Y	VARCHAR2(7)
TEMPORARY	Y	VARCHAR2(1)
GENERATED	Y	VARCHAR2(1)
SECONDARY	Y	VARCHAR2(1)
Total Bytes	approximately 251 bytes	

To begin simply, let's first restrict the number of rows returned by filtering against the **OWNER** column. Let's search for all rows that have objects owned by the user **SYSTEM**. You should try these **SELECT**s from the user **SYS** or **SYSTEM** on your Oracle database.

```
SELECT * FROM dba_objects WHERE owner='SYSTEM';
```

Notice how we restricted the rows returned by simply specifying a **WHERE** clause. How do we limit the number of columns? Listing only those column names that we wish to see in our result set restricts the number of columns in a result set from a **SELECT** command. An example would be if we only wanted to see **OWNER, OBJECT_NAME, OBJECT_TYPE**, and the last time the object was modified: **LAST_DDL_TIME**.

```
SELECT owner, object_name, object_type, last_ddl_time FROM dba_objects
WHERE owner='SYSTEM';
```

Restricting the length of returned columns can be done in one of two ways. If you are in the SQLPLUS environment, you can use **COLUMN** commands to format how each column is displayed. If you are in PL/SQL or other non-interactive environments, then you will have to use Oracle functions to restrict the size or format of a data item. Functions such as **SUBSTR(), RTRIM(), LTRIM(), TRUNC(), TRIM()**, and **TO_CHAR()** can be used to restrict the length or to force formatting of data items. These are single row functions. An example use of functions would be the following:

```
SELECT SUBSTR(owner,1,10) owner,
SUBSTR(object_name,1,10) object_name,
SUBSTR(object_type,1,10) object_type,
TO_CHAR(last_ddl_time,'DD-MON-YYYY HH24:MI') last_ddl_time
FROM dba_objects WHERE owner='SYSTEM';
```

The only problem with using the **SUBSTR()** function is that it slices the exact substring from the specified data item. For example, look at Listing 2.5.

Listing 2.5   Example **SELECT** output using **SUBSTR()**.

```
DMDB:r
  1   select substr(owner,1,10) owner,
  2   substr(object_name,1,10) object_name,
  3   substr(object_type, 1,10) object_type,
  4   to_char(last_ddl_time,'dd-mon-yyyy hh24:mi') last_ddl_time
  5   from dba_objects
  6*  where owner='SYSTEM'
```

```
OWNER       OBJECT_NAM OBJECT_TYP LAST_DDL_TIME
----------  ---------- ---------- ----------------
SYSTEM      AQ$DEF$_AQ VIEW       03-aug-1998 11:56
SYSTEM      AQ$DEF$_AQ VIEW       03-aug-1998 11:56
SYSTEM      AQ$_QIDSEQ SEQUENCE   03-aug-1998 11:53
SYSTEM      AQ$_QUEUES TABLE      03-aug-1998 11:53
SYSTEM      AQ$_QUEUES INDEX      03-aug-1998 11:53
SYSTEM      AQ$_QUEUES INDEX      03-aug-1998 11:53
SYSTEM      USER_PRIVS VIEW       03-aug-1998 12:20
SYSTEM      USER_PROFI TABLE      03-aug-1998 12:20
```

Notice how several objects appear to have identical names and object types (**AQ$_QUEUES**), which is not allowed. Actually, they are all named differently; the **SUBSTR()** function sliced away the unique portion of the names leaving us to scratch our heads over which is which. Some might think that using the **RTRIM** or **TRIM** functions would do the trick; unfortunately, while they trim away the trailing blanks for the data items, they leave the default length as is.

As was stated earlier, inside SQLPLUS we can use the **COLUMN** command (usually shortened to **COL**) to restrict each column's output length. One nice feature of the **COLUMN** command is that it allows the column value to wrap if the column value exceeds the specified format length; thus no data is lost. **COLUMN** also allows you to format and change the default heading values as well as several other advanced features. Let's look at a select using the **COLUMN** commands in SQLPLUS to format the output.

```
COL owner FORMAT a10 HEADING 'Owner'
COL object_name FORMAT a10 HEADING 'Object|Name'
COL object_type FORMAT a10 HEADING 'Object|Type'
COL last_ddl_time FORMAT a16 HEADING 'Last|DDL Time'
SELECT owner, object_name, object_type,
TO_CHAR(last_ddl_time,'DD-MON-YYYY HH24:MI') last_ddl_time
FROM dba_objects
WHERE owner='SYSTEM';
```

The results of the above **SELECT** are shown in Listing 2.6.

Listing 2.6   Example output from a COLUMN formatted command set.
```
DMDB: SELECT owner, object_name, object_type,
  2   TO_CHAR(last_ddl_time,'dd-mon-yyyy hh24:mi') last_ddl_time
  3   FROM dba_objects
  4* WHERE owner='SYSTEM'
```

Owner	Object Name	Object Type	LAST_DDL_TIME
SYSTEM	AQDEF_AQ CALL	VIEW	03-aug-1998 11:56
SYSTEM	AQDEF_AQ ERROR	VIEW	03-aug-1998 11:56
SYSTEM	AQ$_QIDSEQ	SEQUENCE	03-aug-1998 11:53
SYSTEM	AQ$_QUEUES	TABLE	03-aug-1998 11:53
SYSTEM	AQ$_QUEUES _CHECK	INDEX	03-aug-1998 11:53
SYSTEM	AQ$_QUEUES _PRIMARY	INDEX	03-aug-1998 11:53
SYSTEM	AQ$_QUEUE_ TABLES	TABLE	03-aug-1998 11:53
SYSTEM	USER_PRIVS	VIEW	03-aug-1998 12:20
SYSTEM	USER_PROFI LE	TABLE	03-aug-1998 12:20

So, to limit the number of columns returned, we simply list only those columns that we want to see data from in the body of the **SELECT** command. To limit the size of returned columns, we can use internal Oracle functions such as **SUBSTR()**, or if we are using the SQLPLUS interface, we can use the **COLUMN** command to reformat data values without losing information due to truncation. What if we want to enforce an order on returned rows?

Enforcing Order

Order can be imposed on **SELECT** command results sets by use of the **ORDER BY** clause. The **ORDER BY** clause accepts as its argument either a single order column or a set of order columns. The **ORDER BY** clause can also accept positional indicators and column alias values as its arguments. The **ORDER BY** clause can enforce ascending (**ASC**) or descending (**DESC**) orders based on the columns specified. Listing 2.7 shows the results from various **ORDER BY** clauses.

Listing 2.7   Example SELECTs using the ORDER BY clause.

```
SQL> SELECT username, default_tablespace
  *2 FROM dba_users;

USERNAME                          DEFAULT_TABLESPACE
------------------------------    ------------------------------
SYS                               SYSTEM
SYSTEM                            TOOLS
OUTLN                             SYSTEM
MIGRATE                           SYSTEM
```

```
REPMAN                          TOOLS
DBSNMP                          SYSTEM
GRAPHICS_DBA                    GRAPHICS_DATA
AULTM                           USER_DATA
ORDSYS                          SYSTEM

9 rows selected.

SQL> SELECT username, default_tablespace
  2 FROM dba_users
  3 ORDER BY username;

USERNAME                        DEFAULT_TABLESPACE
------------------------------  ------------------------------
AULTM                           USER_DATA
DBSNMP                          SYSTEM
GRAPHICS_DBA                    GRAPHICS_DATA
MIGRATE                         SYSTEM
ORDSYS                          SYSTEM
OUTLN                           SYSTEM
REPMAN                          TOOLS
SYS                             SYSTEM
SYSTEM                          TOOLS

9 rows selected.

SQL> SELECT username, default_tablespace
  2  FROM dba_users
  3  ORDER BY username desc;

USERNAME                        DEFAULT_TABLESPACE
------------------------------  ------------------------------
SYSTEM                          TOOLS
SYS                             SYSTEM
REPMAN                          TOOLS
OUTLN                           SYSTEM
ORDSYS                          SYSTEM
MIGRATE                         SYSTEM
GRAPHICS_DBA                    GRAPHICS_DATA
DBSNMP                          SYSTEM
AULTM                           USER_DATA

9 rows selected.
SQL> SELECT username, default_tablespace
  2  FROM dba_users
  3* ORDER BY default_tablespace,username;
```

USERNAME	DEFAULT_TABLESPACE
GRAPHICS_DBA	GRAPHICS_DATA
DBSNMP	SYSTEM
MIGRATE	SYSTEM
ORDSYS	SYSTEM
OUTLN	SYSTEM
SYS	SYSTEM
REPMAN	TOOLS
SYSTEM	TOOLS
AULTM	USER_DATA

9 rows selected.

In the examples in Listing 2.7, first we see a non-ordered **SELECT**, which will return the rows selected either by inserted order in the table or by indexed order if an index is used to resolve the query. Next, we see a single column **ORDER BY** on the username column using both the default ascending sort and a forced **DESC** (descending) sort. In Listing 2.7, we also see a two-column sort where the return is sorted by default_tablespace and then for each set of values for each default_tablespace value the result set is also sorted by username.

Using **ORDER BY** always results in a **SORT**, which can have a performance impact if the result set exceeds the initialization parameter **SORT_AREA_SIZE** in size or, if the parameter **SORT_AREA_RETAINED_SIZE** is set, if that value is exceeded. The **SORT** can be avoided by having an index on the column that we use to **SORT** the returned values where the index is ordered as we want the result set to be. However, note that the use of the index to resolve the **SORT** can actually result in poorer performance than allowing a memory-based **SORT**, so be careful when using this technique.

In **ORDER BY**, you must use the column name or its position in the **SELECT**; you cannot use the column alias to define the sort column. In **GROUP BY**, you must use the column name. If the column name is not unique, you must use either the table name or the table alias in both commands.

The **GROUP BY** clause is another sort method, however, it is usually used when grouping functions such as **SUM()** or **COUNT()** are used in a **SELECT**. If all columns in the result set are used to sort the result set, then the **GROUP BY** clause can be used to sort the returned rows; otherwise all non-function affected columns must be included in the **GROUP BY** clause. If a one or more columns affected by grouping functions are present in a query along with one or more non-grouped columns, the non-grouped columns must all be present in the **GROUP BY** clause. Listing 2.8 shows several examples using **GROUP BY**.

Listing 2.8   Example SELECTs using the GROUP BY clause.

```
SQL> SELECT username, default_tablespace
  2 FROM dba_users
 *3 GROUP BY default_tablespace,username;

USERNAME                         DEFAULT_TABLESPACE
------------------------------   ------------------------------
GRAPHICS_DBA                     GRAPHICS_DATA
DBSNMP                           SYSTEM
MIGRATE                          SYSTEM
ORDSYS                           SYSTEM
OUTLN                            SYSTEM
SYS                              SYSTEM
REPMAN                           TOOLS
SYSTEM                           TOOLS
AULTM                            USER_DATA

12 rows selected.

SQL> SELECT username, default_tablespace
  2 FROM dba_users
 *3 GROUP BY default_tablespace;

SELECT username, default_tablespace
       *
ERROR at line 1:
ORA-00979: not a GROUP BY expression


SQL> SELECT COUNT(username) users, default_tablespace
  2 FROM dba_users
 *3 GROUP BY default_tablespace
SQL> /

    USERS DEFAULT_TABLESPACE
--------- ------------------------------
        1 GRAPHICS_DATA
        5 SYSTEM
        2 TOOLS
        1 USER_DATA
```

In the examples in Listing 2.8, we see a **GROUP BY** that uses all of the columns returned in the result set. The next example in Listing 2.8 shows the error that will result if a non-grouping function altered column is left out of the column list in the clause. The final example in Listing 2.8 shows a **GROUP BY** with a grouping function applied to a column. Multiple grouping functions can be applied to the same result set; however, their effect will be limited to the major **GROUP BY** subsets. The **GROUP BY** clause has the **HAVING** sub-clause, which is used to restrict the rows returned. Listing 2.9 shows an example of a multi-column **GROUP BY** using multiple grouping functions.

Listing 2.9   Example of a SELECT with multiple groupings and a GROUP BY.

```
SQL> SELECT owner,
  2 COUNT(*) objects, SUM(bytes) bytes
  3 FROM dba_extents
  4 GROUP BY owner
  5 /


OWNER                             OBJECTS     BYTES
------------------------------    --------  --------
GRAPHICS_DBA                           21   8724480
OUTLN                                   6     98304
REPMAN                                176   7208960
SYS                                   670  52912128
SYSTEM                                 61   2662400


5 rows selected.
```

A new feature in Oracle8i is the addition of the **ROLLUP** and **CUBE** functions to the **GROUP BY** clause. These actually allow the summation of data vectors or partitions over an entire **SELECT** statement. By data vectors or partitions, we mean that you can specify the summation over department in an employee table or territory/salesperson in a sales table, for example. Listing 2.10 shows some examples using the **ROLLUP** operator in the **GROUP BY** clause.

Listing 2.10   Example of a SELECT using ROLLUP.

```
SQL> select
  2          owner,
  3          tablespace_name,
  4          sum(bytes)/(1024*1024) total_meg
  5  from dba_extents
  6  group by owner,tablespace_name
  7  /


OWNER                    TABLESPACE_NAME              TOTAL_MEG
------------------------ ---------------------------- ----------
AULTM                    USER_DATA                     .0390625
OEMMAN                   OEM_REPOSITORY                      24
OUTLN                    SYSTEM                         .09375
SYS                      RBS                          13.203125
SYS                      SYSTEM                       55.3828125
```

```
SYSTEM              TOOLS                    2.921875
SYSTEM              USER_DATA               1.3671875

SQL> select
  2          owner,
  3          tablespace_name,
  4          sum(bytes)/(1024*1024) total_meg
  5  from dba_extents
  6  group by rollup (owner,tablespace_name)
  7  /

OWNER                    TABLESPACE_NAME             TOTAL_MEG
------------------------ --------------------------- ----------
AULTM                    USER_DATA                    .0390625
AULTM                                                 .0390625
OEMMAN                   OEM_REPOSITORY                     24
OEMMAN                                                      24
OUTLN                    SYSTEM                        .09375
OUTLN                                                  .09375
SYS                      RBS                          13.203125
SYS                      SYSTEM                      55.3828125
SYS                                                  68.5859375
SYSTEM                   TOOLS                        2.921875
SYSTEM                   USER_DATA                   1.3671875
SYSTEM                                                4.2890625
                                                     97.0078125


SQL> select
  2          decode(grouping(owner),1,'Owner Total',owner) owner,
  3          decode(grouping(tablespace_name), 1,'Tablespace Total',
  4          tablespace_name) tablespace_name,
  5           sum(bytes)/(1024*1024) total_meg
  6  from dba_extents
  7  group by rollup (owner,tablespace_name)
  8  /

OWNER                    TABLESPACE_NAME             TOTAL_MEG
------------------------ --------------------------- ----------
AULTM                    USER_DATA                    .0390625
AULTM                    Tablespace Total             .0390625
OEMMAN                   OEM_REPOSITORY                     24
OEMMAN                   Tablespace Total                   24
OUTLN                    SYSTEM                        .09375
OUTLN                    Tablespace Total              .09375
SYS                      RBS                          13.203125
SYS                      SYSTEM                      55.3828125
SYS                      Tablespace Total            68.5859375
SYSTEM                   TOOLS                        2.921875
```

```
SYSTEM              USER_DATA                 1.3671875
SYSTEM              Tablespace Total          4.2890625
Owner Total         Tablespace Total         97.0078125
```

In the examples shown in Listing 2.10 , we first see a simple group by giving the total bytes for all of the objects owned by a specific owner in the database tablespaces. The second example shows the results of using the **ROLLUP** command. In the second example, note how a blank line is shown giving the subtotal for each owner in each tablespace. To make this more readable, you can use the **GROUPING** clause in the **DECODE** statement. If a value is used in a **GROUP BY ROLLUP**, the resulting value will have a heading of 1; otherwise it will be 0. Thus, we make the third example more readable by use of the **DECODE** and **GROUPING** clauses. The order of column names in the **ROLLUP** is important because it determines the way the total summation will be developed. In our example, the final total summary is for all owners. Had we reversed the order it would have been for all tablespaces.

Listing 2.11 shows the use of the **CUBE** operator. The **CUBE** operator produces not only individual area summary, it also provides overall report summaries. Listing 2.11 shows the use of the **CUBE** operator using the same example selects from Listing 2.10

Listing 2.11   Example grouping using the **CUBE** operator.

```
SQL> select
  2          owner,
  3          tablespace_name,
  4          sum(bytes)/(1024*1024) total_meg
  5  from dba_extents
  6  group by owner,tablespace_name
  7  /
```

OWNER	TABLESPACE_NAME	TOTAL_MEG
AULTM	USER_DATA	.0390625
OEMMAN	OEM_REPOSITORY	24
OUTLN	SYSTEM	.09375
SYS	RBS	13.203125
SYS	SYSTEM	55.3828125
SYSTEM	TOOLS	2.921875
SYSTEM	USER_DATA	1.3671875

```
SQL> select
  2          owner,
  3          tablespace_name,
  4          sum(bytes)/(1024*1024) total_meg
  5  from dba_extents
```

```
6  group by cube (owner,tablespace_name)
7  /
```

OWNER	TABLESPACE_NAME	TOTAL_MEG
AULTM	USER_DATA	.0390625
AULTM		.0390625
OEMMAN	OEM_REPOSITORY	24
OEMMAN		24
OUTLN	SYSTEM	.09375
OUTLN		.09375
SYS	RBS	13.203125
SYS	SYSTEM	55.3828125
SYS		68.5859375
SYSTEM	TOOLS	2.921875
SYSTEM	USER_DATA	1.3671875
SYSTEM		4.2890625
	OEM_REPOSITORY	24
	RBS	13.203125
	SYSTEM	55.4765625
	TOOLS	2.921875
	USER_DATA	1.40625
		97.0078125

```
SQL> select
  2        decode(grouping(owner),1,'Owner Total',owner) owner,
  3        decode(grouping(tablespace_name), 1,'Tablespace Total',
  4        tablespace_name) tablespace_name,
  5         sum(bytes)/(1024*1024) total_meg
  6  from dba_extents
  7  group by cube (owner,tablespace_name)
  8  /
```

OWNER	TABLESPACE_NAME	TOTAL_MEG
AULTM	USER_DATA	.0390625
AULTM	Tablespace Total	.0390625
OEMMAN	OEM_REPOSITORY	24
OEMMAN	Tablespace Total	24
OUTLN	SYSTEM	.09375
OUTLN	Tablespace Total	.09375
SYS	RBS	13.203125
SYS	SYSTEM	55.3828125
SYS	Tablespace Total	68.5859375
SYSTEM	TOOLS	2.921875
SYSTEM	USER_DATA	1.3671875
SYSTEM	Tablespace Total	4.2890625
Owner Total	OEM_REPOSITORY	24

Owner Total	RBS	13.203125
Owner Total	SYSTEM	55.4765625
Owner Total	TOOLS	2.921875
Owner Total	USER_DATA	1.40625
Owner Total	Tablespace Total	97.0078125

From Listing 2.11, we can see that by using the **CUBE** operator the total over the entire report for each subcategory is also calculated along with the overall total.

Another new feature is the **SAMPLE** clause. The **SAMPLE** clause is used to take representative samples of data based on either a percentage of total rows or total blocks being sampled. The **SAMPLE** clause, if improperly used, can lead to erroneous conclusions so be sure to use it within proper statistical analysis guidelines.

The **BLOCK** sub-clause instructs Oracle to perform random block sampling instead of random row sampling.

The value for sample_percent is a number specifying the percentage of the total rows or block count to be included in the sample. The value must be in the range .000001 to 99.

You can only specify **SAMPLE** in a query that selects from a single table. Joins are not supported. When you specify **SAMPLE**, Oracle automatically uses the cost-based optimizer. The rule-based optimizer is not supported with this clause.

Joins

What if we need data from more than one table? As long as a relationship exists between the tables, we can join them in a query statement and pull the related information out of both tables. If no relationship exists, we can form a **SELECT** that gets information from both tables, but the data will be returned in an "all-or-nothing" type arrangement.

Joins can be simple or complex. The simplest join in most cases is the equijoin, which establishes a simple equality or inequality relationship between two tables of the form: tab1.col1 = tab2.col2. The datatypes of the two columns must be the same or convertible into a compatible type. Any forced conversion of datatypes (from number to character, for example) will result in the query not being able to use any indexes associated with the converted column. Listing 2.12 demonstrates several equijoins.

Listing 2.12   Example equijoins.

```
SQL> SELECT a.table_name,b.column_name
  2  FROM dba_tables a, dba_tab_columns b
  3  WHERE a.table_name = b.table_name
  4  AND a.tablespace_name = 'GRAPHICS_DATA';
```

```
TABLE_NAME                    COLUMN_NAME
----------------------------  -----------------------------
GRAPHICS_TABLE                BFILE_ID
GRAPHICS_TABLE                BFILE_TYPE
GRAPHICS_TABLE                BFILE_LOC
GRAPHICS_USERS                USERNAME
GRAPHICS_USERS                USER_FUNCTION
INTERNAL_GRAPHICS             GRAPHIC_ID
INTERNAL_GRAPHICS             GRAPHIC_TYPE
INTERNAL_GRAPHICS             GRAPHIC_BLOB

8 rows selected.

SQL> SELECT a.table_name,b.column_name, c.created
  2  FROM dba_tables a, dba_tab_columns b, dba_objects c
  3  WHERE a.table_name = b.table_name
  4  AND a.table_name = c.object_name
  5  AND a.tablespace_name = 'GRAPHICS_DATA'
  6* AND object_type = 'TABLE';

TABLE_NAME                    COLUMN_NAME                      CREATED
----------------------------  -----------------------------    --------
GRAPHICS_TABLE                BFILE_ID                         11-MAY-99
GRAPHICS_TABLE                BFILE_LOC                        11-MAY-99
GRAPHICS_TABLE                BFILE_TYPE                       11-MAY-99
GRAPHICS_USERS                USERNAME                         23-MAY-99
GRAPHICS_USERS                USER_FUNCTION                    23-MAY-99
INTERNAL_GRAPHICS             GRAPHIC_ID                       11-MAY-99
INTERNAL_GRAPHICS             GRAPHIC_BLOB                     11-MAY-99
INTERNAL_GRAPHICS             GRAPHIC_TYPE                     11-MAY-99

15 rows selected.
```

The examples in Listing 2.12 are a simple two table and three table (well, actually in this case they are views, but the principle is still the same) equijoins. Note that in order to ensure that you get the proper rows returned, there must be $n-1$ join conditions where n is the number of tables. If $n-1$ join conditions are not present, a Cartesian join will be performed against the non-equijoined table. Another important condition that is frequently overlooked is that not only must you have n-1 joins, you must also use n-1 of the tables in those joins.

Another type of join is the outer join. An outer join is when one of the tables participating in the join is deficient in data. An example would be a situation where a department exists but as yet has no employees. In the case where a department exists and has no employees and you want the department to still be listed in a report, an outer join would be required. An outer join is performed when the outer join indicator is placed at the end of the table name for the table deficient in data. The outer join indicator is a plus sign surrounded by parentheses: (+). Listing 2.13 demonstrates an outer join using some simple tables.

Listing 2.13   Example outer join.

```
SQL> SELECT * FROM department;

  DEPTNO DEPT_DESC
-------- ----------------------------------
       1 Administration
       2 Sales
       3 Marketing
       4 Consulting
       5 Training
       6 Remote Monitoring


6 rows selected.

SQL> SELECT * FROM employee;

  EMP_NO   DEPT_NO NAME
-------- -------- ----------------------------------
     100        1 Joe Boss
     101        1 Ann Assistant
     102        1 Fred Fumbles
     103        1 Frank Receives
     104        2 Sam Salesman
     105        2 Eliza Can
     106        2 Bill Cant
     107        3 Sara Smiles
     108        3 John Dont
     109        4 Gilles Gogeter
     110        4 Gomer Newbie


11 rows selected.

SQL> SELECT a.dept_desc, b.emp_no, b.name
  2  FROM department a, employee b
  3  WHERE a.deptno = b.dept_no
  4* ORDER BY dept_no;

DEPT_DESC                           EMP_NO   NAME
------------------------------   -------- ----------------------------
Administration                       100   Joe Boss
Administration                       101   Ann Assistant
Administration                       102   Fred Fumbles
```

```
Administration                103        Frank Receives
Sales                         104        Sam Salesman
Sales                         105        Eliza Can
Sales                         106        Bill Cant
Marketing                     107        Sara Smiles
Marketing                     108        John Dont
Consulting                    109        Gilles Gogeter
Consulting                    110        Gomer Newbie

11 rows selected.

SQL> SELECT a.dept_desc, b.emp_no, b.name
  2  FROM department a, employee b
  3  WHERE a.deptno=b.dept_no(+)
  4* ORDER BY dept_no;


DEPT_DESC                        EMP_NO    NAME
----------------------------     --------  -------------------------------
Administration                   100       Joe Boss
Administration                   101       Ann Assistant
Administration                   102       Fred Fumbles
Administration                   103       Frank Receives
Sales                            104       Sam Salesman
Sales                            105       Eliza Can
Sales                            106       Bill Cant
Marketing                        107       Sara Smiles
Marketing                        108       John Dont
Consulting                       109       Gilles Gogeter
Consulting                       110       Gomer Newbie
Training
Remote Monitoring

13 rows selected.
```

In the example in Figure 2.13, we see two tables, department and employee. Each department in the department table has employees with the exception of Training and Remote Monitoring. In the first join (not using the outer-join indicator), we get back 11 rows—the departments without employees are ignored. When we add the outer join indicator—as is shown in the second **SELECT**—we now get the two empty departments showing up in the output result set as well as the non-empty departments giving us 13 rows.

Self-Joins

A self-join is when a table relates back to itself. This can happen in an employee table where the department and title information is included, or in the classic

BOM (bill-of-materials) breakout problem. A good example of using a self-join is use of the plan_table created by the UTLXPLAN.SQL script for use with the **EXPLAIN PLAN** and **TKPROF** utilities. The plan_table contains the columns **ID** and **PARENT_ID,** which are used to join the table to itself. Another example is the case where a table may have duplicate rows; a query using the **ROWID** hidden column and the column values that cause duplication is used to identify the duplicate rows for removal. Listing 2.15 demonstrates these examples.

Listing 2.14 Example self-joins.

```
DMDB:DESC dba_temp
 Name                            Null?    Type
 ------------------------------  -------- ----

 NAME                                     VARCHAR2(64)
 VALUE                                    NUMBER
 REP_ORDER                                NUMBER

DMDB:EXPLAIN PLAN SET STATEMENT_ID='TEST1'
  2* FOR SELECT * FROM dba_temp WHERE rep_order>5


Explained.

DMDB:COLUMN operation FORMAT a20
DMDB:COLUMN options FORMAT a10
DMDB:COLUMN object_name FORMAT a20
DMDB:SELECT operation,options, object_name, id, parent_id
  2   FROM plan_table
  3   WHERE statement_id='TEST1'
  4* ORDER BY id

OPERATION              OPTIONS     OBJECT_NAME         ID       PARENT_ID
--------------------   ----------  -----------------   -------  --------

SELECT STATEMENT                                        0
TABLE ACCESS           FULL        DBA_TEMP             1        0

DMDB:SELECT LPAD('    ',2*LEVEL)||operation||' '||object_name
query_plan
  2   FROM plan_table WHERE statement_id='TEST1'
  3   CONNECT BY PRIOR id=parent_id
  4   START WITH id=0;

QUERY_PLAN
--------------------------------------------------------------------------

   SELECT STATEMENT
      TABLE ACCESS DBA_TEMP

DMDB:CREATE TABLE test_self_join (id number, desc_id varchar2(10))
```

Table created.

DMDB:INSERT INTO test_self_join VALUES (1,'TEST1');

1 row created.

...

DMDB:INSERT INTO test_self_join VALUES (4,'TEST4')

1 row created.

DMDB:COMMIT;

Commit complete.

DMDB:SELECT * FROM test_self_join;

```
       ID DESC_ID
-------- ----------
        1 TEST1
        1 TEST1
        1 TEST1
        2 TEST2
        3 TEST3
        3 TEST3
        4 TEST4
```

7 rows selected.

```
DMDB:SELECT a.rowid FROM test_self_join a
  2  WHERE a.rowid > (SELECT MIN (b.rowid)
  3  FROM test_self_join b
  4* WHERE b.id=a.id);

ROWID
------------------
AAAC4xAAPAAAADUAAB
AAAC4xAAPAAAADUAAC
AAAC4xAAPAAAADUAAF

DMDB:DELETE FROM test_self_join a
  2  WHERE a.rowid > (SELECT MIN (b.rowid)
  3  FROM test_self_join b
  4  WHERE b.id=a.id);
```

3 rows deleted.

```
DMDB:COMMIT;

Commit complete.

DMDB:SELECT * FROM test_self_join;

        ID DESC_ID
-------- ----------
         1 TEST1
         2 TEST2
         3 TEST3
         4 TEST4

DMDB:DESC sql_garbage
  Name                                  Null?    Type
  ----------------------------------    -------- ----
  USERS                                          VARCHAR2(30)
  GARBAGE                                        NUMBER
  GOOD                                           NUMBER

DMDB:select * from sql_garbage;

  USERS                          GARBAGE   GOOD
  ----------------------------   --------  --------
  ASAP                           680879
  ASAP                                     2182475
  ESTOECKE                                   88203
  JKISKEL                                   214491
  QDBA                                     2456368
  SYS                             33236
  SYS                                      1210234
  SYSTEM                        1245629
  SYSTEM                                    119171

9 rows selected.

DMDB:SELECT
   2     AVG(b.good/(b.good+a.garbage))*100 avg_reuse
   3   FROM sql_garbage a, sql_garbage b
   4   WHERE a.users=b.users
   5     AND a.garbage IS NOT NULL
   6     AND b.good IS NOT NULL;

AVG_REUSE
---------
61.895823
```

In the example, we see three types of self-joins, one using the **CONNECT BY** clause, one using a subquery, and the final using an alias join structure to relate the table to itself. Some items to note about the self-joins in Listing 2.14 are the following:

➤ The **CONNECT BY** must have a root value to start from, in this case the root value is zero.

➤ The subquery must use multiple aliases for the table.

➤ The join of the table to itself using the alias join must also use multiple aliases.

Cartesian Products

If a join is performed and no join condition is specified, a Cartesian product results. A Cartesian product is a result set that is the product of the two tables' total rows. If table "a" has 10 rows and table "b" has 100 rows and a Cartesian product is developed, the resulting result set will have 1000 rows. If a query joins three or more tables, the optimizer may find a way to choose a join order that precludes a Cartesian product, but don't count on it.

Hash Joins and Anti-Joins

Two new types of joins became available in late Oracle7 and Oracle8: the anti-join and the hash join.

The hash join has nothing to do with hash clusters or **TABLE ACCESS HASH** method. A hash join compares two tables in memory. The first table is full table scanned, and a hashing function is applied to the data in memory. Then, the second table is full-table scanned, and the hashing function is used to compare the values. Matching values are returned to the user. The user usually has nothing to do with this process and it is completely optimizer controlled. Generally, hash joins will only gain something for you if you are using parallel query. Generally, the optimizer will use hash joins for small tables, which can be scanned quickly. To use hash joins, the **HASH_JOIN_ENABLED** initialization parameter must be set to **TRUE**.

Several **HASH** parameters affect how hash joins are used. These are the following:

• HASH_JOIN_ENABLED—Set to true to use hash joins.

• HASH_AREA_SIZE—Large value reduces cost of hash joins so they are used more frequently (set to half the square root of the size of the smaller of the two objects, but not less than 1 megabyte). Suggested range is between 8–32 megabytes.

- HASH_MULTIBLOCK_IO_COUNT—Large value reduces cost of hash joins so they are used more frequently. Suggested size is 4.

To use anti-joins, you must set the initialization parameter ALWAYS_ANTI_JOIN to HASH or MERGE. This causes the NOT IN clause in queries to always be resolved using a parallel-hash or parallel-merge anti-join. If the ALWAYS_ANTI_JOIN parameter is set to anything other than HASH or MERGE, the NOT IN will be evaluated as a correlated subquery. You can force Oracle to perform a specific query as an ANTI-JOIN by using the MERGE_AJ or HASH_AJ hints.

Subqueries

We have already looked at subquery examples. We have also learned that if a NOT IN is declared and the initialization parameters aren't set to use the HASH or ANTI_JOIN type of joins, then a correlated subquery is generated to resolve the NOT IN condition. When a subquery is included in a FROM clause, it can also be considered an "inline view." Listing 2.16 shows some examples of subqueries.

Listing 2.15   Example SELECTs using subqueries.

```
DMDB:SELECT COUNT(*) num_owned, a.owner
  2  FROM dba_objects a
  3  WHERE 10<(SELECT COUNT(*) FROM dba_objects b
  4  WHERE a.owner=b.owner)
  5  GROUP BY a.owner;


NUM_OWNED OWNER
---------- ------------------------------
      3016 ASAP
      1954 DMADMIN
        38 EBOND
        14 EDI
      1605 PUBLIC
        67 QDBA
      1407 SYS
        90 SYSTEM


8 rows selected.

DMDB:SELECT COUNT(*) num_owned, a.owner
  2  FROM dba_objects a
  3  WHERE 100<(SELECT COUNT(*) FROM dba_objects b
  4  WHERE a.owner=b.owner)
  5  GROUP BY a.owner;
```

```
     NUM_OWNED OWNER
     ---------- -----------------------------
           3016 ASAP
           1954 DMADMIN
           1605 PUBLIC
           1407 SYS


DMDB:SELECT COUNT(*) num_owned, a.owner
  2   FROM dba_objects a
  3   WHERE a.owner NOT IN (SELECT b.owner FROM dba_objects b
  4   WHERE b.owner LIKE 'SYS%')
  5   GROUP BY a.owner;

  NUM_OWNED OWNER
  -------- ------------------------------
        3016 ASAP
        1954 DMADMIN
          38 EBOND
          14 EDI
        1605 PUBLIC
          67 QDBA


6 rows selected.

DMDB:SELECT COUNT(*) num_owned, a.owner
  2   FROM dba_objects a
  3   WHERE a.owner NOT IN (SELECT b.owner FROM dba_objects b
  4   WHERE b.owner LIKE 'S%')
  5   GROUP BY a.owner;

  NUM_OWNED OWNER
  -------- ------------------------------
        3016 ASAP
        1954 DMADMIN
          38 EBOND
          14 EDI
        1605 PUBLIC
          67 QDBA


6 rows selected.

DMDB:SELECT a.owner FROM (SELECT DISTINCT b.owner FROM dba_objects b
  2   WHERE b.owner LIKE 'S%') a;

OWNER
------------------------------
SYS
SYSTEM
```

In the examples in Listing 2.15, we see several forms of the subquery. First, we see a correlated subquery used to strip out any result sets that don't meet specific criteria (in this case, the owner must own at least 10 objects in the first example and 100 in the second). In the next example in Listing 2.15, we have a subquery that restricts values for all owners whose names start with 'SYS' and then just 'S'. The final example in Listing 2.15 shows a subquery used as an inline view.

Using the SET Operators UNION, UNION ALL, INTERSECT, and MINUS

Sometimes, you may need to merge the results of two disparate queries. In some cases there are no logical ways to join two sets of tables, but we want to display their contents in a single report. How can we accomplish these types of SELECTs without generating Cartesian products? The answers to these problems are the SET operators. The SET operators are UNION, UNION ALL, INTERSECT, and MINUS. A UNION merges the results of two queries, discarding any duplicate rows. A UNION ALL merges the results of two queries, leaving in duplicate values. The INTERSECT merges the results from two queries and leaves only the distinct rows. The MINUS operator returns all distinct rows selected by the first query but not the second. If the column names don't match, aliases must be used. The SET operators cannot be used with the object clauses THE or MULTISET or with the FOR UPDATE clause. Listing 2.16 demonstrates the various SET operators.

Listing 2.16 Example SELECTs using the SET operators.

```
SQL> SELECT object_name FROM dba_objects
  2 WHERE object_type = 'TABLE' AND owner = 'GRAPHICS_DBA';

OBJECT_NAME
-----------------------------------------------------------------
ART
ARTIST_STORE
BASIC_LOB_TABLE
GRAPHICS_TABLE
GRAPHICS_USERS
INTERNAL_GRAPHICS

6 rows selected.

SQL> SELECT object_name FROM dba_objects WHERE owner = 'GRAPHICS_DBA';

OBJECT_NAME
-----------------------------------------------------------------
ART
ARTIST_LIST
```

```
ARTIST_STORE
ARTIST_T
ART_T
BASIC_LOB_TABLE
GET_BFILES
GRAPHICS_SEC
GRAPHICS_SEC
GRAPHICS_TABLE
GRAPHICS_TABLE_SEQ
GRAPHICS_USERS
IMAGE_SEQ
INTERNAL_GRAPHICS
PICTURE_PART_V
PK_INTERNAL_GRAPHICS
SYS_C001192
SYS_C001193
SYS_LOB0000003140C00002$$
SYS_LOB0000003140C00003$$
SYS_LOB0000003146C00003$$

21 rows selected.

SQL> SELECT object_name FROM dba_objects
  2  WHERE object_type = 'TABLE' AND owner = 'GRAPHICS_DBA'
  3  UNION
  4  SELECT object_name FROM dba_objects WHERE owner =
'GRAPHICS_DBA';

OBJECT_NAME
-------------------------------------------------------------------
ART
ARTIST_LIST
ARTIST_STORE
ARTIST_T
ART_T
BASIC_LOB_TABLE
GET_BFILES
GRAPHICS_SEC
GRAPHICS_TABLE
GRAPHICS_TABLE_SEQ
GRAPHICS_USERS
IMAGE_SEQ
INTERNAL_GRAPHICS
PICTURE_PART_V
PK_INTERNAL_GRAPHICS
SYS_C001192
SYS_C001193
```

```
SYS_LOB0000003140C00002$$
SYS_LOB0000003140C00003$$
SYS_LOB0000003146C00003$$


20 rows selected.

SQL> SELECT object_name FROM dba_objects
  2  WHERE object_type = 'TABLE' AND owner = 'GRAPHICS_DBA'
  3  UNION ALL
  4  SELECT object_name FROM dba_objects WHERE owner =
'GRAPHICS_DBA';

OBJECT_NAME
-------------------------------------------------------------------
ART
ARTIST_STORE
BASIC_LOB_TABLE
GRAPHICS_TABLE
GRAPHICS_USERS
INTERNAL_GRAPHICS
ART
ARTIST_LIST
ARTIST_STORE
ARTIST_T
ART_T
BASIC_LOB_TABLE
GET_BFILES
GRAPHICS_SEC
GRAPHICS_SEC
GRAPHICS_TABLE
GRAPHICS_TABLE_SEQ
GRAPHICS_USERS
IMAGE_SEQ
INTERNAL_GRAPHICS
PICTURE_PART_V
PK_INTERNAL_GRAPHICS
SYS_C001192
SYS_C001193
SYS_LOB0000003140C00002$$
SYS_LOB0000003140C00003$$
SYS_LOB0000003146C00003$$


27 rows selected.

SQL> SELECT object_name FROM dba_objects
  2  WHERE object_type = 'TABLE' AND owner = 'GRAPHICS_DBA'
```

```
  3  INTERSECT
  4  SELECT object_name FROM dba_objects WHERE owner =
'GRAPHICS_DBA';

OBJECT_NAME
------------------------------------------------------------------
ART
ARTIST_STORE
BASIC_LOB_TABLE
GRAPHICS_TABLE
GRAPHICS_USERS
INTERNAL_GRAPHICS

6 rows selected.

SQL> SELECT object_name FROM dba_objects
  2  WHERE object_type = 'TABLE' AND owner = 'GRAPHICS_DBA'
  3  MINUS
  4  SELECT object_name FROM dba_objects WHERE owner =
'GRAPHICS_DBA';

no rows selected

SQL> SELECT object_name FROM dba_objects WHERE owner = 'GRAPHICS_DBA'
  2  MINUS
  3  SELECT object_name FROM dba_objects
  4  WHERE object_type = 'TABLE' AND owner = 'GRAPHICS_DBA';

OBJECT_NAME
------------------------------------------------------------------
ARTIST_LIST
ARTIST_T
ART_T
GET_BFILES
GRAPHICS_SEC
GRAPHICS_TABLE_SEQ
IMAGE_SEQ
PICTURE_PART_V
PK_INTERNAL_GRAPHICS
SYS_C001192
SYS_C001193
SYS_LOB0000003140C00002$$
SYS_LOB0000003140C00003$$
SYS_LOB0000003146C00003$$

14 rows selected.
```

The examples in Listing 2.17 show the results of the two non-merged queries and then the various results from using the **SET** operators. Note that the order for the **MERGE** and **MERGE ALL SELECT**s is not important; however, the order for the **INTERSECT** and **MINUS** operators is critical as is demonstrated by the last two examples.

Differences Between SQL and SQLPLUS Commands

You will usually use the SQLPLUS executable to execute your SQL scripts and anonymous PL/SQL blocks. Although the SQLWorksheet is provided by Oracle, it is not covered on the exam, so we do not cover it here.

SQL commands involve data definition language (DDL), Data Manipulation Language (DML), and Data Control Language (DCL) commands. Also bundled with SQL as far as Oracle is concerned are the various flow control and cursor control commands in PL/SQL.

SQLPLUS commands deal with the execution environment and output formatting for execution of your SQL and PL/SQL routines. Example SQLPLUS commands are shown in Table 2.4.

Listing 2.18 shows an example SQL script that uses the major SQLPLUS commands.

Table 2.4 Example SQLPLUS commands.	
Command	**Description**
!	Executes a single host level command (UNIX, NT)
$	Executes a single host level command (OpenVMS)
&(1-n)	Substitutes the user inputted variable in position *n* here
&*user_variable*	Substitutes the user variable here (will prompt for variable if not previously defined or **ACCEPT**ed
. (period)	Ends a substitution variable
/	Executes previous SQL command or terminates PL/SQL routine entry
@	On login, used to specify database alias as part of user/password@alias, or, used to automatically start an external routine as a part of user/password@alias @routine, or used to **GET** and **RUN** a SQL script if used form the command line in SQLPLUS
ACCEPT	Used to ask for a user variable usually used like: **ACCEPT** *variable* **PROMPT "Prompt string for variable"**
APPEND	Used to append to the current line in the buffer. This can be shortened to just A or a.

(continued)

Table 2.4   Example SQLPLUS commands (continued).

Command	Description
ATTRIBUTE	Specifies the display characteristics of a given attribute for an Object Type column, such as the format for NUMBER data. This command can also list current display characteristics for a single attribute or for all attributes of an Object Type.
BREAK	Used to specify **BREAK** values for a report output
BTITLE	Used to specify a report bottom title
CHANGE	Used to replace specific characters or phrases in the current buffer line. This can be shortened to just C or c.
CLEAR	Used to **CLEAR** definitions such as **COLUMN**, **BREAK** or **COMPUTE** definitions; also used to clear the screen or the buffer area
COLUMN	Used to specify column formats; can specify **HEADING**, **FORMAT**, **WORD_WRAP**, **JUSTIFY**, and other column related format issues
COMPUTE	Used to specify computed values such as **SUM**, **AVG**, **COUNT**, on **BREAK** values
CONNECT	Used to connect to a different database or user
COPY	Used to copy values from one table to another or one database to another; can be used for **LONG** datatypes
DEFINE	Used to define variables used in SQL routines
DEL	Used to delete the current line, a specified single (1–n) line or group (x y z) of lines, or a specified range (x–y) of lines from the buffer
DISCONNECT	Used to disconnect from the current database without exiting SQLPLUS; issues an implicit **COMMIT**
EDIT (ED)	Used to invoke the default system editor for the lines contained in the SQL buffer—usually Notepad on NT, vi on UNIX, and edt on OpenVMS
EXECUTE	Used to execute a single PL/SQL procedure or function call
EXIT	Exits the SQLPLUS executable; issues an implicit **COMMIT**
GET	Gets the specified external file and places it in the buffer without execution of the file
HOST	Forks out to the HOST system until an **EXIT** is issued at the HOST level
INPUT (I)	Inputs one line of text at the current location in the SQL buffer
LIST (L)	Lists the contents of the SQL buffer
PASSWORD	Allows change of the user password without echoing it to the terminal

(continued)

Table 2.4	Example SQLPLUS commands *(continued)*.
Command	**Description**
PAUSE	Pauses execution until the Enter key is pressed
PRINT	Prints the specified variable value to the screen
PROMPT	Prompts with the specified text; expects an Enter key stroke to terminate **PROMPT**
REMARK (REM)	Used to enter remarks in a SQL script; can also use a double dash
REPFOOTER	Used to specify a report footer
REPHEADER	Used to specify a report header
RUN	Runs the contents of the SQL buffer
SAVE	Used to save the contents of the SQL buffer to a file
SET	Used to set various environmental variables such as **LINESIZE** (width of page), **PAGESIZE** (number of lines), **ECHO** (echo all commands to screen), **VERIFY** (verify substitutions of variables), and **FEEDBACK** (give messages such as line counts and successful executions)
SPOOL	Used to specify the output file for script or command output
START	Used to load and run a SQL script (identical to the **@** command)
STORE	Saves the attributes of the current SQLPLUS session in an OS file
TIMING	Used to toggle timing on or off for SQL command execution timing
TTITLE	Used to specify a top-title for output
UNDEFINE	Used to undefined a variable
VARIABLE	Used to specify a variable definition
WHENEVER SQLERRORI OSERROR	Used to process errors in the SQL or OS environment

Listing 2.17   Example SQLPLUS script.

```
REM  ************************************************************
REM  NAME: AUTO_CHN.sql
REM  FUNCTION: Run CHAINING.sql for all of a specified users
tables.
REM  NOTES:   Requires a minor mod to CHAINING.sql. See
CHAINING.sql header.
REM  INPUTS:
REM            tabown = Name of owner.
REM  ************************************************************
ACCEPT tabown PROMPT 'Enter table owner: '
```

```
SET TERMOUT OFF FEEDBACK OFF VERIFY OFF ECHO OFF HEADING OFF PAGES
999
SET EMBEDDED ON
COLUMN value NEW_VALUE db NOPRINT
SELECT value FROM v$parameter WHERE name='db_name';
TTITLE 'REM Caining commands'
SPOOL rep_out\auto_chn.gql
SELECT 'START chaining &tabown '||table_name
  FROM dba_tables
 WHERE owner = UPPER('&tabown')
/
SPOOL OFF
TTITLE OFF
SPOOL rep_out\&db\chaining
START rep_out\auto_chn.gql
SPOOL OFF
UNDEF tabown
SET TERMOUT ON FEEDBACK 15 VERIFY ON PAGESIZE 20 LINESIZE 80 SPACE
1
SET EMBEDDED OFF
HOST del rep_out\auto_chn.gql
PAUSE Press enter to continue
EXIT
```

First, we would need to start SQLPLUS and connect to the database in order to run the script:

```
$ sqlplus system/manager@aultdb1 @auto_chain.sql
```

This command executes the SQLPLUS executable, connects to the database specified by the TNSNAMES.SQL file alias aultdb1 using the user **SYSTEM** and password **MANAGER,** and then executes the script AUTO_CHAIN.SQL. If you do not specify the username or password, SQLPLUS will prompt you for them; if you do not specify the database, the database in the environmental variable **ORACLE_SID** will be used by default. We could have left off the script specification and as soon as we logged in, used the @ or **START** commands with the script name to load and run the script.

So what do the lines in the script in Figure 2.20 do for us? Let's look at some of them. First, we have the lines that begin with **REM**, which is short for **REMARK.** Anything in a **REMARK** line is ignored (except for & variables) up to the next linefeed/carriage return. The next line after the remarks is an **ACCEPT** line.

In the **ACCEPT** line, we are accepting a value for the **tabown** variable. The program will prompt for the value using the text, which follows the **PROMPT** portion of the **ACCEPT.**

The next lines are **SET** lines. Notice the different values that can be specified. Generally speaking, **SET** is used to set environmental variables such as number of lines in a page (**PAGESIZE** or **PAGES**), the number of characters in a line (**LINESIZE** or **LINES**), terminal output (**TERMOUT** or **TERM**), feedback on command status (**FEEDBACK**), verification of substitution variables (**VERIFY**), and output column spacing (**SPACE**). Other **SET** variables you may see will be **ECHO** (to turn on or off command echo to the screen) or **EM-BEDDED** (to force the suppression of page feeds on new **SELECT** commands).

The **COLUMN** line is being used to push the value of the "value" column into a variable called **db** using the **NEW_VALUE** specification. The **NOPRINT** option in the **COLUMN** command tells SQLPLUS not to print the value when it is selected. Usually the **COLUMN** command is used to specify a value for **HEADING**, which is used to head the column in a printout, and to specify the **FORMAT** using various text and number formats.

The next line is used to **SELECT** the value column from the **V$PARAMETER** table where the name column value is **db_name**. This result is not printed to screen or file because of the previous **COLUMN** command line. The entry in the value column is shoved into the **db** variable where it can be used in substitution just like other variables.

The **TTITLE** line is being used to place a remark heading in the output. Notice the **TTILE OFF** line near the end of the listing—this turns the **TTITLE** off, or it would be used in all subsequent **SELECT** outputs until a new **TTITLE** was issued or a **TTITLE OFF** was executed.

Next, we have a **SPOOL** command followed by the path to the file into which we want the output placed. The other **SPOOL** commands are identical in function. The **SPOOL OFF** command terminates **SPOOL** commands. Only one **SPOOL** command is active at any given time.

The next **SELECT** command is using dynamic SQL to create a series of commands for all the tables owned by the owner specified in the **tabown** variable. The created command list executes the **CHAINING** script against the specified tables using the **START** command.

Let's go down to the **START** command line. In this line, we load and execute the script we create with the dynamic SQL script.

The next few lines undo the **SET** commands and **UNDEFINE** (**UNDEF**) the variables we have set. Although not required, leaving the environment as you found it is always a good practice, especially if more than one script is to be executed in the same SQLPLUS session.

The final line is the **EXIT** that issues an explicit commit and terminates the SQLPLUS session.

As you can see, the user has enormous control over the SQLPLUS environment and how the output from SQLPLUS is formatted.

Within the SQLPLUS environment, you can also use the **DESCRIBE** command to describe the structure of tables and views and to show the required input and output variables for procedure and functions. When used to describe a table or view, the **DESCRIBE** command displays the table's or view's columns in a **NAME** column, whether or not the column will accept null values in the **NULL?** column, and the full datatype specification of the column. When used to describe a PL/SQL stored object, **DESCRIBE** commands the object's argument names, argument types, whether the argument is an **IN** or **OUT** argument, and if the argument has a default are displayed.

In the SQLPLUS environment, two scripts are used to automatically execute specified commands when a user logs in to SQLPLUS. These two scripts are GLOGIN.SQL and LOGIN.SQL. If it is specified, the GLOGIN.SQL script will be executed by all SQLPLUS logins on a specific host or client. If a LOGIN.SQL script is present in the users login directory, then the LOGIN.SQL script will also be executed by the SQLPLUS login.

All SQLPLUS commands can be shortened to the length that ensures uniqueness for the command. For example, **COLUMN** becomes **COL**, **UNDEFINE** becomes **UNDEF**, **DEFINE** becomes **DEF**, and so forth.

Practice Questions

Question 1

Which clause restricts the groups of rows returned to those groups meeting a specified condition?

- ○ a. **SELECT**
- ○ b. **FROM**
- ○ c. **WHERE**
- ○ d. **GROUP BY**
- ○ e. **HAVING**
- ○ f. **ORDER BY**

The correct answer is e. The **HAVING** clause restricts the groups of rows returned to those groups meeting a specified condition. Answer a is incorrect because a **SELECT** by itself doesn't group results. For that matter, **SELECT** is a command, not a clause. Answer b is incorrect because the **FROM** clause tells **SELECT** where to get its data, and it has nothing to do with ordering or grouping. Answer c is incorrect because the **WHERE** clause has nothing to do with sorting or grouping; it deals with what data to retrieve. Answer d, although concerned with grouping, doesn't by itself restrict the groups; it returns to a specified set, but returns all groups meeting the **SELECT** criteria. Answer f is incorrect because an **ORDER BY** clause orders only returned data; it doesn't restrict the values returned.

Question 2

You query the database with this command:

```
SELECT id_number, 100/nvl(quantity,0)
FROM inventory;
```

Which value is displayed when the quantity value is null?

- ○ a. 0
- ○ b. Command will error out.
- ○ c. The keyword **NULL**
- ○ d. 100

The correct answer is b; the command will error out. Answers a and d are incorrect because any operation involving the **NVL** function will substitute the provided value for the **NULL**; 100/0 is indeterminate, so an error is generated. Answer c is incorrect because a null response is a blank space, not any special keyword. Also, because we are using the **NVL** function, no **NULL** value is present in the answer.

Question 3

> Which operator would be most appropriate to use to search through a group of similar values?
>
> ○ a. **LIKE**
> ○ b. **=**
> ○ c. **BETWEEN**
> ○ d. **IN**

The correct answer is a. **LIKE** is used to search through similar values by appending the % wildcard to either the front, or end, of a search variable. Other wild cards for single character substitution can also be used. Answer b is incorrect because an equality can be used to compare against only a single value, not a list of values. Answer c is incorrect because **BETWEEN** is used to find values inside a specified minimum and maximum value, not inside a list of possible values. Answer d is incorrect because **IN** is used to compare against a list of exact match values.

Question 4

Contents of the PRODUCTS table.					
PRODUCT_ ID	DESCRIPTION	SUPPLIER_ID	STOCK_ ON_HAND	PRICE	SHIP_ DATE
23023	Tennis Balls	1334	255	10.57	10-jun-99
23025	Tennis Rackets	1335	50	34.99	15-jul-99
23021	Elbow Guards	1336	25	5.28	15-jul-99
23026	Shin Guards	1336	50	10.22	15-jul-99
30079	Tennis Shorts	1335	10	32.56	10-jun-99

Using the table above, evaluate this command:

```
SELECT product_id
FROM products
WHERE price BETWEEN 11.00 AND 50.00
ORDER BY description, supplier_id;
```

Which **product_id** would be displayed first?

O a. 30079

O b. 23026

O c. 23025

O d. 23023

The correct answer is c, 23025. Only two of the **PRICE** column values fall into the **BETWEEN** values, so all but 23025 and 30079 are removed based on the **BETWEEN**. Because our first **ORDER BY** is on the **DESCRIPTION** column, the rows will be ordered by that column and then reordered by duplicate **SUPPLIER_ID** values in the default order, which is ascending if not specified. This places the value of Tennis Rackets—23025—at the top of the list.

Question 5

You need to display the column **order_date**, which is a date data type, in this format:

25TH OF FEB 1997

Which **SELECT** statement could you use?

○ a.
```
SELECT order_date('fmDD "OF" MONTH YYYY')
FROM inventory;
```

○ b.
```
SELECT
TO_CHAR(order_date,'fmDDTH "OF" MON YYYY')
FROM inventory;
```

○ c.
```
SELECT
TO_CHAR(order_date,('fmDDspth "OF" MONTH YYYY')
FROM inventory;
```

○ d.
```
SELECT
order_date('fmDDspth "OF" MONTH YYYY')
FROM inventory;
```

The correct answer is b. Answers a and d are incorrect because they are syntactically incorrect; they don't include the **TO_CHAR** function. Answer c is incorrect because its format line is incorrect and can't produce the desired output.

Question 6

You have five tables in a **SELECT** statement, with three join conditions specified for four of the tables. What will happen when the query is run?

- ○ a.   Four of the tables will have their results properly restricted, and the results will be Cartesian-joined to the fifth table.

- ○ b.   Two of the tables will have their contents properly joined and restricted, and the results will be Cartesian-joined to the other two tables.

- ○ c.   Nothing; an error will be returned because you have only three join conditions for five tables.

- ○ d.   An error will be returned because you can't join more than two tables in Oracle.

The correct answer is a. Answer b is incorrect because you have joins between three tables, not just two. Answer c is incorrect because you will get processing, just not what you expect. Answer d is incorrect because the number of tables joined in Oracle is essentially limited to the amount of physical memory you have available on your machine (unlimited).

Question 7

Evaluate this command:

```
SELECT manufacturer_id
"Manufacturer Identification Code", SUM(price)
FROM inventory
WHERE price > 6.00
GROUP BY "Manufacturer Identification Code"
ORDER BY 2
```

Which two clauses will cause errors? [Check all correct answers]

❑ a.
```
SELECT manufacturer_id
"Manufacturer Identification Code", SUM(price)
```

❑ b.
```
FROM inventory
```

❑ c.
```
WHERE price >   6.00
```

❑ d.
```
GROUP BY "Manufacturer Identification Code"
```

❑ e.
```
ORDER BY 2
```

The correct answers are a and d. Answer a is correct because you can't have a column alias longer than 30 characters. Answer d is correct because you can't perform a **GROUP BY** on a column alias. The rest of the clauses shown are correct in their syntax and thus are the incorrect answers.

Question 8

You query the database with this command:

```
SELECT manufacturer_id
FROM inventory
WHERE manufacturer_id LIKE
'%N\%P\%O%' ESCAPE \;
```

For which character pattern is the **LIKE** operator searching?

- ○ a. NPO
- ○ b. N\%P\%O
- ○ c. N\P\O
- ○ d. N%P%O

The correct answer is d. When you're evaluating a **LIKE** statement, always check to see if it includes the **ESCAPE** clause. If there's an **ESCAPE** clause, note which character it specifies to treat as an escape. Any character that's preceded by the escape character will be treated as a normal character and will have no special meaning. In this case, with answer d, the percent signs in front of the P and O characters have been escaped, indicating that they're to be treated as a part of the search string and not as wildcards. The leading and trailing percent signs have not been escaped, so they're treated as wildcards. The other answers are incorrect because they're not what the specified string translates into.

Question 9

Your **parts** table contains a **subassembly** column and a **part_no** column. If you want to find out which parts are contained in which subassemblies, what type of join should you use? [Select the most complete answer]

- ○ a. A self-join
- ○ b. An equijoin
- ○ c. A self-join with an equijoin
- ○ d. A self-join containing a hierarchical query

The correct answer is d. Answer a is incorrect because, although correct in that you need a self-join, it doesn't mention the hierarchical query. Answer b is incorrect because, although you may need to do an equijoin, it doesn't mention the self-join or the hierarchical query. Answer c is incorrect because, although it may be true that you will need a self-join and maybe an equijoin, it doesn't mention the hierarchical query. Answer d is the most complete answer because this query will require a hierarchical query and a self-join.

Question 10

Which clauses cannot contain a subquery? [Choose three]

- ○ a. **WHERE**
- ○ b. **SELECT**
- ○ c. **HAVING**
- ○ d. **ORDER BY**
- ○ e. **GROUP BY**

The correct answers are b, d, and e. Of the clauses listed, only **WHERE** and **HAVING** are allowed to have a subquery.

Need to Know More?

 Oracle Corporation. *Oracle8i Server SQL Reference Manual, Release 3(8.1.7)*. September, 2000, Redwood City, California. Part No. A85397-01. This is the source book for all Oracle SQL for version 8i. You can find this book on the Web, at the time of writing, at **http://technet.oracle.com**. This site has free membership and has all current versions of Oracle documentation available online in Acrobat format (PDF files).

 Ault, Michael R. *Oracle8i Administration and Management*. John Wiley & Sons, 2000, New York, New York. ISBN 0-471-35453-8. This book covers virtually all aspects of Oracle8i administration, including command syntax, tuning, and management topics.

 Honour, Edward, Dalberth, Paul, Kaplan, Ari, and Atul Mehta. *Oracle8 HOW-TO*. Waite Group Press, 1998, Corte Madera, California. ISBN 1-57169-123-5. This book provides an excellent resource for general Oracle how-to information and covers topics from installation to how to use the Web server.

 Oracle Corporation, *SQL*Plus Quick Reference Release 8.1.7*, September, 2000, Redwood City, California. Part No. A82951-01. This quick reference covers all SQLPLUS commands and their use. The DBA should review it and use it daily.

Using Oracle SQL Functions, Expressions, and Conditions

3

Terms you'll need to understand:

✓ DECODE

✓ COMMIT

✓ ROLLBACK

✓ Operators

✓ Expression

✓ Condition

✓ Function

Techniques you'll need to master:

✓ Using operators

✓ Using SQL Expressions in statements

✓ Using intrinsic SQL functions to perform operations and conversions on data

✓ Using and applying **COMMIT** and **ROLLBACK** commands in Oracle to make changes permanent or remove them

In this chapter, I cover the Oracle functions and expression elements. After you study this chapter, you should be able to do the following:

➤ Use Oracle-intrinsic SQL functions

➤ Understand the use of expressions and conditions

➤ Understand **ROLLBACK** and **COMMIT**

DML Elements

The actual command elements that form the DML portion of SQL are few in number; they are **INSERT, UPDATE, DELETE,** and **SELECT.** Oracle also contains operators (unary and binary) and functions. I discuss operators and functions first because they're used to construct parts of the DML commands. The **SELECT** command is covered in this chapter. The other DML commands are covered in later chapters.

Oracle Operators

Oracle has two types of operators: unary and binary. Unary operators operate on only one operand and are shown in the format:

`Operator operand`

A binary operator operates on two operands and generally is shown in the format:

`Operator operand, operand`

Special operators also exist that can operate on more than two operands.

If an operator is given a **NULL** argument, and if it's any operator other than the concatenation operator (a double pipe: ||), its results are **NULL.**

Precedence governs the order in which operands are evaluated. Those with high precedence are evaluated before those with low precedence, and those with equal precedence are evaluated left to right. Precedence is overridden by the use of parentheses. Operators inside of parentheses are evaluated first.

Precedence of operators (from highest to lowest) is as follows:

➤ *(+) and (-)*—Unary operators (positive and negative number indicators) and the **PRIOR** operator

➤ *(*) and (/)*—Multiplication and division operators

➤ *Binary (=)*—Arithmetic operators (such as addition [+] and subtraction [-]) and the concatenation (||) operator

➤ *All comparison operators*—The **NOT, AND,** and **OR** logical operators

 Parentheses always override precedence. Operators inside parentheses are always evaluated first.

Set operators are also supported in Oracle SQL. The set operators are the following:

➤ **UNION**—Shows all nonduplicate results from queries A and B

➤ **UNION ALL**—Shows all results from queries A and B (including duplicates)

➤ **INTERSECT**—Shows common results from queries A and B

➤ **MINUS**—The MINUS operator returns all distinct rows selected by the first query but not the second

 All set operators have equal precedence.

Comparison operators allow the comparison of two values. The comparison operators are the following:

➤ (=)—Does A equal B?

➤ (!=)—Does A not equal B?

➤ (^=)—Does A not equal B?

➤ (<>)—Does A not equal B?

➤ (>)—Is A greater than B?

➤ (<)—Is A less than B?

➤ (>=)—Is A greater than or equal to B?

➤ (<=)—Is A less than or equal to B?

➤ **IN**—Is A in this set?

➤ **NOT IN**—Is A not in this set?

➤ **ANY, SOME**—Combines with certain operators—(=), (!=), (<), (>), (<=), (>=)—and compares a value to each value in a list returned from a query. Evaluates to **FALSE** if no rows are returned.

➤ **ALL**—Combines with certain operators—(=), (!=), (<), (>), (<=), (>=)—and says that a value must relate to the entire list or to the subquery as indicated.

➤ **[NOT] BETWEEN** *x* **AND** *y*—Checks for inclusion between *x* and *y* values, inclusive of the values *x* and *y*.

➤ **EXISTS**—Evaluates to **TRUE** if a subquery returns at least one row.

➤ *X* **[NOT] LIKE** *y* **[ESCAPE** '*z*'**]**—Evaluates to **TRUE** if *x* does not match the pattern *y*. The *y* value can contain the wildcard characters % (percent) and _ (underscore). Any character except % and _ can follow the **ESCAPE** clause to allow comparison against restricted characters such as the wildcards. A wildcard can be used if the ESCAPE character precedes it. The default escape character is the \ character on some platforms.

➤ **IS [NOT] NULL**—Tests for **NULL** values and is the only valid method to test for nulls. **NULL** values cannot be tested for using equality or nonequality operators because, by definition, a **NULL** is undefined.

The logical operator most used in SQL is probably the **AND** operator because it is used to add more conditional clauses to a **WHERE** clause. The logical operator used to search a list of values is the **IN** operator. The operator most used in single-row subqueries is the **equal** operator.

SQL Functions

SQL functions allow the manipulation of values, and they return a result. Functions can have multiple arguments yet always return a single value. Functions have the general format:

```
Function(arg1, arg2, ...)
```

If possible, functions will do implicit conversion of data types if a type other than the one needed is specified to them. Calling most functions with a **NULL** will return a **NULL**. The only functions that don't return a **NULL** are the following:

➤ **CONCAT**—Concatenates strings

➤ **DECODE**—Performs explicit conversions

➤ **DUMP**—Dumps a value

➤ **NVL**—Allows for **NULL** value substitution

➤ **REPLACE**—Allows for string replacement

Functions are either *scalar* (single row) or *aggregate* (group) in nature. A single-row function returns a single result row for each row of a queried table or view. An aggregate function returns a single value for a group of rows.

A single-value function can appear in a **SELECT** statement if the **SELECT** statement doesn't contain a **GROUP BY** clause. Single-value functions can also appear in **WHERE, START WITH,** and **CONNECT BY** clauses. Single-value functions can also be nested.

Group functions can be used in select lists and **HAVING** clauses. If a **SELECT** statement uses group functions, the **GROUP BY** clause must include all columns not affected by group functions.

Functions are divided into **NUMBER, CHARACTER,** and **DATE** functions.

The SQL Numeric Single-Value Functions
In the **NUMBER** functions listed in this section, *n* can be an expression. If the accuracy is not specified in the following list, it can be up to 38 places. The **NUMBER** functions are as follows:

➤ **ABS(*n*)**—Returns the absolute value of *n*.

➤ **ACOS(*n*)**—Returns the arc-cosine of *n*. Accurate to 30 places.

➤ **ASIN(*n*)**—Returns the arc-sine of *n*. Accurate to 30 places.

➤ **ATAN(*n*)**—Returns the arc-tangent of *n*. Accurate to 30 places.

➤ **ATAN2(*n*,*m*)**—Returns the arc-tangent of *n* and *m* outputs in the range of $-pi$ to pi, depending on the signs of *n* and *m*. Results are expressed in radians and are accurate to 30 places.

➤ **BITAND(*m*,*n*)**—Computes an **AND** operation on the bits of *m* and *n*, both of which must resolve to nonnegative integers, and returns an integer. This function is commonly used with the **DECODE** expression.

➤ **CEIL(*n*)**—Rounds *n* up.

➤ **COS(*n*)**—Returns the cosine of *n*. Accurate to 36 places.

➤ **COSH(*n*)**—Returns the hyperbolic cosine of *n*. Accurate to 36 places.

➤ **EXP(*n*)**—Returns *e* raised to the *n*th power (natural log). Accurate to 36 places.

➤ FLOOR(*n*)—Rounds *n* down.

➤ LN(*n*)—Returns the natural log of *n* where *n* is greater than zero. Accurate to 36 places.

➤ LOG(*m,n*)—Returns the logarithm, base *m*, of *n*. The base can be any positive number other than 0 or 1, and *n* can be any positive number. Accurate to 36 places.

➤ MOD(*m,n*)—Returns the remainder of *m* divided by *n*. Returns *m* if *n* is 0.

➤ POWER(*m,n*)—Returns *m* raised to the *n*th power.

➤ ROUND(*n* [,*m*])—Returns *n* rounded to *m* decimal places; *m* can be positive or negative, depending on which side of the decimal you wish to round.

➤ SIGN(*n*)—Returns -1 if *n* is less than 0. Returns 0 if *n* equals 0. Returns 1 if *n* is more than 0.

➤ SIN(*n*)—Returns the sine of *n*. Accurate to 36 places.

➤ SINH(*n*)—Returns the hyperbolic sine of *n*. Accurate to 36 places.

➤ SQRT(*n*)—Returns the square root of *n*. Accurate to 36 places.

➤ TAN(*n*)—Returns the tangent of *n*. Accurate to 36 places.

➤ TANH(*n*)—Returns the hyperbolic tangent of *n*. Accurate to 36 places.

➤ TRUNC(*n* [,*m*])—Returns *n* truncated to *m* decimal places. If *m* is omitted, truncates to zero decimal places.

Numeric functions provide great calculation abilities within Oracle. You can perform almost any arithmetic operation with the proper combination of these functions and operators.

Character Functions That Return Character Values

Oracle also provides a rich function set for character data. Character data—such as **CHAR** and **VARCHAR2** values—can be altered, translated, truncated, or appended to through the use of functions. **VARCHAR2** data types are limited to 4,000 bytes, and **CHAR** data types are limited to 2,000 bytes in Oracle8. If any result exceeds the maximum size for its data type, the result is truncated to that length and no error is returned.

The character functions included in Oracle are the following:

➤ CHR(*n*)—Returns the character having the ASCII-code equivalent to *n* in the current character set for the database.

➤ CONCAT(*char*1, *char*2)—Returns *char*1 concatenated to *char*2.

➤ INITCAP(*char*)—Returns *char* with the first letter of each word in uppercase.

➤ LOWER(*char*)—Returns *char* with all characters lowercase.

➤ LPAD(*char1,n* [,*char2*])—Returns *char*1 left, padded with either blanks or the value of *char2*.

➤ LTRIM(*char*1 [,*set*])—Returns *char*1 left-trimmed of blanks if *set* isn't specified, or trimmed of *set* characters if it is.

➤ NLS_INITCAP(*char* [, '*nlsparams*'])—Returns *char* with all initial letters capitalized. The *nlsparams* entry determines the **NLS_SORT** setting or is set to **BINARY**.

➤ NLS_LOWER(*char* [, '*nlsparams*'])—Returns *char* all lowercase. The *nlsparams* values are the same as for **NLS_INITCAP**.

➤ NLSSORT(*char*[, '*nlsparams*'])—Returns a string of bytes used to sort *char*. The value of *nlsparams* can have the form: **NLS_SORT** = *sort*, where *sort* is a linguistic sort sequence or **BINARY**. If the *nlsparams* setting is left off, the default setting for your session is used.

➤ NLS_UPPER (*char* [, '*nlsparams*'])—Returns *char* all uppercase. The *nlsparams* values are the same as for **NLS_INITCAP**.

➤ REPLACE(*char, search_string* [, *replacement_string*])—In *char*, replaces all instances of *search_string* with the value of *replacement_string*. Removes all instances of *search_string* if no *replacement_string* is specified.

➤ RPAD(*char*1, *n* [,*char2*])—Right-pads *char*1 with the value of *char2*, or with a blank if *char2* isn't specified to a length of *n*.

➤ RTRIM(*char* [,*set*])—Returns *char* with the rightmost characters in *set* removed. If *set* isn't specified, all rightmost blanks are removed.

➤ SOUNDEX(*char*)—Returns the soundex equivalent of the value of *char*. This is useful in searching for words that sound alike but are spelled differently.

➤ SUBSTR(*char m* [,*n*])—Returns the substring located in *char*, starting at *m* and ending at *n*. If *n* isn't specified, it returns the value, starting at *m* and going to the end of the *char* value. The value for *m* can be positive to search forward or negative to search backwards.

➤ SUBSTRB(*char m* [,*n*])—Returns the byte substring located in *char*, starting at *m* bytes and ending at *n*. If *n* is unspecified, it returns the value, starting at *m* bytes and going to the end of the *char* value. The value for *m* can be positive to search forward or negative to search backwards. For single-byte character sets, the effect is the same as with **SUBSTR**.

➤ TRANSLATE(*char*, *from*, *to*)—Returns *char* with the values in *from* translated to the values in *to*.

➤ TRIM(*[LEADING|TRAILING|BOTHtrim_char]| trim_char [FROM] trim_source*)—Enables you to trim leading or trailing characters (or both) from a character string. If *trim_char* or *trim_source* is a character literal, you must enclose it in single quotes. If just *trim_source* is specified, it assumes the space character and trims leading and trailing spaces.

➤ UPPER(*char*)—Returns *char* in all uppercase.

Character Functions That Return Numeric Values

The following functions return numeric values from character inputs. Outputs, such as length or position, are generated by these functions:

➤ ASCII(*char*)—Returns the ASCII equivalent of the first byte of *char*. This is the inverse of the **CHR()** function. If you need to know the value to insert into a **CHR()** for a specific character, use **SELECT ASCII(*char*) FROM DUAL** to get it.

➤ INSTR(*char1*, *char2* [, *n*[, *m*]])—Returns the numeric position of the *m*th occurrence of *char2* in *char1*, starting at the *n*th character. The value of *m* must be positive if specified. If the value is not specified, it defaults to 1 (one). The value of *n*, if negative, says to search backwards. If the value returns zero, the search was not successful.

➤ INSTRB(*char1*, *char2* [, *n*[, *m*]])—Returns the numeric byte position of the *m*th occurrence of *char2* in *char1*, starting at the *n*th byte. The value of *m* must be positive if specified. The value of *n*, if negative, says to search backwards. If the value returns zero, the search wasn't successful. The effect is the same as **INSTR()** for single-byte character sets.

➤ LENGTH(*char*)—Returns the length in characters of *char*. If *char* is a **CHAR**, it includes trailing blanks. If *char* is null, it returns a **NULL**.

➤ LENGTHB(*char*)—Returns the length in bytes of *char*. If *char* is a **CHAR**, it includes trailing blanks. If *char* is null, it returns a **NULL**. It's the same as **LENGTH** for single-byte character sets.

Date and Time Functions

Almost all databases pertain to dates and times. Humans are time-based creatures who want to know "when" as well as "what, who, and how." Databases require the ability to deal with date and time values. Oracle provides numerous date and time functions, including the following:

➤ ADD_MONTHS(*d,n*)—Adds *n* months to date *d*. Returns a **DATE** value.

➤ LAST_DAY(*d*)—Returns the last day of the month that contains date *d*. Returns a **DATE** value.

➤ MONTHS_BETWEEN(*d1, d2*)—Returns either the positive or the negative difference between date *d1* and date *d2*. Returns a numeric value.

➤ NEW_TIME(*d, z1, z2*)—Returns the date and time in time zone *z2* when date *d* is in time zone *z1*.

➤ NEXT_DAY(*d, char*)—Returns the first weekday named by *char* that is later than date *d*. Returns a **DATE** value.

➤ ROUND(*d* [*,fmt*])—Returns date *d* rounded to the unit specified by the *fmt* string. For example, a *fmt* of **YEAR** will return only the year portion of the specified date value.

➤ SYSDATE—Has no arguments and returns the current system date and time. It can't be used in a **CHECK** constraint.

➤ TRUNC(*d* [*,fmt*])—Returns date *d* with the time truncated to the unit specified by the format string *fmt*. If *fmt* is left off, the entire time portion of *d* is removed.

The **ROUND** and **TRUNC** functions use standard date-formatting sequences:

➤ *CC*—Both CC and SCC return one number greater than the first two digits of a four-digit year (for example, returns 20 for 1999).

➤ *SCC*—Returns 20 for 1999.

➤ *SYYYY*—The various forms of the year format round up as of July 1 for any year. Returns 1999 for 1999.

➤ *YYYY*—Returns 1999 for 1999.

➤ *YEAR*—Returns NINETEEN NINETY-NINE for 1999.

➤ *SYEAR*—Returns NINETEEN NINETY-NINE for 1999.

➤ *YYY*—Returns 956 for 1956.

➤ *YY*—Returns 56 for 1956.

➤ *Y*—Returns 6 for 1956.

➤ *IYYY*—Use of the "I" with the year produces the ISO year format. Returns 1956 for 1956.

➤ *IYY*—Returns 956 for 1956.

➤ *IY*—Returns 56 for 1956.

➤ *I*—Returns 6 for 1956.

➤ *Q*—Rounds up on the 16th day of the second month of the quarter. Returns the number of the current quarter.

➤ *MONTH*—Month (rounds up on the 16th day of the month). Returns the month spelled out.

➤ *MON*—First three letters of the month.

➤ *MM*—Numeric month.

➤ *RM*—A really useful format, the roman numeral month.

➤ *WW*—Rounds to the same day of the week as the first day of the year. Gives the current week's number. For August 8, 1999, returns 32.

➤ *IW*—Rounds to the same day of the week as the first day of the ISO year. For August 8, 1999, returns 31.

➤ *W*—Rounds to the same day of the week as the first day of the month, and the number of the week in the month. For August 8, 1999, returns 3.

➤ *DDD*—Day of the year. For August 8, 1999, returns 220.

➤ *DD*—Two-place numeric day (01).

➤ *J*—Julian day (for August 8, 1999, returns 2451399).

➤ *DAY*—Rounds to starting day of the week. Spells out the day (SUNDAY).

➤ *DY*—Abbreviation for day of week (SUN).

➤ *D*—Day (numeric) of week (1).

➤ *HH*—Hour (defaults to 12-hour format); 2 P.M.=02.

➤ *HH12*—Forces 12-hour format (2 P.M.=02).

➤ *HH24*—Forces 24-hour format (2 P.M.=14).

➤ *MI*—Minute.

 Remember that MM is for months and MI is for minutes. If you specify a time value as HH:MM:SS, you will get a constant value returned in the minutes area that will correspond to the current month.

Starting day of the week is determined from the setting of the **NLS_TERRITORY** setting.

Subtraction of two date values (when converted with the **TO_DATE** function) results in the difference in days between the two dates.

Any appropriate date format string can also use the date suffixes shown in Table 3.1.

Special modifiers for date-format models can also be applied to date values. These modifiers are **FM** or **FX** (which can also be lowercase, **fm** and **fx**). The **FM** modifier specifies "fill mode," which suppresses blank padding in the return from a **TO_CHAR** call with a date. The **FX** mode means "format exact"; it requires an exact matching for the character argument and the date-format model of a **TO_DATE** function call. For example:

```
1 SELECT TO_CHAR(SYSDATE, 'fmDDTH')||' of '||TO_CHAR
2   (SYSDATE, 'fmMonth')||', '||TO_CHAR(SYSDATE, 'YYYY') "FM
Example"
3*    FROM DUAL;
AULTDB1:/

FM Example
------------------
1ST of May, 2001
```

While the FX special modifier in the same query would be:

```
  1  SELECT TO_CHAR(SYSDATE, 'fxDDTH')||' of '||TO_CHAR
  2     (SYSDATE, 'fxMonth')||', '||TO_CHAR(SYSDATE, 'YYYY') "FX
Example"
  3*     FROM DUAL
AULTDB1:/

FX Example
----------------------
01ST of May        , 2001
```

Table 3.1	Date suffixes.		
Suffix	**Meaning**	**Example Element**	**Example Value**
TH	Ordinal number	DDTH	4TH
SP	Spelled number	DDSP	FOUR
SPTH or THSP	Spelled, ordinal number	FOURTH	

Conversion Functions

Oracle provides conversion routines for standard data-type conversions. In many cases, Oracle will do implicit conversions for compatible data types; however, it's recommended that explicit conversions be done to prevent performance problems inherent in some implicit conversions. The conversion functions are the following:

➤ CHARTOROWID(*char*)—Converts *char* to Oracle's internal ROWID format. The value of *char* must follow ROWID data type guidelines.

➤ CONVERT(*char, dest_char_set* [,*source_char_set*])—Converts *char* to the character set specified in *dest_char_set*. If *char* is in a different character set than the database default, *source_char_set* must be included to specify the character set of the *char* value.

➤ HEXTORAW(*char*)—Converts the hexadecimal value in *char* to its equivalent RAW value.

➤ NUMTODSINTERVAL (*n, 'char_exp'*)—Converts *n* to an INTERVAL DAY TO SECOND literal. *n* can be a number or an expression resolving to a number. The value for *char_expr* specifies the unit of *n* and must resolve to one of the following string values: 'DAY', 'HOUR', 'MINUTE', 'SECOND'.

➤ NUMTOYMINTERVAL (*n, 'char_exp'*)—Converts number *n* to an INTERVAL YEAR TO MONTH literal. *n* can be a number or an expression resolving to a number. The value for *char_expr* specifies the unit of *n* and must resolve to one of the following string values: 'YEAR', 'MONTH'. This function is restricted to use with analytic functions. It accepts only numbers as arguments, and it returns interval literals.

➤ RAWTOHEX(*raw*)—Converts the raw data value in *raw* to its hexadecimal equivalent.

➤ ROWIDTOCHAR(*rowid*)—Converts the row ID value in *rowid* to its character equivalent.

➤ TO_CHAR(d, [,*fmt* [, *'nlsparams'*]]), TO_CHAR(*label* [, *fmt*]), or TO_CHAR(*number*)—Converts from a date value, *d*, to a character value in the format specified by *fmt*, using any guidelines in the *nlsparams* variable. It can also convert the label specified in *label* to the specified character format in *fmt*, or convert the number value in *number* to a character value. (A *label* is a tag used in Oracle secure server; it is not on the test so unless you use it, don't worry about it.) It also formats using date, number, or label format strings to specify the proper output form.

➤ TO_DATE(*char* [, *fmt* [, *'nlsparams'*]])—Converts the specified character value in *char* to the internal Oracle DATE value as translated via the *fmt* and, if specified, the *nlsparams* value.

➤ TO_LOB(*long_col*)—Converts LONG or LONG RAW values in the column long_column to LOB values. You can apply this function only to a LONG or LONG RAW column, and only in the SELECT list of a subquery in an INSERT statement. Before using this function, you must create a LOB column to receive the converted LONG values. To convert LONGs, create a CLOB column. To convert LONG RAWs, create a BLOB column.

➤ TO_MULTI_BYTE(*char*)—Converts the character value *char* to its equivalent multibyte representation.

➤ TO_NUMBER(*char* [,*fmt* [, *'nlsparams'*]])—Converts the number represented in the character value *char* to a number based on translation in the format string *fmt* (if specified) and the *nlsparams* value.

➤ TO_SINGLE_BYTE(*char*)—Converts the multibyte value in *char* to its single-byte equivalent.

➤ TRANSLATE (*text* USING {*CHAR_CS* | *NCHAR_CS*})—Translates the value of *text* into the character set specified by either *CHAR_CS* or *NCHAR_CS*. Using *CHAR_CS* output is VARCHAR2; using *NCHAR_CS* output is NVARCHAR2.

Other Functions

Other functions in Oracle don't quite fit in any category. These functions are described here:

➤ BFILENAME (*'directory'*,*'filename'*)—Used to create a BFILE entry. The *directory* value is the internal DIRECTORY specification set with the CREATE DIRECTORY command. The *filename* value is the name of the external file containing the external LOB data. The actual operating-system directory used in the BFILENAME function is not verified to exist or to be accessible until the BFILE access is attempted by an application.

➤ DUMP (*expr*[, *return_format* [,*start_position* [, *length*]]])—Returns a VARCHAR2 value containing the data type code, length in bytes, and internal representation of *expr*. The *return_format* tells Oracle to return the value as octal (8), decimal (10), hexadecimal (16), or single characters (17). The *start_position* and *length* values determine which portion of the representation to return.

➤ EMPTY_[B|C]LOB()—Returns an empty **LOB** (either **BLOB** or **CLOB**) locator, which can be used to initialize a **LOB** variable or can be used in an **INSERT** or **UPDATE** statement to create an **EMPTY LOB** value for subsequent use.

➤ GREATEST(*expr* [,*expr*] ...)—Returns the greatest of the specified values.

➤ LEAST(*expr* [,*expr*] ...)—Returns the least of the specified values.

➤ NLS_CHARSET_DECL_LEN(*bytcnt, csid*)—Returns the declaration width, in number of characters, of an **NCHAR** column. The *bytcnt* value is the width in bytes of the columns. The *csid* value is the character set for the column.

➤ NLS_CHARSET_ID(*text*)—Returns the NLS character set number that corresponds to the NLS character set specified by *text*. Use of **CHAR_CS** as the value for *text* returns the server's database character set ID number. **NCHAR_CS** returns the server's national character set.

➤ NLS_CHARSET_NAME(*n*)—Returns the name of the character set with *n* as its ID number. Note that *n* can also be an expression, such as a call to **NLS_CHARSET_ID()**.

➤ NVL(*expr1, expr2*)—Returns *expr1* if *expr1* isn't null, or *expr2* if *expr1* is null. Be careful with any conversion routines or substitution functions when used in mathematical formulas, especially in division. Don't substitute a zero for a **NULL** in division $Y/(NVL(X,0))$, or a divide-by-zero exception will result.

➤ NVL2(*expr1, expr2, expr3*)—If *expr1* is not null, **NVL2** returns *expr2*. If *expr1* is null, **NVL2** returns *expr3*. The argument *expr1* can have any datatype. The arguments *expr2* and *expr3* can have any datatypes except **LONG**. If the datatypes of *expr2* and *expr3* are different, Oracle converts *expr3* to the datatype of *expr2* before comparing them unless *expr3* is a null constant. In that case, a datatype conversion is not necessary. The datatype of the return value is always the same as the datatype of *expr2*, unless *expr2* is character data, in which case the return value's datatype is **VARCHAR2**. Note: If you look this up in the documentation, the example used in the 8.1.7 manual is incorrect because it uses an "&" in a text field. As we all know, Oracle will treat this as a substitution call and will prompt you for a value. Oracle documentalists like to do this and frequently include it in REM areas of their DBMS package headers, causing execution errors.

➤ SYS_CONTEXT(*namespace,attribute [,length]*)—Returns the value of *attribute* associated with the context *namespace*. You can use this function in both SQL and PL/SQL statements. The context *namespace* must already have been created, and the associated *attribute* and its value must also have been set using the **DBMS_SESSION.set_context** procedure. The *namespace* must be a valid SQL identifier. The *attribute* name can be any string, and it is not case-sensitive, but it cannot exceed 30 bytes in length. The data type of the return value is **VARCHAR2**. The default maximum size of the return value is 256 bytes. You can override this default by specifying the optional length parameter. The valid range of values is 1 to 4,000 bytes. (If you specify an invalid value, Oracle ignores it and uses the default.) Oracle8i provides a built-in *namespace* called **USERENV**, which describes the current session.

➤ **SYS_GUID()**—Generates and returns a globally unique identifier (**RAW** value) made up of 16 bytes. On most platforms, the generated identifier consists of a host identifier and a process or thread identifier of the process or thread invoking the function, and a nonrepeating value (sequence of bytes) for that process or thread.

➤ **UID**—Has no arguments and returns the user ID of the current user.

➤ **USER**—Has no arguments and returns the username of the current user.

➤ **USERENV(*option*)**—Returns the specified setting for the current environment. The *option* argument is always surrounded by single quotes. Possible values of *option* are the following:

➤ **ISDBA**—Returns **TRUE** if the OSDBA role is enabled for this user on Unix using OS authentication, or if the user has logged in with the **AS SYSDBA** clause with username and password, or if the user has the group ORA_[<sid>]_DBA on NT and has logged in with no username or password (such as svrmgrl / AS SYSDBA).

➤ **ENTRYID**—Returns the available auditing-entry identifier.

➤ **INSTANCE**—Returns the instance-identification number of the current instance.

➤ **LANG**—Returns the ISO language setting for this session.

➤ **LANGUAGE**—Returns the language and territory used by this session.

➤ **SESSIONID**—Returns your auditing session ID.

➤ **TERMINAL**—Returns the operating system ID of this session's terminal.

➤ **VSIZE(*expr*)**—Returns the number of bytes in the internal representation of *expr*.

Object Reference Functions

Oracle8 object-reference functions manipulate **REF** values in Oracle8 objects (UDTs, or user-defined types). The object-reference functions are:

➤ **DEREF**(*e*)—Returns the object reference of argument *e*. Argument *e* must resolve to a valid **REF** value.

➤ **REFTOHEX**(*r*)—Returns the hexadecimal equivalent of argument *r*.

➤ **MAKE_REF**(*table, key* [*,key*...])—Creates a **REF** to a row of an object view using the value(s) of *key* as the primary key.

Oracle Group Functions

Oracle also provides group functions to act on groups of values, rather than individual items. You should know how to use these functions in conjunction with **SELECT, INSERT, UPDATE,** and **DELETE.** The group functions are the following:

➤ **DISTINCT**—Returns only unique values for the specified data-set grouping.

➤ **ALL**—Returns all values, including duplicates, for the specified data-set grouping.

➤ **AVG([DISTINCT|ALL]** *n*)—Returns the average value for the specified set of numbers. You can exclude duplicates by using **DISTINCT** or include them with **ALL**, which is the default.

➤ **CORR**(*expr1, expr2*) [*OVER (analytical_clause)*]—Returns the coefficient of correlation of a set of number pairs. You can use it as an aggregate or analytic function. Both *expr1* and *expr2* are number expressions. Oracle applies the function to the set of (*expr1, expr2*) after eliminating the pairs for which either *expr1* or *expr2* is null. Then Oracle makes the following computation:

```
COVAR_POP(expr1, expr2) / (STDDEV_POP(expr1) * STDDEV_POP(expr2))
```

The function returns a value of type **NUMBER**. If the function is applied to an empty set, it returns null.

➤ **COUNT**({* | [DISTINCT|ALL] *expr*})—Returns the count of rows (*), distinct values using **DISTINCT**, all values (the default) using **ALL**, or all values that satisfy the values generated from the expression in *expr*.

➤ **COVAR_POP**(*expr1, expr2*) [*OVER (analytical_clause)*]—Returns the population covariance of a set of number pairs. You can use it as an aggregate or analytic function. Both *expr1* and *expr2* are number expressions. Oracle applies the function to the set of (*expr1*, *expr2*) pairs after eliminating all pairs for which either *expr1* or *expr2* is null. Then Oracle makes the following computation:

```
(SUM(expr1 * expr2) - SUM(expr2) * SUM(expr1) / n) / n
```

where *n* is the number of (*expr1*, *expr2*) pairs where neither *expr1* nor *expr2* is null. The function returns a value of type **NUMBER**. If the function is applied to an empty set, it returns null.

➤ **COVAR_SAMP**(*expr1, expr2*) [*OVER (analytical_clause)*]—Returns the sample covariance of a set of number pairs. You can use it as an aggregate or analytic function. Both *expr1* and *expr2* are number expressions. Oracle applies the function to the set of (*expr1*, *expr2*) pairs after eliminating all pairs for which either *expr1* or *expr2* is null. Then Oracle makes the following computation:

```
(SUM(expr1 * expr2) - SUM(expr1) * SUM(expr2) / n) / (n-1)
```

where *n* is the number of (*expr1*, *expr2*) pairs where neither *expr1* nor *expr2* is null. The function returns a value of type **NUMBER**. If the function is applied to an empty set, it returns null.

➤ **GROUPING**(*expr*)—The **GROUPING** function is applicable only in a **SELECT** statement that contains a **GROUP BY** extension, such as **ROLLUP** or **CUBE**. These operations produce superaggregate rows that contain nulls representing the set of all values. You can use the **GROUPING** function to distinguish a null that represents the set of all values in a superaggregate row from an actual null. The *expr* in the **GROUPING** function must match one of the expressions in the **GROUP BY** clause. The function returns a value of 1 if the value of *expr* in the row is a null representing the set of all values. Otherwise, it returns zero. The datatype of the value returned by the **GROUPING** function is Oracle **NUMBER**.

➤ **MAX**([DISTINCT|ALL] *expr*)—Returns the maximum value generated from the expression in *expr*.

➤ **MIN**([DISTINCT|ALL] *expr*)—Returns the minimum value generated from the expression in *expr*. The expression can be numeric or character data. If the value is a character, the sum of the ASCII values for the letters is used to determine what value is minimum.

➤ **REGR**--The linear regression functions are (as of February, 2001, none of these are on the exam):

➤ **REGR_SLOPE**—Returns the slope of the line. The return value is a number and can be null. After the elimination of null (*expr1*, *expr2*) pairs, it makes the following computation:

```
COVAR_POP(expr1, expr2) / VAR_POP(expr2)
```

➤ **REGR_INTERCEPT**—Returns the y-intercept of the regression line. The return value is a number and can be null. After the elimination of null (*expr1*, *expr2*) pairs, it makes the following computation:

```
AVG(expr1) - REGR_SLOPE(expr1, expr2) * AVG(expr2)
```

➤ **REGR_COUNT**—Returns an integer that is the number of non-null number pairs used to fit the regression line.

➤ **REGR_R2**—Returns the coefficient of determination (also called "R-squared" or "goodness of fit") for the regression. The return value is a number and can be null. **VAR_POP**(*expr1*) and **VAR_POP**(*expr2*) are evaluated after the elimination of null pairs. The return values are as follows:

➤ NULL if **VAR_POP**(*expr2*) = 0

➤ 1 if **VAR_POP**(*expr1*) = 0 and **VAR_POP**(*expr2*) != 0

➤ **POWER(CORR**(*expr1*,*expr2*),) if **VAR_POP**(*expr1*) > 0 and **VAR_POP**(*expr2*) != 0

➤ **REGR_AVGX**—Evaluates the average of the independent variable (*expr2*) of the regression line. It makes the following computation after the elimination of null (*expr1*, *expr2*) pairs:

```
AVG(expr2)
```

➤ **REGR_AVGY**—Evaluates the average of the dependent variable (*expr1*) of the regression line. It makes the following computation after the elimination of null (*expr1*, *expr2*) pairs:

```
AVG(expr1)
```

➤ **REGR_SXX** (diagnostic function)—Makes the following computation after the elimination of null (*expr1*, *expr2*) pairs:

```
REGR_COUNT(expr1, expr2) * VAR_POP(expr2)
```

➤ **REGR_SYY**(diagnostic function)—Makes the following computation after the elimination of null (*expr1, expr2*) pairs:

```
REGR_COUNT(expr1, expr2) * VAR_POP(expr1)
```

➤ **REGR_SXY**(diagnostic function)—Makes the following computation after the elimination of null (*expr1, expr2*) pairs:

```
REGR_COUNT(expr1, expr2) * COVAR_POP(expr1, expr2)
```

All **REGR** functions have the same general format:

```
REGR_function(expr1, expr2 ) [OVER (analytical_clause)]
```

➤ **STDDEV([DISTINCT|ALL]** *expr*)—Returns the standard deviation of the values generated from the expression in *expr*. For this function, standard deviation is calculated as the square root of the variance as calculated in the **VARIANCE** function.

➤ **STDDEV_POP**(*expr*) [*OVER (analytical clause)*]—Computes the population standard deviation and returns the square root of the population variance. You can use it as both an aggregate and analytic function. The *expr* is a number expression, and the function returns a value of type **NUMBER**. This function is same as the square root of the **VAR_POP** function. When **VAR_POP** returns null, this function returns null.

➤ **STDDEV_SAMP**(*expr*) [*OVER (analytical clause)*]—Computes the cumulative sample standard deviation and returns the square root of the sample variance. You can use it as both an aggregate and analytic function. The *expr* is a number expression, and the function returns a value of type **NUMBER**. This function is same as the square root of the **VAR_SAMP** function. When **VAR_SAMP** returns null, this function returns null.

➤ **SUM([DISTINCT|ALL]** *expr*)—Returns the sum of the values generated from the expression in *expr*.

➤ **VAR_POP**(*expr*) [*OVER (analytical clause)*]—Returns the population variance of a set of numbers after discarding the nulls in this set. You can use it as both an aggregate and analytic function. The *expr* is a number expression, and the function returns a value of type **NUMBER**. If the function is applied to an empty set, it returns null. The function makes the following calculation:

```
(SUM(expr2) - SUM(expr)2 / COUNT(expr)) / COUNT(expr)
```

➤ VAR_SAMP(*expr*) [*OVER (analytical clause)*]—Returns the sample variance of a set of numbers after discarding the nulls in this set. You can use it as both an aggregate and analytic function. The *expr* is a number expression, and the function returns a value of type **NUMBER**. If the function is applied to an empty set, it returns null. The function makes the following calculation:

```
(SUM(expr2) - SUM(expr)2 / COUNT(expr)) / (COUNT(expr) - 1)
```

This function is similar to **VARIANCE**, except that given an input set of one element, **VARIANCE** returns 0 and **VAR_SAMP** returns null.

➤ VARIANCE([DISTINCT|ALL] *expr*)—Returns the variance of the values generated from the expression in *expr*. The **VARIANCE** function uses the standard *n-1* statistics variance formula.

Analytical Functions in Oracle8i

Oracle has introduced an entire spectrum of analytical functions in Oracle8i, release 8.1.6. however, they are beyond the scope of this book. Most DBAs will never have to deal with the complex analytical functions, and they will not be covered on the OCP exams. However, be aware that they exist and know that you can look them up in the SQL manual should you need them. I do not over them in this book because there are more important topics to get on with.

The expr Clause

In many of the commands, function definitions, and statement definitions, you may see the term *expr*. This clause represents several possible expressions that can be placed in commands, functions, and statements. Not all commands, however, will accept all forms of the *expr* formats. In particular, expressions are used in the following:

➤ **SELECT** select lists

➤ **WHERE** and **HAVING** clauses

➤ **CONNECT BY, START WITH,** and **ORDER BY** clauses

➤ The **VALUES** clause of the **SELECT** statement

➤ The **SET** clause of the **UPDATE** statement

Lists can contain up to 254 expressions. Figures 3.1 through 3.11 show the various forms of the *expr* clause.

The form of the *expr* clause shown in Figure 3.1 is used when the expression represents any of the following: a pseudo-column—such as **LEVEL, ROWID,**

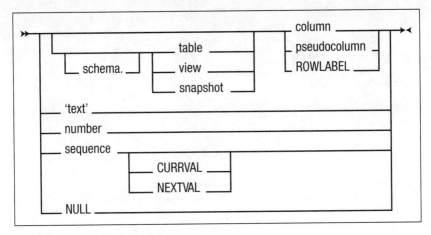

Figure 3.1 Form 1 of the *expr* clause.

or **ROWNUM**—in a table; a constant; a sequence number; or a **NULL** value. Pseudo-column use is restricted to tables. **NCHAR** and **NVARCHAR2** are not valid pseudo-column or **ROWLABEL** data types. **ROWLABEL** is applicable only to trusted Oracle.

The form of the *expr* clause shown in Figure 3.2 is used as a host variable with an optional indicator variable. This form can be used only in embedded SQL or through the Oracle Call Interface (OCI).

The form of the *expr* clause shown in Figure 3.3 is used when you're calling an implicit SQL function.

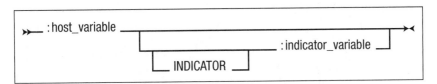

Figure 3.2 Form 2 of the *expr* clause.

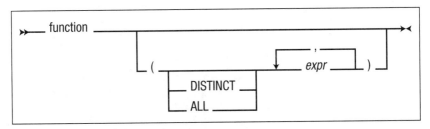

Figure 3.3 Form 3 of the *expr* clause.

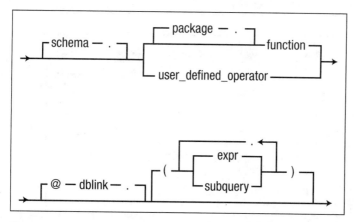

Figure 3.4   Form 4 of the *expr* clause.

The form of the *expr* clause shown in Figure 3.4 is used when you're calling a user-defined function.

The form of the *expr* clause shown in Figure 3.5 is used when a combination of other expressions is required. Some combinations are inappropriate, such as use of a **LENGTH** expression in a **GROUP BY** clause. In the case of an inappropriate combination of expressions, the combination will be rejected.

Form 6 of the *expr* clause is used to call a type constructor when using objects in Oracle. The *type_name* is an object type, and *type_argument_list* is an ordered list of any arguments where the argument types correspond to the type attribute-data types. Any embedded type in the master type will have an embedded type constructor inside form 6. The maximum number of attributes in a type expression is

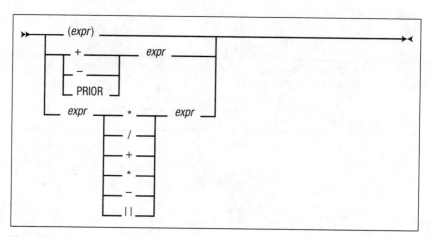

Figure 3.5   Form 5 of the *expr* clause.

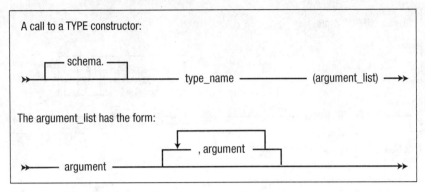

Figure 3.6 Form 6 of the *expr* clause.

999. Nested types—such as **VARRAY** or a nested table specification—can have zero arguments, creating an empty collection.

Form 7 of the *expr* clause is used to cast the collection-typed values of one type into another collection type. The collection that is cast can be the result of an embedded subquery, or it can be a collection type of **VARRAY** or a nested table. The target *type_name* must be an existing, compatible type. If a subquery results in multiple rows, the **MULTISET** keyword must be specified. Scalar **SELECT** operations are not allowed in the subquery of a **CAST** expression.

Form 8 of the *expr* clause is used to return a nested cursor. This is similar to a PL/SQL REF cursor. The nested cursor is opened implicitly when the containing row is fetched from the parent cursor. The nested cursor is closed when:

➤ The user explicitly closes the nested cursor.

➤ Re-execution of the parent cursor occurs.

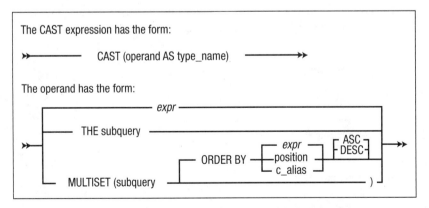

Figure 3.7 Form 7 of the *expr* clause.

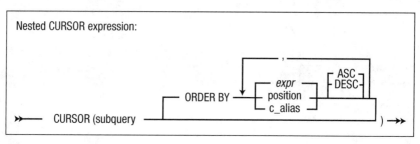

Figure 3.8 Form 8 of the *expr* clause.

➤ The parent cursor is closed.

➤ The parent cursor is canceled.

➤ An error closes the parent cursor, and it is closed during cleanup.

Form 8 can be used only when:

➤ It is in a non-nested **SELECT** statement, except if the **SELECT** is in the parent cursor.

➤ It is in the outermost **SELECT** list of the query.

➤ It is not in a view.

BIND and **EXECUTE** operations cannot be performed on nested queries.

Form 9 of the *expr* clause is used to construct a reference (REF) value. The *argument* is not a table name, but is a table alias as specified in the main statement. The clause returns a REF value, which is bound to the variable or row selected.

Form 10 of the *expr* clause, the **VALUE** expression (don't confuse it with the **VALUES** clause of the **INSERT** command) returns the actual row object from a referenced object. The **VALUE** expression takes a table alias as its argument and returns the corresponding row rather than the REF value.

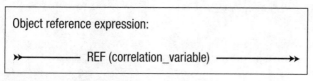

Figure 3.9 Form 9 of the *expr* clause.

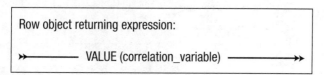

Figure 3.10 Form 10 of the *expr* clause.

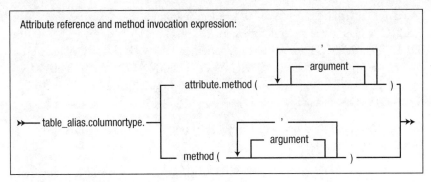

Attribute reference and method invocation expression:

Figure 3.11 Form 11 of the *expr* clause.

Form 11 of the *expr* clause specifies attribute reference and method invocation for types. The *column* value is either a REF or an object column.

When an expression contains a numeric value or a character value enclosed in single quotes, these values are known as *literals*. Literals can be concatenated to other literals or to column values. The simplest literal would be a blank space enclosed with single quotes. Special characters, such as the forward slash (/) and percent sign (%), can be used in a literal if they're preceded by the escape character. An escape character is either the backslash (\) or the character designated with the **ESCAPE** clause in a **LIKE** operator statement.

The DECODE Function

The **DECODE** function is important in that it can be used to perform quasi **if...then** processing inside SQL statements and to enable value specific ordering and translation. Figure 3.12 shows the format to use for the **DECODE** function.

When the **DECODE** function is invoked, Oracle compares *expr* to each *search* value one by one. If the values of *expr* and *search* match, *result* is substituted. If *default* is not specified, the null value is returned; otherwise, *default* is returned.

CONDITION Clauses

The entire purpose of SQL is to allow the insertion, updating, deletion, and retrieval of data. Limiting retrieval of data to just what we want requires some means of limiting the return set of data. The **CONDITION** clauses let you

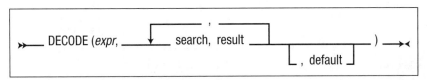

Figure 3.12 The format for the **DECODE** function.

weed out data that's not wanted or needed. Just like the *expr* clause, the CON-DITION clause has several forms. A **CONDITION** clause can be used in **DELETE, SELECT,** or **UPDATE** statements. A **CONDITION** clause can also be used in the **WHERE, START WITH, CONNECT BY,** and **HAVING** clauses of the **SELECT** statement. Figures 3.13 through 3.20 show the various **CONDITION** clauses.

The **CONDITION** clause in Figure 3.13 shows a comparison with expressions or subquery results.

The **CONDITION** clause in Figure 3.14 shows a comparison with any or all members in a list or subquery.

The **CONDITION** clause in Figure 3.15 shows a comparison to test for membership in a group or subquery.

The **CONDITION** clause in Figure 3.16 tests for inclusion in a range.

The **CONDITION** clause in Figure 3.17 tests for nulls. (You must implicitly test for nulls in some situations—such as when you're checking for values not to exist or using **COUNT**—or the rows will be ignored.)

The **CONDITION** clause in Figure 3.18 checks for the existence of rows in a subquery.

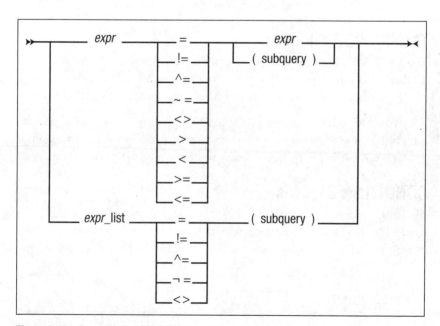

Figure 3.13   Form 1 of the **CONDITION** clause.

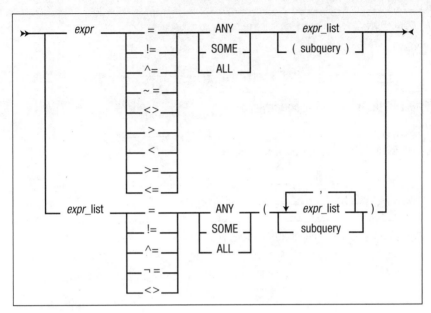

Figure 3.14   Form 2 of the **CONDITION** clause.

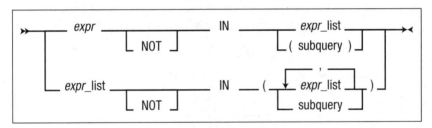

Figure 3.15   Form 3 of the **CONDITION** clause.

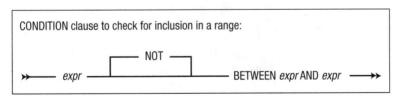

Figure 3.16   Form 4 of the **CONDITION** clause.

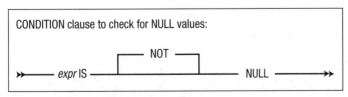

Figure 3.17   Form 5 of the **CONDITION** clause.

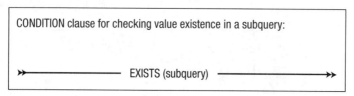

Figure 3.18 Form 6 of the **CONDITION** clause.

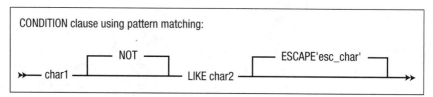

Figure 3.19 Form 7 of the **CONDITION** clause.

The **CONDITION** clause in Figure 3.19 uses tests for pattern matching.

The **CONDITION** clause in Figure 3.20 shows a compound condition.

The **CONDITION** clauses can be combined using logical operators such as **AND, OR,** and **NOT.** Clauses grouped by use of parentheses are checked as a set of conditions that must be met to move on to the next condition.

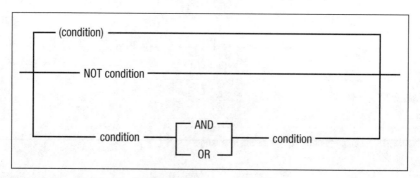

Figure 3.20 Form 8 of the **CONDITION** clause.

The **COMMIT** and **ROLLBACK** Commands

The **COMMIT** command converts temporary records into permanent records. If a user exits from a session normally, a **COMMIT** is automatically performed. Many of the DBMS package procedures provided by Oracle do implicit commits. Implicit **COMMIT** commands are executed by a normal exit from SQLPLUS or when any data definition language (DDL) command is executed (such as **CREATE, ALTER, DROP, TRUNCATE**). Explicit **COMMIT**s are also executed when a Data Control Language (DCL) command is issued (for example, **GRANT** or **REVOKE**).

The **ROLLBACK** command rolls back (undoes the actions) any changes that haven't been committed by a **COMMIT** (either implicit or explicit). An implicit **ROLLBACK** is executed against uncommitted transactions whenever a session terminates abnormally or when a database that has crashed is restarted.

Practice Questions

Question 1

Which single row function can be used on a varchar2?

○ a. **NVL**

○ b. **VARIANCE**

○ c. **ROUND**

○ d. **TRUNC**

○ e. **CORR**

The correct answer is a. Answer b is incorrect because the **VARIANCE** function is used to calculate a variance on numbers. Answer c is incorrect because the **ROUND** function is used to round a numeric answer. Answer d is incorrect because the **TRUNC** function is used with dates and numbers not varchar2. Answer e is incorrect because **the COR function** is used with the new statistics calculations for numeric data, not character data.

Question 2

PRODUCTS					
PROD_ID	DESCRIPTION	SUPPLIER_ID	INVENTORY	COST	RECEIVE_DATE
27025	Labels	avery111	100	2.10	10-jun-99
27027	Cable	canon222	100	0.50	11-oct-99
27023	Pen Set	bic333	80	8.25	19-apr-99
27028	Barrel Pen	blick777	200	2.50	30-oct-99
34081	Copy paper	ibm999	50	20.00	25-jul-99
34096	Address Book	taft666	100	2.50	11-sep-99
27026	Ledger Book	taft666	100	3.50	31-jan-99
47025	Reference Set	wiley000	10	25.00	15-sep-99

Examine the table above.

You attempt to query the database with this command:

```
SELECT 100/NVL(inventory,0)
FROM products;
```

Why does this cause an error when inventory values are null?

○ a. The expression tries to divide by zero.

○ b. The expression tries to divide by a null value.

○ c. The datatypes in the NVL function are incompatible.

○ d. A null value cannot be converted to a normal value.

The correct answer is a. If a null value is found the NVL function will substitute a zero (0) thus causing a divide by zero error. Answer b is what we are trying to avoid with the **NVL** statement. Answer c is incorrect because the datatypes are compatible. Answer d is incorrect because this is the purpose of the **NVL** function.

Question 3

What is the purpose of the **ROLLBACK** command?

○ a. **INSERT** data into the database

○ b. Change existing data in the database

○ c. Make any pending changes permanent in the database

○ d. Move a transaction back to a predetermined statement

○ e. Discard all pending data changes or inserts

The correct answer is e. A **ROLLBACK** command discards all pending data changes or inserts. Answer a is incorrect because this is the purpose of the **INSERT** command. Answer b is incorrect because this is the purpose of the **UPDATE** command. Answer c is incorrect because this is the purpose of the **COMMIT** command (the inverse command from **ROLLBACK**). Answer d is incorrect because this is the purpose of a **SAVEPOINT** command.

Question 4

Retirement is based on the number of years an employee has been employed by the company. You need to create a report showing the employee's name, date of hire, and years of service. Which of the following statements will give the correct report structure and data?

○ a. SELECT first_name|| '|||last_name, date_hired,
                ROUND(SYSDATE)-ROUND(date_hired) Years
                FROM employee;

○ b. SELECT first_name|| '|||last_name, date_hired,
                (ROUND(SYSDATE)-ROUND(date_hired))/12 Years
                FROM employee;

○ c. SELECT first_name|| '|||last_name, date_hired,
                (TRUNC(SYSDATE,'YY')-TRUNC(date_hired,'YY')) Years
                FROM employee;

○ d. SELECT first_name|| '|||last_name, date_hired,
                ROUND(MONTHS_BETWEEN(SYSDATE,date_hired))/12)
                Years
                FROM employee;

The correct answer is d. Answer a is incorrect because the **ROUND** function will produce the number of days between the two dates. Answer b is incorrect because it is taking the number of days and dividing by 12. Answer c is incorrect because it will generate the number of days between the years in the dates but not the value we are looking for.

Question 5

Which of the **to_char()** calls will display a date value formatted like 3RD OF FEBRUARY 2001?

○ a. To_char(date)

○ b. To_char(date,'DDspth OF MONTH YYYY')

○ c. To_char(date,'fmDDth "OF" MONTH YYYY')

○ d. To_char(date,'DDspth 'OF' MONTH YYYY')

The correct answer is c. The fm in the format mask suppresses the zero that would otherwise be displayed with the 3 in the given date output. Answer a will simply convert the date into the current format value for NLS_DATE_FORMAT. Answer b generates a format error. Answer d also generates a format error.

Question 6

You issue the following **SELECT**:

```
SELECT UPPER(CONCAT(SUBSTR(building,1,3),empno))
       FROM emp;
```

Which function will be evaluated first?

○ a. **UPPER**

○ b. **CONCAT**

○ c. **SUBSTR**

The correct answer is c. The function deepest inside the parenthesis will be evaluated first. The other answers are incorrect since they aren't the ones deepest inside the parenthesis.

Question 7

> Which Date arithmetic operation will return a number?
>
> ○ a. To_date('01-Feb-2001')+25
>
> ○ b. TO_DATE('01-jan-2001') – TO_DATE('01-Jan-2000')
>
> ○ c. To_date('03-Dec-2001')-30
>
> ○ d. To_date('01-Oct-2001')+(480/24)

The correct answer is b. Only math with two complete dates will return a number. Answer a is incorrect because it will produce a date. Answer c is incorrect because it will produce a date. Answer d is incorrect because it will produce a date.

Question 8

> You perform the following operations:
>
> 1. Create table **USERS**
>
> 2. Insert 4 records into table **USERS**
>
> 3. Grant **SELECT** privilege on **USERS** to **PUBLIC**
>
> At this point the system crashes (someone unplugged it).
>
> What is the state of the **USERS** table on instance restart?
>
> ○ a. Because no **COMMMIT** was completed before the crash, the **USERS** table wasn't created.
>
> ○ b. Because no **COMMIT** was completed before the crash, no rows were created in the **USERS** table.
>
> ○ c. The **USERS** table has 4 rows in a pending state.
>
> ○ d. The **USERS** table has 4 permanent records.

The correct answer is d. Because the **GRANT** command in Step 3 performs an implicit **COMMIT** command, the records where committed prior to the system crash. Answer a is incorrect since all DDL command perform an implicit **COMMIT** as soon as they are executed. Answer b is incorrect since the GRANT command performs an implicit **COMMIT**. Answer c is incorrect since there is no such thing as a pending state.

Question 9

Evaluate this command:

```
SELECT * FROM emp
WHERE LOWER(last_name)='SCOTT';
```

What result would be expected from this command?

- ○ a. Nothing; an error will be generated.
- ○ b. The command will execute, but no values will be returned.
- ○ c. All employees with a last name of 'scott' will be shown.
- ○ d. All employees with a last name of 'SCOTT' will be shown.

The correct answer is b. Since the command is attempting to compare a value that has been forced into all lowercase by use of the **LOWER** function with an uppercase value it will never return a value. Answer a is incorrect because the statement is syntactically correct. Answer c is incorrect because the comparison clause is matching 'scott' to 'SCOTT'. Answer d is incorrect because the comparison clause is matching 'scott' to 'SCOTT'.

Question 10

Which two commands will cause an implicit **COMMIT** command? (Choose two)

- ❏ a. **GRANT**
- ❏ b. **SELECT**
- ❏ c. **INSERT**
- ❏ d. **UPDATE**
- ❏ e. **CREATE**
- ❏ f. **DELETE**

The correct answers are a and e. Answer a is correct because **GRANT** is a DCL command and DCL always causes an implicit **COMMIT**. Answers b, c, and d are DML, which do not cause implicit commits. Answer e is correct because **CREATE** is a DDL command, which always cause an implicit **COMMIT**. Answer f is incorrect because **DELETE** is a DML command.

Need to Know More?

Oracle Corporation. *Oracle8i Server SQL Reference Manual, Release 3(8.1.7).* September, 2000, Redwood City, California. Part No. A85397-01. This is the source book for all Oracle SQL for version 8i. This book can be found on the Web, at the time of writing, at **http://technet.oracle.com.** This site has free membership and has all current versions of Oracle documentation available online in Acrobat format (PDF files).

Ault, Michael R. *Oracle8i Administration and Management.* John Wiley & Sons. New York, New York, 2000. ISBN 0-471-35453-8. This book covers virtually all aspects of Oracle8i administration, including command syntax, tuning, and management topics.

Honour, Edward, Dalberth, Paul, Kaplan, Ari, and Atul Mehta. *Oracle8 HOW-TO.* Waite Group Press, Corte Madera, California, 1998. ISBN 1-57169-123-5. This book provides an excellent resource for general Oracle how-to information and covers topics from installation to how to use the Web server.

Data Manipulation Language (INSERT, UPDATE, and DELETE)

4

Terms you'll need to understand:

✓ **INSERT**

✓ **UPDATE**

✓ **DELETE**

Techniques you'll need to master:

✓ Using **INSERT** to place data into tables

✓ Using **UPDATE** to change data in tables

✓ Using **DELETE** to perform partial or complete data removal from tables

Database structures, objects, and files aren't useful unless you have a means of putting data into the database, altering stored values, retrieving that data when needed, and removing that data when it's no longer needed. This manipulation of database data is handled with *Data Manipulation Language (DML)* statements. In this chapter, I cover the Oracle DML elements. In this series of certification exams, one focuses entirely on SQL (which consists of Data Definition Language [DDL], Data Manipulation Language [DML], and Data Control Language [DCL]) and Procedural Language—SQL (PL/SQL). You should be able to do the following:

➤ Identify improper command syntax

➤ Analyze tables to determine the SQL needed to generate appropriate result sets

➤ Use Oracle-intrinsic SQL functions

➤ Understand how basic SQL statements operate against a database

It's vital for the database administrator (DBA) to have a complete understanding of SQL, DDL, DML, DCL, and PL/SQL.

DML Elements

The actual command elements that form the DML portion of SQL are few in number: **INSERT, UPDATE, DELETE,** and **SELECT.** The **SELECT** command was covered in Chapter 2. Oracle operators, functions, and conditions statements were covered in Chapter 3.

DML Commands

I cover **INSERT** first because the other commands do you little good if there's no data in the database to manipulate. Insertions can't override constraints, such as **NOT NULL** or **UNIQUE.** Insertions can't specify nonconverted values that can't be implicitly converted to the data type in the destination table.

The INSERT Command

The **INSERT** command is used to add new data into existing database tables, a view's base tables, a table's partition, an object table, or an object view's base table from SQL and PL/SQL. In order to **INSERT** into a table, you must have **INSERT** privilege on the table or have the **INSERT ANY TABLE** system privilege. In order to **INSERT** into a view's base table, the owner of the view must have **INSERT** privilege on the table or have the **INSERT ANY TABLE** system privilege.

The syntax of the **INSERT** command is shown in Figure 4.1.

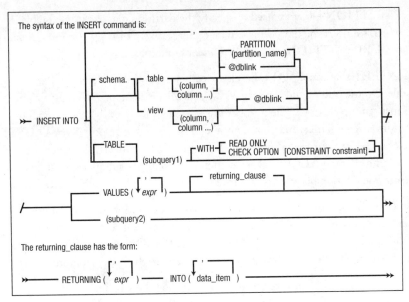

Figure 4.1 The syntax of the **INSERT** command.

The parameters have the following definitions:

➤ *schema*—The owner of the table or view.

➤ *table_name, view_name*—Name of the table or updatable view.

➤ *dbl*—The database link for a remote table or view.

➤ *subquery_2*—A subquery that returns rows or values to be inserted.

➤ *column*—The name(s) of the column(s) in which data will be inserted. If the names are omitted, all the table or view columns must have a matching value or *subquery_2* item.

➤ *expr*—An expression or a list of values corresponding to the inserted values.

➤ **TABLE**—Clause used to flatten a nested object, such as a **VARRAY** or a nested table.

➤ **WITH** clause—Clause used for restricting the subquery; **WITH READ ONLY** specifies that the subquery contents cannot be updated; **WITH CHECK OPTION** prohibits Oracle from making any changes to the table that would not be reflected in the subquery.

➤ *subquery_1*—The query that returns the **VARRAY** or nested table values.

➤ **RETURNING**—Clause used to specify the data items returned (such as **REF** values). This clause cannot be used with parallel DML or with remote objects.

➤ PARTITION—Clause used to specify the partition of a partitioned table in which to insert the data. This can be either a **PARTITION** *partition_name* or **SUBPARTITION** *subpartition_name* combination.

An **INSERT** that uses a **VALUES** clause can insert only a single row of data into a table. On the other hand, a query with a subselect instead of a **VALUES** clause can insert multiple rows. The number of items in a subquery that's used to fetch items for insertion must match the number of items in the column list **VALUES** clause list. Also, the items must be of the same or a convertible data type. If no column list or **VALUES** clause is included, then the subquery must have a one-to-one relation between its returned values and the target table's attributes.

The **INSERT** command is used to add table values, and it can also be used to insert data into an updatable view's base table. If a view is to have data inserted into it, and if that view has a **WITH CHECK OPTION** clause with its definition, then the inserted rows must meet the criteria in the view's defining query.

A view can't have data inserted into it if any of the following are true:

➤ It has a **JOIN**.

➤ It uses a **SET OPERATOR**.

➤ It contains a **GROUP BY** clause.

➤ It uses any group function.

➤ It uses a **DISTINCT** operator.

➤ It has a nested table column.

➤ It has flattened subqueries.

➤ It uses **CAST** and **MULTISET** expressions.

One thing to note is that if a special form of trigger, known as an **INSTEAD-OF** trigger, can allow insert into many views that could not be updated in previous versions.

If you want a join view to be updateable, all of the following conditions must be true:

➤ The **DML** statement must affect only one table underlying the join.

➤ For an **UPDATE** statement, all columns updated must be extracted from a key-preserved table. If the view has the **CHECK OPTION**, join columns and columns taken from tables that are referenced more than once in the view must be shielded from **UPDATE**.

> For a **DELETE** statement, the join can have one and only one key-preserved table. That table can appear more than once in the join, unless the view has the **CHECK OPTION**.

> For an INSERT statement, all columns into which values are inserted must come from a key-preserved table, and the view must not have the **CHECK OPTION**.

The **INSERT** command causes any triggers on the table or underlying tables acted on by the **INSERT** to fire. It can't be used to do the following: force the insertion of data of an incorrect data type or of a nonimplicitly convertible data type into a noncompatible row; violate a **NOT NULL**, **UNIQUE**, or **CHECK** constraint limitation; or violate foreign or primary key constraints.

An **INSERT** statement using a **RETURNING** clause retrieves any inserted rows into the specified PL/SQL or bind variables. **ROWID**s and **REF**s may also be returned in a **RETURNING** clause.

The **UPDATE** Command

The **UPDATE** command is used to change the contents of an existing table row —column or columns or the base columns for an updatable view. You must have **UPDATE** privilege on the table being updated or have the **UPDATE ANY TABLE** system privilege. To update views, the owner of the view must have the **UPDATE ANY TABLE** system privilege.

The syntax for an **UPDATE** command is shown in Figure 4.2.

The parameters have the following definitions:

> *schema*—Owner of the table, view, or snapshot.

> *table_name, view_name, snap*—Table or updatable view or snapshot to be updated.

> *dbl*—A database link to the update item's remote location (if needed).

> *t_alias*—Alias for object name to be used in subqueries and in **WHERE** clauses to make them more readable or more logical. A column or table alias cannot exceed 30 characters.

> *subquery_1*—A subquery that's in the same format as a view definition.

> *subquery_2*—A subquery that returns values to be used to update the object.

> *subquery_3*—A subquery that returns a single value.

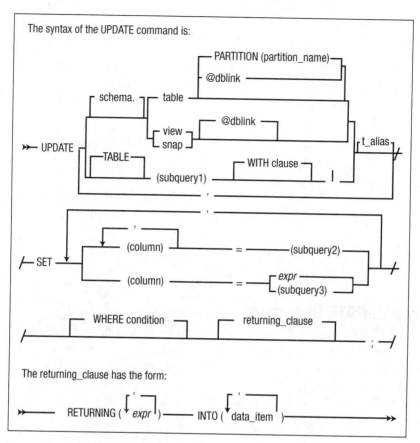

Figure 4.2 Syntax of the **UPDATE** command.

➤ *column*—A column or list of columns to be updated. Lists must be in parentheses. If a column is not mentioned in the clause, that column's value is not updated.

➤ *expr*—New value or values assigned to the subquery or to the column list.

➤ **TABLE**—This clause flattens the corresponding subquery when it returns values from a nested table or **VARRAY**.

➤ **WITH** clause—Clause used for restricting the subquery, the same as an **INSERT WITH** clause.

➤ **RETURNING**—This clause retrieves the rows affected by the **UPDATE** statement. Returned values are limited to scalar, **LOB**, **ROWID**, or **REF** types. The **RETURNING** clause cannot be used with Parallel DML or with remote objects.

➤ **INTO**—Shows Oracle the variables in which the values returned are to be stored.

➤ *Data_item*—This is a PL/SQL variable or bind variable in which to store the returned value. This variable must match the value's data type, or the value's data type must be convertible to the specified data type of the variable.

➤ **WHERE**—A clause used to limit which rows are updated by the **UPDATE** command. If a **WHERE** clause is not specified, then all rows are updated.

➤ **PARTITION**—Clause used to specify the partition of a partitioned table in which to insert the data. This can be either a **PARTITION** *partition_name* or **SUBPARTITION** *subpartition_name* combination.

The **UPDATE** command is used to change table values, and it can be used to update an updatable view's base table. The **UPDATE** command will fire any **UPDATE** triggers that have been specified for the table or any **INSTEAD OF** triggers on an **UPDATE** to a view. If a view is to be updated, and that view has a **WITH CHECK OPTION** clause with its definition, the updated rows must meet the criteria in the view's defining query.

A view can't be updated if any of the following are true unless an **INSTEAD-OF** trigger is created on the view:

➤ It has a **JOIN**.

➤ It uses a **SET OPERATOR**.

➤ It contains a **GROUP BY** clause.

➤ It uses any group function.

➤ It uses a **DISTINCT** operator.

➤ It has flattened subqueries.

➤ It uses nested table columns.

➤ It uses **CAST** and **MULTISET** expressions.

When you're updating a partition or subpartition, you must specify all of the partition columns in the update. (A *partition column* is one out of the possible set of columns that determine how to partition the table.) A partition update that could force a row to migrate will be rejected with an error in Oracle8.0 but will execute in 8i if the partition was created wih **ENABLE ROW MIGRATION**.

If a subquery in an **UPDATE** statement refers back to the updated table, this situation is called a *correlated update,* and the subquery will be evaluated once for each row updated. Usually, to use a subquery to perform a correlated update, you will specify a table alias.

When you're using a **RETURNING** clause, you must be sure to specify scalar return variables for scalar updates and to provide bind arrays for any **UPDATE** that will return multiple rows, or an error will be returned.

The **DELETE** Command

After a table has been loaded with data, you may need to periodically remove rows from the data set that results. This removal of data is accomplished with one of two commands. The **DELETE** command is used to remove some or all rows from a table, and a **ROLLBACK** of the command is allowed if no **COMMIT** is executed. The **TRUNCATE** command is used to remove all rows from a table, and no **ROLLBACK** is allowed.

The syntax of the **DELETE** command is shown in Figure 4.3.

The parameters have the following definitions:

➤ *schema*—Name of the object owner.

➤ *table_name, view_name, table_name:partition_name, table_name:subpartition_name*—Name of the table or view whose base table will have data deleted from it.

➤ *dblink*—Database link to remote instance if the object is not local.

➤ *alias*—Shorthand for the table, view, or subquery, for use in the **WHERE** clause. A column or table alias cannot exceed 30 characters.

➤ *subquery*—A subquery that selects data to be deleted. This subquery is executed, and the resulting rows are deleted. The subquery can't query a table that appears in the same **FROM** clause as the subquery.

➤ **WITH** clause—This **WITH** clause has the same definition as in the **INSERT** command.

➤ **TABLE**—This clause tells Oracle that the column value returned is a nested table and not a scalar value. I prefer to think of it as **THE TABLE**, instead of just **THE**.

➤ **RETURNING**—This clause retrieves the rows affected by the **DELETE** statement. Returned values are limited to scalar, **LOB**, **ROWID**, or **REF** types. The **RETURNING** clause cannot be used with Parallel DML or with remote objects.

➤ **INTO**—Shows Oracle the variables in which the values returned are to be stored.

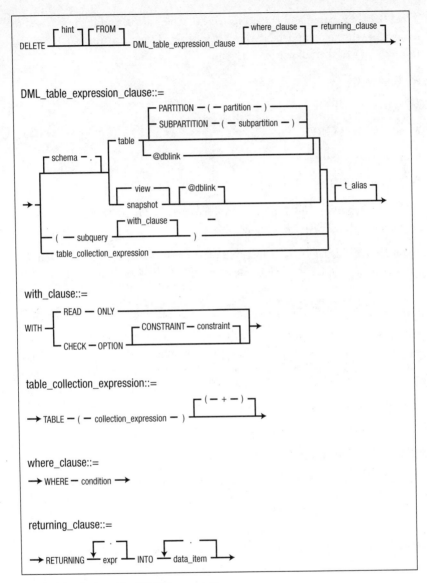

Figure 4.3 Syntax of the **DELETE** command.

➤ *Data_item*—This is a PL/SQL variable or bind variable in which to store the returned value. The variable must match the value's data type, or the value's data type must be convertible to the specified data type of the variable.

➤ **WHERE** condition—Allows deletion of only those rows that meet the specified condition.

The **DELETE** command is used to remove table values, and it can be used to remove rows from an updatable view's base table. A view can't have data deleted from it if any of the following are true:

➤ It has a **JOIN**.

➤ It uses a **SET OPERATOR**.

➤ It contains a **GROUP BY** clause.

➤ It uses any group function.

➤ It uses a **DISTINCT** operator.

A **DELETE** will fire any **DELETE** triggers specified on the tables or underlying tables of the **DELETE** command.

If you **DELETE** data from a specified partition in a partitioned table, you can avoid using a complex **WHERE** clause.

INSERT, UPDATE, and DELETE Examples

In contrast to the many forms of the **SELECT** statement, the other DML commands aren't nearly as complex when you remember that, except for the **SET** operators, many of the other clauses apply to most of the other DML commands. Of course, the sorting and grouping clauses don't apply to the other DML. These exclusions leave the **WHERE** clause and the subqueries with a sprinkling of the object clauses for flavoring.

INSERT Command

The **INSERT** command is used to initially insert data into tables either directly or through views. The **INSERT** command can use subqueries and the **THE** object clause. The **RETURNING** clause can also be used with an **INSERT** command to return inserted values to variables. The **RETURING** clause cannot be used with Parallel DML or with remote objects. Listing 4.1 shows the various forms of the **INSERT** command.

Listing 4.1:   **INSERT** command examples.

```
SQL> CREATE TABLE test1 (table_name varchar2(30), owner varchar2(30));

Table created.

SQL> INSERT INTO test1 SELECT table_name,owner FROM all_tables

11 rows created.
```

```
SQL> COMMIT;

Commit complete.

SQL> INSERT INTO test1 VALUES ('TEST_TABLE','NO_ONE');

1 row created.

SQL> INSERT INTO test1(table_name) VALUES('TEST2_TABLE');

1 row created.

SQL> VAR t1 varchar2(30);
SQL> VAR t2 varchar2(30);
SQL> INSERT INTO test1 VALUES ('TEST3_TABLE','TEST3_OWNER')
  2  RETURNING table_name,owner INTO :t1,:t2;

1 row created.

SQL> PRINT t1

T1
---------------------------------
TEST3_TABLE

SQL> PRINT t2

T2
---------------------------------
TEST3_OWNER
```

The examples in Listing 4.1 show various uses of the **INSERT** command. The first example is an insert using a subquery. The second example in Listing 4.1 shows a blank insert of an entire row. The third example in Listing 4.1 shows a partial row insert. The final example shows the use of the **RETURNING** clause.

UPDATE Command

The **UPDATE** command can change only existing rows—it cannot create new rows. The **UPDATE** clause can use the **WHERE** clause, subqueries, the **RE-TURNING** clause, and the **TABLE** object-related clause. Listing 4.2 shows examples of the **UPDATE** command.

Listing 4.2: Example **UPDATE** commands.

```
SQL> DESC emp
   Name                                       Null?    Type
   ---------------------------------------    -------- ------------------
   ENAME                                               VARCHAR2(100)
   ENUMBER                                             NUMBER
   EDEPT                                               REF OF DEPT_T

SQL> SELECT ename FROM emp;

ENAME
-------------------------------------------------------
Mike Ault
George Petrod
Carol Smith
Francine Lenord

SQL> UPDATE emp SET ename='Michael Ault'
  2  WHERE ename='Mike Ault';

1 row updated.

SQL> COMMIT;

Commit complete.

SQL> COL ename FORMAT a20
SQL> SELECT ename,enumber FROM emp;

ENAME                  ENUMBER
-------------------- --------
Michael Ault                1
George Petrod               3
Carol Smith                 4
Francine Lenord             2

SQL> UPDATE emp SET ename='Frank Lenord' WHERE enumber=2;

1 row updated.

SQL> COMMIT;

Commit complete.

SQL> SELECT ename,enumber FROM emp;
```

```
ENAME                 ENUMBER
--------------------- --------
Michael Ault              1
George Petrod             3
Carol Smith              4
Frank Lenord             2


SQL> UPDATE emp SET assignment='None';

4 rows updated.

SQL> COL assignment FORMAT a10
SQL> SELECT ename,enumber,assignment FROM emp;

ENAME                 ENUMBER ASSIGNMENT
--------------------- -------- ----------
Michael Ault              1 None
George Petrod             3 None
Carol Smith              4 None
Frank Lenord             2 None


SQL> SELECT * FROM assignments;

  ENUMBER COMPANY_NAME
-------- ----------------------------------
        1 Internal
        2 Practical Software, Inc.
        3 The Phone Company
        4 Internal


SQL> UPDATE emp a SET a.assignment=(SELECT b.company_name
  2                                 FROM assignments b
  3                                 WHERE a.enumber=b.enumber);

4 rows updated.

SQL> COL assignment FORMAT a24
SQL> SELECT ename,enumber,assignment FROM emp;

ENAME                 ENUMBER ASSIGNMENT
--------------------- -------- ------------------------
Michael Ault              1 Internal
George Petrod             3 The Phone Company
Carol Smith              4 Internal
Frank Lenord             2 Practical Software, Inc.
```

```
SQL> VAR e VARCHAR2(32)
SQL> UPDATE emp SET ename='Michael R. Ault'
  2  WHERE ename='Michael Ault'
  3  RETURNING ename INTO :e;

1 row updated.

SQL> print e

E
---------------------------------
Michael R. Ault

SQL> DESC art
 Name                            Null?   Type
 --------------------------      ------- -------------------
 PICTURE_DATE                            DATE
 PICTURE_CONTENTS                        PICTURE_PART_V
 ARTIST                                  ARTIST_LIST

SQL> UPDATE TABLE(SELECT artist FROM art a
  2  WHERE a.picture_date='23-aug-99') artists
  3  SET artists.last_name='Smith';

2 rows updated.

SQL> COL artists FORMAT a59
SQL> SELECT TABLE(SELECT artist FROM art a
  2  WHERE a.picture_date='23-aug-99') artists
  3  FROM art;

ARTISTS(LAST_NAME, FIRST_NAME, MIDDLE_INITIAL, SSN)
----------------------------------------------------------------
ARTIST_LIST(ARTIST_T('Smith', 'Mike', 'R', '222-33-4444'),
ARTIST_T('Smith', 'Susan', 'K', '333-44-5555'))

SQL> UPDATE emp SET edept=NULL WHERE edpt IS DANGLING;

1 row updated.
```

In the examples in Listing 4.2, we first see two simple single row **UPDATE**s using the **WHERE** clause to restrict the **UPDATE** to a single row. In the next example in Listing 4.2, the use of **UPDATE** to update a single column in the entire table is shown. The next few examples in Listing 4.2 show the use of a subquery, a **RETURNING** clause, and the **TABLE** clause for a nested table. The final example in Listing 4.2 shows how to set **DANGLING REF** values to **NULL**.

When updating a user-defined type where **REF** values are used, be aware that this can result in working with **DANGLING REF** values. A **DANGLING REF** is when the primary record in the master object is deleted, leaving the **REF** in the secondary object without anything to connect into. Thus, it is **DANGLING**. Performing **REF** and **DEREF** against a **DANGLING REF** can result in errors and in some early releases of Oracle8, instance and system crashes. Always check for **DANGLING REF** values and always ensure that related records are removed when the primary object is deleted. The **IS [NOT] DANGLING** clause should be used if **DANGLING REF** values are suspected.

DELETE Command

The **DELETE** command is used to remove records from tables. The **DELETE** command can use the **WHERE** clause, subqueries, the **RETURNING** clause, and the **TABLE** object-related clause. Listing 4.3 shows examples of the **DELETE** command.

Listing 4.3:   Example **DELETE** commands.

```
SQL> SELECT ename,enumber FROM emp;

ENAME                   ENUMBER
-------------------- --------
Michael R. Ault          1
George Petrod            3
Carol Smith              4
Frank Lenord             2

SQL> DELETE emp;

4 rows deleted.

SQL> SELECT ename,enumber FROM emp;

no rows selected

SQL> ROLLBACK;

Rollback complete.

SQL> SELECT ename,enumber FROM emp;

ENAME                   ENUMBER
-------------------- --------
Michael Ault             1
George Petrod            3
```

```
Carol Smith              4
Frank Lenord             2

SQL> DELETE emp WHERE enumber=1;

1 row deleted.

SQL> SELECT ename,enumber FROM emp;

ENAME                  ENUMBER
-------------------- --------
George Petrod            3
Carol Smith              4
Frank Lenord             2

SQL> ROLLBACK;

Rollback complete.

SQL> DELETE emp e WHERE e.ename=(SELECT d.ename
  2                          FROM emp d WHERE d.enumber=1);

1 row deleted.

SQL> SELECT ename,enumber FROM emp;

ENAME                  ENUMBER
-------------------- --------
George Petrod            3
Carol Smith              4
Frank Lenord             2

SQL> ROLLBACK;

Rollback complete.
SQL> var e1 number
SQL> var e2 varchar2(32)
SQL> DELETE emp e WHERE e.ename=(SELECT d.ename
  2    FROM emp d
  3    WHERE d.enumber=1)
  4    RETURNING enumber,ename INTO :e1,:e2;

1 row deleted.

SQL> PRINT e1
```

```
         E1
--------
         1

SQL> PRINT e2

E2
---------------------------------
Michael Ault

SQL> ROLLBACK;

Rollback complete.

SQL> DELETE TABLE(SELECT artist FROM art a
  2              WHERE a.picture_date='23-aug-99') artists
  3   WHERE artists.first_name='Mike';

1 row deleted.

SQL> SELECT TABLE(SELECT artist FROM art a
  2              WHERE a.picture_date='23-aug-99') artists
  3   FROM art;

ARTISTS(LAST_NAME, FIRST_NAME, MIDDLE_INITIAL, SSN)
-----------------------------------------------------------
ARTIST_LIST(ARTIST_T('Ault', 'Susan', 'K', '333-44-5555'))

SQL> rollback;

Rollback complete.

SQL> r
  1* rollback

Rollback complete.

SQL> SELECT TABLE(SELECT artist FROM art a
  2              WHERE a.picture_date='23-aug-99') artists
  3   FROM art;

ARTISTS(LAST_NAME, FIRST_NAME, MIDDLE_INITIAL, SSN)
-----------------------------------------------------------
ARTIST_LIST(ARTIST_T('Ault', 'Mike', 'R', '222-33-4444'),
ARTIST_T('Ault', 'Susan', 'K', '333-44-5555'))
```

In the examples in Listing 4.3, we first see a simple single row **DELETE** using the **WHERE** clause to restrict the **DELETE** to a single row. In the next example in Listing 4.3, the use of **DELETE** to remove all rows in the entire table is shown. A **DELETE** can also use the **DELETE FROM** form but this is strictly for compliance to the standard and is not a required syntax. The next few examples in Listing 4.3 show the use of a subquery, a **RETURNING** clause, and the **TABLE** clause for a nested table. When deleting from user-defined types where **REF** values are used, be aware that this can result in **DANGLING REF** values. Performing **REF** and **DEREF** against a **DANGLING REF** can result in errors and in some early releases of Oracle8, instance and system crashes. Always check for **DANGLING REF** values and always ensure that related records are removed when the primary object is deleted. The **IS [NOT] DANGLING** clause should be used if **DANGLING REF** values are suspected.

Practice Questions

Question 1

Which command is used to modify existing rows in an existing table?

○ a. **UPDATE**

○ b. **INTO**

○ c. **INSERT**

○ d. **CREATE**

○ e. **ADD**

The correct answer is a. The only command that allows the alteration of existing data is the **UPDATE** command. Answer b is incorrect because **INTO** is actually a required part of the **SELECT** command when it is used in PL/SQL, and it has nothing to do with **INSERT**. Answer c is incorrect because an **INSERT** command is used to insert new rows. Answer d is incorrect because the **CREATE** command is a DDL and not a DML command, and it has nothing to do with putting data into a table. Answer e is incorrect because **ADD** is a part of the DDL command **ALTER** and has nothing to do with insertion of data into tables.

Question 2

Examine the following table:

Products					
PROD_ID	**DESCRIPTION**	**SUPPLIER_ID**	**INVENTORY**	**COST**	**RECEIVE_DATE**
27025	Labels	avery111	100	2.10	10-jun-99
27027	Cable	canon222	100	0.50	11-oct-99
27023	Pen Set	bic333	80	8.25	19-apr-99
27028	Barrel Pen	blick777	200	2.50	30-oct-99
34081	Copy paper	ibm999	50	20.00	25-jul-99
34096	Address Book	taft666	100	2.50	11-sep-99
27026	Ledger Book	taft666	100	3.50	31-jan-99
47025	Reference Set	wiley000	10	25.00	15-sep-99

Evaluate this command:

```
DELETE FROM products
WHERE cost < 3.00 AND receive_date > to_date(15-
    sep-1999, 'dd-mon-yyyy');
```

Which **PROD_ID**s would be deleted? [Check all correct answers]

❏ a. 27027

❏ b. 34096

❏ c. 27028

❏ d. 27026

The correct answers are a and c. None of the other answers meet the criteria of having a **COST** less than 3.00 and a **RECEIVE_DATE** greater than 15-sep-1999.

Question 3

> Evaluate the following command:
>
> ```
> UPDATE emp SET salary=salary*1.05;
> ```
>
> What does this statement accomplish?
>
> ○ a. Insert data into the database.
>
> ○ b. Update all salaries in the emp table to reflect a 5% raise.
>
> ○ c. Update all salaries in the emp table to reflect a 105% raise.
>
> ○ d. Set a specific salary in the emp table to indicate a 5% raise.
>
> ○ e. Nothing, it will generate an error condition.

The correct answer is b. The **UPDATE** command shown would multiple the salary column in the table by a 1.05 factor, which equates to a 5% increase. Answer a is incorrect since it is not inserting data, it is updating data. Answer c is incorrect because 1.05 corresponds to 5%, not 105%. Answer d is incorrect because there was no **WHERE** clause thus all rows were updated. Answer e is incorrect because the statement is syntactically correct.

Question 4

> What command is used to add data to a table?
>
> ○ a. **INSERT**
>
> ○ b. **UPDATE**
>
> ○ c. **CHANGE**
>
> ○ d. **ADD**

The correct answer is a. The only command to add data to a table is **INSERT**. Answer b is incorrect because the **UPDATE** command changes data that is already in a table. Answer c is incorrect because a **CHANGE** command is applicable only to SQLPLUS buffer contents. Answer d is incorrect because an **ADD** command is a subclause in a **ALTER** command and has nothing to do with DML.

Question 5

> Which of the following actions will happen when a **CREATE** command is issued?
>
> ○ a. The system crashes.
>
> ○ b. The system will automatically exit the active session.
>
> ○ c. An automatic **ROLLBACK** is issued.
>
> ○ d. An automatic **COMMIT** is issued.

The correct answer is d. Whenever a DDL command is issued, an automatic COMMIT is generated upon successful completion.

Question 6

> What will happen if an **ALTER** command is issued in the middle of a transaction?
>
> ○ a. The transaction will end.
>
> ○ b. The system will crash.
>
> ○ c. An error will be generated and processing will continue to end of transaction.
>
> ○ d. The results will be deferred until the transaction ends.

The correct answer is a. Because ALTER is a DDL command, any ALTER command will result in a COMMIT upon its completion that will end the current transaction.

Question 7

> What is true about a DML transaction?
>
> ○ a. Only one statement per transaction is allowed.
>
> ○ b. Multiple actions such as a credit and debit can be performed.
>
> ○ c. Automatic **COMMIT** commands are generated after each statement.
>
> ○ d. Transaction logic doesn't apply to DML operations.

The correct answer is b. In DML, multiple DML statements can be entered before a **COMMIT** or **ROLLBACK** terminates the transaction.

Question 8

> You perform the following operations:
>
> 1. Create a table named users
>
> 2. Insert 4 records into table users
>
> 3. Grant **SELECT** privilege on users to **PUBLIC**
>
> At this point the system crashes (someone unplugged it).
>
> What is the state of the users table on instance restart?
>
> O a. Because no **COMMMIT** was completed before the crash, the users table doesn't exist.
>
> O b. Because no **COMMIT** was completed before the crash, the users table doesn't contain any rows.
>
> O c. Four rows are in a pending state for table users.
>
> O d. Four permanent records are in the users table.

The correct answer is d. Because the **GRANT** command in Step 3 performs an implicit **COMMIT** command, the 4 records were committed prior to the system crash. Answers a and b are incorrect because a COMMIT is executed due to the Grant command. Answer c is incorrect because there is no pending state.

Question 9

> Evaluate this command:
>
> ```
> DELETE test_scores;
> ```
>
> Which task will this command accomplish?
>
> O a. Delete the test_scores column
>
> O b. Delete all the values in the columns of the test_scores table that don't have **NOT NULL** constraints
>
> O c. Drop the test_scores table
>
> O d. Delete all records from the test_scores table

The correct answer is d. A **DELETE** command without a **WHERE** clause will remove all rows from the specified table (unless a **ROLLBACK** is executed.) **DELETE** is a DML command, it affects only data. A non-restricted **DELETE** removes all rows from the specified table unless the table is a parent table and child records exist. Because we have not been told that test_scores is a parent table, we have to assume that d is the correct answer to this question.

Question 10

Which commands will cause an implicit **COMMIT** command? [Check all correct answers]

- ❑ a. **GRANT**
- ❑ b. **SELECT**
- ❑ c. **INSERT**
- ❑ d. **UPDATE**
- ❑ e. **CREATE**
- ❑ f. **DELETE**

The correct answers are a and e. Answer a is correct because **GRANT** is a DCL command, which don't always cause an implicit **COMMIT**. Answers b, c, and d are DML, which do not cause implicit **COMMIT**s. Answer e is correct because **CREATE** is a DDL command—DDL commands always cause an implicit **COMMIT**. Answer f is incorrect because **DELETE** is a DML command.

Need to Know More?

 Oracle Corporation. *Oracle8i Server SQL Reference Manual, Release 3(8.1.7)*. September, 2000. Redwood City, California. Part No. A85397-01. This is the source book for all Oracle SQL for version 8i. This book can be found on the Web, at the time of writing, at **http://technet.oracle.com**. This site has free membership and has all current versions of Oracle documentation available online in Acrobat format (PDF files).

 Ault, Michael R. *Oracle8i Administration and Management*. John Wiley & Sons. New York, New York. 2000. ISBN 0-471-35453-8. This book covers virtually all aspects of Oracle8i administration, including command syntax, tuning, and management topics.

 Honour, Edward, Dalberth, Paul, Kaplan, Ari, and Atul Mehta. *Oracle8 HOW-TO*. Waite Group Press, Corte Madera, California. 1998. ISBN 1-57169-123-5. This book provides an excellent resource for general Oracle how-to information and covers topics from installation to how to use the Web server.

Data Definition Language

Terms you'll need to understand:

✓ DDL (Data Definition Language)

✓ Tablespace

✓ Storage parameters

✓ **INITIAL**

✓ **NEXT**

✓ **MINEXTENTS**

✓ **MAXEXTENTS**

✓ **PCTINCREASE**

✓ **PCTFREE**

✓ **PCTUSED**

✓ **INITRANS**

✓ **FREELIST**

✓ **MAXTRANS**

Techniques you'll need to master:

✓ Using all storage parameters

✓ Using the **CREATE** command for all objects (databases, tablespaces, relational tables, indexes, clusters, sequences, views, synonyms, rollback segments, and control files)

The OCP exam covers the storage parameters and their various uses in great detail. A DBA must know all of the ins and outs of the storage parameters, particularly those dealing with the prevention of chaining and fragmentation.

Data Definition Language (DDL) includes all commands used to create, alter, and drop database objects. These objects include tables, indexes, clusters, sequences, triggers, procedures, functions, and packages (including package bodies). The **CREATE** command is used to create all of these objects (with differing modifiers and options). Likewise, the **ALTER** command is used to alter database objects, and the **DROP** command is used to drop them. This first DDL chapter is dedicated to the most complex of these command sets: the **CREATE** command.

The CREATE Command

The **CREATE** command is used to make all database objects. This command and its optional **STORAGE** clause will be the subject of most of the DDL-related questions on the exam. The following shows the syntax of the generic **CREATE** command:

```
CREATE <modifier> object_type object_name
create options,
STORAGE ( storage parameters)
```

The CREATE Command for Databases

All things in an Oracle database reside in the database. Therefore, the first **CREATE** command to discuss is the **CREATE DATABASE** command. Some systems require the user to have the OSDBA or SYSDBA role to use the command. The **CREATE DATABASE** command should not be used on an existing database, or it will be reinitialized to its original empty state and all tables, index, or other user created objects will be lost. Figure 5.1 shows the format for this command.

The **CREATE DATABASE** command has the following parameters:

➤ *database_name*—Name of the database. Composed of a maximum of eight ASCII characters. (You cannot use special characters from European or Asian character sets in a database name.)

➤ *file_specs*—File specifications for data files are of the format: **'filename' SIZE integer K** or **M REUSE**. K is for kilobytes, M is for Megabytes, and **REUSE** specifies to reuse the file if it already exists.

➤ AUTOEXTEND—Used to allow your data files to automatically extend as needed. Be very careful with this command because it can use up a great deal of disk space rather rapidly if a mistake is made during table builds or inserts.

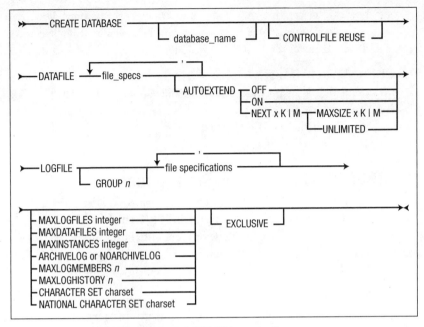

Figure 5.1   The syntax of the **CREATE DATABASE** command.

Note: File specifications for log files depend on the operating system.

➤ **MAXLOGFILES, MAXDATAFILES,** and **MAXINSTANCES**—Set hard limits for the database and should be set to the maximum you ever expect to need.

➤ **MAXLOGMEMBERS** and **MAXLOGHISTORY**—Set hard limits for the number of members in a log group or the maximum number of logs to maintain in the history table in the control file. Pre-8i, the MAXLOGHISTORY was 65535 and instance crash could result from more than 655535 log switches, this has been fixed to nearly unlimited in Oracle8i.

➤ **CHARACTER SET**—Determines the character set that data will be stored in. This value is operating system dependent.

➤ **ARCHIVELOG**—Used to set archive logging.

➤ **NOARCHIVELOG**—Used if you don't need to set archive logging. I suggest creating databases with **NOARCHIVELOG**. Then, after all creation activities are complete, alter the database to **ARCHIVELOG** if desired.

➤ **NATIONAL CHARACTER SET**—Specifies the national character set used to store data in columns specifically defined as **NCHAR, NCLOB,** or **NVARCHAR2**. In earlier releases of Oracle, you can't change the national character set after creating the database; in Oracle8i this is now allowed as long as the old character set is a strict subset of the new one. If not specified, the national character set defaults to the database character set.

The **CREATE DATABASE** command allows the initial specification of database maximum values, such as the maximum allowed number of database data files, log files, and log file groups. It also allows for specification of the initial database data file for the **SYSTEM** tablespace, as well as specification of other data files used with other tablespaces.

The **CREATE** Command for Tablespaces

All objects in an Oracle database are stored in *tablespaces,* which are the units of logical storage for an Oracle database. The **CREATE TABLESPACE** command allows you to create a tablespace and one or more initial data files. It also allows you to specify default storage parameters. Figure 5.2 shows the **CREATE TABLESPACE** syntax.

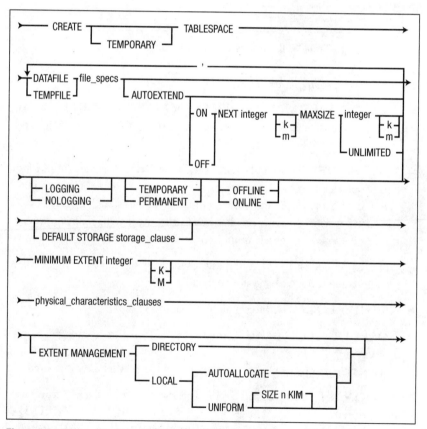

Figure 5.2 The syntax of the **CREATE TABLESPACE** command.

The **CREATE TABLESPACE** command has the following keywords and parameters:

➤ **tablespace_name**—Name of the tablespace to be created.

➤ **DATAFILE**—Specifies the data file or files used to compose the tablespace.

➤ **MINIMUM EXTENT**—Integer clause that controls free-space fragmentation in the tablespace by ensuring that every used and/or free extent size in a tablespace is at least as large as the integer and is a multiple of the integer.

➤ **AUTOEXTEND**—Enables or disables the automatic extension of the data file:

  ➤ **OFF**—Disables **AUTOEXTEND** if it's turned on. **NEXT** and **MAXSIZE** are set to zero. To re-enable the feature after **AUTOEXTEND** is disabled, you must specify values again for **NEXT** and **MAXSIZE** in additional **ALTER TABLESPACE AUTOEXTEND** commands.

  ➤ **ON**—Enables **AUTOEXTEND**.

  ➤ **NEXT**—Specifies disk space to allocate to the data file when more extents are required.

  ➤ **MAXSIZE**—Specifies the maximum disk space allowed for allocation to the data file.

  ➤ **UNLIMITED**—Tells Oracle to set no limit on allocating disk space to the data file.

Note: Be careful with AUTOEXTEND on all versions of Oracle8 and Oracle8i. I say this because in versions of Oracle up to 8.1.7.1, the maximum block allocation for Oracle is 4,194,303 Oracle blocks. This limit on the number of blocks leads to a hard limit on the maximum size of an Oracle data file, which can be silently exceeded by AUTOEXTEND, causing data dictionary corruption. For more information on this and other space-related bugs, see note 112011.1 on http://metalink.oracle.com.

➤ **LOGGING/NOLOGGING**—Specifies the default logging attributes of all tables, indexes, and partitions within the tablespace. **LOGGING** is the default. If **NOLOGGING** is specified, no undo and redo logs are generated for operations that support the **NOLOGGING** option on the tables, indexes, and partitions within the tablespace. The tablespace-level logging attribute can be overridden by logging specifications at the table, index, and partition levels.

➤ **DEFAULT STORAGE**—Specifies the default storage parameters for all objects created in the tablespace.

➤ ONLINE—Makes the tablespace available immediately after creation to users who have been granted access to the tablespace.

➤ OFFLINE—Makes the tablespace unavailable immediately after creation.

Note: If you omit both the ONLINE and OFFLINE options, Oracle creates the tablespace online by default. The data dictionary view DBA_TABLESPACES indicates whether each tablespace is online or offline. Similarly, LOGGING and ONLINE are defaults.

➤ PERMANENT—Specifies that the tablespace will be used to hold permanent objects. This is the default.

➤ TEMPORARY—Specifies that the tablespace will be used only to hold temporary objects—for example, segments used by implicit sorts to handle **ORDER BY** clauses.

➤ EXTENT MANAGEMENT—Can be either **DICTIONARY** (the default) or **LOCAL**. If **LOCAL** management is specified, a bitmap located in the tablespace itself is used to manage extents reducing the load on the **FET$** and **UET$** data dictionary extent management tables and recursive SQL. **LOCAL** managed extents can either be **AUTOALLOCATED** or **UNIFORM**. If **UNIFORM**, the **SIZE** for each extent in K or M can be specified.

The major decisions when you use the **CREATE TABLESPACE** command are the placement of the data files and the specification of the default storage options. You should be familiar with file placement and with what happens to objects created using the default storage options. The **STORAGE** clause and its options are shown in Figure 5.3.

The **STORAGE** clause has the following parameters:

➤ INITIAL—Size in bytes of the initial extent of the object segment. The default value is the size of 5 data blocks. The minimum value is the size of 2 data blocks for nonbitmapped segments or 3 data blocks for bitmapped segments, plus one data block for each free list group you specify. The maximum value depends on your operating system. Oracle rounds values up to the next multiple of the data block size for values less than 5 data blocks, and it rounds up to the next multiple of 5 data blocks for values greater than 5 data blocks.

➤ NEXT—Size for the next extent after **INITIAL** is used. The default is 5 blocks, the minimum is 1 block, and the maximum is 4,095 megabytes. This is the value that will be used for each new extent if **PCTINCREASE** is set to 0.

➤ MINEXTENTS—Number of initial extents for the object. Generally, except for rollback segments, it's set to 1. If a large amount of space is required

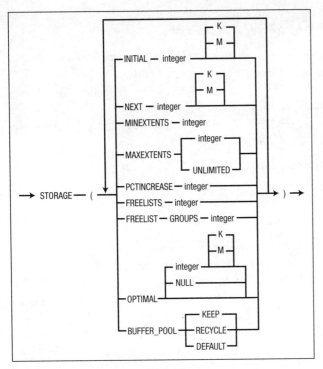

Figure 5.3   The syntax of the **STORAGE** clause.

and if there's not enough contiguous space for the table setting, using a smaller extent size and specifying several extents may solve the problem.

➤ MAXEXTENTS—Largest number of extents allowed for the object. This defaults to the maximum allowed for your block size, as of version 7.3. However, it is possible to set **MAXEXTENTS** to unlimited after version 8, allowing over 2 billion extents. However, Oracle suggests not going over 4,000 extents for a single object.

➤ PCTINCREASE—Parameter that tells Oracle how much to grow each extent after the **INITIAL** and **NEXT** extents are used. A specification of 50 will grow each extent after **NEXT** by 50 percent for each subsequent extent. This means that for a table created with one **INITIAL** and a **NEXT** extent, any further extents will increase in size by 50 percent over their predecessors. In Oracle7.2 and later versions, this parameter is applied only against the size of the previous extent. Increase this value if you don't know how much the table will grow, but know only that it will grow significantly. The value of **PCTINCREASE** indicates a growth *rate* for subsequent extents. A tablespace with a default storage setting for **PCTINCREASE** of zero will not be automatically coalesced by the SMON process.

➤ OPTIMAL—Used only for rollback segments. Specifies the value to which a rollback segment will shrink after extending.

➤ FREELISTS—For objects other than tablespaces, specifies the number of freelists for each of the freelist groups for the table, index, or cluster. The minimum value is 1, and the maximum is block-size dependent. Before version 8.1.6, this could not be reset without re-creating the table; in 8.1.6 and greater, it can be reset dynamically if the COMPATIBLE initialization parameter is set to 8.1.6 at a minimum.

➤ FREELIST GROUPS—Parameter that specifies the number of freelist groups to maintain for a table or index. This parameter is generally meaningful for only parallel server databases and can't be specified unless a database is altered into parallel or shared mode.

➤ BUFFER_POOL *pool_name*—Specifies the area of the buffer pool where the object will be cached. The *pool_name* parameter corresponds to DEFAULT (the value assigned if no BUFFER_POOL parameter is specified); KEEP for objects which should not be aged out of the buffer pool; and RECYCLE for objects that should be rapidly aged out of the buffer pool. The KEEP and RECYCLE pools are sub-sections of the DEFAULT pools and must be configured in the initialization parameters BUFFER_POOL_KEEP and BUFFER_POOL_RECYCLE before they can be used.

Tablespaces are subject to fragmentation as their chief space-related problem. As objects grow and shrink, extents are allocated and dropped. This frequent deallocation of extents results in fragmented tablespaces. In the ALTER command section, I discuss the ALTER TABLESPACE command, which allows coalescence of contiguous free-space areas (deallocated extents that lie next to each other). It is a good practice to use standard extent sizes in a specific tablespace so that any other segment can reuse the released extents from a dropped or re-built object.

New in Oracle8i is the concept of the CREATE TEMPORARY TABLESPACE command. This differs from a CREATE TABLESPACE...TEMPORARY tablespace in that a CREATE TEMPORARY TABLESPACE type tablespace uses TEMPFILES and a CREATE TABLESPACE...TEMPORARY tablespace uses DATAFILES. A CREATE TABLESPACE...TEMPORARY tablespace can be altered to hold PERMANENT objects, whereas a CREATE TEMPORARY TABLESPACE type tablespace cannot. Generally speaking, for a dictionary-managed temporary tablespace use the TEMPORARY clause of CREATE TABLESPACE. For a locally managed temporary tablespace, use CREATE TEMPORARY TABLESPACE. This statement specifies TEMPFILES instead of DATAFILES.

Note: There is a documentation error in the 8.1.7 manuals that incorrectly states that either type of temporary tablespace can be altered back to permanent status. This is incorrect—only those made into temporary tablespace with the TEMPORARY clause of the CREATE TABLESPACE can be altered to permanent status.

You do not specify the **DEFAULT STORAGE** clause for **CREATE TEMPROARY TABLESPACE** tablespaces—if you do not specify **LOCAL** for extent management, **AUTOALLOCATE** is assumed.

Tablespaces created as **CREATE TEMPORARY TABLESPACE** tablespaces that use locally managed extents have temporary data files *(tempfiles)*, which are similar to ordinary data files except that:

➤ Tempfiles are always set to **NOLOGGING** mode.

➤ You cannot make a tempfile read-only.

➤ You cannot rename a tempfile.

➤ You cannot create a tempfile with the **ALTER DATABASE** statement.

➤ Media recovery does not recognize tempfiles:

  ➤ **BACKUP CONTROLFILE** does not generate any information for tempfiles.

  ➤ **CREATE CONTROLFILE** cannot specify any information about tempfiles.

Tempfile information is shown in the dictionary view **DBA_TEMP_FILES** and the dynamic performance view **V$TEMPFILE**, but not in **DBA_DATA_FILES** or the **V$DATAFILE** view.

The **CREATE** Command for Relational and Object Tables

Tables are structures in an Oracle database that contain header and data sections. In Oracle8, the command to create tables has expanded extensively. Tables can now be index-only, partitioned, relational, and object (user-defined type). However, each table still contains the same elements, with the exception of the object table, which uses an **OID** (object identifier) as well as **ROWID**.

The table contains segment and block headers. The segment header contains freelist information, the block header contains transaction entries, and the row header contains row-length and datatype indicators. (The row length is 1 byte if less than 256 bytes; 3 bytes if longer than 256 bytes.) The data, or row sections, contains the actual data values. The header area grows from the bottom up, whereas the data area grows from the top down.

Table placement in relation to other database objects is important for optimal database performance. You should attempt to minimize contention by placing tables away from their associated indexes and away from other I/O-intensive database objects, such as redo logs and rollback segments. A partitioned table (or index) can have up to 65,535 partitions and/or subpartitions.

 For some large tables, you may want to consider using the partitioning and/or subpartitioning options to spread the table across several disks. This is not a labor-intensive operation, but before considering its use, you must thoroughly understand how your data is used.

Because all other database objects depend completely on tables for existence (such as indexes) or operate against tables (functions, procedures, and packages) or provide data for tables (sequences), it makes sense to discuss the **CREATE** command in relation to tables next. Even though object tables are a major feature in Oracle8 and Oracle8i, they aren't covered on the exam. Therefore, if you wish to learn more about them, I suggest using the manuals. Figure 5.4 shows the **CREATE TABLE** command syntax for relational tables.

The **CREATE TABLE** command has the following parameters in Oracle8i:

➤ **schema**—The schema to contain the table. If you omit **schema**, Oracle creates the table in your own schema. In Oracle, **schema** is the same as **username**.

➤ **table**—The name of the table (or object table) to be created. A partitioned table cannot be a clustered table or an object table.

➤ **column**—Specifies the name of a column of the table. A table can have up to 1,000 columns in Oracle8. You can omit column definitions only when you're using the **AS** subquery clause.

➤ **attribute**—Specifies the qualified column name of an item in an object.

➤ **datatype**—The data type of a column. You can omit the **datatype** only if the statement also designates the column as part of a foreign key in a referential integrity constraint. Oracle automatically assigns the column the data type of the corresponding column of the referenced key of the referential-integrity constraint. Object types, **REF object_type**, **VARRAYs**, and nested tables are valid data types. The possible **datatype** specifications are:

➤ **CHAR(*size*)**—Character-type data; maximum size of 2,000 bytes. **CHAR** is blank padded to the specified length. It defaults to 1 byte if the value for size is not specified.

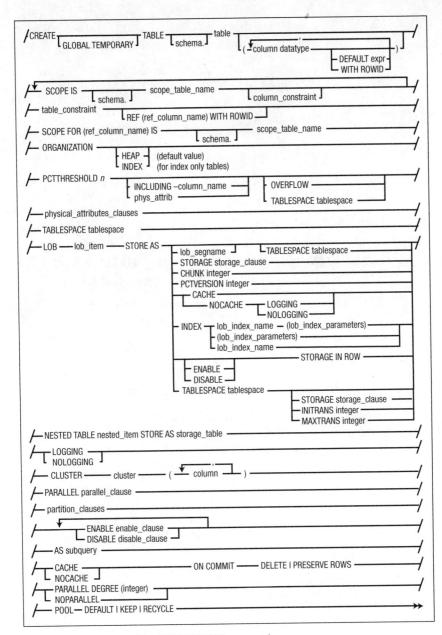

Figure 5.4   The syntax of the **CREATE TABLE** command.

➤ VARCHAR2(*size*)—Variable-length character up to 4,000 bytes. It must have a length specification when declared because it has no default size.

➤ DATE—Date format from 1/1/4712 B.C. to 12/31/4712 A.D. Standard Oracle format is "DD-MON-YY" (e.g. 10-APR-99). A DATE data type is always 7 bytes long.

➤ LONG—Character up to 2 gigabytes long. Only one LONG per table.

➤ RAW(*size*)—Raw binary data, maximum of 2,000 bytes under Oracle8i.

➤ LONG RAW—Raw binary data in hexadecimal format, 2 gigabytes maximum.

➤ ROWID—Internal data type, not user definable. Used to uniquely identify table rows. An extended ROWID is 10 bytes (new in Oracle8). A restricted ROWID is 6 bytes long and is identical to Oracle7 and earlier ROWIDs.

➤ NUMBER(*p,s*)—Numeric data (with *p* being precision and *s* being scale). Defaults to 38 *p*, null *s*. NUMBER columns store as *n*/2 where *n* is the actual length of the number.

➤ DECIMAL(*p,s*)—Same as NUMBER(*p,s*).

➤ INTEGER—Defaults to NUMBER(38), no scale.

➤ SMALLINT—Same as INTEGER.

➤ FLOAT—Same as NUMBER(38).

➤ FLOAT(*b*)—NUMBER with precision of 1 to 126.

➤ REAL—Same as NUMBER(38).

➤ DOUBLE PRECISION—Same as NUMBER(38). If no scale is specified for numeric data types where it's allowed, then the value is treated as a floating point.

The following data types are provided for compatibility, but are treated internally the same as NUMBER:

➤ NUMERIC*(precision, scale)*

➤ DECIMAL*(precision, scale)*

➤ DEC*(precision, scale)*

➤ INTEGER

➤ INT

➤ SMALLINT

➤ FLOAT(*size*)

➤ DOUBLE PRECISION

➤ REAL

The following are Large Object (LOB) data types:

➤ BLOB—Binary large objects; up to 4 gigabytes.

➤ CLOB—Character large objects; up to 4 gigabytes.

➤ NCLOB—National Character large objects; up to 4 gigabytes.

➤ BFILE—Pointer to an external LOB file that can be up to 4 gigabytes.

➤ DEFAULT—Specifies a value to be assigned to the column if a subsequent INSERT statement omits a value for the column. The data type of the expression must match the data type of the column. The column must also be large enough to hold this expression. A DEFAULT expression cannot contain references to other columns, to the pseudo-columns CURRVAL, NEXTVAL, LEVEL, and ROWNUM, or to date constants that are not fully specified.

➤ SCOPE IS *scope_table_name*—Restricts the scope of the column REF values to *scope_table_name*. The REF values for the column must come from REF values obtained from the object table specified in the clause. You can specify only one scope table per REF column. The *scope_table_name* is the name of the object table in which object instances (of the same type as the REF column) are stored. The values in the REF column point to objects in the scope table. You must have SELECT privileges on the table or SELECT ANY TABLE system privileges.

➤ CONSTRAINT *column-constraint*—Used to specify column-level constraints. *Constraints* are limits placed on a table or a column. It's a statement of the format: CONSTRAINT—Name of the constraint type.

Constraints also may be of the form:

➤ NULL CONSTRAINT *constraint_name*

➤ NOT NULL CONSTRAINT *constraint_name*

➤ PRIMARY KEY CONSTRAINT *constraint_name*

➤ UNIQUE CONSTRAINT *constraint_name*

➤ CHECK *condition* CONSTRAINT *constraint_name*

➤ REFERENCES *table name (column name)* CONSTRAINT *constraint_name*

➤ DEFAULT *default_value_clause*

In these formats, the **CONSTRAINT** *constraint_name* is optional. You can use unlimited **CHECK**-type constraints per column, and a **NOT NULL** is converted internally into a **CHECK** constraint by Oracle. A **CHECK** constraint requires that a condition be true or unknown for each value in the column it affects. Check constraints are the only constraints allowed to call system functions such as **USER** or **SYSDATE**. **NOT NULL** constraints can be defined only at the column level. Constraints can be added, enabled, disabled, or dropped.

Tables may also have the additional table-level constraints, as shown here:

```
CONSTRAINT constraint_name FOREIGN KEY (column, column)
   REFERENCES table_name (column, column)
CONSTRAINT constraint_name PRIMARY KEY (column, column)
  USING INDEX TABLESPACE tablespace_name
 STORAGE (storage_clause)
```

The foreign key constraint is enforced such that its values must match its corresponding primary or unique key values. However, indexes aren't automatically generated for foreign keys. Indexes should be maintained on foreign keys to prevent excessive full-table scans and locking issues that can result from foreign key updates. A primary key will automatically have an index-generated name for the constraint. A primary key automatically forces its column or columns to be not null, and if a single column is unique, or a composite set of columns is specified as unique, the resulting set must be unique. Foreign and primary key constraints are referred to as *referential constraints*. Referential integrity violations occur when a parent record is deleted and child records still exist; orphan records are not permitted in the child table of a parent-child relationship where primary and foreign key constraints are in place.

User-defined constraints are used to enforce business rules. Constraints that enforce typing (such as inserts of number-into-number columns) are column constraints. These are generally enforced with no action on the part of the DBA or designer.

Declarative constraints (**NOT NULL, UNIQUE, PRIMARY KEY, FOREIGN KEY**, and **CHECK**), those defined with commands verses, and those enforced by triggers—though they provide instant feedback to the users— can make it difficult to get an overview of which declarative constraints are in effect on the database.

➤ **table_constraint**—Defines an integrity constraint as part of the table definition.

➤ **REF** (*ref_column_name*)—Refers to a row in an object table. For *ref_column_name*, you can specify either a **REF** column name of an object or relational table or an embedded **REF** attribute within an object column.

➤ **WITH ROWID**—Stores the **ROWID** and the **REF** value in a column or attribute. Storing a **REF** value with a **ROWID** can improve the performance of dereferencing operations but will also use more space. Default storage of **REF** values is without **ROWID**s.

➤ **SCOPE FOR** (*ref_column_name*) **IS** *scope_table_name*—Restricts the scope of the **REF** values in *ref_column_name* to *scope_table_name*. The **REF** values for the column must come from **REF** values obtained from the object table specified in the clause. The *ref_column_name* is the name of a **REF** column in an object table or an embedded **REF** attribute within an object column of a relational table. The values in the **REF** column point to objects in the scope table.

➤ **ORGANIZATION HEAP**—Specifies that the data rows of the table are stored in no particular order. This is the default.

➤ **ORGANIZATION INDEX**—Specifies that the table is created as an index-only table. In an index-only table, the data rows are held in an index defined on the primary key for the table.

➤ **PCTTHRESHOLD**—Specifies the percentage of space reserved in the index block for the index-only table row. Any portion of the row that exceeds the specified threshold is stored in the area. If **OVERFLOW** is not specified, then rows exceeding the **THRESHOLD** limit are rejected. **PCTTHRESHOLD** must be a value from 0 to 50. The **TABLESPACE** clause in the **PCTTHRESHOLD** clause specifies the tablespace where the overflow segment is to be stored. The **phys_attrib** clause is the same as with other physical objects.

➤ **INCLUDING** *column_name*—Specifies a column at which to divide an index-only table row into index and overflow portions. All columns that follow *column_name* are stored in the overflow data segment. A *column_name* is the name of either the last primary key column or any non–primary-key column.

➤ **phys_attrib**—This clause gives the physical storage attributes for the object. The physical attributes are:

    ➤ **PCTFREE**—Specifies the percentage of space in each of the table's, object table's **OIDINDEX**, or partition's data blocks reserved for future updates to the table's rows. **PCTFREE** must be a value from 0 to 99. A value of 0 allows the entire block to be filled by inserts of new rows. The default value is 20. This value reserves 20 percent of each block for updates to existing rows and allows inserts of new rows to fill a maximum of 80 percent of each block.

PCTFREE has the same function in the **PARTITION** description clause and in the commands that create and alter clusters, indexes, snapshots, and snapshot logs. The combination of **PCTFREE** and **PCTUSED** determines whether inserted rows will go into existing data blocks or into new blocks. For nonpartitioned tables, the value specified for **PCTFREE** is the actual physical attribute of the segment associated with the table. For partitioned tables, the value specified for **PCTFREE** is the default physical attribute of the segments associated with the table. The default value of **PCTFREE** applies to all partitions specified in the **CRE-ATE** statement (and on subsequent **ALTER TABLE ADD PARTITION** statements) unless you specify **PCTFREE** in the **PARTITION** description clause.

You must understand row chaining and row migration. *Row chaining* is caused when a row is updated and there is insufficient space available to insert the new data. Row chaining usually happens with **VARCHAR2** and **NUMBER** types that can vary in size but more so with **VARCHAR2**. Other data types that may vary in length (such as **RAW**, **LONG**, and **LONG RAW**) can also cause row chaining. Row chaining causes Oracle to perform multiple diskreads to get a single row, usually forcing the read head for the disk to jump from a smooth read to reading all over the disk. This increase in disk I/O can cause extreme performance degradation. A large value for **PCTFREE** can reduce or eliminate row chaining, but it can also reduce increased storage requirements. Remember that unless **PCTUSED** and **PCTFREE** are set so that their sum exactly equals 100—which is not a good idea—an increase or decrease in one may have no effect on the other. Row migration occurs when the length of a row exceeds the total available space in a data block forcing storage of the row in multiple blocks. The only correction for row migration is to re-create the database with a larger block size.

➤ PCTUSED—Specifies the minimum percentage of used space allowed for each data block of the table, the object table **OIDINDEX**, or the overflow data segment of the index-only table. A block becomes a candidate for row insertion when its used space falls below **PCTUSED**. **PCTUSED** is specified as a positive integer from 1 to 99, and it defaults to 40.

PCTUSED has the same function in the **PARTITION** description clause and in the commands that create and alter clusters, snapshots, and snapshot logs. For nonpartitioned tables, the value specified for

PCTUSED is the actual physical attribute of the segment associated with the table. For partitioned tables, the value specified for **PCTUSED** is the default physical attribute of the segments associated with the table partitions. The default value of **PCTUSED** applies to all partitions specified in the **CREATE** statement (and on subsequent **ALTER TABLE ADD PARTITION** statements) unless you specify **PCTUSED** in the **PARTITION** description clause. **PCTUSED** is not a valid table-storage characteristic if you're creating an index-only table (**ORGANIZATION INDEX**). The sum of **PCTFREE** and **PCTUSED** must be less than 100. You can use **PCTFREE** and **PCTUSED** together to use space within a table more efficiently.

➤ **INITRANS**—Specifies the initial number of transaction entries allocated within each data block allocated to the table, object table **OIDINDEX**, partition, **LOB** index segment, or overflow data segment. This value can range from 1 to 255, and it defaults to 1. In general, you should not change the **INITRANS** value from its default.

Each transaction that updates a block requires a transaction entry in the block. The size of a transaction entry depends on your operating system. This parameter ensures that a minimum number of concurrent transactions can update the block and helps avoid the overhead of dynamically allocating a transaction entry.

The **INITRANS** parameter serves the same purpose in the **PARTITION** description clause and in clusters, indexes, snapshots, and snapshot logs as in tables. The minimum and default **INITRANS** value for a cluster or index is 2, rather than 1. For nonpartitioned tables, the value specified for **INITRANS** is the actual physical attribute of the segment associated with the table. For partitioned tables, the value specified for **INITRANS** is the default physical attribute of the segments associated with the table partitions. The default value of **INITRANS** applies to all partitions specified in the **CREATE** statement (and on subsequent **ALTER TABLE ADD PARTITION** statements) unless you specify **INITRANS** in the **PARTITION** description clause.

➤ **MAXTRANS**—Specifies the maximum number of concurrent transactions that can update a data block allocated to the table, object table **OIDINDEX**, partition, **LOB** index segment, or index-only overflow data segment. This limit does not apply to queries. This value can range from 1 to 255, and the default is a function of the data block size. According to Oracle, you should not change the **MAXTRANS** value from its default. If the number of concurrent transactions updating a block exceeds the **INITRANS** value, Oracle dynamically allocates transaction entries in the block until either the **MAXTRANS** value is exceeded or the block has no more free space.

The **MAXTRANS** parameter serves the same purpose in the **PARTITION** description clause, clusters, snapshots, and snapshot logs as in tables. For nonpartitioned tables, the value specified for **MAXTRANS** is the actual physical attribute of the segment associated with the table. For partitioned tables, the value specified for **MAXTRANS** is the default physical attribute of the segments associated with the table partitions. The default value of **MAXTRANS** applies to all partitions specified in the **CREATE** statement (and on subsequent **ALTER TABLE ADD PARTITION** statements) unless you specify **MAXTRANS** in the **PARTITION** description clause.

➤ TABLESPACE—Specifies the tablespace in which Oracle creates the table, partition, **LOB** storage, **LOB** index segment, or overflow data segment of the index-only table. If you omit this option, then Oracle creates the table, partition, **LOB** storage, **LOB** index segment, or partition in the default tablespace of the owner of the schema containing the table.

For nonpartitioned tables, the value specified for **TABLESPACE** is the actual physical attribute of the segment associated with the table. For partitioned tables, the value specified for **TABLESPACE** is the default physical attribute of the segments associated with the table partitions. The default value of **TABLESPACE** applies to all partitions specified in the **CREATE** statement (and on subsequent **ALTER TABLE ADD PARTITION** statements) unless you specify **TABLESPACE** in the **PARTITION** description clause.

➤ STORAGE—Specifies the storage characteristics for the table, partition, **LOB** storage, **LOB** index segment, or overflow data segment of the index-only table. This clause has performance ramifications for large tables. Storage should be allocated to minimize dynamic allocation of additional space. For nonpartitioned tables, the value specified for **STORAGE** is the actual physical attribute of the segment associated with the table. For partitioned tables, the value specified for **STORAGE** is the default physical attribute of the segments associated with the table partitions. The default value of **STORAGE** applies to all partitions specified in the **CREATE** statement (and on subsequent **ALTER TABLE ADD PARTITION** statements) unless you specify **STORAGE** in the **PARTITION** description clause.

➤ OVERFLOW—Specifies that an index-only table's data rows exceeding the specified threshold are placed in the data segment listed in this clause.

➤ LOGGING—Specifies that the creation of the table (and any indexes required because of constraints), partition, or **LOB** storage characteristics will be logged in the redo log file. **LOGGING** also specifies that subsequent operations against the table, partition, or **LOB** storage are logged in the redo file. This is the default. If the database is run in **ARCHIVELOG** mode, media recovery from a backup will re-create the table (and any indexes required because of constraints). You cannot specify **LOGGING** when using **NOARCHIVELOG** mode.

For nonpartitioned tables, the value specified for **LOGGING** is the actual physical attribute of the segment associated with the table. For partitioned tables, the value specified for **LOGGING** is the default physical attribute of the segments associated with the table partitions. The default value of **LOGGING** applies to all partitions specified in the **CREATE** statement (and on subsequent **ALTER TABLE ADD PARTITION** statements) unless you specify **LOGGING** in the **PARTITION** description clause.

Note: According to Oracle, in unspecified future versions of Oracle, the LOGGING keyword will replace the RECOVERABLE option. RECOVERABLE is still available as a valid keyword in Oracle when you're creating nonpartitioned tables, but using it is not recommended. You must specify LOGGING if you're creating a partitioned table.

➤ RECOVERABLE—See **LOGGING**. **RECOVERABLE** is not a valid keyword for creating partitioned tables or **LOB** storage characteristics.

➤ NOLOGGING—Specifies that the creation of the table (and any indexes required because of constraints), partition, or **LOB** storage characteristics will not be logged in the redo log file. **NOLOGGING** also specifies that subsequent operations against the table or **LOB** storage are not logged in the redo file. As a result, media recovery will not re-create the table (or any indices required because of constraints).

For nonpartitioned tables, the value specified for **NOLOGGING** is the actual physical attribute of the segment associated with the table. For partitioned tables, the value specified for **NOLOGGING** is the default physical attribute of the segments associated with the table partitions. The default value of **NOLOGGING** applies to all partitions specified in the **CREATE** statement (and on subsequent **ALTER TABLE ADD PARTITION** statements) unless you specify **NOLOGGING** in the **PARTITION** description clause.

Using this keyword makes table creation faster than using the **LOGGING** option because redo log entries are not written. **NOLOGGING** is not a valid keyword for creating index-only tables.

*Note: In unspecified future versions of Oracle, the **NOLOGGING** keyword will replace the **UNRECOVERABLE** option. **UNRECOVERABLE** is still available as a valid keyword in Oracle when you're creating nonpartitioned tables, but using it is not recommended.*

➤ **UNRECOVERABLE**—See **NOLOGGING**. This keyword can be specified only with the **AS** subquery clause. **UNRECOVERABLE** is not a valid keyword for creating partitioned or index-only tables.

➤ **LOB**—Specifies the **LOB** storage characteristics.

➤ **lob_item**—The **LOB** column name or **LOB** object attribute for which you are explicitly defining tablespace and storage characteristics that are different from those of the table.

➤ **STORE AS** *lob_segname*—Specifies the name of the **LOB** data segment. You cannot use *lob_segname* if more than one *lob_item* is specified.

➤ **CHUNK** *integer*—The unit of **LOB** value allocation and manipulation. Oracle allocates each unit of **LOB** storage as **CHUNK** *integer*. You can also use K or M to specify this size in kilobytes or megabytes. The default value of integer is 1K and the maximum is 32K. For efficiency, use a multiple of the Oracle block size.

➤ **PCTVERSION** *integer*—The maximum percentage of overall **LOB** storage space used for creating new versions of the **LOB**. The default value is 10, meaning that older versions of the **LOB** data are not overwritten until 10 percent of the overall **LOB** storage space is used.

➤ **INDEX** *lob_index_name*—The name of the **LOB** index segment. You cannot use *lob_index_name* if more than one *lob_item* is specified.

➤ **NESTED TABLE** *nested_item* **STORE AS** *storage_table*—Specifies *storage_table* as the name of the storage table in which the rows of all *nested_item* values reside. You must include this clause when you're creating a table with columns or column attributes whose type is a nested table. The *nested_item* is the name of a column or a column-qualified attribute whose type is a nested table. The *storage_table* is the name of the storage table. The storage table is created in the same schema and the same tablespace as the parent table.

➤ **CLUSTER**—Specifies that the table is to be part of the cluster. The columns listed in this clause are the table columns that correspond to the cluster's columns. Generally, the cluster columns of a table are the column or columns that make up its primary key or a portion of its primary key. Specify one column from the table for each column in the cluster key. The columns are matched by position, not by name. Because a clustered table uses the cluster's space allocation, the **PCTFREE, PCTUSED, INITRANS,** or **MAXTRANS** parameters, the **TABLESPACE** option, or the **STORAGE** clause are ignored with the **CLUSTER** option.

➤ **PARALLEL** *parallel_clause*—Specifies the degree of parallelism for creating the table and the default degree of parallelism for queries on the table after it's created. This is not a valid option when you're creating index-only tables.

➤ **partition_clauses**—Specifies how a table is partitioned; a table can be partitioned on ranges, hash, or composite partitioned on both (when subpartitions are used). Even though partitions are an important feature of Oracle8 and 8i, they are not covered in the SQL and PL/SQL exam. They are covered in the upgrade exam. Therefore I don't cover them here. The Oracle SQL manual covers them in detail if you wish to learn more about them.

➤ **ENABLE**—Enables an integrity constraint.

➤ **DISABLE**—Disables an integrity constraint.

Constraints specified in the **ENABLE** and **DISABLE** clauses of a **CREATE TABLE** statement must be defined in the statement. You can also enable and disable constraints with the **ENABLE** and **DISABLE** keywords of the **CONSTRAINT** clause. If you define a constraint but do not explicitly enable or disable it, Oracle enables it by default. You cannot use the **ENABLE** and **DISABLE** clauses in a **CREATE TABLE** statement to enable and disable triggers.

➤ **AS subquery**—Inserts the rows returned by the subquery into the table upon its creation. The number of columns in the table must equal the number of expressions in the subquery. The column definitions can specify only column names, default values, and integrity constraints, not data types. Oracle derives data types and lengths from the subquery. Oracle also follows these rules for integrity constraints:

> ➤ Oracle automatically defines any **NOT NULL** constraints on columns in the new table if those constraints existed on the corresponding columns of the selected table and if the subquery selects the column rather than an expression containing the column.

> ➤ A **CREATE TABLE** statement cannot contain both an **AS** clause and a referential-integrity constraint definition.

> ➤ If a **CREATE TABLE** statement contains both the **AS** clause and a **CONSTRAINT** clause or an **ENABLE** clause with the **EXCEPTIONS** option, Oracle ignores the **EXCEPTIONS** option. If any rows violate the constraint, Oracle does not create the table and returns an error message.

➤ If all expressions in the subquery are columns, rather than expressions, you can omit the columns from the table definition entirely. In this case, the names of the columns in the table are the same as the columns in the subquery.

➤ CACHE—Specifies that the data will be accessed frequently, so the blocks retrieved for this table are placed at the most recently used end of the LRU list in the buffer cache when a full table scan is performed. This option is useful for small lookup tables. CACHE as a parameter in the LOB storage clause specifies that Oracle allocates and retains LOB data values in memory for faster access. CACHE is the default for index-only tables.

➤ NOCACHE—Specifies that the data will not be accessed frequently, so the blocks retrieved for this table are placed at the least recently used end of the LRU list in the buffer cache when a full table scan is performed. For LOBs, the LOB value is not placed in the buffer cache. This is the default behavior except when you're creating index-only tables. This is not a valid keyword when you're creating index-only tables. NOCACHE as a parameter in the LOB storage clause specifies that LOB values are not allocated in memory. This is the LOB storage default.

➤ PARALLEL DEGREE (*integer*)—Used to specify the degree of parallel processing for the table.

➤ NOPARALLEL—Turns off parallel processing for the table.

➤ POOL—With the DEFAULT, KEEP, and RECYCLE options, determines the buffer pool area in which the table will be cached. The DEFAULT pool is the standard Oracle buffer pool. If configured, the optional KEEP and RECYCLE pools provide for keeping objects (the KEEP pool) or having them quickly recycle out of the pool (the RECYCLE pool). If both the KEEP and RECYCLE areas aren't configured, buffer pool behavior is the same as in Oracle7, even if the POOL qualifier is used.

As you can see, there are myriad modifiers and options added to the basic CREATE command.

The CREATE Command for Indexes

Indexes can be created implicitly, such as by specifying unique or primary key constraints, or explicitly with the CREATE INDEX command. Only normal, B-tree-type indexes are created by default. Normally (except in the case of BITMAPPED indexes), you should index only a column or set of columns that contains a wide range of values. If a table is small, an index may decrease the speed of a query against it because small tables may be cached in memory or may better be searched with a full table scan.

In Oracle8i, you can also create function-based indexes. Function-based indexes, as their name implies, are indexes based on deterministic functions or methods. A deterministic function or method is one that will return the same value given the same inputs, no matter who calls it. Almost all Oracle internal functions are deterministic and can therefore be used for a function-based index. Examples of functions that can be used in a function-based index are **UPPER()**, **LOWER()**, **TRIM()**, **DECODE()**, and **TRUNC()**. To use function-based indexes, the initialization parameters **QUERY REWRITE ENABLED** and **QUERY REWRITE INTEGRITY** must be enabled, and the privileges **QUERY REWRITE** or **GLOBAL QUERY REWRITE** must be granted to the index creator. In addition, once the function-based index is created it (and its underlying table) must be analyzed.

The format for the **CREATE INDEX** command is shown in Figure 5.5.

The Oracle8i **CREATE INDEX** clauses have the following keywords and parameters:

➤ UNIQUE—Specifies that the value of the column (or group of columns) in the table to be indexed must be unique. If the index is local nonprefixed (see the **LOCAL** clause, further down in this list), then the index columns must contain the partitioning columns.

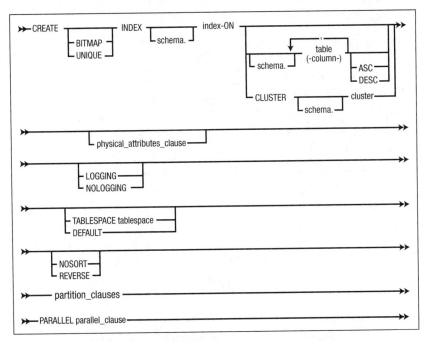

Figure 5.5   The syntax of the **CREATE INDEX** command.

➤ BITMAP—Specifies that the index is to be created as a bitmap, rather than as a B-tree. You cannot use this keyword when you're creating a global partitioned index. Causes the index to be stored as a bitmap and should be used only for low-cardinality data, such as sex, race, and so forth. A **BITMAP** index has a substantial reduction of space usage compared to other types of indexes for low-cardinality data.

➤ **schema**—The schema to contain the index. If you omit **schema**, Oracle creates the index in your own schema.

➤ **index**—The name of the index to be created. An index can contain several partitions. You cannot range-partition a cluster index or an index defined on a clustered table.

➤ **table**—The name of the table for which the index is to be created. If you do not qualify **table** with **schema**, Oracle assumes that the table is contained in your own schema.

If the index is **LOCAL**, the table must be partitioned.

You cannot create an index on an index-only table.

You can create an index on a nested-table storage table.

➤ **column**—The name of a column in the table. An index can have up to 32 columns. A data type of **LONG** or **LONG RAW** cannot be used for indexing.

You can create an index on a scalar object (non-**VARRAY**) attribute column or on the system-defined **NESTED_TABLE_ID** column of the nested-table storage table. If an object-attribute column is specified, the column name must be qualified with the table name. If a nested-table column attribute is specified, then it must be qualified with the outermost table name, the containing column name, and all intermediate attribute names leading to the nested-table column attribute.

Column can also be the name of the column to include in the index, up to a maximum of 32 columns. If more than one column is used, the index is said to be a *composite* or *concatenated* index. Concatenated indexes are generally used to increase performance of a specific query. The order of a concatenated key is important. Only queries that access columns in this order will use the index. For example, table **EXAMPLE** has 16 columns. The first three are used as the concatenated index. Only queries that contain columns 1, 2, 3 or 1, 2, or 1 will use the index.

➤ **ASC** and **DESC**—Creates the index in the designated order. In releases prior to 8.1, only **ASC** (ascending) indexes would be created (although you could specify **DESC**—this was to allow compliance with standards). Oracle treats descending indexes as if they are function-based indexes. You do not need the **QUERY REWRITE** or **GLOBAL QUERY REWRITE** privileges to create them, as you do with other function-based indexes. However, as with other function-based indexes, Oracle does not use descending indexes until you first analyze the index and the table on which the index is defined. To use this feature, the **COMPATIBLE** initialization parameter should have a value 8.1.0.0.0 or higher.

➤ **CLUSTER** *schema.cluster*—Specifies the cluster for which a cluster index is to be created. If you do not qualify *cluster* with *schema*, Oracle assumes that the cluster is contained in your current schema. You cannot create a cluster index for a hash cluster.

➤ **INITRANS** and **MAXTRANS**—Establish values for these parameters for the index. See the **INITRANS** and **MAXTRANS** parameters of the **CREATE TABLE** command.

➤ **TABLESPACE** *tablespace*—The name of the tablespace to hold the index or index partition. If this option is omitted, Oracle creates the index in the default tablespace of the owner of the schema containing the index. This can cause immediate contention if the table and its index are both contained in the default tablespace of the schema owner.

For a partitioned index, this is the tablespace name.

For a **LOCAL** index, you can specify the keyword **DEFAULT** in place of a tablespace name. New partitions added to the **LOCAL** index will be created in the same tablespace(s) as the corresponding partition(s) of the underlying table.

➤ **STORAGE**—Establishes the storage characteristics for the index.

The definitions for the specified parameters are:

The **physical_attributes_clause** contains zero, one, or more of the following:

➤ **PCTFREE** integer

➤ **PCTUSED** integer

➤ **INITRANS** integer

➤ **MAXTRANS** integer

➤ **STORAGE** storage_clause

➤ **PCTFREE**—The percentage of space to leave free for updates and insertions within each of the index's data blocks.

➤ NOSORT—Indicates to Oracle that the rows are stored in the database in ascending order, and therefore Oracle does not have to sort the rows when creating the index. You cannot specify **REVERSE** with this option. If the rows are not in ascending order when this clause is used, an ORA-01409 error is returned and no index is created.

➤ REVERSE—Stores the bytes of the index block in reverse order, excluding the **ROWID**. You cannot specify **NOSORT** with this option.

➤ LOGGING—Specifies that the creation of the index will be logged in the undo and redo logs, and redo and log data will be recorded on activity in this index.

If the index is nonpartitioned, this is the logging attribute of the index.

If the index is partitioned, this is the default logging attribute of the index partitions created. If index is **LOCAL**, this value is used as the default attribute for index partitions created when new partitions are added to the base table of the index.

If the [NO]LOGGING clause is omitted, the logging attribute of the index defaults to the logging attribute of the tablespace in which it resides.

If the database is run in **NOARCHIVELOG** mode, index creation is not logged in the undo and redo log file, even if **LOGGING** is specified. Media recovery from backup and online redo logs will not re-create the index.

If the database is run in **ARCHIVELOG** mode, media recovery from a backup will re-create the index.

➤ NOLOGGING—Specifies that the creation of the index will not be logged in the undo and redo log file. As a result, media recovery will not re-create the index.

If the index is nonpartitioned, this is the logging attribute of the index.

If the index is partitioned, this is the default logging attribute of the index partitions created. If index is **LOCAL**, this value is used as the default attribute for index partitions created when new partitions are added to the base table of the index.

If the [NO]LOGGING clause is omitted, the logging attribute of the index defaults to the logging attribute of the tablespace in which it resides.

Using this keyword makes index creation faster than using the **LOGGING** option because undo and redo log entries are not written.

➤ partition_clause—Specifies partitioning options for the index. Indexes can be **GLOBAL** or **LOCAL** partitioned. Partitioning can be range, hash, or composite (if subpartitions are used.) Partitioning of indexes—an important feature of Oracle8 and 8i—is not covered in the SQL and PL/SQL exam. It is, however, covered in the upgrade exam. If you need more information on index partitioning, the Oracle SQL manual is a great resource.

➤ PARALLEL—Specifies the degree of parallelism for creating the index.

When the **CREATE INDEX** command is used to create a cluster index, an additional type of index known as a *cluster index* can be created. The cluster index is created against the cluster key, which can have a maximum of 32 columns assigned to it. I discuss clusters and their peculiarities more in the next section.

The **CREATE** Command for Clusters

A cluster can be used when values from multiple related tables are always retrieved together. Using a cluster reduces storage requirements and, in some cases, can speed access to data. The major drawback is that—in operations involving updates, inserts, and deletes—performance degradation can occur. The DBA should look at the expected mix of transaction types on the tables to be clustered and cluster only those that are frequently joined and those that don't have numerous updates, inserts, and deletes.

Clusters store shared data values in the same physical blocks (the cluster key values). For tables that are frequently joined, this can speed access; for tables that are frequently accessed separately, joining is not the answer. An exception is when a single table is clustered. A single-table cluster forces the key values for that table into a single set of blocks; thus, accesses of that table can be sped up. Usually, this single-table clustering also uses a hash structure to further improve access times. In Oracle8i, the **CREATE CLUSTER** command has the option of creating a single table cluster.

Oracle7 added an additional cluster feature: the ability to specify a hash cluster. A hash cluster uses a hash form of storage and no index. Hash structures should be used only for static tables. *Hashing* is the process in which a value, either of a unique or a nonunique row, is used to generate a hash value. This hash value is used to place the row into the hashed table. To retrieve the row, the value is simply recalculated. Hashes can be used only for equality operations. The syntax of the **CREATE CLUSTER** command is shown in Figure 5.6.

The **CREATE CLUSTER** command has the following parameters:

➤ cluster_name—Name of the cluster. If the user has DBA privileges, a schema name may be specified (**schema.cluster**).

➤ (column data type, column data type...)—List of columns and their data types; this list is called the *cluster key*. The names of the columns do not have to

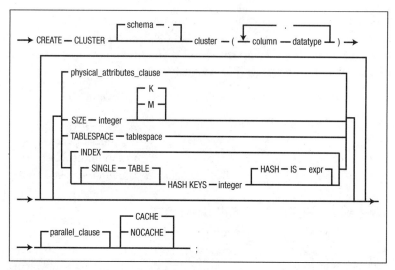

Figure 5.6 The syntax of the **CREATE CLUSTER** command.

match the table column names, but the data types, lengths, and precisions do have to match.

➤ *n*—An integer (not all of the *n*'s are the same value; *n* is just used for convenience).

➤ SIZE—Expected size of the average cluster. This is calculated by 19 + (sum of column lengths) + (1 × number of columns).

SIZE should be rounded up to the nearest equal divisor of your block size. For example, if your block size is 2,048 and the cluster length is 223, round up to 256. This, along with **HASHKEYS**, will limit the number of cluster keys stored in a single data block. If SIZE is small, then the number of keys that can be assigned to a single block will increase, allowing many keys to be assigned to a single block. If you have very few rows for a cluster key, set SIZE to a small value to minimize wasted space in the data block.

➤ STORAGE—Used as the default for the tables in the cluster.

➤ INDEX—Specifies to create an indexed cluster (default).

➤ SINGLE TABLE—Creates a single table cluster.

➤ HASH IS—Specifies to create a hash cluster. The specified column must be a zero precision number.

➤ HASHKEYS—Creates a hash cluster and specifies the number (*n*) of keys. The value is rounded up to the nearest prime number. This value, along with

SIZE, will limit the number of keys stored in a single data block. The number of hash values generated will be **HASHKEYS+1**.

➤ **PCTFREE**—Parameter for clusters that applies only to the cluster and not to the individual tables in the cluster.

The other parameters are the same as for the **CREATE TABLE** command.

To create a cluster, follow these steps:

1. First, issue the **CREATE CLUSTER** command. This creates the definition for the **CLUSTER** in the data dictionary.

2. Create the cluster index by using the following snippet:

```
CREATE INDEX index_name ON CLUSTER cluster_name;
```

Note: You don't specify the columns. The number of columns is taken from the CREATE CLUSTER command that was used to create the named cluster.

3. Create the tables that will be in the cluster. Use the following code:

```
CREATE TABLE cluster table
( column list)
CLUSTER cluster_name (cluster column(s))
```

In this instance, *cluster table* is a table name for a table that will be a part of the cluster, and *column list* is a list of columns for the table, specified identically to the **CREATE TABLE** command's normal format.

Remember that the cluster columns don't have to have the same name, but must be the same data type, size, and precision, and must be specified in the same order as the columns in the **CREATE CLUSTER** command.

The CREATE Command for Sequences

Sequences allow for automatic generation of sequential nonrepeating or, if you desire, repeating integer values for use in keys or wherever numbers of this type should be used. Sequences can be either positive or negative in value and can range from 10e-27 to (10e27)-1 in value. The way in which a sequence increments can be controlled, as can the number of values cached for performance reasons in the shared pool area of the shared global area (SGA) of an instance. The syntax of the **CREATE SEQUENCE** command is shown in Figure 5.7.

The **CREATE SEQUENCE** command has the following parameters:

➤ sequence_name—The name you want the sequence to have. This may include the schema name if the sequence is created from an account with DBA or **CREATE ANY SEQUENCE** privileges.

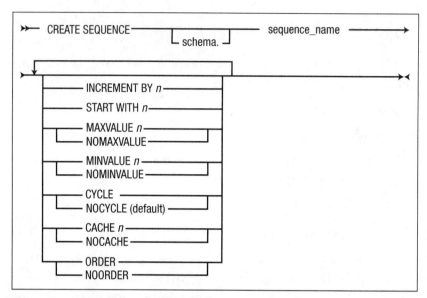

Figure 5.7 The syntax of the **CREATE SEQUENCE** command.

➤ *n*—An integer, positive or negative.

➤ **INCREMENT BY**—Tells the system how to increment the sequence. If it's positive, the values are ascending; if it's negative, values are descending.

➤ **START WITH**—Tells the system what integer to start with.

➤ **MINVALUE**—Tells the system how low the sequence can go. For ascending sequences, it defaults to 1; for descending sequences, the default value is 10e27-1.

➤ **MAXVALUE**—Tells the system the highest value that will be allowed. For descending sequences, the default is 1; for ascending sequences, the default is 10e27-1.

➤ **CYCLE**—Causes the sequence to automatically re-cycle to **MINVALUE** when **MAXVALUE** is reached for ascending sequences. For descending sequences, it will cause the sequence to re-cycle from **MINVALUE** back to **MAXVALUE**.

➤ **CACHE**—Will cache the specified number of sequence values into the buffers in the SGA. This speeds access, but all cached numbers are lost when the database is shut down. Default value is 20; maximum value is **MAXVALUE-MINVALUE**.

➤ **ORDER**—Forces sequence numbers to be output in order of request. When they are used for time stamping, this may be required. In most cases, the sequence numbers are in order anyway, and **ORDER** is not required.

Sequences avoid the performance problems associated with sequencing numbers generated by application triggers of the form, as shown here:

```
DECLARE
TEMP_NO NUMBER;
BEGIN
LOCK TABLE PO_NUM IN EXCLUSIVE MODE NOWAIT;
SELECT MAX(PO_NUM)+1 INTO TEMP_NO FROM SALES ;
END;
```

If the application requires numbers that are exactly in sequence (that is, 1, 2, 3, and so on), this trigger may be your only recourse, because if a statement that refers to a sequence is rolled back (canceled), that sequence number is lost. Likewise, any cached sequence numbers are lost each time a database is shut down.

Sequences can't be accessed directly; you can retrieve their values only by using the pseudo-columns CURRVAL and NEXTVAL. The pseudo-columns can be selected either from DUAL into a holding variable in PL/SQL, or from the table being inserted (via the VALUES clause) into or updated (in the SET clause). A value must first be accessed via the NEXTVAL pseudo-column before the CURRVAL pseudo-column can be accessed.

Uses and Restrictions of CURRVAL and NEXTVAL

The pseudo-columns CURRVAL and NEXTVAL for sequences are used:

➤ With the VALUES clause of an INSERT command

➤ With the SELECT subclause of a SELECT command

➤ In the SET clause of an UPDATE command

CURRVAL and NEXTVAL cannot be used:

➤ In a subquery or in an inline view

➤ In a view or snapshot query

➤ With a DISTINCT clause

➤ With a GROUP BY or ORDER BY clause

➤ In a SELECT command in combination with another SELECT statement with the UNION, INTERSECT, or MINUS set operator

➤ In the WHERE clause

➤ In the DEFAULT column value in a CREATE TABLE or ALTER TABLE command

➤ In a CHECK in a constraint

The **CREATE** Command for Views

Views are stored queries in Oracle that can be treated as tables. Until fairly recently, views were essentially read-only. Now, with certain caveats, views can be updated. They're used to hide or to enhance data structures, to make complex queries easier to manage, and to enforce security requirements. Figure 5.8 shows the syntax of the **CREATE VIEW** command.

The **CREATE VIEW** command has the following parameters:

➤ **view_name**—Name of the view.

➤ **alias**—Valid column name. It doesn't have to be the same as the column it's based on. If aliases aren't used, the names of the columns are used. If a column is modified by an expression, it must be aliased. If four columns are in the query, there must be four aliases.

➤ **subquery**—Any valid **SELECT** statement that doesn't include an **ORDER BY** or **FOR UPDATE** clause. A view can only be based on one or more tables and/or views.

➤ **WITH CHECK OPTION**—Specifies that inserts and updates through the view must be selectable from the view. This can be used in a view based on a view.

➤ **READ ONLY**—Specifies that the view is read-only and can't be changed by using the **INSERT, UPDATE,** or **DELETE** operations.

➤ **CONSTRAINT**—Specifies the name associated with the **CHECK OPTION** constraint.

➤ **FORCE**—Specifies that the view be created even if all permissions or objects it specifies as part of the view aren't available. Before the view can be used, the permissions or objects must be in the database and accessible.

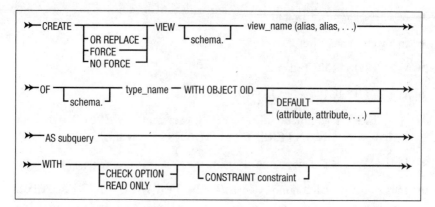

Figure 5.8 The syntax of the **CREATE VIEW** command.

➤ **NO FORCE** (default)—Means that all objects and permissions must be in place before the view can be created.

➤ **OF** *object_type*—Explicitly creates an object view of type *object_type*. The columns in the object view are the same as the top-level attributes of the specified *object_type*. Each row will have an assigned **OID**.

➤ **WITH OBJECT IDENTIFIER**—Specifies the attributes of the row that will be used as a key to uniquely identify each row of the object view. These attributes should correspond to the primary key of the base table. If the base object has an **OID** already, you can specify **DEFAULT**. This is only for Oracle8 and 8i.

A view can usually be used in the following commands:

➤ **COMMENT**

➤ **DELETE**

➤ **INSERT**

➤ **LOCK TABLE**

➤ **UPDATE**

➤ **SELECT**

A view's **SELECT** statement in the subquery can't select a **CURRVAL** or **NEXTVAL** from a sequence or directly access **ROWID, ROWNUM,** or **LEVEL** pseudo-columns. To use the pseudo-columns for a table, a view's **SELECT** must alias them.

A view is just a window to data; it can't store data itself. Views can be used in a SQL statement just like a table can.

You can't update a view if it:

➤ Contains a join.

➤ Contains a **GROUP BY, CONNECT BY,** or **START WITH** clause.

➤ Contains a **DISTINCT** clause or expressions like **AMOUNT+10** in the column list.

➤ Doesn't refer to all **NOT NULL** columns in the table (all **NOT NULLs** must be in the view and assigned a value by the update).

You can update a view that contains pseudo-columns or columns modified by expressions if the update doesn't affect these columns.

You can query the view, **USER_UPDATABLE_COLUMNS,** to find out if the columns in a join view are updateable. Generally speaking, as long as all of the **NOT NULL**s and key columns are included in a join view for a table, that table can be updated through the view.

Note: The concept of a key-preserved table is fundamental to understanding the restrictions on modifying join views. A table is key preserved if every key of the table can also be a key of the result of the join. So, a key-preserved table has its keys preserved through a join. It is not necessary that the key or keys of a table be selected for it to be key preserved. It is sufficient that if the key or keys were selected, then they would also be key(s) of the result of the join.

A join view can have the commands **INSERT, UPDATE,** and **DELETE** used against it if:

➤ The DML affects only one of the tables in the join.

➤ For **UPDATE,** all of the columns updated are extracted from a key-preserved table. In addition, if the view has a **CHECK OPTION** constraint, join columns are shielded from update; so are columns taken from tables that are referred to more than once in the view.

➤ For **DELETE,** there is one and only one key-preserved table in the join, and that table can be present more than once if there is no **CHECK OPTION** constraint on the view.

➤ For **INSERT,** all of the columns are from a key-preserved table, and the views don't have a **CHECK OPTION** constraint.

As with all stored objects, to create a view, the user must have direct grants on all objects that are a part of the view, including those objects that may be used in views and that are used in the new view. The grants used to create a view can't be from a role; they must be direct grants.

Views can cause poor performance if they're nested too deeply. This can easily occur when they're created against the **DBA_, USER_,** or **ALL_** views.

Object Views

To take advantage of the benefits of the new object paradigm in Oracle8, you can make a common relational table into a pseudo-object table by creating what is known as an *object view,* which is directly based on the relational table. The object ID is not system-generated, but is based on columns that you specify.

An example using the **EMP** table would be this:

```
CREATE TYPE emp_t AS OBJECT (
  empno    NUMBER(5),
```

```
ename      VARCHAR2(20),
salary     NUMBER(9,2),
job        VARCHAR2(20));
/
CREATE TABLE emp(
  empno    NUMBER(5) CONSTRAINT pk_emp PRIMARY KEY,
  ename    VARCHAR2(20),
  salary   NUMBER(9,2),
  job      VARCHAR2(20));

CREATE VIEW emp_man OF emp_t
  WITH OBJECT IDENTIFIER (empno) AS
    SELECT empno, ename, salary, job
    FROM emp
    WHERE job='MANAGER';
```

This example creates an object view of **EMP_T** (type) objects corresponding to the employees from the **EMP** table who are managers, with **EMPNO**, the primary key of **EMP**, as the object identifier.

The **CREATE** Command for Synonyms

Synonyms are database shorthand notations that allow long, complex combinations of schema, object name, and connection strings to be reduced to a simple alias. Because synonyms remove the requirement to prefix a table, view, or sequence with a schema name, they perform a simple type of data hiding by allowing tables from one or more schemas to appear to be located in the user's schema. The **CREATE SYNONYM** command syntax is shown in Figure 5.9.

The **CREATE SYNONYM** command has the following parameters:

➤ PUBLIC—Creates a public synonym that can be used by all users. Usually, only DBAs create public synonyms.

➤ synonym_name—Name or alias that you want the object to assume.

➤ schema—Schema in which the object resides.

➤ object_name—Actual name of the object on which the synonym is being created.

➤ @dl—Database link that's used only if the object resides in another database.

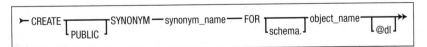

Figure 5.9 The syntax of the **CREATE SYNONYM** command.

The CREATE Command for Rollback Segments

Rollback segments store system undo data, allowing non-committed transactions to be rolled back. Rollback segments can be likened to "before image" logs or journals in other database systems. Rollback segments store the before images of changed data. Large transaction failures can usually be attributed to the following rollback-related problems:

➤ Inadequate space in the rollback segment (usually named **RBS**) tablespace for rollback segment expansion

➤ Improper storage specifications for the rollback segment being used, resulting in that segment exceeding its **MAXEXTENTS** value

➤ Improper scheduling, allowing other transactions to cause Snapshot Too Old errors to occur in the transaction (which can also be caused by an improper **INITRANS** setting)

In addition to the **SYSTEM** rollback segment created when the database is built that is used strictly by the **SYSTEM** tablespace, at least one additional rollback segment must be created. Usually, the number of private rollback segments is determined by determining how many concurrent users will access the database and deciding how many users should be assigned to each rollback segment (by specifying the **MINEXTENTS** value). For example, if you have 100 concurrent users and you want (on average) 20 users per rollback segment, then set the **MINEXTENTS** to 20 for each of 5 rollback segments. For private rollback segments, the calculated ratio of the initialization parameters—**TRANSACTIONS** divided by **TRANSACTIONS_PER_ROLLBACK_SEGMENT**, rounded up to the nearest integer, should be used to determine the number of rollback segments created. The syntax of the **CREATE ROLLBACK SEGMENT** command is shown in Figure 5.10.

The **CREATE ROLLBACK SEGMENT** command has the following parameters:

➤ **rollback_name**—Name of the rollback segment. Must be unique.

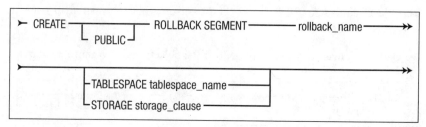

Figure 5.10   The syntax of the **CREATE ROLLBACK SEGMENT** command.

➤ **tablespace_name**—Name of the tablespace in which the segment is to be created. If this name is not specified, the rollback segment is created in the user's default tablespace.

➤ **storage_clause**—Specifies the required storage parameters for the rollback segment. The following guidelines are strongly suggested for its use:

   ➤ **INITIAL = NEXT**—INITIAL sets the size of the initial segment in a rollback segment. **NEXT** sets the size of the next extent in the rollback segment and subsequent extents, assuming that **PCTINCREASE** is set to zero (it will always be zero for rollback segments in Oracle8 because specification of the parameter results in an error). **NEXT** can be modified after the rollback segment is created.

   ➤ **MINEXTENTS = 20** (or your calculated value; 2 is the default on **CREATE ROLLBACK**)—MINEXTENTS sets the minimum number of extents that are initially allocated when the rollback segment is created.

   ➤ **MAXEXTENTS =** —A calculated maximum based on the size of the rollback segment tablespace, the size of rollback segments' extents, and the number of rollback segments. If set to **UNLIMITED**, the **MAXEXTENTS** parameter could allow the rollback segment to use up all available free area in the rollback tablespace (disk space allocated to rollback segments). **MAXEXTENTS** can be modified after the rollback segment is created.

➤ **OPTIMAL**—Reflects the size to which the system will restore the rollback segment by deallocating extents after the rollback segment has been increased by a large transaction. **OPTIMAL** should be set to allow your average-sized transaction to complete without wrapping or causing shrinks. **OPTIMAL** and **MINEXTENTS** can be used by the Oracle server to determine the optimal number of extents for rollback segments. **OPTIMAL** can be modified after the rollback segment is created.

After Oracle7.3, **PCTINCREASE** can no longer be set for rollback segments; in earlier versions, it should always be set to zero.

When a private or public rollback segment is created, it's not online. To be used, it must be brought online by using the **ALTER ROLLBACK SEGMENT** *name* **ONLINE;** command (usually for private rollbacks); or by shutting down the database, modifying the INIT.ORA parameter **ROLLBACK_SEGMENTS**, and restarting the database (for private rollback segments); or by allowing the system to bring the rollback online automatically for public rollback segments. In any case, the INIT.ORA file parameter **ROLLBACK_SEGMENTS** should be altered for private rollback segments if the rollback segment is to be used permanently, or it won't be acquired when the database is shut down and restarted.

The **CREATE** Command for Control Files

The control file is one of the more important files in the Oracle database system. The *control file* is a storage location for the names and places of all physical data files for the system. The control file also acts as a database of the SCN and timestamp information that applies to those data files. Without one functional control file (the first one in the list in the **CONTROL_FILES** parameter), the database won't start up.

Sometimes, it may be necessary for a DBA to re-create a control file. This option can be used in several situations: when a control file has become damaged and no viable copy is available; when a database name must be changed; and when a fixed limit such as **MAX_DATAFILES** has to be altered for a database. If the DBA has good documentation for the database, the **CREATE CONTROLFILE** command can be issued manually; however, it's usually easier to periodically use the **ALTER DATABASE BACKUP CONTROLFILE TO TRACE** command to automatically create a control-file rebuild script.

Practice Questions

Question 1

Evaluate this command:

```
CREATE TABLE sales_items
SELECT id_number, description
FROM inventory
WHERE quantity > 500;
```

Why will this statement cause an error?

○ a. A keyword is missing.

○ b. A clause is missing.

○ c. The **WHERE** clause can't be used for creating a table.

○ d. All of the columns in the inventory table must be included in the subquery.

○ e. The data types in the new table were not defined.

The correct answer is a; the keyword **AS** is missing right before the subquery. Answer b is incorrect because **AS** is a keyword, not a clause. Answer c is incorrect because any valid subquery, including **WHERE** clauses, can be used in a **CREATE TABLE** command. Answer d is incorrect because any portion of a table or set of tables can be selected for use in a new table—you don't have to select all columns. Answer e is incorrect because a table created with a subquery takes on the data types of the selected columns.

Question 2

What is increased when the database contains migrated rows?

○ a. **PCTUSED**

○ b. I/O

○ c. Shared pool size

○ d. **PCTFREE**

The correct answer is b. At first glance, you might be tempted to answer d for this question, but look again. It's not asking how to correct migrated rows (by increasing **PCTFREE** in the affected table)—it's asking what's increased in the database when you have migrated rows. Obviously, the correct answer is b—I/O—because multiple reads are required for each migrated row. Answer a is incorrect because, even if the question asked how to correct migrated rows, you'd never increase **PCTUSED** to correct migrated rows. Answer c is incorrect because migrated rows have nothing whatsoever to do with the shared pool.

Question 3

> The inventory application has tables that undergo numerous deletes. To which value should you set **PCTUSED** for tables of this nature?
>
> ○ a. 20
>
> ○ b. 10
>
> ○ c. 50
>
> ○ d. 0

The correct answer is c. This is actually a trick question. Furthermore, it's a bit ambiguous and is asking for an opinion, not a fact. However, if you remember that the exam developers look for opportunities to plant exaggerations, follow the axiom that if a little is good, a lot must be great. Using this axiom, the correct answer is c, which is the highest value.

Question 4

> What is the size of the first extent if the storage parameters are **INITIAL 50K**, **NEXT 20K**, and **PCTINCREASE 30**?
>
> ○ a. 20K
>
> ○ b. 30K
>
> ○ c. 50K
>
> ○ d. 70K

The correct answer is c. Again, this is a trick question. Exam developers try to confuse you here with too much information. The question asks for the size of the first extent. The correct answer is c because the **INITIAL** value is set to 50K. The **INITIAL** storage parameter sets the size of the first extent.

Question 5

> Which parameter value would you use if your tables will have frequent inserts and deletes?
>
> ○ a. Lower **PCTFREE**
>
> ○ b. Higher **PCTFREE**
>
> ○ c. Lower **PCTUSED**
>
> ○ d. Higher **PCTUSED**

The correct answer is c. This is another trick question. Just from scanning the question, you would probably choose b, assuming that an answer dealing with migrated or chained rows was sought. You'd be incorrect because the key word in the question is "deletes." The parameter that deals directly with deletes is **PCTUSED,** and to allow for inserts and deletes, the value needs to be lowered.

Question 6

> Which constraints are implicitly defined on a primary key column? [Check all correct answers]
>
> ❑ a. **UNIQUE**
>
> ❑ b. **CHECK**
>
> ❑ c. Foreign key
>
> ❑ d. **NOT NULL**

The correct answers are a and d. A little reasoning and recall about the definition of a primary key will give you the answers. A primary key is a **UNIQUE, NOT NULL** identifier for a table's row. Answer b is incorrect since a **CHECK** constraint is not implicitly defined on a primary key. Answer c is not correct since a foreign key is defined based on an existing primary key.

Question 7

> Which parameter value setting will reserve more room for future updates?
>
> ○ a. Lower **PCTFREE**
>
> ○ b. Higher **PCTFREE**
>
> ○ c. Lower **PCTUSED**
>
> ○ d. Higher **PCTUSED**

The correct answer is b. Given Question 5, you may be tempted to answer c, lower **PCTUSED**, but you'd be wrong. The key to this question is the phrase "future updates." The only parameter that provides for future updates is **PCTFREE**, so increasing it reserves room for future updates.

Question 8

> In which statements would you typically use the **CURRVAL** pseudo-column? [Check all correct answers]
>
> ❑ a. **SET** clause of an **UPDATE** command
>
> ❑ b. **SELECT** list of a view
>
> ❑ c. **SELECT** statement with the **HAVING** clause
>
> ❑ d. Subquery in an **UPDATE** statement
>
> ❑ e. **VALUES** clause of an **INSERT** statement

The correct answers are a and e. The pseudo-columns **CURRVAL** and **NEXTVAL** of a sequence can be used only in the **SET** clause of an **UPDATE** command (answer a), in the **VALUES** clause of an **INSERT** statement (answer e), and in the target of an **INSERT INTO** statement. The pseudo-columns can't be used in a view (answer b), or in a subquery (answer d).

Question 9

Which SQL statement creates the **parts_456874_vu** view that contains the ID number, description, and quantity for **manufacturer_id 456874** from the inventory table and does not allow the manufacturer values to be changed through the view?

○ a.
```
CREATE VIEW parts_456874_vu
AS SELECT id_number, description, quantity
FROM inventory
WHERE manufacturer_id = 456874
WITH READ ONLY;
```

○ b.
```
CREATE VIEW parts_456874_vu
AS SELECT id_number, description, quantity
FROM inventory
HAVING manufacturer_id = 456874
WITH READ ONLY;
```

○ c.
```
CREATE VIEW parts_456874_vu
AS SELECT id_number, description, quantity
FROM inventory
WHERE manufacturer_id = 456874
WITH CHECK OPTION;
```

○ d.
```
CREATE VIEW parts_456874_vu
AS SELECT id_number, description, quantity
FROM inventory
WITH CHECK CONSTRAINT;
```

The correct answer is a; it has complete clauses, restricts the view to the proper range of values (those belonging to the **manufacturer_id 456874**), and specifies the proper format **READ ONLY** clause. Answers b and d won't even compile, and answer c doesn't restrict to **READ ONLY**.

Question 10

What is the size of the third extent if the storage parameters are **INITIAL 50K, NEXT 20K**, and **PCTINCREASE 30**?

- O a. 20K
- O b. 26K
- O c. 30K
- O d. 36K
- O e. 40K
- O f. 100K

The correct answer is b. This is a straightforward calculation. Remember that **NEXT** sets the size for the **NEXT** extent, and **PCTINCREASE** is applied after the **INITIAL** and **NEXT** have been utilized against the value of **NEXT**, so the third extent will be **NEXT** + (**NEXT** * **PCTINCREASE**/100) or, in this case, 20 + (20 * 30/100) = 20 + 6 = 26.

Question 11

The size of the **INITIAL** storage parameter for your rollback segments is 1MB. To which value should you set the **NEXT** storage parameter?

- O a. 2MB
- O b. 4MB
- O c. 256KB
- O d. 1MB

The correct answer is d. For rollback segments, generally speaking, the initial should equal the next extent.

Question 12

When you're attempting to control the space allocation and usage of a cluster's data segment, which storage parameter applies to the cluster and not to the individual tables?

○ a. **PCTFREE**

○ b. **MAXTRANS**

○ c. **INITRANS**

○ d. **SIZE**

○ e. **INITIAL**

The correct answer is a. In **CREATE CLUSTER** statements, the **PCTFREE** applies only to the cluster itself, not to the individual tables. The cluster stores the cluster key values. Answers b, c, d and e are incorrect since only **PCTFREE** applies only to the cluster and not to the individual tables in the cluster.

Question 13

Which length will be assigned to a **VARCHAR2** column if it's not specified when a table is created?

○ a. 1

○ b. 25

○ c. 255

○ d. 38

○ e. A column length must be specified for a **VARCHAR2** column.

The correct answer is e. Unlike a **CHAR** column, which has a default value of 1, if a length is not specified, the **VARCHAR2** column has no default and must have a length specified.

Question 14

> If a character column will store 266 bytes, how many bytes will the column header entry be?
>
> ○ a. 0
>
> ○ b. 1
>
> ○ c. 2
>
> ○ d. 3
>
> ○ e. 250
>
> ○ f. 266

The correct answer is d. For character data, the data storage is 1 byte per character, so a column that stores 266 bytes will have a length of 266. However, a column that is greater than 256 bytes will have a 3-byte header entry instead of a 1-byte header entry.

Question 15

> What is the maximum number of columns in a cluster key?
>
> ○ a. 1
>
> ○ b. 2
>
> ○ c. 4
>
> ○ d. 8
>
> ○ e. 16
>
> ○ f. 32

The correct answer is e, 16. Oracle8i limits the number of cluster key columns to 16. The other answers are incorrect since they aren't 16.

Need To Know More?

 Oracle Corporation. *Oracle8i Server SQL Reference Manual, Release 3(8.1.7)*. September, 2000. Redwood City, CA. Part No. A85397-01. This is the source book for all Oracle SQL for version 8i. This book can be found on the Web, at the time of writing, at **http:// technet.oracle.com**. This site has free membership and has all current versions of Oracle documentation available online in Acrobat format (PDF files).

 Ault, Michael R. *Oracle8i Administration and Management*. John Wiley & Sons. New York, NY, 2000. ISBN 0-471-35453-8. This book covers virtually all aspects of Oracle8i administration, including command syntax, tuning, and management topics.

 DBA Pipeline at **www.revealnet.com/** is a great place to ask those last-minute questions and to peruse for up-to-the-minute questions, problems, and solutions.

 RevealNet Oracle Administrator from RevealNet, Inc. is an online reference that provides diagrams with hot links to definitions and examples of all DDL commands. It's one of the fastest online searchable references I've come across (even though I might be a bit prejudiced because I'm its principal author). It's more expensive than a book, at around $300 to $400; however, you'll use it long after the books have been put away. You can download it from **www.revealnet.com/**.

DDL: Using The ALTER, COMMENT, and DROP Commands

Terms you'll need to understand:

✓ **ALTER** command

✓ **COMMENT** command

✓ **DROP** command

Techniques you'll need to master:

✓ Using the **ALTER** command to alter the characteristics of database objects that can be changed

✓ Using the **COMMENT** command to document your database objects

✓ Using the **DROP** command to remove obsolete objects

This chapter is devoted to the following DDL commands: **ALTER, COMMENT,** and **DROP**. Like **CREATE**, the **ALTER** command has numerous incarnations. Because it is the most complex of the remaining DDL commands, I cover it first. The **ALTER** command allows changes in various aspects of database objects and allows additions to and removals from existing objects. The **COMMENT** command allows for documentation of database objects. The **DROP** command allows obsolete objects to be removed. All of these commands are important, and DBAs must be familiar with their various aspects.

The ALTER Command

The **ALTER** command is used to alter the characteristics of database objects that can be changed. (For the purpose of this chapter, a change is defined as an alteration of structure or characteristics, not simply a recompile.) The **ALTER** command is used with databases, instances (SYSTEM), tablespaces, tables, indexes, clusters, and sequences. Procedures, functions, packages, package bodies, triggers, and views can be recompiled only through the use of the **ALTER** command, as shown in this code snippet:

```
ALTER object_type schema.object_name COMPILE;
```

One thing to remember about any DDL command—such as **ALTER, DROP,** or **CREATE**—is that it results in an implicit **COMMIT** command. An implicit **COMMIT** command causes any uncommitted changes to be committed to the database, so if you perform **INSERT, UPDATE,** or **DELETE** commands and then issue a **CREATE, ALTER,** or **DROP** command, the previous commands will be committed.

The ALTER Command for Databases

Even the best-designed database eventually has to be changed. New log group member files may need to be added, data files may need to be renamed or moved, archive logging status may need to be changed, and so forth. These are all accomplished with the **ALTER DATABASE** command. The syntax for this command is shown in Figure 6.1.

The **ALTER DATABASE** command has the following options and variables:

➤ **database_name**—The database name. It can be a maximum of eight characters long. If the name is not specified, the value in the init.ora file will be used.

➤ **MOUNT**—Indicates that the database is available for some DBA functions but not for normal functions. In an Oracle8 or Oracle8i database, initialization parameters are used to tell Oracle whether an instance is exclusive or shared. In Oracle8 or Oracle8i, you can also mount the standby database or a

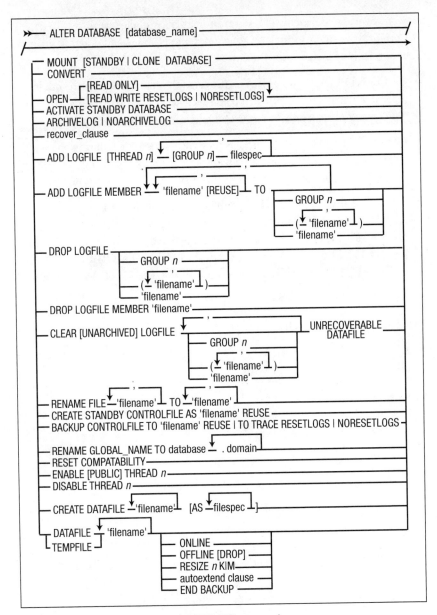

Figure 6.1   The syntax of the **ALTER DATABASE** command.

clone database (used in backup and recovery). A mounted database cannot have the **CREATE CONTROLFILE** command issued against it. To use the **RENAME FILE** option in this command, you must mount the database.

➤ **STANDBY DATABASE**—With version 7.3 and newer, this command operates against a hot-standby database. A *hot-standby database* is one that is left in recovery mode; archive logs are automatically applied against it to keep it current. It's usually located on a second, remote server, and it acts as an automatic failover instance for the current one.

➤ **CLONE DATABASE**—Oracle8 provided the capability to open and mount a clone database that is used in some recovery scenarios. See *Oracle8 DBA: Backup and Recovery Exam Cram* by Debbie Wong for more details.

➤ **CONVERT**—New in Oracle8, **CONVERT** is used only during an in-place conversion from version 7.*x* to version 8 or from Oracle8 to Oracle8i. This clause should only be issued when the database to be converted is not mounted.

➤ **OPEN**—Mounts the database and opens it for general use, either with **RESETLOGS** if an incomplete recovery was performed or with **NORESETLOGS** (the default). **OPEN** has two modes in Oracle8i: either **READ WRITE** (the default) or **READ ONLY**. The **RESETLOGS** or **NORESETLOGS** options can be used only with the **READ WRITE** clause.

➤ **ACTIVATE STANDBY DATABASE**—Used to activate a standby database.

➤ **ARCHIVELOG, NOARCHIVELOG**—Turns archive logging on or off.

➤ **ADD LOGFILE THREAD**—Adds a thread of redo to a Parallel Server instance.

➤ **filespec**—A file specification in the format of:

```
'file_name' SIZE n K or M REUSE
```

where:

➤ **file_name** is an operating-system-specific full path name.

➤ **SIZE** *n* sets the size *n* in bytes, kilobytes, or megabytes.

➤ **K** or **M** is an integer expressed in kilobytes or megabytes.

➤ **REUSE** specifies to reuse the existing file if there is one. **REUSE** is optional and is used if the file specified already exists and is the proper size. If the file is not the correct size, an error will result.

➤ **ADD LOGFILE MEMBER**—Adds a log file member to an existing group.

➤ **'filename'**—A full path file name.

➤ **DROP LOGFILE**—Drops an existing log group.

➤ **DROP LOGFILE MEMBER**—Drops an existing log member.

➤ CLEAR LOGFILE—Reinitializes a specified online redo log and, optionally, does not archive the cleared redo log. **CLEAR LOGFILE** is similar to adding and dropping a redo log except that the command can be issued even if there are only two logs for the thread; it can also be issued for the current redo log of a closed thread. **CLEAR LOGFILE** can't be used to clear a log needed for media recovery. If you have to clear a log containing a redo after the database checkpoint, then incomplete media recovery will be necessary. The current redo log of an open thread can never be cleared. Switching logs in the closed thread can clear the current log of a closed thread.

Note: If the CLEAR LOGFILE command is interrupted by a system or instance failure, the database may hang. If this happens, you must reissue the command after you restart the database. If the failure occurred because of I/O errors accessing one member of a log group, that member can be dropped and other members added.

➤ UNARCHIVED—Must be specified if you want to reuse a redo log that was not archived. Note that specifying **UNARCHIVED** will make backups unusable if the redo log is needed for recovery.

➤ UNRECOVERABLE DATAFILE—Must be specified if the tablespace has a data file offline and if the unarchived log must be cleared to bring the tablespace online. If this is the case, then the data file and the entire tablespace must be dropped after the **CLEAR LOGFILE** command completes its work.

➤ RENAME—Renames the specified database file. This command is also used when a file must be moved from one location to another because of media failure.

➤ CREATE STANDBY CONTROLFILE AS—Creates a control file for use with the standby database.

➤ BACKUP CONTROLFILE—This can be used in two ways: first, to make a recoverable backup copy of the control file (**TO** '*file_name*'), and second, to make a script to rebuild the control file (**TO TRACE**). The **TO TRACE** option can also be used to create a template script that can be used, among other things, to create a database rename script and to show the procedures needed to recover if you have read-only tablespaces in the database.

➤ RENAME GLOBAL_NAME TO—Changes the global name of the database. A rename automatically flushes the shared pool but doesn't change data concerning your global name in remote instances, connect strings, or database links.

➤ RESET COMPATIBILITY—Marks the database to be reset to an earlier version of Oracle when the database is next restarted. This will render archived redo logs unusable for recovery.

Note: This option will not work unless you have successfully disabled Oracle8 features that affect backward compatibility.

➤ ENABLE THREAD/DISABLE THREAD—Allows the enabling and disabling of redo log threads (used only for parallel databases).

➤ CREATE DATAFILE—Creates a new data file in place of an old one. You can use this option to re-create a data file that was lost with no backup. The 'file_name' must identify a file that was once a part of the database. The 'filespec' specifies the name and size of the new data file. If you omit the AS clause, Oracle creates the new file with the same name and size as the file specified by 'file_name'.

➤ DATAFILE or TEMPFILE—Allows you to perform manipulations—such as resizing, turning autoextend on or off, and setting backup status—against the data files or temporary files in the instance. Temporary files are new in Oracle8i.

The ALTER DATABASE command option that you should be most aware of is the ALTER DATABASE BACKUP CONTROLFILE command. Study the difference between when a control file is backed up to trace and when it's physically backed up.

When a control file is backed up to trace, a script file is created that allows the re-creation of the control file. The script created by a BACKUP TO TRACE command can also be used to rename an existing database or to document the steps required to recover the database, especially if read-only tablespaces are used. When a CONTROLFILE is backed up to a file, it can be used to recover the database as a backup copy of the CONTROLFILE at that point in time. For more details, see *Oracle8 DBA: Backup and Recovery Exam Cram.*

You also need to understand when the RESETLOGS option is used with the ALTER DATABASE OPEN command. RESETLOGS is used only after an incomplete media recovery is performed.

 Whenever an **OPEN RESETLOGS** is required, you should immediately back up the database because previous archive logs won't be able to be used for future recovery operations.

The ALTER SYSTEM Command

A special DDL command, ALTER SYSTEM, is used to alter the characteristics of the actual database environment. The alterations are in effect only until the database is shut down and restarted. In spite of its importance to database operations, the test mentions very little of the **ALTER SYSTEM** command, if anything at all. We cover it for completeness, but for an explanation of all options, please refer to the SQL manual.

*Note: Although the **ALTER SYSTEM** command is not actually used to modify data structures, this seems like the logical place to cover the command because it is a derivation of the **ALTER** command.*

The syntax of the **ALTER SYSTEM** command is shown in Figure 6.2.

The **ALTER SYSTEM** command has the following clauses and options:

➤ **ARCHIVE LOG**—Manually archives redo log files, or enables or disables automatic archiving, depending on the clause specified.

➤ **CHECKPOINT**—Performs either a **GLOBAL** (all open instances on the database) checkpoint or a **LOCAL** (current instance) checkpoint.

➤ **CHECK DATAFILES**—Verifies access to data files. If **GLOBAL** is specified, all data files in all instances accessing the database are verified accessible. If **LOCAL** is specified, only the current instance's data files are verified.

➤ **DISCONNECT SESSION**—Allows a disconnection rather than a kill of a database session. Use with the **IMMEDIATE** clause is applicable for the **DISCONNECT** clause only if there are no outstanding transactions, at which point the command behaves identically to the **KILL SESSION IMMEDIATE** command.

➤ **ENABLE DISTRIBUTED RECOVERY**—Enables distributed recovery.

➤ **DISABLE DISTRIBUTED RECOVERY**—Disables distributed recovery.

➤ **ENABLE RESTRICTED SESSION**—Allows only those users with the **RESTRICTED SESSION** privilege to log in to the database.

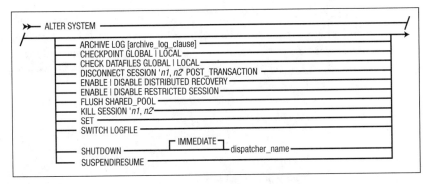

Figure 6.2   The syntax of the **ALTER SYSTEM** command.

➤ DISABLE RESTRICTED SESSION—Allows any user to log on to the instance.

➤ FLUSH SHARED_POOL—Forces a flush of nonpinned (objects not currently being used) and nonkept (objects not kept using the **DBMS_ SHARED_POOL** procedure) objects in the shared pool.

➤ KILL SESSION—Kills an active database session. Use of the **IMMEDIATE** clause causes the session to be immediately killed without waiting for impending I/O.

➤ SET *set_clause*—The **SET** clause allows many initialization parameters and other setup parameters to be dynamically altered. You can see the list of parameters that can be changed in the SQL manual. This is not covered on the exam.

➤ SWITCH LOGFILE—Switches the active log file groups.

➤ SUSPEND|RESUME—Used to **SUSPEND** or **RESUME** database I/O operations including **SELECT** commands. **SUSPEND** is used to allow backup without having to deal with transactions. The tablespaces being backed up should be in backup mode prior to issuing the **SUSPEND** command. This clause is new in Oracle8i.

➤ SHUTDOWN [IMMEDIATE] *dispatcher_name*—Used only with Oracle multi-threaded server (MTS) to shutdown a MTS dispatcher process. If you specify **IMMEDIATE**, the dispatcher immediately stops accepting new connections, and Oracle terminates all existing connections through that dispatcher. After all sessions are cleaned up, the dispatcher process literally shuts down. If you do not specify **IMMEDIATE**, the dispatcher immediately stops accepting new connections but waits for all its users to disconnect and for its entire database links to terminate. This clause is new in Oracle8i.

A Detailed Look at ARCHIVE LOG Clauses

In Oracle8 and Oracle8i, the **ARCHIVE LOG** command is removed from SVRMGR and is placed under the **ALTER SYSTEM** command. The new command has additional clauses to handle the more complex archive log scheme in Oracle8 and Oracle8i. The syntax handles the threads and groups associated with the new archive logs. The new syntax is as follows:

```
ALTER SYSTEM ARCHIVE LOG clause;
ARCHIVE LOG clauses:
      [THREAD n]
      [SEQUENCE n] [TO 'location']
      [CHANGE n] [TO 'location']
      [CURRENT] [TO 'location']
```

```
[GROUP n] [TO 'location']
[LOGFILE 'file_name'] [TO 'location']
[NEXT] [TO 'location']
[ALL] [TO 'location']
[START] [TO 'location']
[STOP]
```

The **ARCHIVE LOG** command has the following clauses:

► **THREAD**—Specifies the specific redo-log thread to affect. If this isn't specified, then the redo-log thread of the current instance is affected.

► **SEQUENCE**—Archives the redo-log group that corresponds to the integer specified by the integer given as the argument.

► **CHANGE**—Corresponds to the System Change Number (SCN) for the transaction you want to archive. It will force archival of the log containing the transaction with the SCN that matches the integer given as the argument in the **CHANGE** argument.

► **GROUP**—Manually archives the redo logs in the specified group. If both **THREAD** and **GROUP** are specified, the group must belong to the specified thread.

► **CURRENT**—Causes all nonarchived redo-log members of the current group to be archived.

► **LOGFILE**—Manually archives the group that contains the file specified by '**filespec**'. If a thread is specified, the file must be in a group contained in the thread specified.

► **NEXT**—Forces manual archival of the oldest online redo log that requires it. If no thread is specified, Oracle archives the oldest available unarchived redo-log file group.

► **ALL**—Archives all online archive logs that are part of the current thread and that haven't yet been archived. If no thread is specified, then all unarchived logs from all threads are archived.

► **START**—Starts automatic archiving of redo-log file groups. This applies only to the thread assigned to the current instance. This command also modifies the control file so that the archive status is recorded and used the next time the database is started.

► **TO**—Specifies where to archive the logs. This must be a full path specification.

► **STOP**—Disables automatic archiving of redo-file log groups. This command applies to your current instance.

You should be familiar with the **ALTER SYSTEM** command and its effects on archive logging, so you need to learn these command options backwards and forwards.

The ALTER Command for Tablespaces

Tablespaces can be altered to add data files, change online status, change recoverability, change backup status, and change the default storage characteristics for the tablespace. The command to perform these tablespace changes is the **ALTER TABLESPACE** command; its syntax is shown in Figure 6.3.

The **ALTER TABLESPACE** command has the following keywords and parameters:

➤ **tablespace_name**—Name of the tablespace to be altered.

➤ LOGGING|NOLOGGING—Turns on or off default-level logging for this tablespace. This setting is overridden by any table- or index-level logging settings.

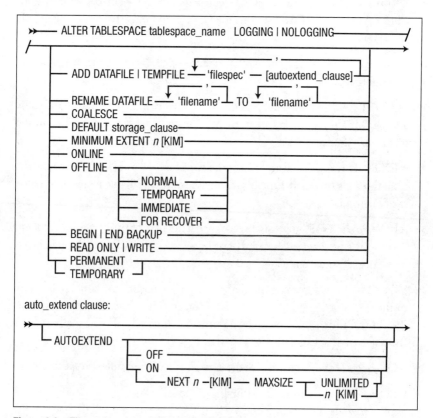

Figure 6.3 The syntax of the **ALTER TABLESPACE** command.

➤ ADD DATAFILE|TEMPFILE—Adds the data file or temp file specified by '**filespec**' to the tablespace. (See the syntax description of '**filespec**'.) You can add a data file or temp file while the tablespace is online or offline but be sure that the data file is not already in use by another database or the operation will fail. You should back up the control file after any change to the database's physical structure. Data files are added only to normal (permanent tablespaces or temporary tablespaces create with the **CREATE TABLESPACE... TEMPORARY** command). Temp files are added to tablespaces created with the **CREATE TEMPORARY TABLESPACE** command.

➤ AUTOEXTEND—Enables or disables the autoextending of the size of the data file in the tablespace. The options for **AUTOEXTEND** are as follows:

  ➤ OFF—Disables **AUTOEXTEND** if it's turned on. **NEXT** and **MAXSIZE** are set to zero. Values for **NEXT** and **MAXSIZE** must be respecified in further **ALTER TABLESPACE AUTOEXTEND** commands.

  ➤ ON—Enables **AUTOEXTEND**.

  ➤ NEXT—Sets the size (in bytes) of the next increment of disk space to be automatically allocated to the data file when more extents are required. You can also use **K** or **M** to specify this size in kilobytes or megabytes. The default is one data block.

  ➤ MAXSIZE—Sets the maximum disk space allowed for automatic extension of the data file.

  ➤ UNLIMITED—Sets no limit on allocating disk space to the data file.

➤ RENAME DATAFILE—Renames one or more of the tablespace's data files. Take the tablespace offline before renaming the data file. Each '**file_name**' must fully specify a data file, using the conventions for file names on your operating system. This clause associates the tablespace with only the new file rather than the old one. The clause doesn't actually change the name of the operating-system file; you must change the name of the file through your operating system. Temp files cannot be renamed.

➤ COALESCE—Combines all contiguous free extents into larger contiguous extents for each data file in the tablespace. The benefit of a manual COALESCE is that it is committed immediately. The space transaction for an automatic COALESCE will not be committed until eight COALESCE operations have been performed by SMON. If PCTINCREASE is set to a nonzero value, the SMON process will perform this operation automatically. SMON wakes up every five minutes to perform automatic COALESCE operations. This is documented in Note 1070504.6 from **http://metalink.oracle.com**.

Note: COALESCE can't be specified with any other command option.

➤ DEFAULT *storage_clause*—Specifies the new default storage parameters for objects subsequently created in the tablespace.

➤ MINIMUM EXTENT—Sets the size of the minimum extent for the entire tablespace.

➤ ONLINE—Brings the tablespace online.

➤ OFFLINE—Takes the tablespace offline and prevents further access to its segments. The options for OFFLINE are as follows:

➤ NORMAL—Performs a checkpoint for all data files in the tablespace. All of these data files must be online. You don't need to perform media recovery on this tablespace before bringing it back online, but you must use this option if the database is in NOARCHIVELOG mode.

➤ TEMPORARY—Performs a checkpoint for all online data files in the tablespace but does not ensure that all files can be written. Any offline files may require media recovery before you bring the tablespace back online.

➤ IMMEDIATE—Does not ensure that tablespace files are available and does not perform a checkpoint. You must perform recovery on the tablespace before bringing it back online.

➤ FOR RECOVER—Takes offline the production database tablespaces in the recovery set. Use this option when one or more data files in the tablespace are unavailable.

The default is NORMAL. If you're taking a tablespace offline for a long time, you may want to reassign any users who have been assigned to the tablespace (as either a default or a temporary tablespace) to some other tablespace. Users can't allocate space for objects or sort areas in the tablespaces that are offline. You can reassign users to new default and temporary tablespaces with the ALTER USER command.

➤ BEGIN BACKUP—Signifies that an online backup is to be performed on the data files that compose this tablespace. This option doesn't prevent users from accessing the tablespace. You must use this option before beginning an online backup. You don't need to use this option on a read-only tablespace. BEGIN BACKUP can be used only in ARCHIVELOG mode. The BEGIN BACKUP command suspends updates to the header block of the data files for the referenced tablespace, and changes to any block for the tablespace cause the entire block to be written to the redo log the first time it is changed, and change vectors are written from then on.

While the backup is in progress, you can't do the following:

➤ Take the tablespace offline normally

➤ Shut down the instance

➤ Begin another backup of the tablespace

➤ **END BACKUP**—Signifies that an online backup of the tablespace is complete. Use this option as soon as possible after completing an online backup. If a tablespace is left in **BACKUP** mode, the database will think it needs recovery the next time the database is shut down and started, and you might not be able to recover. You don't need to use this option on a read-only tablespace, and this option can't be specified unless the database is in **ARCHIVELOG** mode.

➤ **READ ONLY**—Signifies that no further write operations are allowed on the tablespace. Read-only tablespaces provide two benefits: After the initial data backup, the data no longer has to be backed up, and no redo or rollback is generated in the use of read-only tablespaces.

➤ **READ WRITE**—Signifies that write operations are allowed on a previously read-only tablespace.

➤ **PERMANENT**—Specifies that the tablespace is to be converted from a temporary one to a permanent one. A permanent tablespace is one in which permanent database objects are stored. This is the default when a tablespace is created.

➤ **TEMPORARY**—Specifies that the tablespace is to be converted from a permanent to a temporary one. A temporary tablespace is one in which no permanent database objects can be stored.

At least one of the lines following the **ALTER TABLESPACE** command must be supplied. The definitions for most of the arguments are the same as those for the **CREATE** command.

The ALTER Command for Tables

Tables can be altered to add columns; change column types and lengths; or add, change, or drop column or table constraints. A table's storage characteristics can also be altered (for subsequent extents or data blocks only). The syntax of the **ALTER TABLE** command is shown in Figure 6.4.

The **ALTER TABLE** command has the following parameters:

➤ **add_column_options**—Allows you to add a column or constraint to a table or cluster table. You cannot add columns to a nested table.

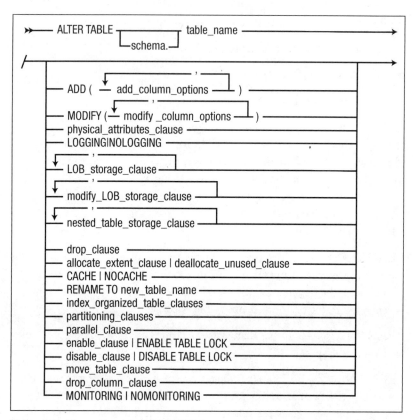

Figure 6.4 The syntax of the **ALTER TABLE** command.

➤ **modify_column_options**—Allows you to modify the definition of an existing column. You cannot modify columns of an index-only table.

➤ **Drop_column_clause**—New in Oracle8i, you can now mark columns as unused, or drop them altogether. The clause consists of either a **SET UNUSED** command with appropriate column name(s) and options or a **DROP [UNUSED] COLUMN[S] [columns]** command with appropriate options. However, this clause is not covered on the exam. Be very careful with this command because after a column is marked as unused, it is difficult to recover from if a mistake was made, and it's impossible to recover from a **DROP [UNUSED] COLUMN[S]** command. A **DROP UNUSED COLUMNS** command drops all unused columns from the specified table.

➤ **Move_clause**—New in Oracle8i, this clause allows a table to be moved from one tablespace to another or to be simply rebuilt in place if no target tablespace is specified. The clause consists of a **MOVE [ONLINE]** command with appropriate modified **physical_attribute_clause, parallel_clause,** or **LOB_storage_clauses.** If the **ONLINE** specification is used, users may still access the table while it is being moved. The **ONLINE** clause can be used only for a nonpartitioned index-organized table. If you specify **MOVE,** it must be the first clause. For an index-organized table, the only clauses outside this clause that are allowed are the **physical_attribute_clause** and the **parallel_clause.** For heap-organized tables, you can specify those two clauses and the **LOB_storage_clauses.** You cannot **MOVE** an entire partitioned table (either heap or index organized). You must move individual partitions or subpartitions. This clause is not covered on the test.

➤ **physical_attributes_clause**—Allows you to modify the following physical attributes: **PCTFREE, PCTUSED, PCTINCREASE, MAXEXTENTS, INITRANS, MAXTRANS,** and **NEXT.** Changes to any of these affect only new blocks, not existing blocks, in a table.

➤ **LOGGING|NOLOGGING**—Allows you to reset the logging attribute of the table.

➤ **LOB_storage_clause**—Allows you to modify the **LOB** storage associated with the table.

➤ **nested_table_storage_clause**—Allows you to reset the nested storage table storage for a nested table.

➤ **drop_clause**—Used to drop an integrity constraint.

➤ **allocate_extent_clause**—Allows you to force the allocation of a new table extent and to specify its location.

➤ **deallocate_unused_clause**—Used to deallocate unused extents from a table.

➤ **CACHE|NOCACHE**—When set to **CACHE,** causes the table to be maintained in the most recently used side of the LRU list.

➤ **RENAME**—Takes the place of the **RENAME** command in previous releases and allows renaming of the table.

➤ **index_organized_table_clauses**—Allows you to specify that this table is an index-only table.

➤ **partitioning_clauses**—Allows you to modify the table's partitions, if it has any.

➤ **parallel_clause**—Allows you to turn on and off parallel activities on the table and allows you to set the degree of parallelism for the table. The **parallel_clause** has the syntax shown in Figure 6.5.

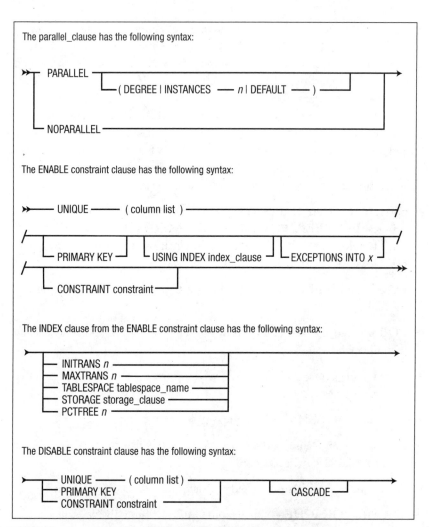

The parallel_clause has the following syntax:

The ENABLE constraint clause has the following syntax:

The INDEX clause from the ENABLE constraint clause has the following syntax:

The DISABLE constraint clause has the following syntax:

Figure 6.5   The syntax of some of the **ALTER TABLE** command's clauses.

➤ MONITORING|NOMONITORING—New in Oracle8i, this clause enables tracking of **INSERT, UPDATE** and **DELETE** gross activity on a table. The values for these changes to the table are then used by the **DBMS_STATS** package to determine when a table should be re-analyzed.

The **PARALLEL** clause has the following parameters:

➤ DEGREE—Specifies that this is a parallel query operation. The *n*, an integer value, tells the number of parallel query slaves to allocate for a single level of parallel operations on this object. Note that multiples of this value may be used if the operation involves sorting.

➤ INSTANCES—Specifies this is a parallel server object where n (an integer) specifies the number of parallel instances to use to cache the object.

➤ DEFAULT—Specifies to use the default settings for degree of parallel for the instance.

➤ ENABLE/DISABLE TABLE LOCK—Clauses that allow you to turn on and off the capability of placing DML and DDL locks in a parallel server environment.

The **ENABLE** constraint clause of the **ALTER TABLE** command has the syntax shown in Figure 6.5.

The **ENABLE** clause is used to enable constraints. When enabling a primary key or unique key, always specify the **index_clause** and especially the **TABLESPACE** clause to prevent the required index from being created in the table's tablespace. The clause has the following parameters:

➤ UNIQUE—Enables the column list as a unique constraint creating the required index.

➤ PRIMARY KEY—Enables the primary key constraint (if any) defined on the table.

➤ USING INDEX—Used to specify the index-specific parameters for **UNIQUE** and **PRIMARY KEY** indexes.

➤ EXCEPTIONS INTO x—Sends data on any rows not meeting the constraint requirements into the table represented by x.

➤ CONSTRAINT *constraint*—Enables the constraint named by the clause.

The **INDEX** clause from the **ENABLE** constraint clause has the syntax shown in Figure 6.5. The **INDEX** clause parameters are the same as those defined in the **CREATE TABLE** and **CREATE INDEX** commands. The **DISABLE** constraint clause has the syntax shown in Figure 6.5

Specifying the **CASCADE** option with either **DISABLE** or **DROP** allows Oracle to cascade the operation to all dependent integrity constraints. **DISABLE** turns a constraint off (note that for **UNIQUE** and **PRIMARY KEY** constraints, this also drops the related indexes). **ENABLE** or **ADD** turns a constraint on or creates it. For **UNIQUE** or **PRIMARY KEY** constraints, an index will be created. If the index clause is not specified, the index is created in the default tablespace of the creator with the default storage characteristics of that tablespace.

ALTER TABLE Specifics

The following are tasks you can accomplish with the **ALTER TABLE** command:

➤ Use the **ADD** clause to add columns that have null values to any table.

➤ Use the **MODIFY** clause to increase the size of columns or to change the precision of numeric columns.

➤ Use the **MODIFY** clause to change columns with all null values so that the columns are shorter or have a different data type.

➤ Use the **DROP COLUMN** or **SET UNUSED** clauses to drop a column or mark it as unused.

➤ **MOVE** a table to a new tablespace or rebuild it in place.

➤ Alter the **PCTFREE, PCTUSED, INITRANS,** or **MAXTRANS** values for any table.

➤ Use the **STORAGE** clause to alter the storage parameters for any table.

➤ Use the **PARALLEL** clause to change or remove the parallelism of a table.

➤ Use **CACHE** or **NOCACHE** to specify whether a table is to be cached.

➤ Use the **DROP** clause to remove a constraint.

➤ Use the **DEFAULT** value clause to add a default value to any column.

➤ Use the **DISABLE** clause to disable a constraint. (This is the only way to disable a constraint.) When the **CASCADE** option is specified with **DISABLE**, it also disables all dependent integrity constraints.

➤ Use the **DEALLOCATE UNUSED** clause to deallocate space that is not being used. (You can use the **KEEP** option to specify a safety margin above the high-water mark.)

➤ Use the **ENABLE** clause to enable a constraint that was created as disabled. (The **ENABLE** clause can be used only in **CREATE** and **ALTER TABLE** commands.)

➤ Use the **ADD CONSTRAINT** clause to add a primary, not null, check, or foreign key constraint to an existing table.

The tasks you can't perform with the **ALTER TABLE** command include:

➤ Modify a column that has values to be shorter or to be a different data type than it already is.

➤ Add a **NOT NULL** column to a table that has rows in a single step operation with only the **ALTER TABLE** command.

➤ Alter a column to **NOT NULL** if it has rows with null values in that column.

➤ Rename a column.

➤ Change a column's data type to an incompatible data type.

The **ALTER TABLE** command allows the allocation of new extents with specification of size and placement (in different data files, if desired) and deallocation of unused extents. When you deallocate unused extents, the bytes reserved for future inserts above the high-water mark are set using the **KEEP** clause of the **DEALLOCATE** clause.

If a table will grow at a rate that makes calculation of exact sizing difficult, increase the value of the **PCTINCREASE** parameter. Usually I suggest doing space calculations as accurately as possible, applying a 50 percent fudge factor to allocate enough space, and setting **PCTINCREASE** to zero. However, in some situations, the only way to handle extreme table growth is to use a high **PCTINCREASE**.

In this chapter, I've covered the clauses that are most important for you to know. For details on clauses that haven't been covered in detail, see the references at the end of the chapter.

The ALTER Command for Clusters

Clusters are altered with the **ALTER CLUSTER** command. With this command, you can change only the sizing and storage parameters; you cannot add or remove columns. The syntax of the command is shown in Figure 6.6.

The definitions for the **ALTER CLUSTER** parameters are the same as those for the **CREATE TABLE, CREATE CLUSTER**, and storage clause parameters.

You need to know only how these parameters relate to tables.

The ALTER Command for Indexes

Indexes are altered with the **ALTER INDEX** command. Indexes can have their physical storage clauses altered, and they can be rebuilt. You can't add, modify, or remove columns from an existing index by using the **ALTER INDEX** command. To change an index's columns, you must drop and re-create the index. The syntax of the **ALTER INDEX** command is shown in Figure 6.7.

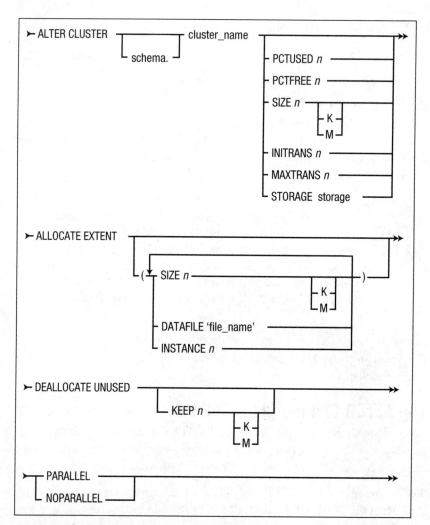

Figure 6.6 The syntax of the **ALTER CLUSTER** command.

The parameters for the **index_physical_attributes_clause** are zero or one or more of the following:

➤ PCTFREE *n*

➤ INITRANS *n*

➤ MAXTRANS *n*

➤ STORAGE *storage_clause*

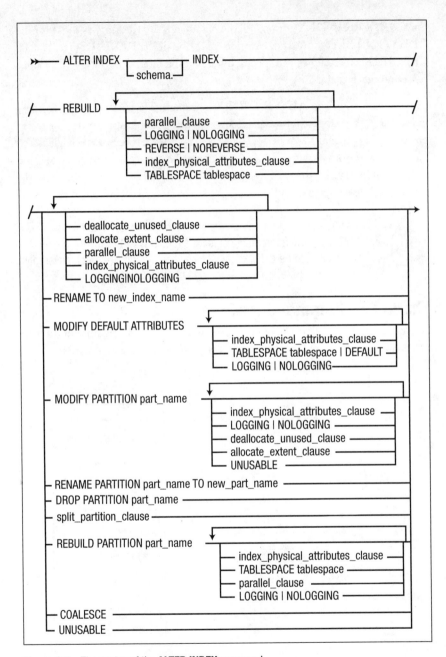

Figure 6.7   The syntax of the **ALTER INDEX** command.

For the **ALTER INDEX** command, the parameters are the same as those for the **CREATE TABLE** command, with the exception of the **REBUILD** clause. The **REBUILD** clause allows the specified index to be rebuilt on the fly in versions 7.3.*x* and newer databases.

The major uses of the **ALTER INDEX** command are to deallocate oversized index space, to change the storage characteristics of an existing index, or to rebuild existing indexes. Notice that you can use the **TABLESPACE** clause to move an index from its existing location to a new location. New to Oracle8i is the **COALESCE** clause, which allows Oracle to merge the contents of index blocks where possible to free blocks for reuse.

 It's not important for you to know the partition-related additions to the **ALTER INDEX** command (including the **UNUSABLE** clause), so they're not discussed here. For details on clauses that haven't been covered in detail, see the references at the end of the chapter.

The ALTER Command for Sequences

Sequences can be altered to change minimum, maximum, caching, and increment values. The syntax of the **ALTER SEQUENCE** command is shown in Figure 6.8.

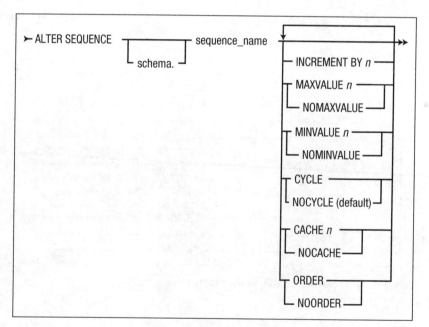

Figure 6.8   The syntax of the **ALTER SEQUENCE** command.

Only future sequence numbers are affected by the **ALTER SEQUENCE** command. To alter the **START WITH** clause, you must drop and re-create the sequence. For ascending sequences, the **MAXVALUE** can't be less than the current sequence value. For descending sequences, the **MINVALUE** can't be greater than the current sequence value.

The **ALTER** Command for Rollback Segments

The only items that can be altered for a rollback segment are the items that deal with storage characteristics or rollback-segment status and size. Rollback segments can be altered to affect the **NEXT, OPTIMAL,** and **MAXEXTENTS** storage parameters. Rollback segments can be taken **OFFLINE** or placed **ONLINE**. Using the **SHRINK** clause, you can shrink rollback segments either to a specified size or to the value of **OPTIMAL** if the size isn't specified. The syntax of the ALTER ROLLBACK SEGMENT command is shown in Figure 6.9.

> Although you can't change a view by using an **ALTER** command, you can re-create it without loss of privilege grants by using the **CREATE OR REPLACE** command. So, to alter a view, you must redefine the entire specification for the view by using the **CREATE OR REPLACE** command. Using this command removes the need to first drop the view and then re-creates it and regrants privileges.

The **COMMENT** Command

Although the **COMMENT** command may not be a true DDL command, it fits in with the **ALTER** commands, so I'll cover it here. The **COMMENT** command adds comments—at the table, view, or column levels—to the data dictionary. The comments entered with the **COMMENT** command can be seen by using the **DBA_TAB_COMMENTS** and **DBA_COL_COMMENTS** views or their

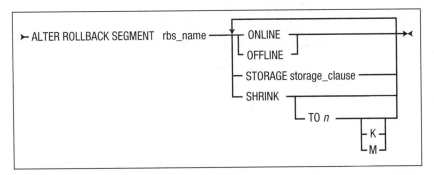

Figure 6.9   The syntax of the **ALTER ROLLBACK SEGMENT** command.

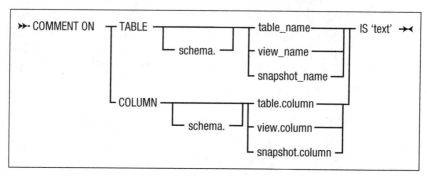

Figure 6.10   The syntax of the **COMMENT** command.

related **USER_** and **ALL_** series of views. The syntax of the **COMMENT** command is shown in Figure 6.10.

Using the **COMMENT** command is an excellent way to document your application tables, views, snapshots, and columns internally, so a simple query using the **DBA_**, **USER_**, or **ALL_** views will produce documentation concerning the purpose of a table, view, snapshot, or individual column.

The DROP Command

The only way to drop an object (other than an index explicitly tied to a constraint) is to use the **DROP** command. The **DROP** command is used to remove tables, indexes, clusters, tablespaces, sequences, stored objects, and synonyms. Any command that frees up space—such as a **DROP** command, a **TRUNCATE** command, or an **ALTER** command with a **DEALLOCATE** clause—can result in tablespace fragmentation. The general syntax of a **DROP** command is shown in Figure 6.11.

The **DROP** command has the following options:

➤ **object_type**—Type of object to drop. Accepted object types are:

  ➤ TABLE (can use **CASCADE CONSTRAINTS**)

  ➤ TABLESPACE (can use **INCLUDING CONTENTS**)

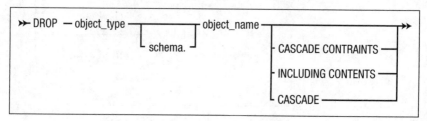

Figure 6.11   General syntax of the **DROP** command.

➤ USER (can use CASCADE)

➤ PACKAGE (only entire packages or package bodies; can't drop individual package items)

➤ PROCEDURE

➤ FUNCTION (only standalone; can't drop individual package items)

➤ TRIGGER

➤ SYNONYM

➤ DATABASE LINK

➤ VIEW

➤ TYPE

➤ schema—Owner of the object to be dropped (usually required only if you are not the owner; then, you must have adequate DROP privileges against the object or have been granted the privilege database wide with the DROP ANY... type privilege).

➤ object_name—Name of the object to be dropped.

➤ CASCADE CONSTRAINTS—Tells Oracle to drop any related foreign key constraint for a parent table. If ON DELETE CASCADE is in effect, all related rows will also be dropped from child tables.

➤ INCLUDING CONTENTS—Forces a drop for tablespaces and their objects, even if the tablespace still contains objects.

➤ CASCADE—Allows users who still have objects in the database to be dropped. This option drops the users' objects along with the users.

A DROP command is a DDL command and can't be rolled back. Any dropped object must be re-created if the DROP command was issued in error. If you find yourself frequently dropping and creating the same table, consider making the table permanent and just issuing TRUNCATE commands. If a table that is frequently created and dropped is shared among several users, add a trigger to populate a session identifier (sessionid) column and then just delete the rows from that user when the user is finished.

Practice Questions

Question 1

Which SQL command syntax would you use to remove the view **parts_vu**?

○ a. **DELETE VIEW parts_vu;**

○ b. **DELETE parts_vu;**

○ c. **DROP parts_vu;**

○ d. **DROP VIEW parts_vu;**

The correct answer is d; it's the only one of the listed commands that uses the correct syntax. Answer a has incorrect syntax. Answer b will delete the data contained in the underlying tables for view **parts_vu** if the criteria allowing deletion are fulfilled. Answer c doesn't supply the **object_type** required by the syntax for the **DROP** command.

Question 2

Evaluate this SQL command:

```
ALTER TABLESPACE users COALESCE;
```

Which background process performs the same task?

○ a. **PMON**

○ b. **SMON**

○ c. **DBWR**

○ d. **LGWR**

The correct answer is b, **SMON**. **SMON** performs space management as part of its system monitoring tasks. Answer a is incorrect because **PMON** cleans up process-related areas and does no space management at the system level. Answer c, **DBWR**, is incorrect because **DBWR** performs dirty buffer writes and does no space management functions at all. Answer d, **LGWR**, is incorrect because **LGWR** writes out the log buffer and checkpoint data but performs no space management functions.

Question 3

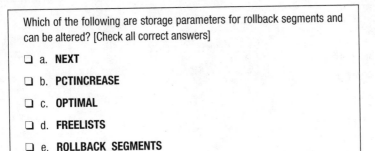

Which of the following are storage parameters for rollback segments and can be altered? [Check all correct answers]

❑ a. **NEXT**

❑ b. **PCTINCREASE**

❑ c. **OPTIMAL**

❑ d. **FREELISTS**

❑ e. **ROLLBACK_SEGMENTS**

The correct answers are a, **NEXT**, and c, **OPTIMAL**. Answer b is incorrect because since Oracle7.3, **PCTINCREASE** is no longer a modifiable parameter for rollback segments—it's set to zero and can't be changed. Answer d is incorrect because **FREELISTS** aren't set for rollback segments. Answer e is incorrect because **ROLLBACK_SEGMENTS** is an initialization parameter for the instance, not a storage parameter for rollback segments.

Question 4

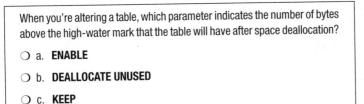

When you're altering a table, which parameter indicates the number of bytes above the high-water mark that the table will have after space deallocation?

○ a. **ENABLE**

○ b. **DEALLOCATE UNUSED**

○ c. **KEEP**

○ d. **ALLOCATE EXTENT SIZE**

The correct answer is c, **KEEP**. **KEEP** is the correct answer because when you're altering a table, the **KEEP** parameter indicates the number of bytes above the high-water mark that the table will have after space deallocation. Answer a is incorrect because **ENABLE** is used to enable constraints or triggers and has nothing to do with space management. Answer b, although dealing with space management, has nothing to do with the amount of space retained above the high-water mark. Answer d concerns extent allocation, not deallocation, so it is also incorrect.

Question 5

A change to which storage parameter will affect only subsequently added data blocks?

○ a. **INITRANS**

○ b. **MAXTRANS**

○ c. **INITIAL**

○ d. **MINEXTENTS**

The correct answer is a, **INITRANS**. The answer is correct because **INITRANS** has to be set before a block is loaded with data; it is the initial size of the transaction area. Answer b, **MAXTRANS**, will apply to all extents, not just subsequently added ones. Answers c and d, **INITIAL** and **MINEXTENTS**, are set when the object is created—they can't be changed unless the object is dropped and re-created.

Question 6

Which clause would you use in an **ALTER TABLE** command to drop a column from a table?

○ a. **REMOVE**.

○ b. **DROP COLUMN**.

○ c. **DELETE**.

○ d. **ALTER**.

○ e. A column can't be dropped from a table.

The correct answer is b—you use **DROP COLUMN** to drop a column from a table. Answer a is incorrect because there's no **REMOVE** clause in an **ALTER TABLE** command; answer c is incorrect because there's no **DELETE** option for the **ALTER TABLE** command; and answer d is incorrect because there's no **ALTER** clause for the **ALTER TABLE** command. Of course, answer e is incorrect as of Oracle8i.

Question 7

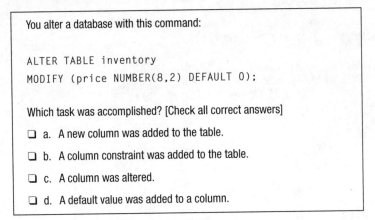

The correct answer is d. This is also a trick question because from common understandings (or perhaps I should say, misunderstandings), there are several correct answers. However, only d is the right answer. Answer a is incorrect because the code uses a **MODIFY** clause, which works only on existing columns. Answer b may be considered correct in some circles because the default value is considered a constraint in some references and is viewed with the same views as other constraints, but this answer is not technically correct. Answer c might also be correct, but because we don't have an exhibit to compare the **NUMBER (8,2)** with, we can't be sure, so we must assume that this answer is also incorrect. The only answer that is 100 percent correct is answer d.

Question 8

Which **ALTER** statement would you use to add a primary key constraint on the **manufacturer_id** column of the inventory table?

○ a.
```
ALTER TABLE INVENTORY
MODIFY manuacturer_id CONSTRAINT PRIMARY KEY;
```

○ b.
```
ALTER TABLE inventory
MODIFY CONSTRAINT PRIMARY KEY manufacturer_id;
```

○ c.
```
ALTER TABLE inventory
ADD CONSTRAINT PRIMARY KEY (manufacturer_id);
```

○ d.
```
ALTER TABLE inventory
ADD CONSTRAINT manufacturer_id PRIMARY KEY;
```

The correct answer is c. Answer c is correct because it uses the proper syntax using the **ADD CONSTRAINT** clause. Answer a is incorrect because it uses the incorrect syntax. Only a **NOT NULL** constraint can be added or removed by using a column constraint syntax in an **ALTER TABLE** command. Answer b is incorrect because you can't modify a constraint. Besides, the question says to *add* a primary key, not modify it. Answer d is incorrect because it doesn't specify the column with **PRIMARY KEY**. If a column had been specified in answer d, a primary key constraint named **manufacturer_id** would have been created.

Question 9

You logged on to the database to update the inventory table. After your session began, you issued three **UPDATE** commands; then, you issued an **ALTER TABLE** command to add a column constraint. You were just about to issue a **COMMIT** command when the system crashed. Which changes were made to the inventory table?

- ○ a. Only the **UPDATE** commands
- ○ b. Only the **ALTER TABLE** command
- ○ c. Both the **UPDATE** commands and the **ALTER TABLE** command
- ○ d. None

The correct answer is c. Answer c is correct because **ALTER TABLE** causes an implicit commit that marks the records as committed and alters the table as commanded. This is almost a trick question because the question is checking whether or not you understand that an implicit commit is issued before and after each DDL command. Answer a is incorrect because we know that the **UPDATE** preceded the **ALTER TABLE**, and the **ALTER TABLE** does an implicit commit, committing both sets of operations. Answer b is incorrect because we know that the **UPDATE** commands that preceded the **ALTER TABLE** command were covered by its implicit commit. Answer d is incorrect because we know that a DDL command always does an implicit commit, so both sets of operations were committed.

Question 10

You issue this command:

```
ALTER TABLESPACE data
ADD DATAFILE 'e:\oracle5\data\ortest1\data02.dbf'
    SIZE 10m;
```

What is the result of this command on the database?

- ○ a. None.
- ○ b. A tablespace is added.
- ○ c. The physical database configuration is altered.
- ○ d. The logical database configuration is altered.

The correct answer is c. This command adds a physical file to the database physical structure. Answer a is incorrect because the database is affected. Answer b is incorrect because the code is altering an existing tablespace, not adding a new one. Answer d is incorrect because the code is altering an existing tablespace's physical configuration, not changing its logical one.

Question 11

What does the **COMMENT ON TABLE** command do?

○ a. Assigns a table alias

○ b. Adds a comment column to a table

○ c. Adds a comment about a column to the data dictionary

○ d. Adds a comment about a table to the data dictionary

The correct answer is d. The **COMMENT** command has the **ON TABLE** qualifier, so it is for a **TABLE**. Answer a is incorrect because alias assignment is done only in DML, not DDL, statements. Answer b is incorrect because a column can be added to a table by using only the **ALTER TABLE** command. Answer c is incorrect because the **COMMENT ON COLUMN** command, not the **COMMENT ON TABLE** command, is used to insert column comments into the database data dictionary.

Need To Know More?

 Oracle Corporation. *Oracle8i Server SQL Reference Manual, Release 3(8.1.7)*. September, 2000. Redwood City, CA. Part No. A85397-01. This is the source book for all Oracle SQL for version 8i. This book can be found on the Web, at the time of writing, at **http://technet.oracle.com**. This site has free membership and has all current versions of Oracle documentation available online in Acrobat format (PDF files).

 Ault, Michael R. *Oracle8i Administration and Management*. John Wiley & Sons. New York, NY, 2000. ISBN 0-471-35453-8. This book provides a comprehensive look at Oracle8 and Oracle8i management. Use it for command syntax definitions for all **CREATE** commands. The book also contains numerous examples for partitions, index-only tables, and nested tables, as well as for the new object features.

 Ault, Michael R. *Oracle8 Black Book*. The Coriolis Group, Scottsdale, AZ, 1998. ISBN 1-57610-187-8. This how-to book on the new features of Oracle8 provides extensive examples using all features of Oracle8, including **PARTITIONS, LOBs**, and JAVA.

 Honour, Dalberth, and Mehta Kaplan. *Oracle8 How-To*. Waite Group Press, Corte Madera, CA, 1998. ISBN 1-57169-123-5. An excellent book for information on all aspects of Oracle8.

The Oracle Data Dictionary

Terms you'll need to understand:

✓ Data dictionary

✓ Metadata

✓ Virtual table

✓ Dynamic performance table (DPT)

✓ Dynamic performance view (DPV)

✓ View

✓ Packages

✓ Procedures

✓ Functions

✓ SQL

Techniques you'll need to master:

✓ Mining the data dictionary

✓ Structuring the data dictionary

In Chapter 6, you learned about altering database objects. In this chapter, we look at the guts of the Oracle system: the data dictionary.

Overview of the Oracle Data Dictionary

The Oracle data dictionary stores the information required for the Oracle system to operate. This information includes all the details about the structures that make up the items we think of as being in a database. The data dictionary is *data about data*, or *metadata*, as it is more popularly called. Metadata details data types, lengths, precisions, and what data items are contained in which objects. All details of tables, indexes, synonyms, views, grants, roles, and so forth are contained in the data dictionary. An expert with a few minutes' access to your data dictionary will know more about your database than you could have told them in the same amount of time. This is one reason why the **SYS** and **SYSTEM** user passwords should be instantly changed and jealously guarded after installation is complete.

 Oracle sets the **SYSTEM** and **SYS** passwords to **MANAGER** and CHANGE_ON_INSTALL, respectively; you should always reset them.

Oracle C Structs and V$ Views

Some of you may be surprised to learn that Oracle is written in C. However, the main structures (called *structs*) are actually C struct blocks. These normally aren't visible to users; indeed, you have to define a view against them to even be able to describe them. Listing 7.1 is a partial list of the major C structs, commonly called the X$ tables. These sometimes change from release to release, sometimes even within point releases.

Listing 7.1   Partial list of X$ tables.

```
NAME
- - - - - - - - - - - - - - - - - - - - - - - - - - -
X$KQFTA
X$KQFVI
X$KQFVT
X$KQFDT
X$KQFCO
X$KCVFHONL
X$KCVFHMRR
X$KGLTABLE
X$KGLBODY
X$KGLTRIGGER
```

```
X$KGLINDEX
X$KGLCLUSTER
X$KGLCURSOR
```

Until recently, these structs were only documented internally, and little documentation about them was available. Now, by detective work in the virtual performance view structures documented in the virtual view **V$FIXED_VIEW_DEFINITION**, we can see their names (from a query against the SYS-owned virtual table, **V$FIXED_TABLE**) and get an idea of what each struct is used for.

You probably don't need to be concerned with the base C structs, but you should study the virtual views (the **V$** views) that use them extensively; these are called *dynamic performance tables (DPTs)* or *dynamic performance views (DPVs)*.

 I must stress the importance of knowing all you can about all of the **V$** views; they make your life as an Oracle DBA much easier.

An example of a DPT from a query against the **V$FIXED_VIEW_DEFINITION** table is shown in Listing 7.2. In Oracle8, the base views' names were changed to **GV$**, and an instance number was added to each. For simplicity's sake, however, I show the view as it would appear if the **V$** view were the top level (99 percent of you will never use parallel servers, where the instance number is important).

Listing 7.2   Example V$ table and its definition.

```
VIEW_NAME              VIEW_DEFINITION
------------------     ------------------------------------------
V$DATAFILE             select
                       fe.indx+1,decode(bitand(fe.festa,19),0,
                       'OFFLINE',1,'SYSOFF',
                       2,'ONLINE',3,'SYSTEM',16,'RECOVER',18,
                       'RECOVER','UNKNOWN'),
                       decode(bitand(fe.festa, 12),
                       0,'DISABLED',4,'READ ONLY',12,
                       'READ WRITE','UNKNOWN'),
                       to_number(fe.fecps),fh.fhfsz*fe.febsz,
                       fe.fecsz*fe.febsz,fn.fnnam from x$kccfe
                       fe,x$kccfn fn, x$kcvfh fh where
                       fe.fedup!=0 and fe.indx+1=fn.fnfno   and
                       fn.fntyp=3 and fh.hxfil=fn.fnfno and
                       fn.fnnam is not null
```

The **X$** tables generally won't be used by the DBA, and for the most part, they will not be covered on the test. The **X$** tables sometimes change dramatically between releases; don't depend on the above list being the same as you would get from your instance.

Generally speaking, the **V$** tables are used to show transitory performance information based on the underlying C structs, known as the **X$** tables. These DPTs are the only views in Oracle where the data will change almost every time you select from them. This dynamism is why they are called *dynamic* performance tables or views. Because they are based on C structs that are an integral part of the kernel of Oracle, they're also available in a mounted, but not open, database. Except for a few special DPTs built by optional scripts as needed, the **V$** DPTs are created by internalized procedures when the database is built.

The only data-structure information contained in the **X$** and **V$** objects is information that would be used in recovery, and the only information needed for recovery concerns the physical data files (**V$DBFILE**) and the redo logs (**V$LOGHIST** and **V$LOGFILE**). Other than these few views, the others concern performance statistics. The actual metadata is stored in database tables identical in structure to the tables and objects they document.

General database users usually don't need to access the **V$** DPTs. Some DPTs, such as the **V$DATABASE** view, do contain useful information, such as the Oracle version and database name, for general users. I usually grant select permission to the public user for this view and verify that a public synonym is available.

You should know the following **V$** DPTs:

➤ **V$RECOVERY_STATUS**—This view was added to version 7.3 to allow the DBA to track the status of media recovery.

➤ **V$RECOVERY_FILE_STATUS**—This view was added to version 7.3 to allow the DBA to query the status of media recovery.

➤ **V$DB_OBJECT_CACHE**—This view provides information on the amount of sharable memory used by a cached PL/SQL object.

➤ **V$SYSSTAT**—This view has a plethora of system-level statistics. Statistics such as **sorts (memory)** tell how many times a particular type of operation has been performed since startup. Generally speaking, sort location tracking is vital for most applications, and sorts should be done in memory whenever possible, especially for Online Transaction Processing (OLTP) applications. This view is also used to monitor client/server traffic statistics. When tuning the system global area (SGA), you can use this view with the **V$BUFFER_ POOL and V$BUFFER_POOL_STATISTICS** views to evaluate the effect of an increase or decrease in the size of the database buffer cache.

➤ **V$LATCH**—This view contains information on latches and locks. The **SLEEPS** column indicates the number of times that a process waited for a latch. For example, information on the requests for latches that were willing to wait (**WILLING_TO_WAIT** column) is contained in the **MISSES** and **GETS** columns of this view. If you suspect that latch contention is happening, issue a query against this view's **SLEEPS** column to display the number of times a process has waited for a particular latch.

➤ **V$CACHE**—This view is normally used only in parallel-server installations. However, it's useful in more situations than that because you can use it to analyze the database buffer cache in both exclusive and shared server modes. The view shows only objects currently being cached. This view is created by the catparr.sql script, which must be run in addition to the standard catproc.sql script for it to be created.

➤ **V$SYSTEM_EVENT**—This view contains information on system-wide events and is used by the utlbstat and utlestat scripts as a source of statistics. System status, such as the need to increase the redo log buffer size (**LOG_BUFFER**), can be ascertained by looking at the system events (in this case, "log buffer space") listed in this view. Another system event that DBAs should watch for is the "buffer busy waits" event, which indicates contention for the database buffer cache. The total number of event waits for each category is shown in this view.

➤ **V$TRANSACTION**—This view contains information on all transactions in the database. Along with the **V$SESSION** view, **V$TRANSACTION** can be used to get details about a specific user transaction.

➤ **V$SESSION**—This view documents all sessions currently attached to the database. It contains columns that indicate if the session is causing lock contention and, if so, in which row. Because their values are required by the **ALTER SYSTEM KILL SESSION** command, the **SERIAL#** and **SID** columns are useful if you need to kill a user session.

➤ **V$SESSION_EVENT**—This view contains information on session-level events and is used by the utlbstat and utlestat scripts as a source of statistics. It's also useful for determining whether I/O contention exists for the redo log files. Information such as system-wide waits per session is here as well.

➤ **V$LOGFILE**—This view contains the list of all redo log files and their locations. When used with the **V$DBFILE** view, its output is used to provide input to the **CREATE CONTROLFILE** command.

➤ **V$DBFILE**—This view contains the names and locations of all database data files. When used with the **V$LOGFILE** view, it provides the data for input to the **CREATE CONTROLFILE** command. It also provides information used to generate the commands used during a backup operation to back up the physical database data files. This information is also contained in the **DBA_DATA_FILES** view.

➤ **V$LIBRARYCACHE**—This view documents activity in the shared pool library caches. The ratio of **RELOADS** to **PINS** for a specific type of cache should always be less than 1 percent in a properly tuned database. The **RELOADS** column represents the number of object definitions that have been aged out of the library cache for lack of space. The **PINS** column represents the executions of an item in the library cache. The **GETHITRATIO** column should always show a value of greater than 0.9 in an ideally tuned database.

➤ **V$SESSION_WAIT**—This view contains information on session waits and is used by the utlbstat and utlestat scripts as a source of statistics. The wait times, indicated in the **WAIT_TIME** column, record a session's last wait time if the initialization parameter **TIMED_STATISTICS** is set to **TRUE** or **ALTER SYSTEM** is used to reset the parameter to **TRUE**.

➤ **V$SORT_SEGMENT**—This view is a map to the sort extent pool (SEP); it contains such items as the total extents for the **TEMP** tablespace areas, and it's used to monitor sort segments in the **TEMP** tablespace. Each time an unused extent is found in the SEP, the column **EXTENT_HITS** is incremented by one.

➤ **V$BUFFER_POOL_**— This view is new in 8 and 8i databases and stores information about the multiple buffer pools available in 8 and 8i (**DEFAULT**, **KEEP** and **RECYCLE**.)

➤ **V$BUFFER_POOL_STATISTICS**—This view is new in 8 and 8i and stores the critical statistics for monitoring the multiple pools in 8 and 8i. This view's statistics should be used to calculate the hit ratio for the buffer pools, rather than the values from **V$SYSSTAT**. The values in **V$SYSSTAT** also contain read information that is not applicable to hit ratios.

➤ **V$WAITSTAT**—This view contains information on wait statistics, such as high free-list contention. Entries greater than zero in the **VALUE** column indicate possible contention for that resource if the initialization parameter **TIMED_STATISTICS** is set to **TRUE** or **ALTER SYSTEM** is used to reset the parameter to **TRUE**.

For some reason, Oracle likes to refer to rollback segments by the term *undo*, so any references to undo headers or blocks are referring to rollback segments.

The Oracle $ (Dollar) Tables

The final level of the Oracle internals (other than the views based upon them) is collectively known as the *$ tables* or *dollar tables*. Oracle sometimes refers to them as the *base data dictionary tables*. They're called dollar tables because, initially, all of them ended with a dollar sign (the clusters would end with the pound sign[#]) (for example, **COL$**, **TAB$**, **IND$**, and so on). But lately, Oracle has moved away from this standard, so identifying the actual data dictionary tables can often be difficult. (This is a good reason not to place anything in the **SYSTEM** tablespace that isn't a part of the data dictionary or that doesn't belong to the **SYS** user.) The dollar tables are built by the sql.bsq script, which until recently was a hands-off item. Oracle has finally allowed us to edit the sql.bsq script to improve storage parameters for the dollar tables and indexes (in early Oracle7 releases, this was done by experienced DBAs but not supported by Oracle itself). I suggest that you look over the sql.bsq script because it has some interesting internal documentation that shines light into Oracle's data dictionary. Most of the tables created by the sql.bsq script contain comments on each of the table attributes (columns) detailing the column's purpose. Table 7.1 shows some of the names and descriptions of the dollar tables for a version 8.1.6 Oracle database.

Generally speaking, access to dollar tables should be restricted to DBA personnel. Users, however, can use the next set of views I discuss: the **DBA_**, **USER_** and **ALL_** set of data dictionary views. If you select the **DBA_TABLES** view for all tables owned by **SYS**, you can get a complete listing of the $ tables.

Table 7.1 Some of the dollar tables and their descriptions.	
Table Name	**Description**
ACCESS$	Access table for database objects.
ARGUMENT$	Procedure argument table; describes procedural arguments.
ATEMPTAB$	Temporary table used by Oracle8; don't mess with it.
ATTRCOL$	Oracle8 table that stores information about user-defined type (UDT) attributes used in columns.
ATTRIBUTE$	Oracle8 table that stores details about UDT attributes.
AUD$	Audit trail table, which contains entries for all audited actions.
AUDIT$	Audit options table, which tracks auditing actions activated.
AUDIT_ACTIONS	Contains descriptions of auditable actions.
BOOTSTRAP$	Table used during instance startup.
CCOL$	Table of all constraint columns for the database.
CDEF$	Table of all constraint definitions in the database.
CLU$	Table of all clusters in the database.
COL$	Contains descriptions of all columns used in the database.

(continued)

Table 7.1   Some of the dollar tables and their descriptions *(continued)*.

Table Name	Description
COLLECTION$	Contains information about collection types (**VARRAY**s and nested tables).
COLTYPE$	Contains information on columns that contain types rather than regular data types.
COM$	Contains all object and column comments for the database.
CON$	Contains all constraint names in the database.
DBMS_ALERT_INFO	Contains data on user-defined alerts created by **DBMS_ALERT**.
DBMS_LOCK_ALLOCATED	Contains information about locks allocated with **DBMS_LOCK**.
DEFROLE$	Shows all default roles assigned to users in the database.
DEPENDENCY$	Shows all interobject dependencies in the database.
DIR$	Contains information about directories.
DUAL	Single-column, single-value table used for nondirected selects.
DUC$	Table for procedure tracking in the database.
ERROR$	Shows current errors for all users in the database.
EXPACT$	Shows functions to run against tables during export.
FET$	Shows all free extents in the database.
FILE$	Shows all files for the database tablespaces.
HISTGRM$	Shows specifications for histograms used in the database.
HIST_HEAD$	Contains all database histogram header data.
ICOL$	Contains all database index columns.
INCEXP	Incremental export support table.
INCFIL	Shows incremental export file names and users.
INCVID	Contains the identifier for the last valid incremental export.
IND$	Shows all database indexes.
INDPART$	Shows all index partitions in the database.
JOB$	Contains all database-defined jobs.
KOPM$	Oracle8i metadata table.
LIBRARY$	Contains **LIBRARY** definitions for an Oracle8 database.
LINK$	Shows all database links.
LOB$	Shows Oracle8 **LOB** definitions.
METHOD$	Shows UDT method definitions for Oracle8.
MIGRATE$	Used during Oracle7-to-Oracle8 migration.

(continued)

Table 7.1 Some of the dollar tables and their descriptions *(continued)*.	
Table Name	**Description**
MLOG$	Shows all snapshot local master tables.
MLOG_REFCOL$	Tracks filter columns for snapshot logs.
NOEXP$	Contains a list of tables that will not be exported.
NTAB$	Contains information on all nested tables in the database.
OBJ$	Shows all database objects.
OBJAUTH$	Shows table authorizations.
OBJPRIV$	Shows privileges granted to objects in the database.
OID$	Contains all object identifiers in the database (Oracle8 only).
PARAMETER$	Tracks all parameters for methods in UDTs.
PARTCOL$	Tracks partition key columns for partitioned tables.
PARTOBJ$	Tracks all partitioned objects; has a one-to-many relationship with **PARTCOL$**.
PENDING_SESSIONS$	Child table for **PENDING_TRANS$**.
PENDING_SUB_SESSIONS$	Child table for **PENDING_SESSIONS$**.
PENDING_TRANS$	Table of pending or in-doubt transactions.
PROCEDURE$	Table of database procedures.
PROFILE$	Table of database profile resource mappings.
PROFNAME$	Table of database profile names.
PROPS$	Table of database fixed properties.
RESOURCE_COST$	Table of resource costs used with profiles.
RESOURCE_MAP	Maps resource numbers to resource names.
SEG$	Maps all database segments.
SEQ$	Shows all database sequences.
SLOG$	Shows all snapshots on local masters.
SNAP$	Shows all local snapshots.
SNAP_COLMAP$	Contains snapshot aliasing information.
SOURCE$	Stores source code for all stored objects in the database.
SYN$	Shows all synonyms in the database.
SYSAUTH$	Shows all system privilege grants for the database.
SYSTEM_PRIVILEGE_MAP	Maps system privilege numbers to privilege names.
TAB$	Table of all database tables.
TABLE_PRIVILEGE_MAP	Maps table privilege numbers to table privilege names.
TABPART$	Contains information on all table partitions.

(continued)

Table 7.1 Some of the dollar tables and their descriptions *(continued)*.	
Table Name	**Description**
TRIGGER$	Contains all trigger definitions for the database.
TRIGGERCOL$	Maps triggers to the columns they work against.
TRUSTED_LIST$	Lists trusted users for trusted DB links in Trusted Oracle.
TS$	Shows all tablespaces for the database.
TSQ$	Shows all tablespace quota grants in the database.
TYPE$	Contains data on all **TYPE**s (UDTs) defined in the database.
TYPED_VIEW$	Contains information on typed views (used to map relational tables into object-oriented structures).
TYPE_MISC$	Table of miscellaneous type data (UDT).
UET$	Shows all used extents in the database.
UGROUP$	Contains information on rollback segment groups.
UNDO$	Shows all rollback segments for the database.
USER$	Shows all user definitions for the database.
VIEW$	Shows all view definitions for the database.
_default_auditing_options_	Maps all default auditing option numbers to names.

The Data Dictionary User Views: DBA_, USER_, and ALL_

Usually the view hierarchy flows from the C structs to the **V$** DPTs and from the dollar tables to the **DBA_**, **USER_**, and **ALL_** views. Sometimes shortcuts are taken and the C structs and dollar tables are both used, but rarely. Generally, the **DBA_** and other views of their type are based on the dollar tables.

The **DBA_** views are the DBA's windows into the data dictionary. These views contain the condensed versions of the dollar tables in readable format. The **USER_** views provide a window into the user-owned object details in the data dictionary, and the **ALL_** views contain information on every object that the user has access to or has the privilege of using. In most cases, the views in the different hierarchies are identical except that a nonmeaningful column (such as **OWNER** in the **USER_** views) may be excluded.

You usually keep the **DBA_** views from users by not declaring public synonyms against them. However, a knowledgeable user, if they want or need to, can get information from the views with a query, using the SYS schema prefix.

For the purpose of the exam, you can safely assume the views to be identical (unless the question is on how they differ!) and apply information gleaned about the **DBA_** views to the others.

In this section, we limit our discussion to the **DBA_** views. Table 7.2 lists some of these and their purposes.

For the most part, the names of the views are self-explanatory. For example, the **DBA_TABLES** view shows the details of all tables in the database. However, although some may have accurate names, they still may confuse inexperienced DBAs. For example, views with the word "RESOURCE" in them apply to database profiles because resources are the part and parcel of profiles.

Table 7.2 Some Oracle8i DBA views and their descriptions.	
View Name	**Description**
DBA_BLOCKERS	Contains information on all sessions that are blocking other sessions. Built by the catblock.sql script.
DBA_CATALOG	Shows all database tables, views, synonyms, and sequences.
DBA_CLUSTERS	Shows descriptions of all clusters in the database.
DBA_CLUSTER_HASH_EXPRESSIONS	Shows hash functions for all clusters.
DBA_CLU_COLUMNS	Maps table columns to cluster columns.
DBA_COL_COMMENTS	Lists all entered column comments for all tables and views.
DBA_COL_DESCRIPTION	Shows descriptions of columns of all tables and views.
DBA_COL_PRIVS	Shows all grants on columns in the database.
DBA_COLL_TYPES	Contains information on all collection types, such as nested tables and **VARRAY**s.
DBA_CONSTRAINTS	Shows constraint definitions on all tables.
DBA_CONS_COLUMNS	Contains information about accessible columns in constraint definitions.
DBA_DATA_FILES	Contains information about database files.
DBA_DB_LINKS	Shows all database links in the database.
DBA_DDL_LOCKS	Contains information on all database DDL locks; built by the catblock.sql script.
DBA_DML_LOCKS	Contains information on all database DML locks; built by the catblock.sql script.

(continued)

Table 7.2 Some Oracle8i DBA views and their descriptions *(continued)*.

View Name	Description
DBA_DEPENDENCIES	Shows dependencies to and from objects.
DBA_ERRORS	Shows current errors on all stored objects in the database.
DBA_EXP_FILES	Shows descriptions of export files.
DBA_EXTENTS	Shows extents composing all segments in the database.
DBA_FREE_SPACE	Shows free extents in all tablespaces.
DBA_FREE_SPACE_COALESCED	Shows statistics on coalesced space in tablespaces.
DBA_INDEXES	Shows descriptions of all indexes in the database.
DBA_IND_COLUMNS	Shows columns composing indexes on all tables and clusters.
DBA_IND_PARTITIONS	Contains information on all index partitions in the database.
DBA_JOBS	Shows all jobs in the database.
DBA_JOBS_RUNNING	Shows all jobs in the database that are currently running; joins **V$LOCK** and **JOB$**.
DBA_LGLLOCK	Contains information on internal KGL locks; built by the catblock.sql script.
DBA_LOBS	Contains information on all database **LOBs** (Large Objects, such as **BLOB**, **CLOB**, and **NCLOB** data types).
DBA_LOCK	Contains information on all locks or latches and all outstanding requests for locks or latches in the database; created by catblock.sql.
DBA_LOCK_INTERNAL	Contains information on all database internal locks; built by the catblock.sql script.
DBA_NESTED_TABLES	Contains information on all nested table objects.
DBA_OBJECTS	Shows all objects in the database.
DBA_OBJECT_SIZE	Shows sizes, in bytes, of various PL/SQL objects.
DBA_PART_COL_STATISTICS	Contains information on all the partition key columns in the database, as well as their histogram information.
DBA_PART_HISTOGRAMS	Contains information on all partitioned table histograms.
DBA_PART_INDEXES	Contains information on all partitioned indexes in the database.

(continued)

Table 7.2   Some Oracle8i DBA views and their descriptions *(continued)*.

View Name	Description
DBA_PART_KEY_COLUMNS	Contains information on all partition keys in the database.
DBA_PART_TABLES	Contains information on all partitioned tables in the database.
DBA_PROFILES	Displays all profiles and their limits.
DBA_ROLES	Shows all roles that exist in the database.
DBA_ROLE_PRIVS	Shows roles granted to users and roles.
DBA_ROLLBACK_SEGS	Shows descriptions of rollback segments.
DBA_SEGMENTS	Shows storage allocated for all database segments.
DBA_SEQUENCES	Shows descriptions of all sequences in the database.
DBA_SOURCE	Shows the source of all stored objects in the database.
DBA_SYNONYMS	Shows all synonyms in the database.
DBA_SYS_PRIVS	Shows system privileges granted to users and roles.
DBA_TABLES	Shows descriptions of all tables in the database.
DBA_TABLESPACES	Shows descriptions of all tablespaces.
DBA_TAB_COLUMNS	Shows columns of user's tables, views, and clusters.
DBA_TAB_COL_STATISTICS	Contains statistical data for each column in each table in the database.
DBA_TAB_COMMENTS	Contains all table-level comments for the database.
DBA_TAB_HISTOGRAMS	Contains a row for each table that is using a histogram in the database.
DBA_TAB_PARTITIONS	Contains information on all partitions for all partitioned tables in the database.
DBA_TAB_PRIVS	Shows all grants on objects in the database.
DBA_TRIGGERS	Shows all triggers in the database.
DBA_TRIGGER_COLS	Shows column usage in all triggers.
DBA_TS_QUOTAS	Shows tablespace quotas for all users.
DBA_UPDATABLE_COLUMNS	Shows descriptions of database view updatable columns.
DBA_USERS	Contains information about all users of the database.
DBA_VIEWS	Shows text of all views in the database.
DBA_WAITERS	Contains information on all sessions that are waiting on a lock, as well as the session they are waiting on; built by the catblock.sql script.

Oracle Add-On Tables and Utility Scripts

Numerous scripts are housed in the $ORACLE_HOME/rdbms/admin directory on Unix and in the %ORACLE_HOME%\rdbms80\Admin directories on Windows 98 and Windows NT. Many scripts are automatically run by the catalog.sql and catproc.sql scripts during automated database builds or must be run manually during a manual build; others are optional. The optional scripts provide help in tuning the database, checking lock problems, and adding useful tables that a DBA should know about.

The catalog.sql script creates all of the commonly used data dictionary views. Scripts such as cataudit.sql (which creates the audit tables and is run by catproc.sql) have their antiscripts; for example, the antiscript for cataudit.sql is catnoaud.sql. Generally, an antiscript will have "no" embedded in its name and will be used to undo whatever its opposite script performed.

The catproc.sql script also runs virtually all of the dbms*.sql and prvt*.plb scripts, including dbmsutil.sql, which builds the **DBMS_APPLICATION_INFO** package and other useful utilities. The following scripts are considered extra but are extremely useful:

➤ *utlchain.sql*—This script creates the default table for storing the output of the **ANALYZE... LIST CHAINED ROWS** command.

➤ *utldtree.sql*—This procedure, view, and temporary table allows you to see all objects that are (recursively) dependent on the given object. Note that you'll see only objects for which you have permission.

➤ *utlbstat.sql and utlestat.sql*—These are companion scripts. The utlestat.sql script generates the delta statistics based on the initial statistics loaded using utlbstat.sql. These scripts are used to generate the report.txt output file of statistics used for tuning.

➤ *utlexcpt.sql*—This script creates the **EXCEPTIONS** table used to hold table-entry information that causes conflicts when you're creating constraints. The row ID, table name, owner, and violated constraints are listed.

➤ *utllockt.sql*—This script generates a simple lock wait-for graph. This script prints the sessions in the system that are waiting for locks and the locks that they are waiting for. The printout is tree structured. If a session ID is printed immediately below and to the right of another session, it's waiting for that session. The session IDs printed on the left side of the page are the ones everyone is waiting for.

➤ *dbmspool.sql and prvtpool.plb*—These scripts build the **DBMS_SHARED_POOL** package of procedures for managing the shared pool. This package contains procedures for monitoring and pinning objects such as large packages or procedures in the shared pool.

➤ *utltkprf.sql*—This script grants public access to all views used by **TKPROF** with the **verbose=y** option, and it creates the **TKPROFER** role.

➤ *utlxplan.sql*—This script creates the table (**PLAN_TABLE**) that is used by the **EXPLAIN PLAN** statement. The **EXPLAIN** statement used in the **SET AUTOTRACE ON** command in SQL*Plus requires the presence of this table to store the descriptions of the row sources. The data in **PLAN_TABLE** is used to query and evaluate SQL statements using the **EXPLAIN** clause with the **AUTOTRACE** command, without using tracing or **TKPROF**.

➤ *catblock.sql*—This script creates many useful views about database locks. These views are:

➤ **DBA_KGLLOCK**

➤ **DBA_LOCK** (with synonym **DBA_LOCKS**)

➤ **DBA_LOCK_INTERNAL**

➤ **DBA_DML_LOCKS**

➤ **DBA_DDL_LOCKS**

➤ **DBA_WAITERS**

➤ **DBA_BLOCKERS**

The creation of a database is not complete until several scripts have been run. These scripts create the data dictionary views and install the procedure options and utilities. The catalog.sql script creates the most commonly used data dictionary views. The catproc.sql script creates the procedural options and utilities (**DBMS_** packages). In addition to these "must have" scripts, you should also run the catblock.sql, the dbmspool.sql, and the prvtpool.plb scripts. I also suggest that you run the catparr.sql script, which installs the parallel server views, because some of these views are useful for tuning purposes.

Exam questions about the data dictionary and Oracle internals will mostly be in the realm of tuning and monitoring. Your biggest problem will be that you'll tend to outsmart yourself. You'll say, "Naw, the answer can't be that, that's too easy." Remember, the data dictionary was designed to be easy to use (at least at the higher levels), so objects are named for the items they contain.

An example of what I'm talking about is the use of the **DBA_** views. If you review, you'll notice a trend: **DBA_TABLES** monitors all tables,

USER_TABLES monitors a single user's tables, and **ALL_TABLES** monitors all tables that a user has access to. Likewise, the **V$** views are named for the functions they perform; the **V$DBFILES** view shows database data files, **V$INSTANCE** gives instance-specific values, **V$SESSION** monitors sessions, and so forth. With a little experience, and by keeping your head, you can derive most of the answers from the questions.

Practice Questions

Question 1

> Which data dictionary view would you query to display information related to profiles?
>
> O a. **RESOURCE_COST**
> O b. **USER_USERS**
> O c. **DBA_CONSTRAINTS**
> O d. **USER_CONSTRAINTS**

The correct answer is a. This is a trick question because it involves one of the few tables that don't reflect its true purpose, even though its name is accurate. To answer this question, you need to know what a profile is and know that it uses values called resources. Once you know that a profile has resources assigned to it, the only one possible answer is a, **RESOURCE_COST**.

Question 2

> Which view could you query to display users with **CREATE PROCEDURE** privileges?
>
> O a. **DBA_USER_PRIVS**
> O b. **DBA_SYS_PRIVS**
> O c. **DBA_COL_PRIVS**
> O d. **USER_TAB_PRIVS_RECEIVED**

The correct answer is b. If you know that **CREATE PROCEDURE** is a SYSTEM-level privilege, you should know that you'll query the **DBA_SYS_PRIVS** view. This question can be considered a trick question. A quick glance and a general knowledge of how Oracle names work might lead you to choose answer a, **DBA_USER_PRIVS**. However, this view doesn't exist. Once you eliminate a, you can also quickly eliminate answers c and d because they deal with column (**COL**) and table (**TAB**) privileges.

Question 3

Which category of data dictionary views does not have an **OWNER** column?

○ a. **USER_**.

○ b. **DBA_**.

○ c. **ALL_**.

○ d. All categories of data dictionary views have an **OWNER** column.

The correct answer is a, **USER_**. Because the **USER_** views are for objects in which the user is the owner, an **OWNER** column isn't needed. Answer b is incorrect because **DBA_** views show all objects for which they were created, and an **OWNER** column would be mandatory. Likewise, because the **ALL_** views show all objects for which a user has access, an **OWNER** column is required in this type of view as well. Therefore, answer c is incorrect. You should know that answer d is incorrect.

Question 4

Which data dictionary view could a user query to display the number of bytes charged to their username?

○ a. **ALL_USERS**.

○ b. **USER_USERS**.

○ c. **DBA_TS_QUOTAS**.

○ d. **USER_TS_QUOTAS**.

○ e. Only the DBA can display the number of bytes charged to a user.

The correct answer is d. This question refers to a quota. Once you understand this, you can apply the naming convention rules. The question asks what data dictionary view can a *user* query. This means that we're looking for a **USER_** view. Quotas are placed on tablespaces, so we're looking for a view for tablespaces (**TS_**) and a view about quotas. The only view name that meets the above criteria is answer d, **USER_TS_QUOTAS**.

Question 5

Which view would you query to display the users who have been granted **SYSDBA** and **SYSOPER** system privileges?

○ a. **USER_USERS**

○ b. **ALL_USERS**

○ c. **V$PWFILE_USERS**

○ d. **DBA_USERS**

The correct answer is c, **V$PWFILE_USERS**. This view is used only to identify users who've been granted **SYSDBA** and **SYSOPER**. If you know the **DBA_USERS** view, you know that it contains a username, default and **TEMP** tablespaces, a profile assignment, and other user-related data, but it contains no privilege information or grant information. Therefore, any views related to the **DBA_** view (**USER_USERS** or **ALL_USERS**) won't have any privilege or grant information. With these two tidbits, we've eliminated three of four answers. In this case, we are left with answer c.

Question 6

Which script file creates the base data dictionary tables?

○ a. utlmontr.sql

○ b. catexp.sql

○ c. sql.bsq

○ d. cataud.sql

○ e. catproc.sql

The correct answer is c, sql.bsq. Again, if you don't know the answer right off, with a little name sleuthing, you can eliminate the incorrect answers. You should realize that the utlmontr.sql script is probably for utilities and concerns monitoring, not data dictionary base tables. The catexp.sql script is probably about catalogs (that is, views or tables) and exports. Again, this is not a data dictionary base table type of item. The cataud.sql script deals with a catalog and probably auditing. Finally, you could venture an educated guess that the catproc.sql script concerns catalogs and procedures, not a base-level item. This leaves the sql.bsq script, answer c. One way to remember that sql.bsq is about data dictionary base tables is to equate the "b" in bsq with base.

Question 7

Which package can you use to pin large objects in the library cache?

○ a. **STANDARD**

○ b. **DBMS_STANDARD**

○ c. **DIUTL**

○ d. **DBMS_SHARED_POOL**

The correct answer is d. This question requires you to remember that the library cache is another name for the shared pool. The only answer that concerns the shared pool is d, **DBMS_SHARED_POOL**. The **DBMS_SHARED_POOL** package is used to monitor, pin and unpin stored objects such as packages, procedures, functions, triggers, sequences and cursors in the shared pool. The specific procedure in **DBMS_SHARED_POOL** that performs the pinning operation is the **DBMS_SHARED_POOL.KEEP** procedure.

Question 8

Which Oracle fixed view can you query to get the status of media recovery?

○ a. **V$CONTROLFILE**

○ b. **V$RECOVERY_FILE_STATUS**

○ c. **V$DATAFILE**

○ d. **V$RECOVERY_STATUS**

The correct answer is d. The **V$RECOVERY_STATUS** view shows the status of media recovery. In this question, you have to answer the question exactly. Both **V$RECOVERY_FILE_STATUS** and **V$RECOVERY_STATUS** show recovery status, so we can eliminate the other V$ DPTs shown by using name conventions. However, **V$RECOVERY_FILE_STATUS** shows the status of the database's data files during recovery, so that answer is incorrect.

Need To Know More?

Ault, Michael R. *Oracle8i Administration and Management.* John Wiley & Sons. New York, NY. 2000. ISBN 0-471-35453-8. This book covers virtually all aspects of Oracle8i administration, including the definitions of all **DBA_**, **V$**, and **$** tables, as well as other data-dictionary related topics.

Oracle8i Reference Release 2 (8.1.6). Oracle Corporation, Redwood Shores, CA. December, 1999. Part Number A76961-01. This Oracle manual provides information about the **V$** views and the **DBA_** views and their uses.

Adams, Steve, *Oracle8i Internal Services.* O'Reilly and Associates. Cambridge, MA. November, 1999. ISBN 1-565-92598-X. Not for the faint of heart. A down-and-dirty look at the Oracle internals. Adams has dissected the **X$** and other important system structures for Oracle and shows it all.

Controlling User Access: DCL Commands

Terms you'll need to understand:

✓ Grants

✓ System privileges

✓ Object privileges

✓ Roles

✓ Profiles

Techniques you'll need to master:

✓ Creating and managing users

✓ Granting system and object privileges

✓ Revoking grants

✓ Creating and granting roles

✓ Understanding the use of profiles for password and
resource management

Database access begins with the creation of user records. The users are then assigned—either directly or through roles—specific rights to perform actions. The rights to perform actions are called *system* and *object privileges*. System privileges are rights to perform actions in the database. Object privileges are access rights to an object (table, index, synonym, procedure, and so on) within the database, including the columns within tables.

In this chapter, I explain how you use object and system privileges, along with roles, to manage users and objects. In the process of explaining the use of the Data Control Language (DCL) commands, I also cover the creation, alteration, and dropping of users. Although this involves some inclusion of DDL commands, I believe this isn't catastrophic because the DDL involved is central to the DCL commands discussed.

Users

For a user to access your database, an account must be created in the Oracle database for the user. The exceptions to this are the **SYS, SYSTEM,** and several other users that are created by Oracle when the database is created. In the sections that follow, I discuss the creation, alteration, and dropping of users for the Oracle database.

Creating Users

To create a user, you must have the **CREATE USER** privilege. You can create users with Server Manager or at the command line in SQL*Plus. The command syntax for creating a user is illustrated in Figure 8.1.

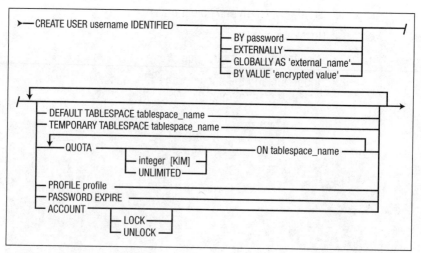

Figure 8.1   The syntax for creating a user.

Here is an example:

```
CREATE USER  james  IDENTIFIED BY    abc1
DEFAULT TABLESPACE  users
TEMPORARY TABLESPACE  temp
PASSWORD EXPIRE
QUOTA  1M ON  users
PROFILE  enduser  ;
```

You need to assign each new user a password or indicate that operating system authentication will be used. Passwords are stored in the database in encrypted format and cannot be read by any user. The use of operating system authentication means that after a user has logged in at the operating system level, no username or password will be required when that user logs in to the Oracle database. Users who are not assigned an Oracle password are designated as **IDENTIFIED EXTERNALLY**. Oracle depends on the operating system for authentication of the user. To use external authentication with other than the default username prefix of "OPS$", you must set the **OS_AUTHENT_PREFIX** in the database parameter file. In Oracle8 and Oracle8i, you can also create the user in a locked state or with a pre-expired password. The **BY VALUE** clause allows you to reset a user's password to a previous encrypted value; this clause is used when you're transferring a user manually from one database to another.

Password expiry options are set using a **PROFILE**, which I discuss later.

The **IDENTIFIED GLOBALLY** clause is used to tell Oracle that the user authentication is obtained from a central authority, such as the Oracle Security Server.

When you create a user, you can designate a specific tablespace to be the *default tablespace* for that user. The designation of a default tablespace means that all the objects created by that user will be placed in that tablespace unless the user specifically indicates that the database object be placed in another tablespace. If no default tablespace is indicated for a user, the system tablespace will be the default for that user.

When you create a user, you can also designate a specific tablespace to be the *temporary tablespace*. The temporary tablespace is used for any database actions that require the use of a workspace for storing intermediate results of actions, such as sorting.

If no temporary tablespace is indicated for a user, the system tablespace will be used. When you designate a default tablespace, a temporary tablespace, or a quota on a tablespace, this does not implicitly grant any system or object privileges on the default tablespace, but the user is granted unlimited quota on the designated temporary tablespace. You can use the **QUOTA** clause to give a user permission to create objects in tablespaces.

Note: I suggest that the only users who are left with the system tablespace as their default tablespace are users—such as SYS and DBSNMP—that are created and maintained internally by Oracle processes. All users should have an explicitly assigned temporary tablespace to prevent sorting from occurring in the system tablespace. Another suggestion is to move the AUD$ table into a separate tablespace if auditing is used.

As the database administrator (DBA), you can access the **DBA_USERS** view for information on all users. Each user can access the **USER_USERS** view (which is the same as the **DBA_USERS** view except it leaves out the password field) for information related to them. Table 8.1 shows the data stored in the **DBA_USERS** view.

To enable a user to create objects in a tablespace, you need to specify a quota for that user on that tablespace. The tablespace quota can be limited to a specific number of kilobytes or megabytes or can be designated as unlimited. An unlimited quota indicates that the user can have any portion of a tablespace that is not already in use by another user. If the user is not assigned the **UNLIMITED TABLESPACE** system privilege, and the assigned limit is reached, the user will no longer be able to create additional objects or insert rows into any objects they own in that tablespace. One thing to remember is that the **RESOURCE** and

Table 8.1 Data dictionary view for user data.	
Column	Definition
DBA_USERS	
username	Oracle login name for the user.
user_id	Oracle unique user id number.
password	An encrypted password or **IDENTIFIED EXTERNALLY**.
account_status	The account status when password expiry functions are used.
lock_date	Date that the expiry function locked the account.
expiry_date	Date that the password will expire if expiry parameters are set.
default_tablespace	Tablespace assigned as the default for the user.
temporary_tablespace	Tablespace assigned for actions requiring a workspace.
created	Date that the user was created within the Oracle database.
initial_rsrc_consumer_group	The resource group that this user is assigned to by default.
external_name	If external validation is used, this user's external name.

DBA roles automatically grant **UNLIMITED TABLESPACE**, so use them only when they're absolutely required.

The **DBA_TS_QUOTAS** view provides tablespace quota information for all users in the database. The **USER_TS_QUOTAS** view provides tablespace quota information for the current user and contains the same information without the user name, because it is restricted to the user who queries the view. When you query **DBA_TS_QUOTAS** or **USER_TS_QUOTAS**, a designation of −1 in the **max_bytes** and **max_blocks** columns indicates that the user has unlimited quota on that tablespace. Table 8.2 shows the data dictionary views associated with quotas.

Altering Users

To change a user record, you must have the **ALTER USER** privilege. You can alter users with Oracle Enterprise Manager (OEM) or at the command line in SQL*Plus or svrmgrl. The command line syntax for altering a user is shown in Figure 8.2.

Here is an example:

```
ALTER  USER bill IDENTIFIED BY  xyz2
DEFAULT TABLESPACE  users
TEMPORARY TABLESPACE temp
QUOTA  1M  ON  users
PROFILE  enduser
DEFAULT ROLE ALL
ACCOUNT UNLOCK;
```

After a user is created, the only thing that a person with **ALTER USER** privilege cannot alter for that user is the username. The password, default tablespace, temporary tablespace, quota on a tablespace, profile, locked state, global name, password expiration state, and default role can all be altered by someone with the **ALTER USER** system privilege.

Table 8.2 Data dictionary view DBA_TS_QUOTAS.	
Column	**Definition**
DBA_TS_QUOTAS	
tablespace_name	Name of the tablespace
username	Name of the user
bytes	Number of bytes assigned to that user
max_bytes	Maximum number of bytes allowed for the user, or −1 for unlimited
blocks	Number of blocks assigned to that user
max_blocks	Maximum number of blocks allowed for the user, or −1 for unlimited

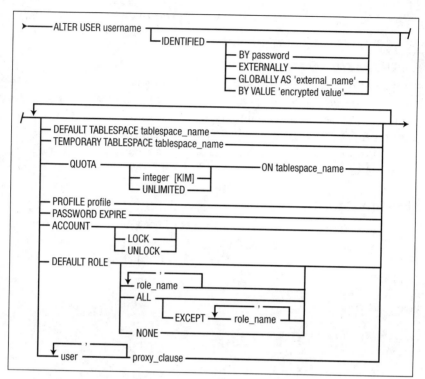

Figure 8.2 The syntax for altering a user.

Each user can alter the Oracle password you initially assigned to that user record when you created it, provided that the user is not identified externally (via the operating system). In addition to the end user, users with the **ALTER USER** system privilege can issue the **ALTER USER** command to change any user's password. A user with the **ALTER USER** system privilege can also change the use of operating system authentication. Any changes to the password will take effect the next time that user logs into Oracle.

When you change the default tablespace for a user, all future objects created by that user will be created in the new default tablespace you designated (unless otherwise specified by the user when the object is created). Remember that the user must have a quota in the tablespace to create new objects in that tablespace. If a user reaches the maximum number of bytes assigned (specified in the quota), then only a user with the **ALTER USER** system privileges will be able to increase the quota limit for the user.

The **proxy_clause** lets you control the ability of a **proxy** (an application or application server) to connect as the specified user and to activate all, some, or none of the user's roles. This is not covered on the exam.

Dropping Users

To drop a user, you must have the **DROP USER** system privilege. You can drop users with Server Manager or at the command line in SQL*Plus. The command line syntax for dropping a user is illustrated in Figure 8.3.

Here is an example:

```
DROP USER edward CASCADE;
```

If a user owns any database objects, you can drop that user only by including the **CASCADE** keyword in the **DROP USER** command. The **DROP USER** command with the **CASCADE** keyword drops the user and all objects owned by that user. If you are using OEM to drop a user, you need to indicate that the associated schema objects be included in the command to drop the user. If a user owns objects and you fail to include **CASCADE**, you will receive an error message, and the user will not be dropped. If a user is currently connected to the database, you cannot drop that user until she exits. After a user is dropped, all information on that user and all objects owned by that user are removed from the database.

After you have issued the command to drop a user, you cannot perform a rollback to recreate the user and his objects. **DROP USER** is a DDL command, which cannot be rolled back.

If you need the objects created by a user you want to drop, you can revoke the **CREATE SESSION** system privilege to prevent the user from logging on, instead of dropping the user. You can also copy the objects to another user by importing the objects from an export made before you drop the user. To prevent the problem of dropping a user without losing your application tables, all application tables should be owned by a separate application schema instead of by an actual database user schema.

Grants

Two types of privileges can be granted:

➤ System privileges

➤ Object privileges

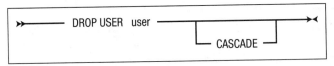

Figure 8.3 The syntax for the **DROP USER** command.

System privileges enable a user to perform a particular system wide action or to perform a particular action on a particular type of object. For example, the privilege to create a table (**CREATE TABLE**) or to insert rows into any table (**INSERT ANY TABLE**) are system privileges.

Object privileges enable a user to perform a particular action on a specific object, including tables, views, sequences, procedures, functions, and packages. For example, the privilege to insert rows into a particular table is an object privilege. Object privilege grants always include the name of the object for which the privilege is granted. Object privileges extend down to the level of individual columns in a table. These privileges are discussed in the following sections.

System Privileges

All users require the **CREATE SESSION** privilege to access the database. This privilege is automatically granted to all users in the **CONNECT** role grant when you use OEM to create the users. If you create the user in command-line mode, you must remember to explicitly grant each user the **CREATE SESSION** system privilege either directly or through a role. Figure 8.4 shows the syntax for the **GRANT** command. Here is an example of the command used to grant **CREATE SESSION** and **CREATE TABLE** privileges:

```
GRANT  create session, create table
TO  annie
WITH ADMIN OPTION;
```

Rules about system privilege grants also include the granting of roles that have been created.

System privileges can be granted to other users when the initial grant made includes **WITH ADMIN OPTION**.

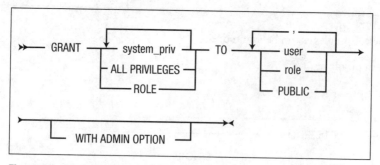

Figure 8.4   The syntax for the **GRANT** command for system privileges.

More than 80 distinct privileges exist—most of which are self-explanatory. Table 8.3 lists all the system privileges, as listed in RevealNet's Oracle Administration product (used with its permission).

Table 8.3   Oracle database system privileges.

System Privilege	Allows Grantee To . . .
For Clusters:	
CREATE CLUSTER	Create clusters in grantee's schema.
CREATE ANY CLUSTER	Create a cluster in any schema except **SYS**. Behaves similarly to **CREATE ANY TABLE**.
ALTER ANY CLUSTER	Alter clusters in any schema except **SYS**.
DROP ANY CLUSTER	Drop clusters in any schema except **SYS**.
For Contexts:	
CREATE ANY CONTEXT	Create any context namespace.
DROP ANY CONTEXT	Drop any context namespace.
For Database Links:	
CREATE DATABASE LINK	Create private database links in grantee's schema.
CREATE PUBLIC DATABASE LINK	Create public database links.
DROP PUBLIC DATABASE LINK	Drop public database links.
For Databases:	
ALTER DATABASE	Alter the database.
ALTER SYSTEM	Issue **ALTER SYSTEM** statements.
AUDIT SYSTEM	Issue **AUDIT sql_statements** statements.
For Directories:	
CREATE ANY DIRECTORY	Create directory database objects.
DROP ANY DIRECTORY	Drop directory database objects.
For Dimensions:	
CREATE DIMENSION	Create dimensions in the grantee's schema.
CREATE ANY DIMENSION	Create dimensions in any schema.
ALTER ANY DIMENSION	Alter dimensions in any schema.
DROP ANY DIMENSION	Drop dimensions in any schema.
For Indexes:	
CREATE INDEX	In the grantee's schema, create an index on any table in the grantee's schema, or create a domain index.

(continued)

Table 8.3   Oracle database system privileges *(continued)*.

System Privilege	Allows Grantee To . . .
CREATE ANY INDEX	In any schema except **SYS**, create a domain index or create an index on any table.
ALTER ANY INDEX	Alter indexes in any schema except **SYS**.
DROP ANY INDEX	Drop indexes in any schema except **SYS**.
For Indextypes:	
CREATE INDEXTYPE	Create an indextype in the grantee's schema.
CREATE ANY INDEXTYPE	Create an indextype in any schema.
ALTER ANY INDEXTYPE	Modify indextypes in any schema.
DROP ANY INDEXTYPE	Drop an indextype in any schema.
EXECUTE ANY INDEXTYPE	Reference an indextype in any schema.
For Libraries:	
CREATE LIBRARY	Create external procedure/function libraries in grantee's schema.
CREATE ANY LIBRARY	Create external procedure/function libraries in any schema except **SYS**.
DROP LIBRARY	Drop external procedure/function libraries in the grantee's schema.
DROP ANY LIBRARY	Drop external procedure/function libraries in any schema except **SYS**.
For Materialized Views (which are identical to SNAPSHOTS)	
CREATE MATERIALIZED VIEW	Create a materialized view in the grantee's schema.
CREATE ANY MATERIALIZED VIEW	Create materialized views in any schema.
ALTER ANY MATERIALIZED VIEW	Alter materialized views in any schema.
DROP ANY MATERIALIZED VIEW	Drop materialized views in any schema.
QUERY REWRITE	Enable rewrite using a materialized view or create a function-based index, when that materialized view or index references tables and views that are in the grantee's own schema.
GLOBAL QUERY REWRITE	Enable rewrite using a materialized view or create a function-based index, when that materialized view or index references tables or views in any schema.
For Operators:	
CREATE OPERATOR	Create an operator and its bindings in the grantee's schema.
CREATE ANY OPERATOR	Create an operator and its bindings in any schema.

(continued)

Table 8.3 Oracle database system privileges *(continued)*.	
System Privilege	**Allows Grantee To . . .**
DROP ANY OPERATOR	Drop an operator in any schema.
EXECUTE ANY OPERATOR	Reference an operator in any schema.
For Outlines:	
CREATE ANY OUTLINE	Create outlines that can be used in any schema that uses outlines.
ALTER ANY OUTLINE	Modify outlines.
DROP ANY OUTLINE	Drop outline.
For Procedures:	
CREATE PROCEDURE	Create stored procedures, functions, and packages in grantee's schema.
CREATE ANY PROCEDURE	Create stored procedures, functions, and packages in any schema except **SYS**.
ALTER ANY PROCEDURE	Alter stored procedures, functions, or packages in any schema except **SYS**.
DROP ANY PROCEDURE	Drop stored procedures, functions, or packages in any schema except **SYS**.
EXECUTE ANY PROCEDURE	Execute procedures or functions (standalone or packaged). Refer to public package variables in any schema except **SYS**.
For Profiles:	
CREATE PROFILE	Create profiles.
ALTER PROFILE	Alter profiles.
DROP PROFILE	Drop profiles.
For Roles:	
CREATE ROLE	Create roles.
ALTER ANY ROLE	Alter any role in the database.
DROP ANY ROLE	Drop roles.
GRANT ANY ROLE	Grant any role in the database.
For Rollback Segments:	
CREATE ROLLBACK SEGMENT	Create rollback segments.
ALTER ROLLBACK SEGMENT	Alter rollback segments.
DROP ROLLBACK SEGMENT	Drop rollback segments.
For Sequences:	
CREATE SEQUENCE	Create sequences in grantee's schema.

(continued)

Table 8.3 Oracle database system privileges *(continued).*

System Privilege	Allows Grantee To . . .
CREATE ANY SEQUENCE	Create sequences in any schema except **SYS**.
ALTER ANY SEQUENCE	Alter any sequence in the database.
DROP ANY SEQUENCE	Drop sequences in any schema except **SYS**.
SELECT ANY SEQUENCE	Refer to sequences in any schema except **SYS**.
For Sessions:	
CREATE SESSION	Connect to the database.
ALTER RESOURCE COST	Set costs for session resources.
ALTER SESSION	Issue **ALTER SESSION** statements.
RESTRICTED SESSION	Log on after the instance is started using the SQL*Plus **STARTUP RESTRICT** statement.
For Snapshots:	
CREATE SNAPSHOT	Create snapshots in grantee's schema.
CREATE ANY SNAPSHOT	Create snapshots in any schema except **SYS**.
ALTER ANY SNAPSHOT	Alter any snapshot in the database.
DROP ANY SNAPSHOT	Drop snapshots in any schema except **SYS**.
For Synonyms:	
CREATE SYNONYM	Create synonyms in grantee's schema.
CREATE ANY SYNONYM	Create private synonyms in any schema except **SYS**.
CREATE PUBLIC SYNONYM	Create public synonyms.
DROP ANY SYNONYM	Drop private synonyms in any schema except **SYS**.
DROP PUBLIC SYNONYM	Drop public synonyms.
For Tables:	
CREATE ANY TABLE	Create tables in any schema except **SYS**. The owner of the schema containing the table must have space quota on the tablespace to contain the table.
ALTER ANY TABLE	Alter any table or view in the schema.
BACKUP ANY TABLE	Use the Export utility to incrementally export objects from the schema of other users.
DELETE ANY TABLE	Delete rows from tables, table partitions, or views in any schema except **SYS**.
DROP ANY TABLE	Drop or truncate tables or table partitions in any schema except **SYS**.

(continued)

Table 8.3   Oracle database system privileges *(continued).*

System Privilege	Allows Grantee To . . .
INSERT ANY TABLE	Insert rows into tables and views in any schema except **SYS**.
LOCK ANY TABLE	Lock tables and views in any schema except **SYS**.
UPDATE ANY TABLE	Update rows in tables and views in any schema except **SYS**.
SELECT ANY TABLE	Query tables, views, or snapshots in any schema except **SYS**.
For Tablespaces:	
CREATE TABLESPACE	Create tablespaces.
ALTER TABLESPACE	Alter tablespaces.
DROP TABLESPACE	Drop tablespaces.
MANAGE TABLESPACE	Take tablespaces offline and online, and begin and end tablespace backups.
UNLIMITED TABLESPACE	Use an unlimited amount of any tablespace. This privilege overrides any specific quotas assigned. If you revoke this privilege from a user, the user's schema objects remain, but further tablespace allocation is denied unless authorized by specific tablespace quotas. You cannot grant this system privilege to roles.
For Triggers:	
CREATE TRIGGER	Create a database trigger in grantee's schema.
CREATE ANY TRIGGER	Create database triggers in any schema except **SYS**.
ALTER ANY TRIGGER	Enable, disable, or compile database triggers in any schema except **SYS**.
DROP ANY TRIGGER	Drop database triggers in any schema except **SYS**.
ADMINISTER DATABASE TRIGGER	Create a trigger on **DATABASE**. (You must also have the **CREATE TRIGGER** or **CREATE ANY TRIGGER** privilege.)
For Types:	
CREATE TYPE	Create object types and object type bodies in grantee's schema.
CREATE ANY TYPE	Create object types and object type bodies in any schema except **SYS**.
ALTER ANY TYPE	Alter object types in any schema except **SYS**.
DROP ANY TYPE	Drop object types and object type bodies in any schema except **SYS**.

(continued)

Table 8.3 Oracle database system privileges *(continued)*.

System Privilege	Allows Grantee To ...
EXECUTE ANY TYPE	Use and refer to object types and collection types in any schema except **SYS** and invoke methods of an object type in any schema if you make the grant to a specific user. If you grant **EXECUTE ANY TYPE** to a role, users holding the enabled role will not be able to invoke methods of an object type in any schema.
For Users:	
CREATE USER	Create users. This privilege also allows the creator to assign quotas on any tablespace, set default and temporary tablespaces, and assigns a profile as part of a **CREATE USER** statement.
ALTER USER	Alter any user. This privilege authorizes the grantee to change another user's password or authentication method, assign quotas on any tablespace, set default and temporary tablespaces, and assign a profile and default roles.
BECOME USER	Become another user. (Required by any user performing a full database import.)
DROP USER	Drop users.
For Views:	
CREATE VIEW	Create views in grantee's schema.
CREATE ANY VIEW	Create views in any schema except **SYS**.
DROP ANY VIEW	Drop views in any schema except **SYS**.
Miscellaneous Privileges:	
ANALYZE ANY	Analyze any table, cluster, or index in any schema except **SYS**.
AUDIT ANY	Audit any object in any schema except **SYS** by using **AUDIT schema_objects** statements.
COMMENT ANY TABLE	Comment on any table, view, or column in any schema except **SYS**.
FORCE ANY TRANSACTION	Force the commit or rollback of any in-doubt distributed transaction in the local database. Induce the failure of a distributed transaction.
FORCE TRANSACTION	Force the commit or rollback of grantee's in-doubt distributed transactions in the local database.
GRANT ANY PRIVILEGE	Grant any system privilege.

(continued)

Table 8.3   Oracle database system privileges (continued).

System Privilege	Allows Grantee To ...
SYSDBA	Perform **STARTUP**, **SHUTDOWN**, **ALTER DATABASE** (open, mount, back up, or change character set), **CREATE DATABASE ARCHIVELOG**, and **RECOVERY** operations. Includes the **RESTRICTED SESSION** privilege.
SYSOPER	Perform **STARTUP**, **SHUTDOWN**, **ALTER DATABASE** (open/mount/backup), **ARCHIVELOG**, and **RECOVERY** operations. Includes the **RESTRICTED SESSION** privilege.

As the DBA, you can access the **DBA_SYS_PRIVS** view for information on the system privileges granted to users. The format of this view is shown in Table 8.4.

Users can see information related to them by accessing the corresponding user view: **USER_SYS_PRIVS**.

The rules for how system level grants take effect are easy:

➤ If you grant a privilege to a **user**, the user can immediately exercise the privilege.

➤ If you grant a privilege to a **role**, users who have been granted and have enabled the role can immediately exercise the privilege. Other users who have been granted the role can enable the role and exercise the privilege.

➤ If you grant a privilege to **PUBLIC**, all users can immediately perform operations authorized by the privilege.

Oracle provides a shortcut for specifying all system privileges at once:

➤ Specify **ALL PRIVILEGES** to grant all the system privileges listed in Table 8.3.

The rules for how **ROLE**s are granted are:

➤ If you grant a role to a **user**, the user can immediately enable the role and exercise the privileges in the role's privilege domain.

Table 8.4   Contents of the DBA_SYS_PRIVS data dictionary view.

Column	Definition
grantee	Oracle login name or role that received the privilege.
privilege	The system privilege granted to the user or role.
admin_option	Indicates **YES** if the grantee can pass along the privilege or **NO** if the grantee cannot pass along the system privilege.

➤ If you grant a role to another **role**, users who have been granted the grantee role can enable it and exercise the privileges in the granted role's privilege domain.

➤ If you grant a role to **PUBLIC**, all users can immediately enable the role and exercise the privileges in the role's privilege domain.

Object Privileges

Object privileges define a user's rights on existing database objects. All grants on objects take effect immediately.

To grant an object privilege, you must be the owner of the object, have been granted **WITH GRANT OPTION** on that object for that privilege, or have the system privilege **GRANT ANY PRIVILEGE**. You can also grant access to all users by granting the privilege to **PUBLIC**. Figure 8.5 shows the syntax for the **GRANT** command used to grant object level privileges. The **GRANT** command is also used to grant privileges on **DIRECTORY, JAVA, LIBRARY, TYPE** and other special objects.

Here is an example:

```
GRANT select
ON   bob.emp
TO   derek;
```

As the DBA, you can access the **DBA_TAB_PRIVS** view for information on the object privileges granted to users. You should note that although it is named **DBA_TAB_PRIVS**, this view also includes information on all objects to which

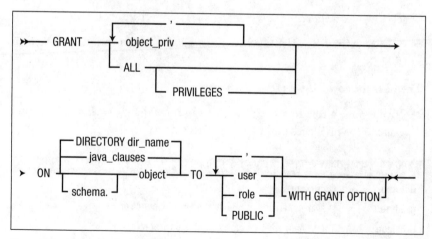

Figure 8.5 The syntax for the **GRANT** command used for a table-level or snapshot-level grant.

Table 8.5 Contents of the DBA_TAB_PRIVS data dictionary view.

Column	Definition
grantee	Oracle login name or role that received the privilege
owner	Owner of the table
table_name	Name of the table, view, Java source, directory, library, package, procedure, function or sequence
grantor	Oracle login name of the person granting the privilege
privilege	System privilege granted to the user
grantable	Indicates **YES** if the grantee can pass along the privilege or **NO** if the grantee cannot pass along the system privilege

privileges may be granted such as procedures, packages, functions, directories, libraries, views and sequences, as well as tables. Table 8.5 shows the contents of this view.

By accessing the corresponding user view **USER_TAB_PRIVS** users can see information on objects for which they are the owner, grantor, or grantee. By using the **ALL_TAB_PRIVS** view, users can see information for all objects for which **PUBLIC** or those users are the grantees.

An object owner can grant the following object privileges to other users:

➤ ALTER

➤ DELETE

➤ INDEX

➤ INSERT

➤ REFERENCES

➤ SELECT

➤ UPDATE

➤ EXECUTE (for stored functions, procedures, packages, libraries, UDTs, operators, and indextypes)

➤ READ (for **DIRECTORY**)

All grants on objects and the revoking of those grants are valid immediately, even if a user is currently logged in to the database. The **SELECT** privilege can be granted only on tables, views, and snapshots. The **EXECUTE** privilege is used for packages, procedures, functions, libraries, UDTs, operators, and indextypes.

Remember that packages, procedures, and functions are always executed with the permissions of the owner of that package, procedure, or function.

By granting other users **INSERT, UPDATE, DELETE,** and **SELECT** privileges on your table, you allow them to perform that action on the table. By granting users the **ALTER** privilege, you allow them to modify the structure of your table or create a trigger on your table. By granting users the **INDEX** privilege, you allow them to create indexes on your table.

The **REFERENCES** privilege differs from the other privileges in that it does not actually grant the capability to change the table or data contained in the table. The **REFERENCES** privilege allows users to create foreign key constraints that refer to your table.

The **READ** privilege is only for **DIRECTORY** objects used to read **BFILE** objects from directories external to the database.

A user can access the **USER_TAB_PRIVS_RECD** view for information on table privileges where that user is the grantee. The corresponding **ALL_TAB_PRIVS_RECD** view includes all grants on objects where that user or **PUBLIC** is the grantee. Table 8.6 shows the contents of the **USER_TAB_PRIVS_RECD** view.

A user can access the **USER_TAB_PRIVS_MADE** view for information on table privileges that he has granted to others. The corresponding **ALL_TAB_PRIVS_MADE** view includes information on all the grants that user has made, as well as grants by others on that user's objects. Table 8.7 shows the contents of the **USER_TAB_PRIVS_MADE** view.

Column Privileges

Only **INSERT, UPDATE,** and **REFERENCES** privileges can be granted at the column level. When granting **INSERT** at the column level, you must include all the **NOT NULL** columns in the row. Figure 8.6 shows the syntax for granting object privileges at the column level.

Table 8.6   Contents of the USER_TAB_PRIVS_RECD data dictionary view.

Column	Definition
owner	Owner of the table
table_name	Name of the table, view, or sequence
grantor	Oracle login name of the person granting the privilege
privilege	System privilege granted to the user
grantable	Indicates **YES** if the grantee can pass along the privilege or **NO** if the grantee cannot pass along the object privilege

Table 8.7	Contents of the USER_TAB_PRIVS_MADE data dictionary view.
Column	**Definition**
grantee	Oracle user granted the privilege
table_name	Name of the table, view, or sequence
grantor	Oracle login name of the person granting the privilege
privilege	System privilege granted to the user
grantable	Indicates **YES** if the grantee can pass along the privilege or **NO** if the grantee cannot pass along the object privilege

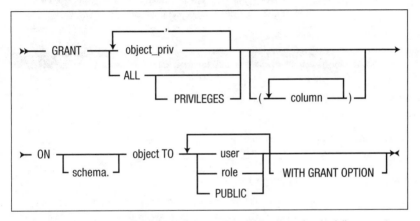

Figure 8.6 The syntax for the **GRANT** command used for column-level privilege grants.

Here is an example:

```
GRANT  update(emp_name)
ON  edwin.emp
TO  joan;
```

As the DBA, you can access the **DBA_COL_PRIVS** view for information on the column-level object privileges granted to users. Table 8.8 shows the contents of the **DBA_COL_PRIVS** view.

Users can access the **USER_COL_PRIVS_RECD** view for information on column-level object privileges that have been granted to them. The **ALL_COL_PRIVS_RECD** view includes information on all column privileges that have been granted to them or to **PUBLIC**. The format of the **USER_COL_PRIVS_RECD** view is shown in Table 8.9.

Users can access the **USER_COL_PRIVS_MADE** view for information on column privileges that they have granted to others. The corresponding **ALL_COL_PRIVS_MADE** view includes information on all columns where

Table 8.8	Contents of the DBA_COL_PRIVS data dictionary view.
Column	**Definition**
grantee	Oracle login name or role that received the privilege
owner	Owner of the table
table_name	Name of the table
column_name	Name of the column
grantor	Oracle login name of the person granting the privilege
privilege	System privilege granted to the user
grantable	Indicates **YES** if the grantee can pass along the privilege or **NO** if the grantee cannot pass along the object privilege

Table 8.9	Contents of the USER_COL_PRIVS_RECD data dictionary view.
Column	**Definition**
owner	Oracle user (schema) that owns the table
table_name	Name of the table
column_name	Name of the column
grantor	Oracle login name of the person granting the privilege
privilege	System privilege granted to the user
grantable	Indicates **YES** if the grantee can pass along the privilege or **NO** if the grantee cannot pass along the column-level object privilege

the user is the owner or the grantor. The contents of the USER_COL_PRIVS_MADE view are shown in Table 8.10.

Users can access information on all columns where they are the grantor, grantee, or owner, or where access has been granted to **PUBLIC** with the corresponding **ALL_TAB_PRIVS_MADE** and **ALL_TAB_PRIVS_RECD** views.

Table 8.10	Contents of the USER_COL_PRIVS_MADE data dictionary view.
Column	**Definition**
grantee	Oracle user granted the privilege
table_name	Name of the table
column_name	Name of the column
grantor	Oracle login name of the person granting the privilege
privilege	System privilege granted to the user
grantable	Indicates **YES** if the grantee can pass along the privilege or **NO** if the grantee cannot pass along the column-level object privilege

View Grants

Views can have the **SELECT, INSERT, UPDATE,** and **DELETE** grants issued against them. To perform **SELECT, INSERT, UPDATE,** or **DELETE** operations against views (where it is allowed), you must grant the privileges for the underlying tables to the users you want to have these privileges.

The information on grants made to views is located in the same views as for tables.

Other Grants

The only allowed grant for sequences is **SELECT.** For procedures, functions, packages, libraries, and user-defined types, you may grant only **EXECUTE** privileges. The only allowed grant for a directory is **READ,** and it is the only object that has a **READ** grant.

Revoking Grants

When you use **WITH ADMIN OPTION** to pass system privileges to others, revoking the system privileges from the original user will cause them to not cascade. The system privileges granted to others must be revoked directly. In contrast, when you use **WITH ADMIN OPTION** to pass object privileges to others, the object privileges are revoked when the grantor's privileges are revoked.

 It is important to note that only object privileges will cascade when revoked; system privileges will not. The revocation of privilege is from the current user down the chain and does not recurse up the chain.

When the **WITH ADMIN OPTION** or **WITH GRANT OPTION** has been included in a grant to another user, the privilege cannot be revoked directly. You must revoke the privilege and then issue another grant without **WITH ADMIN OPTION** or **WITH GRANT OPTION.**

The command-line syntax for revoking a system privilege is shown in Figure 8.7.

In this format, roles are counted the same as system privileges and are grouped with users.

Here are some examples:

```
REVOKE    create table
FROM    judy;

REVOKE create table
FROM developer_role;

REVOKE dba
FROM monitor_role;
```

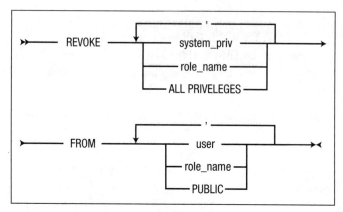

Figure 8.7 The syntax for revoking a system privilege.

To revoke an object privilege, you must be the owner of the object, have used the **WITH GRANT OPTION** privilege to grant that privilege to that user, or have the **GRANT ANY PRIVILEGE** system privilege.

You can revoke object and system privileges with Server Manager or at the command line in SQL*Plus. The command-line syntax for revoking an object privilege is shown in Figure 8.8.

Here is an example:

```
REVOKE  select
ON  mike.emp
FROM  stan;
```

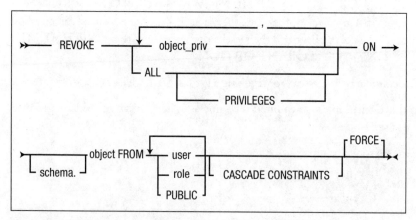

Figure 8.8 The syntax for revoking an object privilege.

When the object privilege **REFERENCES** has been granted, you must specify **CASCADE CONSTRAINTS** to drop the foreign key constraints that were created.

Roles

Using roles has several benefits, including:

➤ Reducing the number of grants and thereby making it easier to manage security

➤ Dynamically changing the privileges for many users with a single grant or revoke

➤ Selectively enabling or disabling privileges and grants, depending on the application

Roles can be used for granting most system and object privileges. Privileges granted through a role cannot be used for creating objects (views, packages, procedures, and functions). You need to grant privileges directly to the user for this.

Creating Roles

A *role* is a collection of grants, privileges, and other roles that can be granted as a unit to users or other roles. In order to use a role, you need to create the role first and then grant system and object privileges to that role. When you create the role, you have three password options:

➤ No authentication

➤ Operating system authentication

➤ Password authentication

You can set operating system authentication either when you create the role or by using the database initialization parameters **OS_ROLES=TRUE** and **REMOTE_OS_ROLES=TRUE**. If you are using the multithreaded server option, you cannot use operating system authentication for roles.

To create a role, you must have the **CREATE ROLE** system privilege. You can create roles with OEM or at the command line in SQL*Plus or svrmgrl. The command-line syntax for creating a role is shown in Figure 8.9.

You can also identify a role globally by using the **GLOBALLY** keyword in the **IDENTIFIED** clause. This means that the role will be authenticated by the Oracle Security Server.

Here is an example:

```
CREATE ROLE  appusers
NOT  IDENTIFIED;
```

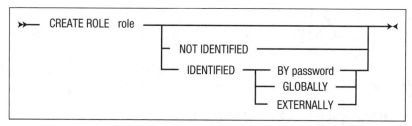

Figure 8.9   The syntax for creating a role.

To alter a role, you must have the **ALTER ANY ROLE** system privilege or have been granted the role with **WITH ADMIN OPTION**. The creator of any role automatically has the **WITH ADMIN OPTION** for that role.

Granting Roles to Users and Privileges to Roles

To grant a role to a user, you must either be the creator of that role or have the **GRANT ANY ROLE** privilege. You can grant roles to users by using OEM or at the command line in SQL*Plus or svrmgrl. Grants to roles will not take effect for a user if that user is currently logged into the database with that role. When the user exits or sets another role, the changes will take effect. After roles have been granted to a user, they can be enabled and disabled.

Figure 8.10 shows the syntax for granting roles to users.

Here is an example:

```
GRANT  enduser
TO  patrick;
```

The command-line syntax for granting privileges to a role is the same as the syntax for granting privileges to a user. Figure 8.11 shows the syntax for granting system privileges to roles.

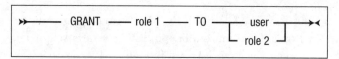

Figure 8.10   The syntax for granting roles to users.

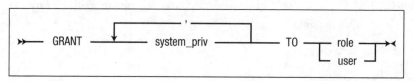

Figure 8.11   The syntax for granting system privileges to roles.

Here is an example:

```
GRANT create session
TO   enduser;
```

Figure 8.12 shows the syntax for granting object privileges to roles.

Here is an example:

```
GRANT select
ON  john.emp
TO  enduser;
```

The only system privilege that cannot be granted to a role is the **UNLIMITED TABLESPACE** grant; however, it is implicitly granted whenever the **DBA** or **RESOURCE** role grant is made to a user. Grants on objects can be passed to other users or to roles if the grantee has been given the **WITH GRANT OPTION** privilege. However, you cannot assign to a role a privilege that includes the **WITH GRANT OPTION** privilege. The **INDEX** and **REFERENCES** privileges cannot be granted to a role; they must be granted only to a user. You can grant that role to a user or to another role. However, you cannot grant a role to itself even indirectly.

You can look at the data dictionary tables shown in Table 8.11 for information on the views for reviewing a roles system and object privileges.

The **ROLE_TAB_PRIVS** view shown in Table 8.12 provides information on tables and column grants to roles.

Setting Roles

When a user is created, the default for active roles is set to **ALL**. The default **ALL** means that all the roles granted to individual users are active. The DBA can

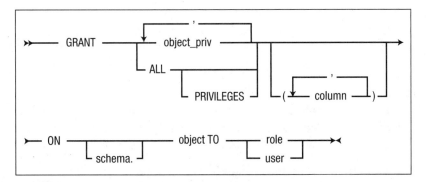

Figure 8.12 The syntax for granting object privileges to roles.

Table 8.11 Data dictionary views for roles.

Column	Definition
DBA_ROLES	
role	Name of the role
password_required	Yes, No, Global, or—for operating system authentication—External
DBA_ROLE_PRIVS	
grantee	Name of the user or role receiving the grant
granted_role	Name of the role
admin_option	Y if it was granted with the admin option
default_role	Y if this is the grantee's default role
ROLE_ROLE_PRIVS	
role	Name of the role receiving the role grant
granted_role	Name of the different role granted to the role listed in this row
admin_option	Indicates that the role was granted with the admin option
ROLE_SYS_PRIVS	
role	Name of the role receiving the system privilege
privilege	System privilege being granted
admin_option	Indicates that the grant was given with the admin option

Table 8.12 Contents of the ROLE_TAB_PRIVS data dictionary view.

Column	Definition
role	Name of the role
owner	Owner of the table, view, or sequence
table_name	Name of the table, view, or sequence
column_name	Name of the column within the table, if applicable
privilege	Object privilege granted to that role
grantable	**YES** if it was granted with the admin option; **NO** otherwise

change the default with an **ALTER USER** command. A user can enable multiple roles at one time and then either use the **SET ROLE** command to switch between roles or use the **SET ROLE ALL** command to activate all roles. The **SET ROLE ALL** command will not work if any of the roles assigned to that user requires either a password or operating system authentication.

The command-line syntax for setting roles is shown in Figure 8.13.

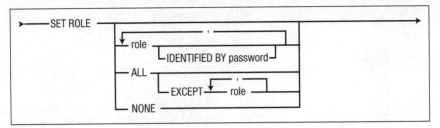

Figure 8.13   The syntax for setting roles.

Here is an example of setting a role:

```
SET ROLE master_dba IDENTIFIED BY dba2001;
```

Users can look at the **SESSION_ROLES** view to find the roles that are currently enabled for them. Users can look at the **SESSION_PRIVS** view to see the
privileges available to their session.

If you determine that all control of roles will be at the operating system level, you
can set the database initialization parameter **OS_ROLES** equal to **TRUE**. All
roles must still be created first in the database. Any grants you previously made
using the database command line or Server Manager are still listed in the data
dictionary, but they cannot be used and are not in effect. If the use of roles is
determined at the operating system level, the multithreaded server option cannot
be used.

You can use the **MAX_ENABLED_ROLES** parameter in the database initialization file to set the number of roles that you will allow any user to have enabled
at one time.

 The **SYS** user is given each role as it is created; you must set **MAX_
ENABLE_ROLES** to the total number you create, or you may get an
error. In other situations such as upgrade, you will want to increase
MAX_ENABLED_ROLES to at least 50.

Special Roles

When you install the Oracle executables, Oracle creates the following two roles:

➤ OSOPER

➤ OSDBA

When you create the database, Oracle creates the following three roles:

➤ CONNECT

➤ RESOURCE

➤ DBA

When you execute the sql.bsq script, Oracle creates the following two roles:

➤ EXP_FULL_DATABASE

➤ IMP_FULL_DATABASE

When the views and packages for Recovery Manager are created, Oracle creates the following five roles:

➤ SELECT_CATALOG_ROLE

➤ EXECUTE_CATALOG_ROLE

➤ DELETE_CATALOG_ROLE

➤ RECOVER_CATALOG_ROLE

➤ RECOVERY_CATALOG_OWNER

Finally, with the addition of the advanced queuing option, Oracle creates the following two roles:

➤ AQ_ADMINISTRATOR_ROLE

➤ AQ_USER_ROLE.

Next, I explain these special roles and how they are used for database maintenance.

OSOPER and OSDBA

The **OSOPER** and **OSDBA** roles are created at the operating system level when Oracle is installed. They cannot be granted. The **OSOPER** and **OSDBA** roles are needed to perform database operations when the database is not mounted, and therefore the data dictionary is not accessible. You use **OSOPER** and **OSDBA** roles when you use **CONNECT INTERNAL** to connect to the database using Server Manager.

Users with the **OSOPER** role can perform the following database management commands:

➤ STARTUP

➤ SHUTDOWN

➤ ALTER DATABASE OPEN/MOUNT

➤ ALTER DATABASE BACKUP CONTROLFILE

➤ ALTER TABLESPACE BEGIN/END BACKUP

➤ ARCHIVE LOG

➤ RECOVER

The **OSDBA** role has all of the privileges of the **OSOPER** role. In addition, the **OSDBA** role has all system privileges granted with **WITH ADMIN OPTION** to allow whoever has it to grant system privileges to other users. The **OSDBA** role is used to create the database and for time-based recovery processes. Both the **OSOPER** and **OSDBA** roles include the **RESTRICTED SESSION** system privilege.

If you intend to allow remote users to **CONNECT INTERNAL,** you need to set the **REMOTE_LOGIN_PASSWORDFILE** option in your database parameter file to either **EXCLUSIVE** or **SHARED.** The user will then connect in Server Manager with the **AS SYSDBA** or **AS SYSOPER** clause at the end of the **CONNECT** command (such as **CONNECT SYS AS SYSDBA**). The privileges assigned to **SYSDBA** correspond to those for **OSDBA.** The privileges assigned to **SYSOPER** correspond to **OSOPER.** Using an external operating system file, the operating system verifies the password provided. This external file is generated using the **ORAPWD** utility. When the password for the **SYS**— and indirectly the **INTERNAL**—accounts is changed with the **ALTER USER** command, the changes are mapped to the operating system password file.

CONNECT, RESOURCE, and DBA Roles

The **CONNECT, RESOURCE,** and **DBA** roles are predefined roles that are available for backward compatibility. These are created by Oracle when the database is created. When you create a user with OEM, the **CONNECT** role is automatically granted to that user.

The following system privileges are granted to the **CONNECT** role:

➤ ALTER SESSION

➤ CREATE CLUSTER

➤ CREATE DATABASE LINK

➤ CREATE SEQUENCE

➤ CREATE SESSION

➤ CREATE SYNONYM

➤ CREATE TABLE

➤ CREATE VIEW

When you grant a user the **RESOURCE** role, that user is granted the **UNLIMITED TABLESPACE** system privilege as well. The following system privileges are granted to the **RESOURCE** role:

➤ CREATE CLUSTER

➤ CREATE PROCEDURE

➤ CREATE SEQUENCE

➤ CREATE TABLE

➤ CREATE TRIGGER

➤ CREATE TYPE

The **DBA** role includes all system privileges (95 separate grants), the capability to grant those system privileges to others, and **UNLIMITED TABLESPACE**. If the **EXP_FULL_DATABASE** and **IMP_FULL_DATABASE** roles have been created, they are granted implicitly with the **DBA** role, as are the **DELETE**, **EXECUTE**, and **SELECT_CATALOG_ROLE** roles.

You can grant additional privileges to or revoke privileges from the **CONNECT**, **RESOURCE**, and **DBA** roles, just as you would with any other role that you created.

Export and Import Roles

Oracle provides a script named catexp.sql, which creates the **EXP_FULL_DATABASE** and **IMP_FULL_DATABASE** roles. You can grant these roles to a user who will be executing the Export and Import utilities.

The **EXP_FULL_DATABASE** role has the **SELECT ANY TABLE** and **BACKUP ANY TABLE** system privileges. In addition, this role has **INSERT**, **DELETE**, and **UPDATE** privileges on the **SYS.INCVID, SYS.INCFIL**, and **SYS.INCEXP** tables.

The **IMP_FULL_DATABASE** role has the **BECOME USER** system privilege.

Profiles

Profiles are a named set of resource limits. By setting up profiles with defined limits on resources, you can set limits on the system resources used. Profiles are very useful in large, complex organizations with many users. By creating and assigning profiles to users, you can regulate the amount of resources used by each database user. In Oracle8, password attributes were added into profiles.

Creating Profiles

By default, when you create users, they are given the default profile. The default profile provides unlimited use of all resources. The syntax to create a profile is shown in Figure 8.14.

Possible values for the **resource_parameters** specifications in Figure 8.14 (you can specify multiple parameters per command) are as follows:

```
[SESSIONS_PER_USER n|UNLIMITED|DEFAULT]
[CPU_PER_SESSION n|UNLIMITED|DEFAULT]
[CPU_PER_CALL n|UNLIMITED|DEFAULT]
[CONNECT_TIME          n|UNLIMITED|DEFAULT]
[IDLE_TIME             n|UNLIMITED|DEFAULT]
[LOGICAL_READS_PER_SESSION n|UNLIMITED|DEFAULT]
[LOGICAL_READS_PER_CALL    n|UNLIMITED|DEFAULT]
[COMPOSITE_LIMIT           n|UNLIMITED|DEFAULT]
[PRIVATE_SGA               n [K|M]|UNLIMITED|DEFAULT]
```

The specifications are used as follows:

➤ **SESSIONS_PER_USER**—Used to limit the number of open database sessions a user can have concurrently.

➤ **CPU_PER_SESSION**—Used to limit the total CPU resource used by a single session. This value is not additive across parallel query slaves.

➤ **CPU_PER_CALL**—Used to limit the total CPU used in a single call from a single session.

➤ **CONNECT_TIME**—Used to limit the total time a session can stay connected to the database.

➤ **IDLE_TIME**—Used to limit the amount of time an inactive session will remain logged in to the database.

➤ **LOGICAL_READS_PER_SESSION**—Used to limit the number of logical reads a single session can perform. This limit is not additive across parallel query slaves.

➤ CREATE PROFILE profile LIMIT resource_parameters | password_parameters ──; ──→

Figure 8.14   The syntax to create a profile.

➤ **LOGICAL_READS_PER_CALL**—Used to limit the number of logical reads in a single call from a single process.

➤ **COMPOSITE_LIMIT** — Used to specify the value for the composite limit. The composite limit is a combination limit based on **CPU_PER_SESSION, CONNECT_TIME, LOGICAL_READS_PER_SESSION** and **PRIVATE_SGA.**

➤ **PRIVATE_SGA** — Specifies the number of bytes in the private space of the shared global area (SGA) that can be used by this session. This limit applies only if they are using the multi-threaded server architecture and allocating private space in the SGA for their session.

Possible values for the **password_parameters** specifications in Figure 8.14 (Oracle8 and above) are as follows:

```
[FAILED_LOGIN_ATTEMPTS  expr|UNLIMITED|DEFAULT]
[PASSWORD_LIFE_TIME      expr|UNLIMITED|DEFAULT]
[PASSWORD_REUSE_TIME     expr|UNLIMITED|DEFAULT]
[PASSWORD_REUSE_MAX      expr|UNLIMITED|DEFAULT]
[PASSWORD_LOCK_TIME      expr|UNLIMITED|DEFAULT]
[PASSWORD_GRACE_TIME     expr|UNLIMITED|DEFAULT]
[PASSWORD_VERIFY_FUNCTION function_name|NULL|DEFAULT]
```

The specifications are used as follows:

➤ **FAILED_LOGIN_ATTEMPTS**—Used to set the number of times a user can enter an improper password before the account is locked.

➤ **PASSWORD_LIFE_TIME**—Used to set the period of time in days that a password is valid.

➤ **PASSWORD_REUSE_TIME**—Used to set the minimum period of time in days before a password can be reused.

➤ **PASSWORD_REUSE_MAX**—Used to set the number of times a password may be reused.

➤ **PASSWORD_LOCK_TIME**—Used to set the amount of time an account will be locked after **FAILED_LOGIN_ATTEMPTS** has been exceeded.

➤ **PASSWORD_GRACE_TIME**—Used to set the time in days that a user has to reset her password after **PASSWORD_LIFE_TIME** has been exceeded.

➤ **PASSWORD_VERIFY_FUNCTION**—Used to name the function used to verify that a password is complex enough.

Password parameters have the following restrictions:

➤ **Expr** must resolve to either an integer value or an integer number of days.

➤ If PASSWORD_REUSE_TIME is set to an integer value, PASSWORD_ REUSE_MAX must be set to UNLIMITED.

➤ If PASSWORD_REUSE_MAX is set to an integer value, PASSWORD_ REUSE_TIME must be set to UNLIMITED.

➤ If both PASSWORD_REUSE_TIME and PASSWORD_REUSE_MAX are set to UNLIMITED, Oracle uses neither of these password resources.

➤ If PASSWORD_REUSE_MAX is set to DEFAULT and PASSWORD_ REUSE_TIME is set to UNLIMITED, Oracle uses the PASSWORD_ REUSE_MAX value defined in the DEFAULT profile.

➤ If PASSWORD_REUSE_TIME is set to DEFAULT and PASSWORD_ REUSE_MAX is set to UNLIMITED, Oracle uses the PASSWORD_ REUSE_TIME value defined in the DEFAULT profile.

➤ If both PASSWORD_REUSE_TIME and PASSWORD_REUSE_MAX are set to DEFAULT, Oracle uses whichever value is defined in the DEFAULT profile.

For example:

```
CREATE PROFILE  enduser  LIMIT
CPU_PER_SESSION              60000
LOGICAL_READS_PER_SESSION    1000
CONNECT_TIME                 30
PRIVATE_SGA                  102400
CPU_PER_CALL                 UNLIMITED
COMPOSITE LIMIT              60000000
FAILED_LOGIN_ATTEMPTS        3
PASSWORD_LIFE_TIME           90
PASSWORD_REUSE_TIME          180
PASSWORD_LOCK_TIME           3
PASSWORD_GRACE_TIME          3
PASSWORD_VERIFY_FUNCTION Verify_function_one;
```

You can assign a profile to a user when you create the user or by altering the user. The syntax to alter the profile for a user is as follows:

```
ALTER USER PROFILE profile;
```

For example:

```
ALTER USER scott
PROFILE appuser;
```

You must have the **CREATE PROFILE** system privilege to create a profile. To alter a profile, you must be the creator of the profile or have the **ALTER PROFILE** system privilege. To assign a profile to a user, you must have the **CREATE USER** or **ALTER USER** system privilege.

Profiles and Resource Limits

The default cost assigned to a resource is unlimited. By setting resource limits, you can prevent users from performing operations that will tie up the system and prevent other users from performing operations. You can use resource limits for security to ensure that users log off the system and do not leave the session connected for long periods of time. You can also assign a composite cost to each profile. The system resource limits can be enforced at the session level, at the call level, or both.

The *session level* restrictions are from the time the user logs into the database until the user exits. The *call level* restrictions are for each SQL command issued. Session-level limits are enforced for each connection. When a session-level limit is exceeded, only the last SQL command issued is rolled back, and no further work can be performed until a commit, a rollback, or an exit is performed. Table 8.13 lists the system resources that can be regulated at the session level.

Note that if you use parallel query option (PQO), the resources are applied to each new session, not accumulated over all of the sessions that a parallel operation uses.

Table 8.13 Resources regulated at the session level.	
System Resource	**Definition**
CPU_PER_SESSION	Total CPU time; expressed in hundreds of seconds
SESSIONS_PER_USER	Number of concurrent sessions allowed for a user
CONNECT_TIME	Allowed connection time; expressed in minutes
IDLE_TIME	Inactive time allowed on the server; expressed in minutes
LOGICAL_READS_PER_SESSION	Number of data blocks read, including both physical and logical reads from memory and disk
PRIVATE_SGA	Bytes of SGA used in a database with the multithreaded server; expressed in K or MB

You can combine the **CPU_PER_SESSION, LOGICAL_READS_PER_ SESSION, CONNECT_TIME,** and **PRIVATE_SGA** system resources to create a **COMPOSITE LIMIT.**

Call-level limits are enforced during the execution of each SQL statement. When a call-level limit is exceeded, the last SQL command issued is rolled back. All the previous statements issued are still valid, and the user can continue to execute other SQL statements. The following system resources can be regulated at the call level:

➤ **CPU_PER_CALL**—For the CPU time allowed for the SQL statement

➤ **LOGICAL_READS_PER_CALL**—For the number of data blocks read for the SQL statement

You can assign a cost to a resource by using the **ALTER RESOURCE COST** command. Resource limits that you set explicitly for a user take precedence over the resource costs in an assigned profile. The command-line syntax for this command is shown in Figure 8.15.

For example:

```
ALTER RESOURCE COST CONNECT_TIME 100;
```

The **ALTER RESOURCE COST** command specifies the weights Oracle uses to calculate the total resource cost used for a session. Oracle calculates the total resource cost by multiplying the amount of each resource used in the session by the resource's weight and summing the results for all four resources. Both the products and the total cost are expressed in units called *service units.*

Although Oracle monitors the use of other resources, only the four specified in Figure 8.15 contribute to the total resource cost for a session.

The weight that you assign to each resource in Figure 8.15 determines how much the use of that resource contributes to the total resource cost. Using a resource with a lower weight contributes less to the cost than using a resource with a higher weight. If you do not assign a weight to a resource, the weight defaults to 0 and the use of the resource does not contribute to the cost. The weights you assign apply to all subsequent sessions in the database.

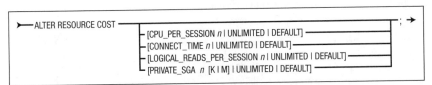

Figure 8.15 The syntax of the **ALTER RESOURCE COST** command.

After you have specified a formula for the total resource cost, you can limit this cost for a session with the **COMPOSITE_LIMIT** parameter of the **CREATE PROFILE** command. If a session's cost exceeds the limit, Oracle aborts the session and returns an error. If you use the **ALTER RESOURCE COST** command to change the weight assigned to each resource, Oracle uses these new weights to calculate the total resource cost for all current and subsequent sessions.

Use of resource limits is set in the database initialization parameter **RESOURCE_LIMIT=TRUE**. By default, this parameter is set to false. This parameter can be changed interactively with an **ALTER SYSTEM** command.

The **DBA_PROFILES** view provides information on all the profiles and the resource limits for each profile. The **RESOURCE_COST** view shows the unit cost associated with each resource. Each user can find information on his resources and limits in the **USER_RESOURCE_LIMITS** view. Table 8.14 describes these data dictionary views.

Altering Profiles

If you have the **CREATE PROFILE** or **ALTER PROFILE** system privilege, you can alter any profile, including the Oracle-created **DEFAULT** profile. You can alter a profile to change the cost assigned to each resource. The syntax to alter a profile is shown in Figure 8.16.

Table 8.14   Data dictionary views for resources.

Column	Definition
DBA_PROFILES	
Profile	The name given to the profile
Resource_name	The name of the resource assigned to the profile
Limit	The limit placed on the profile
RESOURCE_COST	
Resource_name	The name of the resource
Unit_cost	The cost assigned
USER_RESOURCE_LIMITS	
Resource_name	The name of the resource
Limit	The limit placed on the user

➤—ALTER PROFILE profile LIMIT resource_parameters I password_parameters—; →

Figure 8.16   The syntax to alter a profile.

The possible values for the **resource_parameters** specifications are as follows:

```
[SESSIONS_PER_USER  n|UNLIMITED|DEFAULT]
[CPU_PER_SESSION    n|UNLIMITED|DEFAULT]
[CPU_PER_CALL       n|UNLIMITED|DEFAULT]
[CONNECT_TIME       n|UNLIMITED|DEFAULT]
[IDLE_TIME          n|UNLIMITED|DEFAULT]
[LOGICAL_READS_PER_SESSION n|UNLIMITED|DEFAULT]
[LOGICAL_READS_PER_CALL    n|UNLIMITED|DEFAULT]
[COMPOSITE_LIMIT           n|UNLIMITED|DEFAULT]
[PRIVATE_SGA               n [K|M|UNLIMITED|DEFAULT]]
```

The possible values for the **password_parameters** specifications are:

```
[FAILED_LOGIN_ATTEMPTS expr|UNLIMITED|DEFAULT]
[PASSWORD_LIFE_TIME    expr|UNLIMITED|DEFAULT]
[PASSWORD_REUSE_TIME   expr|UNLIMITED|DEFAULT]
[PASSWORD_REUSE_MAX    expr|UNLIMITED|DEFAULT]
[PASSWORD_LOCK_TIME    expr|UNLIMITED|DEFAULT]
[PASSWORD_GRACE_TIME   expr|UNLIMITED|DEFAULT]
[PASSWORD_VERIFY_FUNCTION function_name|NULL|DEFAULT]
```

For example:

```
ALTER PROFILE enduser LIMIT
CPU_PER_SESSION 60000
LOGICAL_READS_PER_SESSION 1000
CONNECT_TIME 60
PRIVATE_SGA 102400
CPU_PER_CALL UNLIMITED
COMPOSITE LIMIT 60000000;
```

To disable a profile during a session, you must have the **ALTER SYSTEM** privilege. A limit that you set for the session overrides the previous limit set by the profile. To reset the profile to the limit originally set by the database, set the limit to **DEFAULT**. The following code shows how the resource limit checking can be turned on (using **TRUE**) or off (using **FALSE**) through use of the **ALTER SYSTEM** command:

```
ALTER SYSTEM SET RESOURCE_LIMIT = TRUE|FALSE;
```

For example:

```
ALTER SYSTEM SET RESOURCE_LIMIT = TRUE ;
```

Profiles and Passwords

A feature added in Oracle8 allows the capability to control password expiry and password complexity and validity. You also use profiles to control passwords. Table 8.15 lists the password control attributes in a profile and their definitions.

Oracle also provides a template PL/SQL procedure for use in creating your own password complexity and verification function. The example PL/SQL procedure is located in $ORACLE_HOME/rdbms/admin/utlpwdmg.sql on Unix and in %ORACLE_HOME%\rdbms80\admin\utlpwdmg.sql on NT. Other than the required input and return variables, the password verification function can be as simple, or as complex, as you want it to be.

Table 8.15 Password control attributes in a profile.

Attribute	Description
FAILED_LOGIN_ATTEMPTS	Specifies the number of failed attempts to log into the user account allowed before the account is locked.
PASSWORD_LIFE_TIME	Limits the number of days the same password can be used for authentication. The password expires if it is not changed within this period, and further connections are rejected.
PASSWORD_REUSE_TIME	Specifies the number of days that the current password can be reused. If you set **PASSWORD_REUSE_TIME** to an integer value, you must set **PASSWORD_REUSE_MAX** to **UNLIMITED**.
PASSWORD_REUSE_MAX	Specifies the number of password changes required before the current password can be reused. If you set **PASSWORD_REUSE_MAX** to an integer value, you must set **PASSWORD_REUSE_TIME** to **UNLIMITED**.
PASSWORD_LOCK_TIME	Specifies the number of days an account will be locked after the specified number of consecutive failed login attempts.
PASSWORD_GRACE_TIME	Specifies the length of a grace period: the number of days in which a warning is issued and login is allowed. If the password is not changed during the grace period, the password expires.
PASSWORD_VERIFY_FUNCTION	Allows a PL/SQL password-complexity verification script to be passed as an argument to the **CREATE PROFILE** statement. Oracle provides a default script, but you can create your own routine or use third-party software instead. **FUNCTION** is the name of the password-complexity verification routine. **NULL** indicates that no password verification is performed and is the default value.

Practice Questions

Question 1

> What is displayed when you query **USER_USERS**?
>
> ○ a. Information about all users of the database
>
> ○ b. Information about the current user
>
> ○ c. Tablespace quotas for all users
>
> ○ d. Tablespace quotas for the current user

The correct answer is b. Views prefixed with **USER** will give information relevant to the current user only, which explains why answer a and c are incorrect. Answer d is incorrect because quota information is not contained in the **USER_USERS** view.

Question 2

> Which keyword, when added to a **DROP USER** command, will remove all objects contained in a user's schema?
>
> ○ a. **DEFAULT**
>
> ○ b. **QUOTA**
>
> ○ c. **CASCADE**
>
> ○ d. **EXCEPT**

The correct answer is c. If a user owns objects, he cannot be dropped unless you explicitly include the **CASCADE** option in the **DROP USER** command. Dropping a user and keeping the user's objects in the database is not possible. You can export the user's objects and import them into another user record, or another user can use his **SELECT** privileges on the objects to copy them before the first user is dropped. After a **DROP USER** statement is issued, it cannot be rolled back. The only keyword allowed in a **DROP USER** is **CASCADE**, so all of the other answers are incorrect.

Question 3

> Which view would you query to display the number of bytes charged to each user?
>
> ○ a. **USER_USERS**
> ○ b. **ALL_USERS**
> ○ c. **DBA_USERS**
> ○ d. **USER_TS_QUOTAS**
> ○ e. **DBA_TS_QUOTAS**

The correct answer is e. The **DBA_TS_QUOTAS** view lists the number of bytes for each user. This view also includes the maximum bytes as set by the quota assigned to the user. Note the wording of this question. It asks how you would obtain tablespace usage information for each user. You can eliminate **USER_TS_QUOTAS**, answer d, because it will give tablespace usage information on the current user only. Answers a, b, and c are incorrect because the **USERS** series of views do not give quota information. Pay special attention to whether the question asks for statistics on the current user or all users.

Question 4

> Evaluate this command:
>
> ```
> ALTER USER jennifer
> QUOTA 0 ON SYSTEM;
> ```
>
> Which task will this command accomplish?
>
> ○ a. Remove user Jennifer
> ○ b. Drop user Jennifer's objects from **SYSTEM** tablespace
> ○ c. Revoke user Jennifer's tablespace quota on **SYSTEM** tablespace
> ○ d. Allocate tablespace to user Jennifer

The correct answer is c. Jennifer may have quotas on several tablespaces, and this command will revoke Jennifer's usage on the **SYSTEM** tablespace only. A process of elimination is used. The command in this question will not remove or drop the user Jennifer (answers a and b). It will not allocate tablespace to Jennifer (answer d). The only applicable answer is c.

Question 5

When you're creating a user, which step can be skipped if the user will not be creating any objects?

- ○ a. Assign a username and password.
- ○ b. Assign a default tablespace.
- ○ c. Assign a tablespace for temporary tables.
- ○ d. Assign a default profile.

The correct answer is b. Be sure to read this question carefully. Notice the words "will not be creating any objects." If a default tablespace is not explicitly assigned, the **SYSTEM** tablespace will be the implicit default. However, if a user will not be creating objects, he will not actually be placing anything in the **SYSTEM** tablespace. Answer a is incorrect since a username and password must always be explicitly stated. Answer d is incorrect since that if a profile is not created, the default profile is implicitly assigned; but that is true regardless of whether the user is going to create objects. Answer c is incorrect since the temporary tablespace will also be implicitly assigned (as **SYSTEM**) but since the temporary tablespace is not used for tables, it is irrelevant. However, it's not a good practice to leave general users assigned to the **SYSTEM** tablespace as their default or for temporary assignments.

Question 6

Who needs a DBA assigned usage quota?

- ○ a. The owner of an object that is read-only
- ○ b. A user who is about to create a table
- ○ c. A user who only reads data from an object owned by another user
- ○ d. A user who is inserting data into an object owned by another user

The correct answer is b. Inserting data into an object owned by another user will use the quota of the user who owns the object. Answer a is incorrect because if the object is read-only, no quota is assigned. Answer c is incorrect because if a user only reads information, that user doesn't need quota because the only space used for a read is temporary (if a sort is required), and temporary tablespace quota is assigned automatically. Answer d is incorrect because data inserted into another user's object uses her quota.

Question 7

> What does the option **EXTERNALLY** do when you're using the **CREATE USER** command to create a user?
>
> ○ a. Allow the user remote access
>
> ○ b. Allow the user network access
>
> ○ c. Allow the user to access the database without a password
>
> ○ d. Requires that the user's password be verified by the operating system

The correct answer is d. When you create a user with **IDENTIFIED EXTERNALLY**, you do not specify a password. The username and password are verified by the operating system. The other answers are incorrect because they do not describe the purpose of **EXTERNALLY**.

Question 8

> Jennifer used **WITH GRANT OPTION** to grant a privilege to Sharon. Sharon granted the privilege to Jacob. If Jennifer's privilege is revoked, who else will lose privileges?
>
> ○ a. Only Sharon.
>
> ○ b. Only Jacob.
>
> ○ c. Both Sharon and Jacob.
>
> ○ d. No one else will lose privileges.

The correct answer is c. **WITH GRANT OPTION** indicates that an object privilege was granted. Remember that when an object privilege is revoked, the revocation cascades to all the users who received the privilege from that user. Since the answer is that both will lose their privileges. This means that any answer that doesn't say this is incorrect; thus a, b, and d are incorrect.

Question 9

> Jennifer used **WITH ADMIN OPTION** to grant a privilege to Sharon. Sharon
> granted the privilege to Jacob. If Jennifer's privileges are revoked, who else
> will lose privileges?
>
> ○ a. Only Sharon.
>
> ○ b. Only Jacob.
>
> ○ c. Both Sharon and Jacob.
>
> ○ d. No one else will lose privileges.

The correct answer is d. **WITH ADMIN OPTION** indicates that a system
privilege was granted. Revoking system privileges from a user does not cascade to
others.

Question 10

> Which characteristic describes a role?
>
> ○ a. Can only consist of object privileges
>
> ○ b. Is owned by the DBA
>
> ○ c. May be granted to any role except itself
>
> ○ d. May be granted to itself

The correct answer is c. Both system and object privileges can be granted to a
role, and a role can be granted to another user. However, recursive grants of a role
to itself are not allowed. Answer a is incorrect since a **ROLE** can consist of object
and system grants. Answer b is incorrect, since no one owns a role, it is a system
object. Answer d is incorrect since a role may not be granted to itself.

Question 11

> Which command could you use to set a default role for a user?
>
> ○ a. **CREATE ROLE**
>
> ○ b. **ALTER USER**
>
> ○ c. **CREATE USER**
>
> ○ d. **SET ROLE**

The correct answer is b. It is correct that you can set a default role for a user when the user is created. However, the question implies that the user and role are already created. Answer a, **CREATE ROLE**, is used to create a role initially, not to change an existing user. Answer c, **CREATE USER**, is used to create a user, not to alter a user's properties, such as default roles. Answer d, **SET ROLE**, is used to turn on a nondefault role that a user may have assigned to him.

Need To Know More?

 Ault, Michael R. *Oracle8i Administration and Management.* John Wiley & Sons. New York, New York, 2000. ISBN 0-471-35453-8. Chapter 9 discusses objects, privileges, and user administration.

 Honour, Dalberth, and Mehta Kaplan. *Oracle8 How-To.* Waite Group Press, Corte Madera, California, 1998. ISBN 1-57169-123-5. Chapters 3 and 8 discuss users and security.

 Oracle Corporation. *Oracle8i Server SQL Reference Manual, Release 3(8.1.7).* September, 2000, Redwood City, California. Part No. A85397-01. This is the source book for all Oracle SQL for version 8i. You can find this book on the Web, at the time of writing, at **http://technet.oracle.com**. This site has free membership and has all current versions of Oracle documentation available online in Acrobat format (PDF files).

 Oracle Corporation. *Oracle8i Administrator's Guide Release 2 (8.1.6)* December 1999, Redwood City, California. Part No. A76956-01. You can find this book on the Web, at the time of writing, at **http://technet.oracle.com**. This site has free membership and has all current versions of Oracle documentation available online in Acrobat format (PDF files).

 All Oracle documentation is available online at **http://technet.oracle.com**. Membership is free.

9

Structure of a
PL/SQL Program

Terms you'll need to understand:

✓ Anonymous PL/SQL block
✓ Declarative section
✓ Executable section
✓ Exception handling
✓ Procedure
✓ Function
✓ Package header
✓ Package body
✓ Implicit cursor
✓ Explicit cursor

Techniques you'll need to master:

✓ Creating anonymous PL/SQL blocks
✓ Creating procedures
✓ Creating functions
✓ Creating packages
✓ Using implicit and explicit cursors

One of the most important additions to Oracle has been PL/SQL. In normal SQL, you deal with single- or multiple-value sets only. In SQL, you can't conditionally insert, update, or select values based on multiple-condition sets (for example, if value *A* is 6, then make *B* currentcount+1; or if *A* is 7, make *B* currentcount–1). Also, you can't do single-line processing of a set of values in SQL. All of this functionality—conditional processing, flow control, and single-line set processing—came along when Oracle added PL/SQL. Both directly support DML commands; special Oracle-provided packages must be employed to use DDL commands in PL/SQL. Unlike SQL, PL/SQL also allows for exception handling routines.

The PL/SQL Engine

The PL/SQL engine processes PL/SQL blocks submitted from the Server Manager. The PL/SQL blocks are parsed into the procedural statements and SQL statements. These parsed statements are processed by passing the procedural statements to the Procedural Statement Executor inside the engine, which also processes data that is local to the application and then passes the SQL statements, as needed, to the Oracle8i server SQL Statement Executor.

Memory Use and PL/SQL

Another timesaving feature of PL/SQL is that it allows a correctly written, parsed program to be used many times. A PL/SQL package, function, procedure, and trigger, once used, will remain in memory until it's no longer frequently accessed. Hence, PL/SQL objects are collectively known as *stored objects*. In addition, PL/SQL uses the advantageous block structure that allows for compartmentalization of programs by function. By wrapping many SQL lines into one PL/SQL program, client/server applications reduce network traffic because a PL/SQL program is sent as one transaction to the database, not as multiple, smaller transactions. The PL/SQL engine can also be incorporated into other program sets, such as those involving forms and reports, thereby reducing transaction processing in these programs as well. A PL/SQL subprogram must contain a header, an executable section, and an **END** command.

PL/SQL Basics

PL/SQL uses the block concept contained within a **BEGIN...END;** construct. An unnamed PL/SQL block that's used either as standalone in SQL*Plus, or as part of a trigger, is known as an *anonymous PL/SQL block*. These anonymous blocks can be used in all Oracle environments. The **BEGIN...END;**, usually called the *executable section*, is the only required part of a PL/SQL program; it must begin with the keyword **BEGIN** and end with the keyword **END** followed by a semicolon. All **BEGIN...END;** keywords must be balanced.

A database trigger is a PL/SQL program (actually an anonymous PL/SQL block) that's associated with a table and that is executed (or fired) automatically based on a predefined action such as **INSERT, UPDATE,** or **DELETE** against the table. In Oracle8i, triggers are allowed against database actions such as log on, log off, and DDL actions.

A complete PL/SQL program consists of the following:

➤ *A declaration section*—Where variables, cursors, and constants are defined

➤ *An executable section*—Where the program logic is performed

➤ *An exception handling section*—Where errors are handled

An anonymous PL/SQL program can consist of a **BEGIN...END;** block, a **DECLARE** section and **BEGIN...END;** block, or a **DECLARE, BEGIN...END;,** and exception section. Anonymous PL/SQL programs can be as short as a single line or span dozens of pages and be as complex as any procedure, function, or trigger. You must include an executable statement within the **BEGIN...END;** statements for a block to be valid. The simplest anonymous PL/SQL block would be the following:

```
BEGIN
NULL;
END;
```

Of course, it doesn't do anything. (**NULL** is an executable statement in PL/SQL and is used to fill in when you don't have any processing to do but must have a PL/SQL block, such as in some **EXCEPTION** situations.)

By definition, any stored PL/SQL block (that is, the PL/SQL program is stored in the data dictionary tables and doesn't need to be read from an external file) is a named PL/SQL block. A named PL/SQL block can be a procedure or a function. Beginning with Oracle 7.3, trigger definitions are stored objects even though they contain anonymous PL/SQL blocks. The simplest PL/SQL named object (hence, a stored object) would be the following:

```
PROCEDURE start_it IS
BEGIN
NULL;
END start_it;
```

The reason why a **PROCEDURE**—and not a **FUNCTION**—is the simplest stored object is that a **FUNCTION** must return a value and hence must include a **RETURN** statement as well as a **NULL**. Although the purpose of such a stored object isn't really clear right now, I show you what it can be used for in a little bit.

Related PL/SQL procedures and functions can be combined into stored structures called *packages*. PL/SQL packages consist of a header section that declares all publicly available contents of the package and their variables and the package body, which contains the actual package definitions and any private objects, which aren't usable outside of the package. When any publicly available part of a package is used, the entire package is read into memory and made available.

In many cases, multiple users who access the same application will use a package. In this situation, the package should be read into memory and *pinned* (removed from the aging algorithm) to keep it in memory. To prevent shared pool fragmentation, this preloading of packages should be done before any ad hoc SQL generation occurs. To this end, a procedure similar to the **start_it** procedure shown in the earlier snippet should be included in all packages, so a simple call to the **start_it** procedure inside the package loads the entire package into memory where it can be pinned using the **DBMS_SHARED_POOL.KEEP** procedure. In 8i, the mere act of pinning the object will call it into memory and the additional step of calling it using a null procedure is not required.

PL/SQL Procedures

PL/SQL procedures are stored, named objects that can return zero, one, or many values to the calling process. However, only one row of values can be returned from a single procedure call. Procedure variables used for sending variables into the program and for receiving values from the program are specified at the start of the program and designated as **IN** (input variables only that can't have their values altered by the program, so they're treated as constants); **OUT** (output variables that are set by the program during execution); and **IN OUT** (variables that are used for both input and output of values.)

When creating procedures, the next line after the end of the procedure definition must be a forward slash (/) to tell Oracle to compile the procedure. The last statement of a PL/SQL procedure must end with a semicolon.

As was demonstrated with the **start_it** procedure, neither input nor output is required from a procedure. A procedure also doesn't require a declarative section. In fact, the only required part of a procedure is the **PROCEDURE** line and the executable block.

Procedures are created using the **CREATE PROCEDURE** command. The syntax for the **CREATE PROCEDURE** command is shown in Figure 9.1.

External procedures are not covered on the exam.

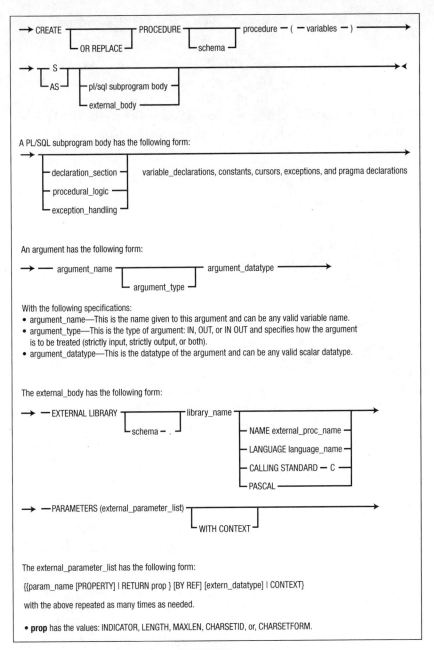

A PL/SQL subprogram body has the following form:

variable_declarations, constants, cursors, exceptions, and pragma declarations

An argument has the following form:

With the following specifications:
- argument_name—This is the name given to this argument and can be any valid variable name.
- argument_type—This is the type of argument: IN, OUT, or IN OUT and specifies how the argument is to be treated (strictly input, strictly output, or both).
- argument_datatype—This is the datatype of the argument and can be any valid scalar datatype.

The external_body has the following form:

The external_parameter_list has the following form:

{{param_name [PROPERTY] | RETURN prop } [BY REF] [extern_datatype] | CONTEXT}

with the above repeated as many times as needed.

- **prop** has the values: INDICATOR, LENGTH, MAXLEN, CHARSETID, or, CHARSETFORM.

Figure 9.1   Syntax for the **CREATE PROCEDURE** command.

The clauses and variables for the **CREATE PROCEDURE** command are defined as follows:

➤ **CREATE [OR REPLACE]**—Causes SQL to create a procedure. If **OR REPLACE** is not used and if the procedure exists, an error will result. The **OR REPLACE** allows for in-place altering of a procedure without affecting any of its grants or dependencies. The **CREATE [OR REPLACE]** must be at the beginning of the statement for the procedure to be created or replaced in SQL*Plus.

➤ **schema**—Name of owner for the procedure. Defaults to current user.

➤ **procedure_name**—Name for the procedure (must follow standard table-naming conventions).

➤ **variables**—Variable declarations in a comma-separated list. A variable declaration has the following format:

```
variable_name   variable_characteristic variable_type
```

For example:

```
(role_name IN VARCHAR2, newpass IN VARCHAR2)
```

Notice that no size information is specified, only the datatype of the variable is specified, and that each variable is declared independently. The previous sentence will answer many of the questions you will see on the exam: Memorize it. Multiple declarations can't be attached to a single type specification; each variable must have its own type of specification. The **variable_characteristic** is either **IN, OUT,** or **IN OUT**. An **IN** variable acts as a constant and can be an expression. **OUT** variable can only be written to and is used to return a value to the calling process; and **IN OUT** is used to pass in a value, then after the value has been changed, return it to the calling process. The **variable_type** must be specified or an error will result. If the variable characteristic isn't defined, it defaults to **IN**.

➤ **AUTHID DEFINER|CURRENT_USER** – This clause tells Oracle that the procedure is either executed in the permission context of the **DEFINER** (creator) of the procedure or of the person's user (**CURRENT_USER**) that is executing the procedure. The **AUTHID** defaults to **DEFINER** if not specified.

➤ **IS** or **AS**—Some tools will balk at using **IS**, some will balk at using **AS**, and some don't care, so be watchful when using coding tools. One of these keywords must be specified or an error will result.

➤ **variable declaration**—A variable declaration of the following form:

```
variable_name  datatype;
```

Variable names must follow the rules for table names, with only one variable name per datatype declaration. The datatype is any allowed PL/SQL datatype. The declaration must end with a semicolon. For example:

```
Test_date    DATE;
   Test_score   NUMBER;
   Retest_date  DATE;
```

Multiple variable declarations per a single datatype line are not allowed. For example:

```
Test_date, retest_date    DATE:
```

is not allowed.

➤ **constants**—Similar to a variable definition, except the keyword **CONSTANT** must be declared. A constant's value can't be changed after it is set unless it's redeclared inside a subsequent block. A constant declaration looks like this:

```
passing_score CONSTANT NUMBER := 68;
```

In this example, the variable **passing_score** is assigned the value of 68 as a numeric datatype. The := compound symbol in PL/SQL is used to show assignment; the = sign is used to show equality only.

➤ **cursors**—If a SQL statement will retrieve multiple values, you should set it as a cursor using a cursor declaration. The cursor declaration has the following form:

```
CURSOR cursor_name (input_variables) IS executable_sql_statement;
```

For example:

```
CURSOR get_stat(stat IN VARCHAR2) IS
    SELECT name,value
    FROM v$sysstat
    WHERE name = stat;
```

The input variables to a cursor can't have a dimension specified. **CHAR**, **VARCHAR2**, and **NUMBER** are allowed, but **CHAR(2)**, **VARCHAR2(20)**, or **NUMBER(10,2)** would be rejected with a format error if you tried to use them.

➤ **exception declaration**—An exception is an error handling routine. Numerous predefined exceptions don't need to be declared in your program, but any user-defined exceptions must be declared in this section. An exception declaration looks like this:

```
exception_name EXCEPTION;
```

The exception name follows the naming guidelines. User-defined exceptions must be explicitly called using the **RAISE** command. Implicit exceptions are invoked automatically when they occur.

➤ **pragma declaration**—A **PRAGMA EXCEPTION_INIT** declaration usually goes hand in hand with the exception declaration. A *pragma* is a PL/SQL interpreter directive that remaps standard Oracle errors into user-defined errors. The pragma call is formatted like this:

```
PRAGMA EXCPEPTION_INIT(exception_name, error_number)
```

For example:

```
PRAGMA EXCEPTION_INIT(table_not_found, -904);
```

➤ **procedural_logic**—The procedural logic (also known as the executable section) is the collection of SQL and PL/SQL statements used to manipulate data in the database wrapped in **BEGIN...END;** blocks. These blocks can be nested to any depth up to the maximum allowed size of a stored procedure. The **RAISE** command for use in exceptions can only be used in the procedural logic or executable section of a PL/SQL program. Remember that the last line of any PL/SQL program must end in a semicolon.

➤ **exception handlers**—In the final section of a PL/SQL procedure (or an individual block), you process exceptions. The exception handling, although a good practice, isn't required. The exception section of a procedure performs error trapping. All user-defined exceptions must be defined in the declaration section of the procedure before they can be raised or used. An exception processing section is formatted like this:

```
EXCEPTION
    WHEN exception_name THEN
    Error_handling_code
END;
```

For example:

```
EXCEPTION
    WHEN table_not_found THEN
    INSERT INTO error_log
    VALUES (sysdate,'Table '||table_name||' not found');
END;
```

Procedures allow complex processing to be reduced to a single procedure call statement. Procedures also enforce uniform processing techniques and ensure that good standards are followed. By forcing use of procedures, you'll encourage code reuse and allow reuse of stored code from the shared pool, thus improving performance. In a client/server environment, use of procedures forces processing to the server and reduces network traffic. Listing 9.1 shows a simple **CREATE PROCEDURE** command.

Listing 9.1   Example **CREATE PROCEDURE** command.

```
CREATE OR REPLACE PROCEDURE populate_table
AUTHID CURRENT_USER AS
 var_col    VARCHAR2(4000);
 num_col    NUMBER;
 date_col   DATE;
 i          NUMBER;
BEGIN
 FOR i IN 1..4000000 LOOP
  dbms_random.initialize(i);
  num_col:=dbms_random.random;
  var_col:=gen_string(4000);
  INSERT INTO test_analyze VALUES(num_col,var_col,sysdate);
  COMMIT;
 END LOOP;
 dbms_random.terminate;
END;
```

Some things to note in Listing 9.1 are the calls to both **FUNCTION**s (lines num_col:=dbms_random.random; and var_col:=gen_string(4000);) and the calls to other procedures (lines dbms_random.initialize(i); and dbms_random.terminate;).

The new external procedure format available since Oracle8i allows reference to an external C sharable library function. The C function must be in a DLL or shared library module that is referenced by a **LIBRARY** definition internal to Oracle.

PL/SQL Functions

PL/SQL functions allow multiple inputs and must return a single value. This characteristic of functions—that they must return a value—is the major difference between a function and a procedure. Functions can either be standalone, or they can be placed in packages. If a function is to be used outside of its package, it must have its purity defined to the Oracle system through use of the **PRAGMA RESTRICT_REFERENCES** call in the package header right after the functions declaration. The **CREATE FUNCTION** command syntax is shown in Figure 9.2.

External functions are not covered on the exam.

The following are the definitions for the clauses and variables in the **CREATE FUNCTION** command:

➤ **schema**—Name of the function owner.

➤ **declaration_section**—Any locally defined variables, constants, exceptions, or cursors.

➤ **functional_logic**—Contains code used for processing in the function.

➤ **exception_handling**—Exception handling code for the function.

➤ **name**—Same as the name specified for the function.

➤ **expr**—Expression to be returned to the calling user. The expression can be as simple as a local variable name or as complex as a mathematical equation that returns a value calculated from input values.

Functions are used to manipulate data and return a single value. Functions by definition can't alter a package's state, a program's state, or a data item's state. This means functions can't be used to write data or change the state of the system or database. This non-altering of system items is referred to as a function's purity. A function must contain a **RETURN** statement. In Oracle8i, the restrictions on a function's purity have been eased somewhat but still apply in many cases. Listing 9.2 shows a simple function used to return strings of random characters for use in populating test tables.

Listing 9.2   Example **CREATE FUNCTION**.

```
CREATE OR REPLACE FUNCTION gen_string(strn_len IN NUMBER)
RETURN VARCHAR2 AUTHID CURRENT USER AS
    pi   NUMBER := 3.141592653589793238462643 ;
    seed NUMBER ;
    ret_string     VARCHAR2(4000);
    ret_len        INTEGER;
```

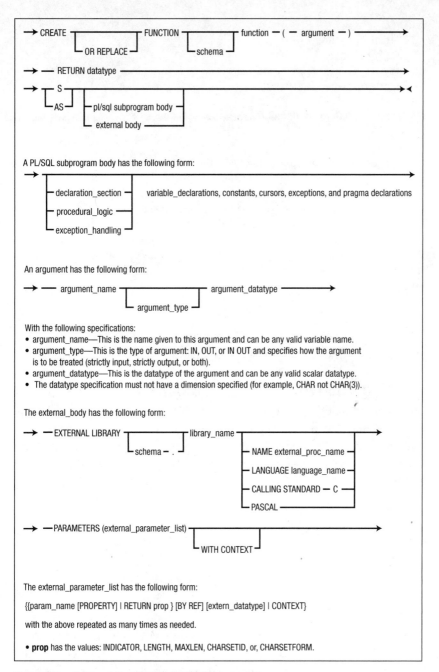

A PL/SQL subprogram body has the following form:

variable_declarations, constants, cursors, exceptions, and pragma declarations

An argument has the following form:

With the following specifications:
- argument_name—This is the name given to this argument and can be any valid variable name.
- argument_type—This is the type of argument: IN, OUT, or IN OUT and specifies how the argument is to be treated (strictly input, strictly output, or both).
- argument_datatype—This is the datatype of the argument and can be any valid scalar datatype.
- The datatype specification must not have a dimension specified (for example, CHAR not CHAR(3)).

The external_body has the following form:

The external_parameter_list has the following form:

{{param_name [PROPERTY] I RETURN prop } [BY REF] [extern_datatype] I CONTEXT}

with the above repeated as many times as needed.

- **prop** has the values: INDICATOR, LENGTH, MAXLEN, CHARSETID, or, CHARSETFORM.

Figure 9.2   Syntax of the **CREATE FUNCTION** command.

```
BEGIN
  IF strn_len>4000 THEN
   ret_len:=4000;
  ELSE
   ret_len:=strn_len;
  END IF;
   SELECT TO_NUMBER(TO_CHAR(hsecs))/8640000 INTO seed FROM v$timer;
   /*0<=seed < 1*/
   ret_string := NULL ;
       seed := POWER(pi + seed,5)-TRUNC(POWER(pi + seed,5));
       ret_len:=CEIL(ret_len*seed);
       FOR   j   IN 1..ret_len LOOP
          seed := POWER(pi + seed,5)-TRUNC(POWER(pi + seed,5));
          ret_string := ret_string||CHR( 64 + 1 + TRUNC (seed *
             26)) ;
       END LOOP;
RETURN ret_string;
END;
```

Some things to note in Listing 9.2 are the calls to **FUNCTION**s with the **SELECT** command and how **FUNCTION** calls are used in the various equations.

Creating Anonymous PL/SQL Blocks

Anonymous PL/SQL blocks are used inside SQL routines, triggers, or directly from operating system files. Anonymous PL/SQL blocks can be used to do virtually anything that procedures and functions can, with the exception that they aren't stored in the database. An anonymous PL/SQL block has the following general form:

```
DECLARE
   Declarations
BEGIN
   Executable section
EXCEPTION
   Exception handlers
END;
```

The only required portion of an anonymous PL/SQL block is the **BEGIN...END;** block with the executable section. Notice that the code has no **CREATE OR RE-PLACE** command; anonymous blocks are built directly in SQL*Plus or directly as a text file using a system editor. Anonymous PL/SQL blocks can be called from any of Oracle's executable environments and are executed by either reading them into the SQL*Plus buffer with a **GET** command and then executing a **RUN, R,** or by entering a backslash (/) command followed by an enter or return keystroke.

Anonymous PL/SQL is especially useful in SQL*Plus scripts where complex processing is required, but where the frequency of use doesn't warrant a stored procedure or function. Of course, triggers are also built using anonymous PL/SQL blocks. An example of an anonymous PL/SQL block is shown in Listing 9.3.

Listing 9.3   Example anonymous PL/SQL block.

```
DECLARE
 v_new_tech_id  NUMBER:=879563;
 v_old_tech_id  NUMBER:=874512;
 v_rows_updated NUMBER:=0;
BEGIN
UPDATE service
        SET technician_id=v_new_tech_id
        WHERE technician_id=v_old_tech_id;
v_rows_updated:=SQL%ROWCOUNT;
END;
/
```

Exception Handling

By proper coding techniques, such as the use of exception processing, you can eliminate application hangs due to errors. Any user-defined exception or error must be implicitly invoked by use of the **RAISE** command. For example:

```
BEGIN
    ---- processing ----
    IF inventory_count < min_stocking_value THEN
       RAISE need_to_reorder;
    END IF;
    ---- processing ----
END;
```

A special form of exception is known as the **OTHERS** exception. The **OTHERS** exception should be a part of any set of exceptions. It traps any nonspecific error that happens so that you can exit gracefully from your routine. The **WHEN OTHERS** clause is allowed only in an exception section of a procedure, function, or anonymous PL/SQL block. Listing 9.4 shows a simple procedure with exception handling.

Listing 9.4   Procedure using exception handling.

```
CREATE OR REPLACE PROCEDURE kill_session ( session_id IN VARCHAR2,
serial_num IN VARCHAR2) AUTHID DEFINER
AS
 cur INTEGER;
 ret INTEGER;
 string VARCHAR2(100);
```

```
BEGIN
  string :=
        'ALTER SYSTEM KILL SESSION
'||''''||session_id||','||serial_num||'''';
    cur := dbms_sql.open_cursor;
    dbms_sql.parse(cur,string,dbms_sql.native);
    ret := dbms_sql.execute(cur)   ;
    dbms_sql.close_cursor(cur);
EXCEPTION
  WHEN OTHERS THEN
      RAISE_application_error(-20001,'Error in execution',TRUE);
      IF dbms_sql.is_open(cur) THEN
        dbms_sql.close_cursor(cur);
      END IF;
END;
/
```

Using Cursors

Explicit cursors are predefined, multirow-returning SQL statements. Cursors are processed explicitly through the use of **OPEN**, **FETCH**, and **CLOSE** commands or through the use of cursor loops. An **OPEN** command parses the cursor code and calls the rows identified by the query. FETCH processes the cursor code to retrieve one row from the selected set of rows, and the values are inserted into a record or set of variables specified with an **INTO** clause. CLOSE closes the cursor, releasing any memory assigned to the cursor. A cursor loop has the following format:

```
FOR rec_id IN cursor_id LOOP
---- processing ----
END LOOP;
```

One advantage of the cursor **FOR** loop is that no **OPEN, FETCH,** or **CLOSE** commands are required for cursor control, which is handled by the loop logic.

The *rec_id* must be a suitably defined record structure or properly typed variable to hold what is returned from the cursor. The *cursor_id* is the name of the cursor. The effect of issuing this type of command is to open and parse, then fetch rows from the cursor until no more records are found, at which time, the cursor loop ends.

Implicit Cursors

An implicit cursor is automatically defined when any SQL statement is issued. An implicit cursor will result in two fetches against the database: One to get an indication if more than one row will be returned (if there is, you get an implicit exception raised) and the next to actually get the row. Implicit cursors can only be used to process one row at a time.

Cursor Attributes

Explicit cursors have built-in attributes that allow tracking of their status. These cursor attributes are as follows:

➤ **Cursor_name%FOUND**—Before the first fetch on an opened cursor, this is **NULL**, and if the latest fetch is successful, **%FOUND** becomes **TRUE**. This shouldn't be checked until after a fetch has executed.

➤ **Cursor_name%ISOPEN**—Before a cursor is opened, this is **FALSE**. If the cursor has been opened, and if it's still open, this will yield **TRUE**.

➤ **Cursor_name%NOTFOUND**—If the last fetch yields a row, this is **FALSE**, and if the last fetch was unsuccessful, this becomes **TRUE**.

➤ **Cursor_name%ROWCOUNT**—Returns the count for the number of rows fetched thus far. Before a cursor is opened, this yields a **NULL**. Before the first fetch, this yields zero. If **%ROWCOUNT** is checked before a cursor is opened, it will raise the **INVALID_CURSOR** exception. Until a cursor is closed, the **%ROWCOUNT** will contain the last valid count of records fetched.

Cursor attributes can also be used with the most current SQL statement (implicit cursor) by appending "SQL" to the front of their name instead of the name of the cursor. With the exception that no **OPEN** or **FETCH** logic is needed, the attributes work identically with an implicit or explicit cursor. Cursors will be covered in more detail in Chapter 10.

Practice Questions

Question 1

What does the Procedural Statement Executor within the PL/SQL engine do?

- ○ a. Separates the SQL statements and sends them to the SQL Statement Executor
- ○ b. Processes server-side data
- ○ c. Processes data that is local to the application
- ○ d. Passes blocks of PL/SQL to the Oracle8i server

The correct answer is c. Answer c is correct because one of the Procedural statement executor's functions is to process data that is local to the application. Answer a is incorrect because this is a function of the PL/SQL engine but not the Procedural Statement Executor inside the engine. Answer b is incorrect because the server-side data is processed by the Oracle8i server. Answer d is incorrect because this is a function of the Server Manager, not the PL/SQL engine or its subcomponent, the Procedural Statement Executor.

Question 2

> Evaluate this procedure:
>
> ```
> PROCEDURE price_increase
>     (v_quote    IN BOOLEAN,
>      v_stock    IN BOOLEAN,
>      v_approval   IN OUT BOOLEAN)
> IS
> BEGIN
>    V_approval:=v_quote AND v_stock;
> END;
> ```
>
> If **v_quote** equals **NULL**, and **v_stock** equals **NULL**, which value is assigned to **v_approval**?
>
> ○ a. **TRUE**
>
> ○ b. **FALSE**
>
> ○ c. **NULL**
>
> ○ d. None of the above

The proper response is c, because **NULL** and **NULL** results in a **NULL**. Answer a is incorrect because to evaluate to **TRUE**, both would have to be **TRUE**. Answer b is incorrect because to evaluate to **FALSE**, both would have to be **FALSE**, or one **TRUE** and one **FALSE**. Answer d is incorrect because a Boolean value is only allowed to be **TRUE, FALSE**, or **NULL**.

Question 3

> In which section of a PL/SQL block is a **WHEN OTHERS** clause allowed?
>
> ○ a. Header
>
> ○ b. Declarative
>
> ○ c. Executable
>
> ○ d. Exception
>
> ○ e. None of the above

The proper answer is d. The **WHEN OTHERS** clause is an exception handling clause. Answer a is incorrect because the **WHEN OTHERS** clause is only allowed in an exception section and is used to process implicit exceptions that aren't specifically covered by **WHEN** statements in the exception section. Answers b and c are incorrect for the same reason as answer a.

Question 4

Evaluate this cursor statement:

```
DECLARE
    CURSOR price_cursor
            (v_price NUMBER(8,2)) IS
        SELECT id_number, description,
        manufacturer_id
        FROM inventory
        WHERE price > v_price;
```

Why will this statement cause an error?

- O a. A parameter isn't defined.
- O b. The size of the variable can't be specified.
- O c. A **WHERE** clause can't be used in a cursor statement.
- O d. The **SELECT** statement is missing the **INTO** clause.

The proper answer is b, because only a variable's type—and not any size information—is specified in the input variable section. Answer a is incorrect because all required parameters *are* specified. Answer c is incorrect because a **WHERE** clause *is* allowed in cursor statements. Answer d is incorrect because, in a cursor statement, the **INTO** clause must *not* be specified. The **INTO** clause is only specified in a **SELECT** statement used as an implicit cursor in PL/SQL; this is an explicit cursor.

Question 5

When will a **SELECT** statement in a PL/SQL block raise an exception?

- O a. When it retrieves only one row
- O b. When it retrieves more than one row
- O c. When the datatypes within the **SELECT** statement are inconsistent
- O d. When the **SELECT** statement is missing a required clause

Answer b is the correct answer. An exception will be raised if an implicit cursor retrieves more than one row. Answer a is incorrect because an implicit cursor (a **SELECT** statement in a PL/SQL block) by definition is allowed to return only a single row. Answers c and d are incorrect because this type of error will not allow the PL/SQL program unit to be successfully compiled. If you can't compile the code, it can't execute, and if it can't execute, it can't raise an exception.

Question 6

> Which types of commands are supported by PL/SQL?
>
> ○ a. DDL.
>
> ○ b. DCL.
>
> ○ c. DML.
>
> ○ d. No commands are supported by PL/SQL.

The answer to this question is c, DML (or Data Manipulation Language). Answer a, DDL, is incorrect because Data Definition Language is not directly supported in PL/SQL. To use DDL, you must use one of the special support packages, such as DBMS_SQL or DBMS_UTILITY. Answer b, DCL, is incorrect because data control language (Oracle security-related commands) cannot be specified directly in PL/SQL. Answer d is incorrect because answer c is correct.

Question 7

> Which PL/SQL program construct must return a value?
>
> ○ a. Anonymous block
>
> ○ b. Stored function
>
> ○ c. Stored procedure
>
> ○ d. Database trigger
>
> ○ e. Application trigger

The correct answer is b. A **FUNCTION** must always return a value by definition. Answer a is incorrect because an anonymous PL/SQL block is incapable of returning a value; there's no syntax for it. Answer c is incorrect because the major difference between a function and a procedure is that a function must return a value, whereas a procedure doesn't have to. Answers d and e are incorrect because, again, the syntax and functionality of a trigger doesn't permit the return of values.

Question 8

> Which PL/SQL subprogram components are required? [Check all correct answers]
>
> ❏ a. Header
>
> ❏ b. Declarative
>
> ❏ c. Executable
>
> ❏ d. Exception handling
>
> ❏ e. End

The correct answers are a, c, and e. The only required sections in a PL/SQL program are **HEADER, EXECUTABLE** and **END**. Answer b is incorrect because a declarative section is not required. Answer d is incorrect because you aren't required to put exception handing into your application (even though it's a good idea). Remember, our simplest procedure would be:

```
CREATE PROCEDURE start_it AS     < This is
                                   the header
BEGIN
    NULL;
END;           < From the BEGIN to
                 the END is the executable
                 section. Every block must
                 have a BEGIN and END.
```

Question 9

Using SQL*Plus, you attempt to create a procedure using this command:

```
    PROCEDURE price_increase
    (v_percent_increase    NUMBER)
IS
BEGIN
    UPDATE inventory
    SET price = price * v_percent_increase;
    COMMIT;
END;
```

Why does this command cause an error?

O a. A parameter mode was not declared.

O b. The procedure does not return a value.

O c. The **CREATE OR REPLACE** clause is missing.

O d. A datatype is not specified.

This is a trick question because many people will not understand what the question is asking. Remember, if it isn't shown in the question, then it isn't there. In this case, the **CREATE OR REPLACE** command line is not shown. Answer c is the correct answer. Answer a is incorrect because the mode will default to **IN** if not specified. Answer b is incorrect because procedures don't have to return values, only functions have to return values. Answer d is incorrect because a datatype (**NUMBER**) is clearly specified.

Question 10

Which PL/SQL program construct is associated with a database table and is fired automatically?

O a. Anonymous block

O b. Stored function

O c. Stored procedure

O d. Database trigger

O e. Application trigger

O f. Application procedure

Answer d is the correct answer. Answer d is correct because a table trigger is the only stored object that will be automatically executed when a table is accessed. Answer a is incorrect because an anonymous block, although used to create the code in a trigger, can't by itself be invoked by an action taken against a database table. Answer b is incorrect because a stored function must be explicitly called from another program unit or from the command line; it can't be tied to a table to happen automatically. Answer c is incorrect for the same reasons as answer b. Answer e is incorrect because an application trigger is fired by an application action, not a table action. Answer f is incorrect because an application procedure must be explicitly called from an application.

Question 11

Which clause is required in a **SELECT** statement within a PL/SQL block?

○ a. **WHERE**

○ b. **INTO**

○ c. **GROUP BY**

○ d. **HAVING**

○ e. **ORDER BY**

The correct answer is b, **INTO**. Answer b is correct because an **INTO** is required if a **SELECT** is used inside a block. The **INTO** may only be omitted if the **SELECT** is part of a **CURSOR** definition. Answer a is incorrect because a **WHERE** clause isn't required for a **SELECT** statement. Answer c is incorrect because the **GROUP BY** clause isn't allowed in an implicit cursor (a PL/SQL **SELECT** statement) because a **SELECT** statement inside a PL/SQL returns only one value by definition. Answer d is incorrect because a **SELECT** statement inside a PL/SQL returns only one value by definition, and the **HAVING** clause is used with the **GROUP BY**, which is for a multivalue return. Answer e is incorrect because by definition a **SELECT** statement inside a PL/SQL block returns only one value.

Question 12

Using SQL*Plus, you create this procedure:

```
CREATE OR REPLACE PROCEDURE price_increase
    (v_manufacturer_id IN NUMBER,
     v_percent_increase IN NUMBER)
IS
    v_rows_update BOOLEAN;
BEGIN
    UPDATE inventory
           SET price = price * v_percent_increase
           WHERE manufacturer_id = v_manufacturer_id;
    v_rows_updated:=SQL%NOTFOUND;
END;
```

What value will be assigned to **v_rows_updated**?

- ○ a. **TRUE**, if any prices were changed
- ○ b. **TRUE**, if no prices were changed
- ○ c. **FALSE**, if no prices were changed
- ○ d. **NULL**

The correct answer is b. Answer b is correct since if the **UPDATE** did not update any rows then were none found and the **SQL%NOTFOUND** cursor variable will be set to **TRUE** for the implicit cursor used to perform the **UPDATE**. Answer a is incorrect because **%NOTFOUND** will evaluate to **TRUE** only if no prices were changed. Answer c is incorrect because if prices weren't changed, the value would be **TRUE**. Answer d is incorrect because **%NOTFOUND** will be set to either **TRUE** or **FALSE**, based on the results of the **UPDATE** command that precedes it.

Need To Know More?

Feuerstein, Steven. *Oracle PL/SQL Programming*. O'Reilly & Associates, 1995. ISBN 1-56592-335-9. This book is considered one of the seminal references on PL/SQL. Although the advanced edition of this book is also a must-have for any serious PL/SQL developer, this earlier edition is probably the better choice for studying for the OCP-DBA exam.

Owens, Kevin. *Building Intelligent Databases With Oracle PL/SQL, Triggers, and Stored Procedures*. Prentice-Hall PTR, 1996. ISBN: 0-13-443631-8. An excellent reference for all phases of PL/SQL use and development.

Urman, Scott and Tim Smith. *Oracle PL/SQL Programming*. Osborne-McGraw Hill, 1996. ISBN: 0-07882-176-2. This is a good Oracle PL/SQL reference from Oracle Press.

Oracle Corporation. *Oracle8i Server SQL Reference Manual, Release 3(8.1.7)*. September, 2000, Redwood City, California. Part No. A85397-01. This is the source book for all Oracle SQL for version 8i. This book can be found on the Web, at the time of writing, at **http://technet.oracle.com**. This site has free membership and has all current versions of Oracle documentation available online in Acrobat format (PDF files).

PL/SQL Users Guide and Reference Release 8.1, Oracle Corporation, December 1999. Part No. A77069-01. This is the source book for PL/SQL. This book can be found on the Web, at the time of writing, at **http://technet.oracle.com**. This site has free membership and has all current versions of Oracle documentation available online in Acrobat format (PDF files).

Using Control Structures in PL/SQL

- -

Terms you'll need to understand:

✓ IF...THEN...ELSE...ELSIF...END IF

✓ LOOP...END LOOP

✓ WHILE

✓ FOR

✓ CURSOR

✓ GOTO

✓ NULL

Techniques you'll need to master:

✓ Creating **IF...THEN...ELSIF...ELSE...END IF** constructs

✓ Creating **LOOP...END LOOP** constructs

✓ Creating **WHILE** loops

✓ Creating **FOR** loops

✓ Creating **CURSOR** loops

✓ Using **GOTO** and **NULL** statements

PL/SQL is short for procedural language SQL. Procedural means that the steps of processing are taken in a logical, straightforward manner. This logical manner means that there must be flow control statements that allow conditional logic, which in PL/SQL is controlled with loop structures. The loop structures in PL/SQL are the **IF, LOOP, WHILE, FOR, CURSOR, GOTO**, and **NULL** command constructs.

PL/SQL Flow Control

Flow control—the use of loops and logic control, such as **IF...THEN...ELSE**—was the primary reason PL/SQL was created. SQL, though great for set processing, was found lacking when it came to structure. Indeed, SQL isn't designed to be structured. A non-procedural language such as plain SQL cannot solve many programming problems. PL/SQL is the solution for these types of problems.

PL/SQL loop control is executed through several types of loop control statements; the easiest is the **LOOP...END LOOP;** construct. This simple structure is augmented through additional control clauses, such as **WHILE, EXIT**, and **EXIT WHEN**. PL/SQL also supports the **FOR...LOOP...END LOOP;** construct that allows iteration control, as well as the **WHILE...LOOP...END LOOP;** construct for conditional control; and the **CURSOR** loop for control based on cursors.

IF...THEN...ELSE Structures

The **IF...THEN...ELSE...ELSIF...END IF** structure allows a single-pass conditional statement to be created. The conditions are always evaluated against the Boolean **TRUE** to determine if processing should be done or if control should pass to the next section. The full syntax for the **IF...THEN...ELSE** construct is as follows:

```
IF condition1 THEN
    Sequence of statements
ELSIF condition2 THEN
    Sequence of statements
ELSE
    Final sequence of statements
END IF;
```

The condition statements can be simple or complex equalities or Boolean values. If the condition in the statement yields a **TRUE**, the sequence of statements that follow it are executed. If the condition is **FALSE**, the processing passes down the decision tree of **ELSIF**s (only one is shown, you can apply as many as are needed) to the final **ELSE** and **END IF**. The only required part of the structure is the **IF...END IF;**. Be sure that the **END IF** is two separate words, or an error will result. Notice also that the term is **ELSIF**, not **ELSEIF** or **ELSE IF**. Finally, the final **ELSE**, if present, has no condition associated with it; it shows the final decision in the decision tree if all others are **FALSE**. If the **ELSE** isn't present, the control passes back into the program body.

An **IF...THEN...ELSE** construct would not be used to set all records to a new value, even if those records met a specific criteria. An **IF...THEN...ELSE** would be used where a record or set of records was each updated based on a set of differing conditions. For example:

```
IF x=1 THEN
Y:=2;
ELSIF x=2 THEN
Y:=3;
ELSE
Y:=4;
END IF;
```

A Simple **LOOP...END LOOP**; Construct

The most simple loop structure is the **LOOP...END LOOP;**. Note that unless control is passed either from an **EXIT, EXIT WHEN,** or exception generation, a **LOOP...END LOOP** structure is an infinite loop. Never depend on an exception to throw you out of a loop. The actual structure of **LOOP...END LOOP;** looks like the following:

```
<<label_name>>
LOOP
    Sequence of statements
END LOOP label_name;
```

For example:

```
X:=0
<<counter_loop>>
LOOP
  EXIT WHEN x=10;
  X:=X+1;
END LOOP counter_loop;
```

The *label_name* is not required, but for a nested loop structure, its use makes debugging easier.

By using the **EXIT** command, simple loops become more controllable, as shown here:

```
<<label_name>>
LOOP
    Sequence of statements
    IF condition THEN EXIT label_name;
END LOOP label_name;
```

The condition can also be built into the **EXIT** by using the **WHEN** statement:

```
<<label_name>>
LOOP
    Sequence of statements
    EXIT label_name WHEN condition;
END LOOP label_name;
```

You can also use alternate forms of **EXIT** and **WHEN**, such as:

```
WHEN condition EXIT;
```

The WHILE Loop

Another useful form of the loop is the **WHILE** loop. The **WHILE** loop allows specification of a condition at the start of the loop, and until the condition is met, the loop executes. Unlike an **IF** statement, which only processes its set of statements if the condition it tests for is **TRUE**, a **WHILE** loop will execute its contained statements until its limiting condition is **FALSE**. Use the **WHILE** loop when an exact count of items to be processed is not available, which means that the loop must continue until finished. The form for a **WHILE** loop is as follows:

```
WHILE condition LOOP
    Sequence of statements
END LOOP;
```

Always be sure that the limiting condition will be reached. A statement inside the **WHILE** loop must itself initiate the setting of the Boolean condition, or you've created an infinite loop. Note that you can also use the **WHILE NOT** condition **LOOP** form.

The FOR Loop

The **FOR** loop is used to process for a specific number of iterations. The order of iteration can be set to either the default ascending order (1, 2, 3) or to reverse order (3, 2, 1). The format of the **FOR** loop is as follows:

. . . .

```
FOR index IN [REVERSE] lower_bound..higher_bound LOOP
    Sequence of statements
END LOOP;
```

Notice that **STEP** commands aren't used, as they are in some languages that allow alteration of the iteration interval. In PL/SQL, the iteration interval is always 1. To use intervals, you can use the **MOD(***m,n***)** command within an **IF...END IF** structure or if some other means of iteration control is implemented. The loop iteration control variable is treated as a constant and cannot be reassigned a value inside the loop. The lower or upper bounds can be replaced with variables. Note that the **EXIT** command and its alternate structures using **WHEN** can be used inside the **FOR** loop structure to force a premature exit from the loop.

PL/SQL assigns the values of the bounds to temporary **PLS_INTEGER** variables, and, if required, rounds the values to the nearest integer. The range of a **PLS_INTEGER** is $-2^{**}31 .. 2^{**}31$. So, if a bound evaluates to a number outside that range, you get a *numeric overflow* error when PL/SQL attempts the assignment.

A special form of the **FOR** loop is the **CURSOR FOR** loop. A cursor loop has the following format:

```
FOR rec_id IN cursor_id LOOP
---- processing ----
END LOOP;
```

One advantage of the cursor **FOR** loop is that no **OPEN, FETCH,** or **CLOSE** commands are required for cursor control, which is handled by the loop logic.

The *rec_id* must be a suitably defined record structure or properly typed variable to hold what is returned from the cursor. The *cursor_id* is the name of the cursor. The effect of issuing this type of command is to open and parse, then fetch rows from the cursor until no more records are found, at which time the cursor loop ends. An example cursor **FOR** loop would be as follows:

```
DECLARE
    endpoint analysis.result1%TYPE;
    CURSOR endpoint IS
        SELECT reagent1,reagent2,reagent3,analysis_name, units
        FROM results_table WHERE test_num = 1;
BEGIN
    FOR el_rec IN endpoint LOOP
        /* calculate analysis result and store the results */
        result := el_rec.reagent2 / (el_rec.reagent1 +
            el_rec.reagent3);
        INSERT INTO analysis VALUES (
```

```
            result1, e1_rec.analysis_name, e1_rec.units);
  END LOOP;
  COMMIT;
END;
```

In this example, the cursor *endpoint* is used to define the implicit record *e1_rec*. When the loop is executed, the results that have the *test_num* value of 1 will be cycled through, and each set of retrieved values are inserted into the record *e1_rec* and processed.

When the cursor **FOR** loop is executed, the *cursor_id* that is used cannot belong to an explicit cursor name already opened by an **OPEN** statement or another *cursor_id* declared in an enclosing cursor **FOR** loop. The cursor is used to create an implicitly defined record. Before each iteration of the **FOR** loop, the PL/SQL engine fetches one set of values into the implicitly declared record. The record is defined only inside the loop. You cannot refer to the implicit record's fields outside of the cursor **FOR** loop.

The set of statements inside the loop is executed once for each row that satisfies the statement associated with the cursor. When you leave the loop, the cursor is closed automatically—even if an **EXIT** or **GOTO** statement is used to leave the loop prematurely or an exception is raised inside the loop.

The GOTO and NULL Statements

The **GOTO** statement is also present in PL/SQL. Luckily it's infrequently used and is not a crucial statement. A **GOTO** is an unconditional branch. You can't use **GOTO** in an **IF**, **LOOP**, or sub-block. As a general rule, overuse of **GOTO** will result in unreadable spaghetti code. Use of a GOTO usually indicates improperly structured code causing an unplanned branch. Too many unplanned branches leads to hard to decipher code.

The **NULL** is the only executable command that doesn't do anything. In fact, not doing anything is its purpose. I already showed you one possible use of the **NULL** in the **start_it** procedure in Chapter 9. Another is for testing and also for placement inside an exception block where you want to handle an exception that has been raised, but except for exiting the block, you don't want to take any other action. A common use of the **NULL** is in a **WHEN OTHERS** exception block.

Practice Questions

Question 1

> Which type of loop construct would you use to add an unknown number of users to a users table?
>
> ○ a. **FOR**
>
> ○ b. **IF...THEN...ELSE**
>
> ○ c. **CURSOR**
>
> ○ d. **WHILE**

The correct answer is d. A **WHILE** loop is used when you don't know the number of items you will be processing. Answer a is incorrect because a **FOR** loop uses a counter where the number of items processed must be known before you start the loop. Answer b is in correct because an **IF** structure is good only for a single pass. Answer c is incorrect because we have not been told the source of the information; it may work if we were drawing from a load table, but not if we were using **UTL_FILE** to get information from an external file.

Question 2

> What would be an appropriate label for a loop?
>
> ○ a. #proc_loop1
>
> ○ b. /proc_loop1
>
> ○ c. @proc_loop1
>
> ○ d. <<proc_loop1>>

The correct answer is d. A loop label is enclosed by <<>> dual sets of angle brackets. All of the other answers are incorrect because they don't show double sets of angle brackets.

Question 3

Evaluate this **IF** statement:

```
IF iso_weight<85 THEN
   per_rad := 0;
ELSIF iso_weight>85 THEN
   per_rad := 100;
ELSIF iso_weight>260 THEN
   comment := 'Not Likely';
ELSE
   comment := 'impossible';
END IF;
```

What will the result be if the **iso_weight** is 85?

○ a. **per_rad** will be set to 0.

○ b. **per_rad** will be set to 100.

○ c. **comment** will be set to 'Not Likely'.

○ d. **comment** will be set to 'impossible'.

The correct answer is d. Because none of the conditions involving 85 specifies an "=" sign as well as the "<" or ">" sign, 85 will not be evaluated, and you will get the **ELSE** result. Answer a is incorrect because this will occur only if the value is less than 85. Answer b is incorrect because this will occur only if the value is greater than 85. Answer c is incorrect because the **ELSIF** that it results from will never be reached, because its answer set is encompassed by the greater-than-85 answer set.

Question 4

What happens in an **IF...THEN...ELSE** statement when the value is **TRUE**?

○ a. Control is passed on to the next **ELSIF** or **ELSE** of the construct.

○ b. The statements after the **THEN** are executed.

○ c. The control is passed to the next executable statement after the **END IF**.

○ d. Nothing. **IF...THEN...ELSE** doesn't depend on Boolean values.

The correct answer is b. A **TRUE** result from the specified condition in the **IF** or **ELSIF** results in the statements after the **THEN** being processed, and control is then passed to the next executable statement after the **END IF**. Answer a is incorrect because this is what happens if the result of the condition is **FALSE**. Answer c is incorrect because this happens only after a set of statements has been executed because of a **TRUE** result, or if none of the conditions in the construct evaluated to **TRUE**. Answer d is incorrect because the **IF** construct *does* use Boolean values.

Question 5

Evaluate this **IF** statement:

```
IF iso_weight<=85 THEN
   per_rad := 0;
ELSIF iso_weight>85 THEN
   per_rad := 100;
ELSIF iso_weight>260 THEN
   comment := 'Not Likely';
ELSE
   comment := 'impossible';
END IF;
```

What will the result be if the **iso_weight** is 270?

O a. **comment** will be set to 'impossible'.

O b. **per_rad** will be set to 0.

O c. **comment** will be set to 'Not Likely'.

O d. **per_rad** will be set to 100.

The correct answer is d. Because the writer of this **IF** didn't place an upper bound on the >85 **ELSIF** and 270>85, then this condition will be satisfied before the >260 condition, and its actions will be taken. Answer a is incorrect because this **ELSE** will never be reached unless a negative value for **iso_weight** is entered. Answer b is incorrect because 270>85. Answer c is incorrect because this **ELSIF** will never be evaluated to **TRUE** because the >85 will catch any instance of **iso_weight** in its range before it can be reached.

Question 6

> Evaluate the following **WHILE** loop:
>
> ```
> v_num := in_num;
> WHILE v_num >= 16
> LOOP
>     v_hex := hextab (MOD (v_num, 16)) || v_hex;
>     v_num := TRUNC (v_num / 16);
> END LOOP;
> v_hex := hextab (MOD (v_num, 16)) || v_hex;
> out_hex := v_hex;
> ```
>
> How many times will the loop execute if **in_num** is set to 256?
>
> ○ a. 1
>
> ○ b. 2
>
> ○ c. 3
>
> ○ d. 16

This is actually a trick question. You have to understand not only what the **WHILE** loop does but what the modulus (**MOD**) function does. The answer is b. The loop is traversed twice for 256 because 256 modulus 16 yields 0, and then the **TRUNC** of 256/16 yields 16. Because this sets **v_num** = 16, the loop is processed one more time yielding a **MOD** of 0 and a **TRUNC** of 1. Because 1 is less than 16, the **WHILE** loop exits. Answer a is incorrect because the value of **in_num** would have to be <16 for the loop to process only once. Answer c is incorrect because the value of **in_num** would have to be greater than 4,096 for the loop to execute three times. Answer d is incorrect because the **in_num** value would have to be greater than 1.84467440737e19 to achieve 16 loop executions.

Question 7

Evaluate the following function:

```
FUNCTION gen_pword
RETURN VARCHAR2 AS
    pi       NUMBER := 3.14159265358979323846264 ;
    seed     NUMBER ;
    pwd      VARCHAR2(6);
    pwd_len  NUMBER := 6;
BEGIN
    SELECT TO_NUMBER(TO_CHAR(hsecs)) / 8640000 INTO
      seed FROM v$timer ;
    pwd := NULL ;
        FOR  j  IN 1..pwd_len LOOP
            seed := POWER(pi + seed,5)   - TRUNC
    (POWER(pi + seed,5) );
            pwd := pwd || CHR( 64 + 1 + TRUNC (seed *
    26)) ;
        END LOOP;
RETURN pwd;
END;
```

How many times will the loop execute?

○ a. You can't determine the answer from the information given.

○ b. 3.

○ c. 6.

○ d. Once for each letter of the input password.

The correct answer is c. This function returns a password with a length of six as set by the **pwd_len NUMBER := 6** line. The **pwd_len** value is used to control the loop execution. Answer a is incorrect because the information is given. Answer b is incorrect because **pwd_len** is set to six. Answer d is incorrect because this function gives you a six-place password and has no input.

Question 8

Evaluate this **IF** statement:

```
IF iso_weight<=85 THEN
  per_rad := 0;
ELSIF iso_weight BETWEEN 85 and 260 THEN
  per_rad := 100;
ELSIF iso_weight>260 THEN
  comment := 'Not Likely';
ELSE
  comment := 'impossible';
END IF;
```

What will cause a result of **comment := 'impossible'**?

O a. An **iso_weight** of less than 1.

O b. An **iso_weight** greater than 260.

O c. You can never get this result.

O d. An **iso_weight** of 0.

The correct answer is c. Because the line **iso_weight<=85** is unbounded in the lower direction, and the line **iso_weight>260** is unbounded in the upper direction, you can never get to the **comment:='impossible'**. Answer a is incorrect because this is satisfied by the first condition. Answer b is incorrect because this is satisfied by the third condition. Answer d is incorrect because this is also satisfied by the first condition.

Question 9

What causes a PL/SQL **WHILE** loop to terminate?

O a. A Boolean variable or expression evaluates to **TRUE**.

O b. A Boolean variable or expression evaluates to **FALSE**.

O c. A Boolean variable or expression evaluates to **NULL**.

O d. Control is passed to the **EXIT** statement.

O e. The specified number of iterations have been performed.

The correct response is b. Answer b is correct because a WHILE loop is only ended implicitly when it returns a FALSE value. Answer a is incorrect because a **WHILE** condition must evaluate to **FALSE** for the loop to terminate. Answer c is incorrect for the same reason as answer a. Answer d is incorrect because a **WHILE** loop doesn't have an **EXIT** statement. Answer e is incorrect because only a **FOR** loop terminates on a specified number of iterations, and we're talking about a **WHILE** loop.

Question 10

Evaluate this incomplete loop:

```
LOOP
    INSERT INTO inventory (id_number,
                           description)
       VALUES (v_id_number, v_description);
    V_counter := v_counter +1;
```

Which statement will need to be added to conditionally stop the execution of the loop?

○ a. **END LOOP**.

○ b. **EXIT**.

○ c. **EXIT WHEN**.

○ d. **END**.

○ e. No statement is needed.

The correct answer is c. The only answer given that allows a conditional end to the loop is the **EXIT WHEN** clause. All of the other values would either generate a syntax error or force an explicit (not conditional) end to the loop. Answer a is incorrect because, although **END LOOP** ends the loop structure, it doesn't end loop processing. Answer b is incorrect because although **EXIT** will terminate loop processing, it won't do it conditionally unless paired with **WHEN**. Answer d is incorrect because just placing an **END** at this point without an **END LOOP** will cause a syntax error. Answer e is incorrect because an **EXIT WHEN** is required.

Need To Know More?

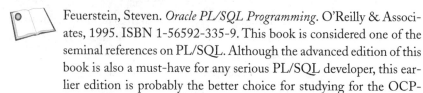

Feuerstein, Steven. *Oracle PL/SQL Programming*. O'Reilly & Associates, 1995. ISBN 1-56592-335-9. This book is considered one of the seminal references on PL/SQL. Although the advanced edition of this book is also a must-have for any serious PL/SQL developer, this earlier edition is probably the better choice for studying for the OCP-DBA exam.

Owens, Kevin. *Building Intelligent Databases With Oracle PL/SQL, Triggers, and Stored Procedures*. Prentice-Hall PTR, 1996. ISBN: 0-13-443631-8. An excellent reference for all phases of PL/SQL use and development.

Urman, Scott and Tim Smith. *Oracle PL/SQL Programming*. Osborne-McGraw Hill, 1996. ISBN: 0-07882-176-2. This is a good Oracle PL/SQL reference from Oracle Press.

Oracle Corporation. *Oracle8i Server SQL Reference Manual, Release 3(8.1.7)*. September, 2000. Redwood City, CA. Part No. A85397-01. This is the source book for all Oracle SQL for version 8i. This book can be found on the Web, at the time of writing, at **http://technet.oracle.com**. This site has free membership and has all current versions of Oracle documentation available online in Acrobat format (PDF files).

Oracle Corporation. *PL/SQL Users Guide and Reference Release 8.1*. December 1999. Redwood City, CA. Part No. A77069-01. This is the source book for PL/SQL. This book can be found on the Web, at the time of writing, at **http://technet.oracle.com**. This site has free membership and has all current versions of Oracle documentation available online in Acrobat format (PDF files).

Michael R. Ault. *Oracle8 Black Book*. Coriolis Group Books, 1998. ISBN No. 1-57610-187-8. This book tells how to use all of the Oracle8 features including LOBs, Collections, and UDTs.

Working with Composite Datatypes in PL/SQL

Terms you'll need to understand:

✓ RECORD

✓ %TYPE

✓ %ROWTYPE

✓ TABLE

Techniques you'll need to master:

✓ Using composite datatypes

✓ Creating a **RECORD**

✓ Creating a **%TYPE**

✓ Creating a **%ROWTYPE**

✓ Creating a PL/SQL **TABLE**

✓ Using Composite datatypes

Composite Datatypes in PL/SQL

A composite datatype has components that can be individually manipulated. Composite datatypes are **RECORD**s, **%ROWTYPE**s, **TABLE**s, nested **TABLE**s, and **VARRAY**s.

A **RECORD** is a group of items, differing in datatype, which are stored in fields. **RECORD**s can be handled as a single item instead of having to deal with multiple individual datatypes. A special form of a **RECORD** is created by the **%ROWTYPE** declaration, which is used to create a **RECORD** that is identical to a row in a table, just as the **%TYPE** declaration is used to define a scaler that is identical to a table row individual data item.

A PL/SQL **TABLE** is a composite datatype sometimes called an index-by **TABLE**. A PL/SQL **TABLE** is a collection of scaler values or composite types much like a nested table. However, unlike a nested table that can have a physical representation in the database, a PL/SQL **TABLE** exists only in memory while it is being used in a PL/SQL routine. A PL/SQL **TABLE** is indexed using a **BINARY INTEGER**.

A nested **TABLE** is a collection of multiple scaler values or types that is not of a predetermined size and that is allowed to be sparse. A nested **TABLE** is stored out of line with the normal data in a table and uses a constructor method to populate its values.

A **VARRAY**, or varying array, is a collection of scaler values or types that is of a predetermined size. A **VARRAY** can also be based on a cursor. A **VARRAY** uses a constructor function to build its records. A **VARRAY** is not allowed to be sparse.

Because **VARRAY**s and nested **TABLE**s won't be covered on the test, we do not cover them in detail. The major composite datatypes you will have to deal with on the exam will be **RECORD**s and PL/SQL **TABLE**s.

PL/SQL RECORDs

A PL/SQL record is a collection of logically related data types that is accessed as a unit in a PL/SQL program. **RECORD**s are similar in PL/SQL and 3GLs that use records. The general properties of a **RECORD** are as follows:

➤ A **RECORD** can be defined in the declarative part of any package, subprogram, or block of a PL/SQL program.

➤ Each **RECORD** can have a virtually unlimited number of fields.

➤ Fields that have not been initialized are **NULL**.

➤ A **RECORD** can be a subcomponent of another **RECORD**.

➤ **RECORD** fields can be initialized to a value or set to **NOT NULL**; if set to **NOT NULL**, they must be initialized.

➤ A **RECORD** field can have an associated **DEFAULT** values clause.

A PL/SQL record is defined using the syntax in Figure 11.1.

An example creation of a **RECORD** is shown in Listing 11.1.

Listing 11.1   Example RECORD-creation statement.

```
TYPE message_rectype IS RECORD
    (item_type  INTEGER
    ,Mvarchar2  VARCHAR2(4093)
    ,Mdate      DATE NOT NULL DEFAULT SYSDATE
    ,Mnumber    NUMBER
    ,Mrowid     ROWID
    ,Mraw       RAW(4093)
    );
```

If your **RECORD** structure is identical to a table row, you can use the **%ROWTYPE** declaration to define a **RECORD** that is identical to the referenced table's row. For example:

```
Tab_rec        dba_tables%ROWTYPE;
```

This defines a **RECORD** called **tab_rec** that has the same structure as a row in the view **DBA_TABLES**. This type of **RECORD** is useful when you will be fetching entire rows from a view or table.

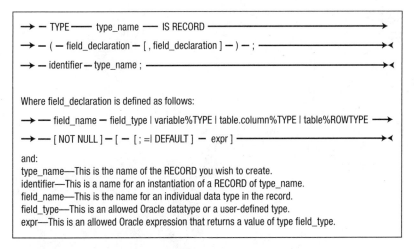

Figure 11.1   Syntax for defining a PL/SQL record.

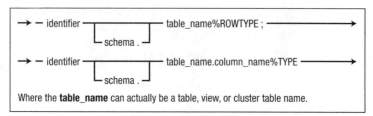

Figure 11.2 Syntax for use of **%ROWTYPE** and **%TYPE**.

Note: If you combine a %ROWTYPE with any other declaration in a RECORD, you cannot use the RECORD to define a PL/SQL TABLE because a PL/SQL TABLE may not contain a table or record with composite fields.

The **%ROWTYPE** declaration forces the record to match the specified table row structure. The **%TYPE** declaration forces the data item to be the identical datatype specified for the table and column referenced in the declaration. The general formats for these types of declaration are shown in Figure 11.2.

The advantages to using **%ROWTYPE** and **%TYPE** are as follows:

➤ The number and datatype of the underlying database column or columns need not be known.

➤ The number and datatype of the underlying database column or columns may change at runtime.

➤ **%ROWTYPE** makes selecting an entire row from a table very easy, especially if the table row is large or complex in structure.

Accessing PL/SQL RECORDs

Individual data items in a PL/SQL **RECORD** are accessed via dot notation. For example, Listing 11.2 shows how to access a **RECORD** called **tab_rec**.

Listing 11.2   Example access of RECORD structures.

```
TYPE tab_rec IS RECORD
(table_owner dba_tables.owner%TYPE,
 table_name dba_tables.table_name%TYPE,
 tablespace_name dba_tables.tablespace_name%TYPE);
```

The fields would be addressed individually as follows:

```
tab_rec.table_owner
tab_rec.table_name
tab_rec.tablespace_name
```

To assign values to a **RECORD**, you can use it as a target of a **CURSOR** or **SELECT INTO**, or you can use the individual fields as the target of assignments, as shown in Listing 11.3.

Listing 11.3   Example use of **RECORD** in assignments.

```
SELECT owner, table_name, tablespace_name INTO tab_rec FROM
dba_tables
WHERE owner=user;

-- OR -

CURSOR get_tab_rec  IS
SELECT owner, table_name, tablespace_name FROM dba_tables WHERE
owner=user;

OPEN get_tab_rec;
LOOP
  FETCH get_tab_rec INTO tab_rec;
  EXIT WHEN get_tab_rec%NOTFOUND;
…
END LOOP;

-- OR --

Tab_rec.table_name:='EMP';
Tab_rec.table_own:='SCOTT';
Tab_rec.tablespace_name:='USERS'
```

If a **RECORD** is instantiated in a block or subprogram, it ceases to exist when you exit the block or subprogram.

*Note: If you create a user defined **RECORD** and another %ROWTYPE record has an identical structure, they are not equivalent and cannot be assigned to each other.*

Creating and Using PL/SQL TABLEs

PL/SQL objects of type **TABLE** are known as PL/SQL **TABLE**s, which are memory constructs and have no physical representation on the Oracle system disks. Oracle PL/SQL **TABLE**s are used like single dimension arrays in 3GL programs. PL/SQL **TABLE**s are always indexed using **BINARY_INTEGERS**. The **BINARY_INTEGER** datatype has the range −2,147,483,647 to +2,147,483,647. This **BINARY_INTEGER** index value can be manually assigned to not start at 1 for record definition. A PL/SQL **TABLE** can be sparse, that is, it can have unoccupied elements surrounded by occupied elements, just like a standard relational or object table.

A PL/SQL **TABLE** consists of a scaler or **RECORD** declaration and a **BINARY_INTEGER** index. The **RECORD** can be a **%ROWTYPE**, but if it is a composite **RECORD**, it cannot be used in a PL/SQL **TABLE**. For example:

```
DECLARE
TYPE test_rec IS RECORD (
  Dba_tab  dba_tables%ROWTYPE);
TYPE test_rec_tab IS TABLE OF test_rec
INDEX BY BINARY_INTEGER;
BEGIN
NULL;
END;
```

will generate a *PLS 00507: a PLSQL Table may not contain a table or a record with composite fields* error. Whereas the following code will not:

```
DECLARE
TYPE test_rec_tab IS TABLE OF dba_tables%ROWTYPE
INDEX BY BINARY_INTEGER;
BEGIN
NULL;
END;
```

PL/SQL **TABLE**s do not have a fixed size; they can increase in size dynamically up to the limitations of the memory context in which they are created. This dynamic ability of PL/SQL **TABLE**s to expand is both a benefit and a bane. The dynamic ability to expand is a benefit in that you don't have to know the number of data elements before the table is used (unlike a **VARRAY**, whose size is fixed). However, the bane of dynamic sizing in PL/SQL **TABLE**s is that if you place too much into memory, you can exceed process global area (PGA) or user global area (UGA) space limitations. The command to create a PL/SQL **TABLE** is shown in Figure 11.3.

So, as you can see from Figure 11.3, this is a two-step process: First you create the PL/SQL **TABLE** type definition and then you declare the actual table based on the type declaration.

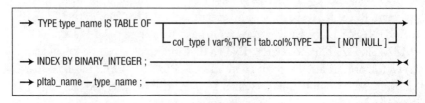

Figure 11.3 Syntax for PL/SQL **TABLE** creation.

After a PL/SQL **TABLE** is created, you access the individual table elements by specifying their integer index values. Listing 11.4 demonstrates this access concept.

Listing 11.4   Example access of PL/SQL **TABLE** elements.

```
SQL>desc dba_temp
 Name                                          Null?    Type
 ---------------------------------------- -------- ------------
 NAME                                                   VARCHAR2(64)
 VALUE                                                  NUMBER
 REP_ORDER                                              NUMBER

SQL>SET SERVEROUTPUT ON
SQL>DECLARE
 2:   TYPE dba_rec IS RECORD (temprec dba_temp%ROWTYPE);
 3:   TYPE val_tab_type IS TABLE OF dba_temp%ROWTYPE
 4:   INDEX BY BINARY_INTEGER;
 5:   dba_tab val_tab_type;
 6:   CURSOR get_val IS
 7:     SELECT * FROM dba_temp;
 8:   i INTEGER:=1;
 9:   BEGIN
10:   FOR dba_rec IN get_val LOOP
11:     dba_tab(i):=dba_rec;
12:     dbms_output.put_line('Value: '||to_char(i)||
13:     ' '||to_char(dba_tab(i).VALUE));
14:     i:=i+1;
15:   END LOOP;
16: END;
17: /

Value: 1 0
Value: 2 3.7750072484778196578718469121484482575
Value: 3 24.2899295004254284672420080223653822787
Value: 4 .9915313353861016584781528800758353544741
...
```

So, in Listing 11.4, we see a table **DBA_TEMP** that is used to define a **RECORD** using **%ROWTYPE** and to define a PL/SQL **TABLE**. The **RECORD** is used in a PL/SQL **FOR** loop (covered in Chapter 12) to insert rows into the PL/SQL **TABLE dba_tab**, which is based on the **TABLE TYPE val_tab_type**. The Oracle-provided package **DBMS_OUTPUT** is then used to show a specific column value from inside the PL/SQL **TABLE** record just created. Notice how, for a specific row in the PL/SQL **TABLE**, you use just the integer index, but for a specific column in the row, you specify the integer followed by a dot and then the column name. Therefore, **dba_tab(i).value** would reference the row represented by the *i*th value of the index for the table, whereas **dba_tab(i).value** represents the information stored in the column "value" for the *i*th row. The format **pl_tab(i).col_name** is correct, whereas **pl_tab.col_name(i)** will generate an *PLS-00302: component "col_name" must be declared* error.

PL/SQL **TABLE** Methods

PL/SQL TABLES have built-in Oracle methods associated with them. A *method* is a function or procedure associated with a specific **TYPE**. In this case, the **TYPE** is a PL/SQL **TABLE**. The methods that are built for each PL/SQL **TABLE** type are shown in Table 11.1.

The methods in Table 11.1 are used to make processing using PL/SQL TABLEs easier. The format for calling a PL/SQL **TABLE** method is shown in Figure 11.4.

Table 11.1 PL/SQL TABLE methods.	
Method	**Purpose**
EXISTS(n)	Returns **TRUE** if the referenced PL/SQL **TABLE** element exists.
COUNT	Returns the number of elements in the PL/SQL **TABLE**.
FIRST or **LAST**	Returns the **FIRST** or the **LAST** value of the **BINARY_INTEGER** for the PL/SQL **TABLE** that is currently occupied by data.
PRIOR(n)	Returns the index value for the first occupied element prior to the value of **n**.
NEXT(n)	Returns the index value for the first occupied element that is next after the value of **n**.
EXTEND(n,i)	Used to increase the size of a PL/SQL **TABLE** by **n** values. If **i** is specified, the value at **i** is used to populate the **n** values, otherwise they are **NULL**. If no values for **n** or **i** are specified, the table is extended by 1 value.
TRIM or **TRIM(n)**	Used to remove one element (**TRIM**) from the end of the table, or **n** (**TRIM(n)**) values from the end of the table.
DELETE, DELETE(n), or **DELETE(m,n)**	Used to delete all values (**DELETE**), a single specified value (**DELETE(n)**), or a range (**DELETE(m,n)**) values from a PL/SQL **TABLE**.

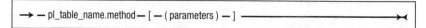

— pl_table_name.method — [— (parameters) —]

Figure 11.4 Syntax for PL/SQL **TABLE** methods.

Practice Questions

Question 1

> Which type of PL/SQL construct would you use to read an unknown number of users from a users table into memory?
>
> ○ a. A **RECORD** created with the **%TYPE** declaration
>
> ○ b. A **RECORD** created with an **INTEGER** and a **%ROWTYPE** datatype declarations
>
> ○ c. An identifier defined from a **TABLE TYPE** declaration
>
> ○ d. A **GLOBAL TEMPORARY** table

The correct answer is c. A PL/SQL **TABLE** is created by a **TABLE TYPE** declaration and a PL/SQL **TABLE** is used when you don't know the number of items you will be processing. Answer a is incorrect because a **%TYPE** declaration is used only for a single scaler value. Answer b is incorrect because a **RECORD** defined using a composite datatype (the **%ROWTYPE**) is not allowed to be used in a PL/SQL **TABLE**. Answer d is incorrect because a **GLOBAL TEMPORARY** table is a physical, not a memory or PL/SQL, construct.

Question 2

> Which is not a benefit of a **%TYPE** declaration?
>
> ○ a. You need to know the datatype of the underlying database column.
>
> ○ b. You don't need to know the size of the underlying database column.
>
> ○ c. The size of the underlying database column may change at runtime.
>
> ○ d. The datatype of the underlying database column may change at runtime.

The correct answer is a. The **%TYPE** declaration is used because you don't need to know the underlying datatype . All of the other answers are incorrect because they are advantages of the **%TYPE** declaration.

Question 3

Evaluate this program fragment:

```
DECLARE
TYPE user_tab_rec IS RECORD (
db_user    dba_users.username%TYPE,
DBA_TAB   dba_tables%ROWTYPE);
TYPE user_rec_tab IS TABLE OF test_rec
INDEX BY BINARY_INTEGER;
Tab_rec dba_tables%ROWTYPE;
Obj_owner dba_objects.owner%TYPE;
begin
(processing)
end;
```

What line will generate an error?

- ○ a. TYPE user_tab_rec IS RECORD (

    db_user dba_users.username%TYPE,

    DBA_TAB dba_tables%ROWTYPE);

- ○ b. TYPE user_rec_tab IS TABLE OF test_rec

    INDEX BY BINARY_INTEGER;

- ○ c. Tab_rec dba_tables%ROWTYPE;

- ○ d. Obj_owner dba_objects.owner%TYPE;

The correct answer is b. The line in b attempts to define a PL/SQL TABLE TYPE using a record that contains a composite datatype, which is not allowed. Answers a, c, and d are incorrect because they will not generate any errors when compiled.

Question 4

What method should be used to find the next index value of a PL/SQL **TABLE** that has data?

○ a. **COUNT**

○ b. **NEXT(n)**

○ c. **PRIOR(n)**

○ d. **LAST**

The correct answer is b. A call to the **NEXT** method returns the **NEXT** highest value of the index for the PL/SQL **TABLE** that is not **NULL**. Answer a is incorrect because **COUNT** returns the **COUNT** of the **NOT NULL** values in the PL/SQL **TABLE**. Answer c is incorrect because a call to the **PRIOR** method returns the previous value of the index for the PL/SQL **TABLE** that is not **NULL**. Answer d is incorrect because the **LAST** method returns the **LAST** index value that is not **NULL** for the PL/SQL **TABLE**.

Question 5

Evaluate this code fragment:

```
DECLARE
TYPE user_rec_tab IS TABLE OF dba_users%ROWTYPE
INDEX BY INTEGER;
Tab_rec dba_tables%ROWTYPE;
Obj_owner dba_objects.owner%TYPE;
begin
(processing)
end;
```

Why will this code generate an error?

○ a. You can't use a PL/SQL **TABLE** in a **DECLARE**.

○ b. You can't combine a **%TYPE** and a **%ROWTYPE** declaration in the same **DECLARE** section.

○ c. At least one **CURSOR** must be defined per PL/SQL anonymous PL/SQL block.

○ d. The PL/SQL **TABLE** should be indexed by **BINARY_INTEGER**.

The correct answer is d. A PL/SQL **TABLE** must be indexed by a **BINARY_INTEGER** by definition. Answer a is incorrect because you are allowed to use a PL/SQL **TABLE** in the **DECLARE** section. Answer b is incorrect because you can have as many **%TYPE** and **%ROWTYPE** declarations as needed in the same **DECLARE**. Answer c is incorrect because you aren't required to have explicit cursor definitions in a PL/SQL block.

Question 6

> You need to get all of the rows and columns of the **DBA_OBJECTS** view with a single **SELECT**. Which declaration will allow this?
>
> ○ a. dba_obj_rec   dba_objects.all%TYPE;
>
> ○ b. TYPE dba_obj_rec IS RECORD (obj_rec dba_objects%ROWTYPE);
>
> ○ c. TYPE dba_obj_tab IS TABLE OF dba_objects%ROWTYPE INDEX BY
>   BINARY_INTEGER;
>
> ○ d. dba_obj_rec   dba_objects%ROWTYPE;

The correct answer is c. In order to store an entire table with a single **SELECT**, you would need a PL/SQL **TABLE** in which to store the values. Answer a is incorrect because there is no **tab_name.all%TYPE** and, **%TYPE** specifies only that one column be used as a model for the identifier specified. Answer b is incorrect because a **RECORD** of **%ROWTYPE**, even if it was placed in the **TABLE TYPE** specification, would cause an error. Answer d is incorrect because you could store only one row at a time in the identifier, and it can't be used in a **TABLE** specification.

Question 7

> Which statement about PL/SQL records is true?
>
> ○ a. Records can have as many fields as needed.
>
> ○ b. Records cannot be defined **NOT NULL**.
>
> ○ c. Nested records cannot be accessed.
>
> ○ d. The individual data items in a record must be logically related and
>   of a similar datatype.

The correct answer is a. Records in PL/SQL are allowed to have as many fields as needed. Answer b is incorrect because records *can* be defined as **NOT NULL**.

Answer c is incorrect because nested records *can* be accessed by specification of their index integer. Answer d is incorrect because the data items in a record can be of any allowed datatype and don't have to be logically related.

Question 8

Examine this section of a PL/SQL declaration block:

```
TYPE user_rec_type IS TABLE OF dba_users%ROWTYPE
INDEX BY BINARY_INTEGER;
User_rec_tab user_rec_type;
```

Evaluate this statement:

```
User_rec_tab(5).username:='Mike';
```

Which statement is true?

- ○ a. The statement sets the username to 5 in the **user_rec_tab** wherever it equals 'Mike'.
- ○ b. The statement sets all of the usernames where the record number is between 1 and 5 inclusive in the **user_rec_tab** to 'Mike'.
- ○ c. The statement assigns the username column of record number 5 in the **user_rec_tab** to 'Mike'.
- ○ d. It will error out because the proper format is **pl_tab_name.col_name(i)**, not **pl_tab_name(i).col_name**.

The correct answer is c. Because the record indicator is set to 5 and the dot notation lists the column username, the assignment sets that records column to the specified value. Answer a is incorrect because 5 is the record indicator, not the assignment value. Answer b is incorrect because there is no way to specify a range in a simple assignment statement involving a PL/SQL **TABLE**. Answer d is incorrect because the specified format is the correct one.

Question 9

Which statement about using a PL/SQL **%ROWTYPE** declaration to define a PL/SQL **RECORD** is **TRUE**?

○ a. The attribute cannot be used to declare a record that is to be populated with a **SELECT ... INTO** statement.

○ b. The number and datatypes of the underlying table must be known.

○ c. The number and datatype of columns may change at runtime.

○ d. The **%ROWTYPE** cannot be used to create a record based on a view.

The correct answer is c. The main advantage to using **%ROWTYPE** is that it automatically adjusts to changes in the number or type of columns in the underlying table at runtime. Answer a is incorrect because a **%ROWTYPE** works well with a **SELECT...INTO**, especially when the entire row (*) is being selected. Answer b is incorrect because the underlying number and datatypes of the columns don't have to be known. Answer d is incorrect because the **%ROWTYPE** can be used against tables, views, and clustered tables.

Question 10

In the executable section of a PL/SQL procedure, you find this line:

```
Phone_rec(10):='770-555-1212';
```

What task does this accomplish?

○ a. A constant is assigned a value.

○ b. The first 10 records in the **phone_rec** PL/SQL **TABLE** have been set to '770-555-1212'.

○ c. The tenth value of the **phone_rec** PL/SQL **TABLE** has been set to '770-555-1212'.

○ d. The **phone_rec TABLE** has been created with 10 elements, each set to '770-555-1212'.

The correct answer is c. The **phone_rec TABLE**'s index value is set to 10, which means that the tenth record will take the assigned value. Answer a is incorrect because this is not a constant assignment statement. Answer b is incorrect because there is no way to set a range of PL/SQL **TABLE** records to a specific value in a simple assignment statement. Answer d is incorrect because the **TABLE** must already exist for us to access it or use it in an assignment statement.

Need To Know More?

 Feuerstein, Steven. *Oracle PL/SQL Programming*. O'Reilly & Associates, 1995. ISBN 1-56592-335-9. This book is considered one of the seminal references on PL/SQL. Although the advanced edition of this book is also a must-have for any serious PL/SQL developer, this earlier edition is probably the better choice for studying for the OCP-DBA exam.

 Oracle Corporation. *Oracle University, Introduction to Oracle: SQL and PL/SQL, Student Guide Volume 2*, Redwood City, California, Part No. M08945. This is the manual that the test is derived from—what better place to get information?

 Oracle Corporation. *Oracle8i Server SQL Reference Manual, Release 3(8.1.7)*. September, 2000, Redwood City, California. Part No. A85397-01. This is the source book for all Oracle SQL for Version 8i. This book can be found on the Web, at the time of writing, at **http://technet.oracle.com**. This site has free membership and has all current versions of Oracle documentation available online in Acrobat format (PDF files).

 PL/SQL Users Guide and Reference Release 8.1, Oracle Corporation, December 1999. Part No. A77069-01. This is the source book for PL/SQL. This book can be found on the Web, at the time of writing, at **http://technet.oracle.com**. This site has free membership and has all current versions of Oracle documentation available online in Acrobat format (PDF files).

Use of Explicit Cursors in PL/SQL

Terms you'll need to understand:

✓ Explicit cursor

✓ Implicit cursor

✓ **OPEN**

✓ **FETCH**

✓ **CLOSE**

✓ Cursor variables

✓ Cursor **FOR** loop

Techniques you'll need to master:

✓ Creating an explicit cursor

✓ Using an implicit cursor

✓ Using **OPEN**, **FETCH**, and **CLOSE** with implicit cursors

✓ Using cursor variables

✓ Using a cursor **FOR** loop

Cursors

A cursor is a memory area used to hold an executable statement. Cursors are either explicitly declared or implicitly created whenever a SQL statement is executed. Implicit cursors are declared for all PL/SQL **SELECT** and **DML** statements. Explicit cursors are declared and named by the programmer. Implicit cursors created for SQL **SELECT** statements can fetch only a single record. Explicit cursors must be used whenever multiple rows must be retrieved using a **SELECT**.

Oracle uses private SQL areas to execute SQL statements. Using explicit cursors, the programmer names and controls these private SQL areas. If the SQL statement is not declared in a cursor, the Oracle server creates a cursor to hold it. The implicit cursor is called the *SQL cursor*.

A special type of cursor, called a *recursive cursor*, is opened for DDL statements, such as a **CREATE TABLE**, that need to do recursive updates to data dictionary tables. These recursive cursors are used to perform recursive calls.

A user can open as many implicit and explicit cursors as needed up to the value of the initialization parameter **OPEN_CURSORS**, which controls the number of cursors any single user session can have open at the same time.

The user process performs the management of private SQL areas. The allocation and deallocation of private SQL areas depends largely on which application tool you are using.

A private SQL area continues to exist until its corresponding cursor is closed, or the statement handle is freed. Although Oracle frees the runtime area after the statement completes, the persistent area stays open. You should close all open cursors that will not be used again in order to free the persistent area and to minimize the amount of memory required for users of the application.

Explicit cursors are controlled using the **OPEN, FETCH,** and **CLOSE** commands. The server holds the control of implicit cursors internally. Whether they are explicit or implicit, you use cursor variables to get status information about cursors from the server. The cursor variables are listed in Table 12.1.

Table 12.1	Cursor variables.
Variable	Definition
%ISOPEN	Evaluates to **TRUE** if the cursor is open
%NOTFOUND	Evaluates to **TRUE** if the most recent fetch does not return a row
%FOUND	Evaluates to **TRUE** if the most recent fetch returns a row; complement of %NOTFOUND
%ROWCOUNT	Evaluates to the total number of rows returned so far

Implicit Cursors

Implicit cursors are created whenever a SQL statement is executed and no explicit cursor has been declared. Explicit cursors can be declared only for **SELECT** statements. **INSERT, UPDATE**, and **DELETE** statements are controlled via implicit cursors. Implicit cursors are executed twice with a SQL **SELECT** statement. The first execution determines if the cursor will return more than one row. If more than one row is returned, the **TOO_MANY_ROWS** exception is raised. The second execution fetches the row into the active set and returns it to the variables that are the target of the **INTO** portion of the **SELECT** command. You use the prefix *SQL* to reference the cursor variables for an implicit cursor.

Other than executing implicit cursors and processing the **TOO_MANY_ROWS** exception in an exception handler, you have little control over them as they are implicitly opened, fetched from, and closed. Therefore, let's move on to explicit cursors.

Explicit Cursors

An explicit cursor must be declared any time a cursor will retrieve more than a single row. The explicit cursor allows the fetching of individual rows from a multirow result set. An explicit cursor can do the following:

➤ Keep track of which row is currently being processed

➤ Allow you to control how a cursor is processed

➤ Process beyond the first row and allow row-by-row processing of a result set

Explicit cursors are controlled with four commands:

➤ CURSOR—Used to declare the **CURSOR**

➤ OPEN—Used to execute the query, bind any variables, and gather the active set

➤ FETCH—Used to retrieve single rows from the active set

➤ CLOSE—Used to release the **CURSOR** after processing is complete

You must test after each row is fetched from the active set to see if it is the last so that you can **CLOSE** the **CURSOR** if needed. Figure 12.1 demonstrates this process through use of a flow diagram.

After a **CURSOR** has been closed, it may be reopened to process a second active set based on different values of any bind variables used.

Declaration of Explicit Cursors

Cursors are declared using the **CURSOR** statement. A **CURSOR** contains a standard SQL statement (without the **INTO** required in an implicit **SELECT**

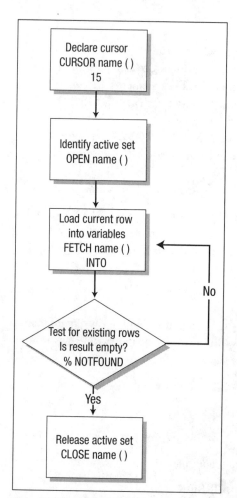

Figure 12.1 Explicit **CURSOR** Command.

inside a PL/SQL routine); this SQL statement can be as simple or as complex as allowed by the SQL **SELECT** syntax. The command for declaring a **CURSOR** is shown in Figure 12.2.

The SQL **SELECT** statement can include **ORDER BY** if a specific order of row processing is required. After a **CURSOR** is declared, it must be opened using the **OPEN** command in order to allow processing to continue.

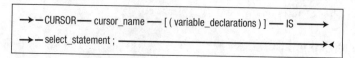

Figure 12.2 Syntax of the **CURSOR** command.

Opening Explicit Cursors

Cursors, after they have been declared, are opened using the **OPEN** command. If a **CURSOR** has been declared that uses variables, these variables must be assigned values before the **CURSOR** is opened. The syntax of the **OPEN** command is shown in Figure 12.3.

A variable may be passed into the **CURSOR** only if it has been assigned a value before the **CURSOR** is opened. A **CURSOR** must be closed before it can be reopened. Once declared, a **CURSOR** doesn't have to be redeclared within its current context. A **CURSOR** can only be fetched from if it has been opened. The **OPEN** command causes the following processing steps to be executed:

1. Dynamically allocate memory for a context area to contain critical processing information.

2. Parse the **SELECT** statement.

3. Bind the variables by tying their names to a memory address containing a value.

4. Identify the active set and note that no values are retrieved into variables.

5. Reposition the pointer to just before the first row in the active set.

If the **SELECT** contains a **FOR UPDATE** clause, the **OPEN** also locks the rows in the active set.

Appropriately enough, you fetch rows from the active set created by the opening of the **CURSOR** by using the **FETCH** command.

Fetching from an **OPEN CURSOR**

After a **CURSOR** is **OPEN**, you use the **FETCH** command to retrieve the results from the active set one row at a time. The target of a **FETCH** command can be a set of individual variables, a **RECORD**, or a PL/SQL **TABLE**. The **FETCH** must have a target that matches the number and order of—and is compatible with—the datatypes of the returned row of the active set, or an error will be generated when the **FETCH** is checked for syntax before execution. The syntax of the **FETCH** command is shown in Figure 12.4.

```
→─ OPEN cursor_name ── [ ( def_variable ── [ , def_variable...] ── ) ] ; ────────►◄
```

Figure 12.3   Syntax of the **OPEN** command.

```
→─ FETCH cursor_name ── INTO ── variable1 ── [ , variable2...] ; ────►◄
```

Figure 12.4   Syntax of the **FETCH** command.

The variable list can be replaced with an attribute that is defined as a **RECORD**, as long as that **RECORD** matches the structure of the returned values and has compatible datatypes.

The **FETCH** command executes these actions:

➤ Advances the pointer in the active set to the next row

➤ Reads the current row into the output PL/SQL variables

After a record is fetched, the value of the **%NOTFOUND CURSOR** variable should be checked to determine if the **FETCH** returned any values. If values were returned, the row can be processed and the control passed back to the commands before the **FETCH** in the **LOOP**.

After all of the rows are processed from the active set, you use the **CLOSE** command to **CLOSE** the **CURSOR**.

Closing an Opened Cursor

After an explicit cursor has completed its purpose, it should be explicitly closed. A cursor will be implicitly closed on exit from a procedure, package, or function or exit from the processing environment. In some cases, an explicit cursor may be held open if the information in the cursor is needed for other cursors to operate, even if it is explicitly closed if the processing block in the PL/SQL object is not ended. Cursors are explicitly closed with the **CLOSE** command. The format for the **CLOSE** command is shown in Figure 12.5.

A procedure showing the complete processing cycle for a cursor is shown in Listing 12.1.

Listing 12.1   **Example full cycle for a cursor.**

```
CREATE OR REPLACE PROCEDURE do_pin AS
--
CURSOR get_packs IS                       <-- Declare Cursor
SELECT
        object_name
FROM
        dbutil_kept_objects;
--
pack_name VARCHAR2(64);
--
BEGIN
        OPEN get_packs;                   <-- Open Cursor
        LOOP
                FETCH get_packs INTO pack_name; <-- Fetch Cursor
                EXIT WHEN get_packs%NOTFOUND;   <-- Check for empty
```

```
            DBMS_OUTPUT.PUT_LINE('Pinning '||pack_name);
            DBMS_SHARED_POOL.KEEP(pack_name);
        END LOOP;
        CLOSE get_packs;                        <-- Close cursor
END do_pin;
```

Advanced Concepts

We have already discussed the essentials of cursor processing. Now we turn our attention towards more advanced concepts involving cursors. The first topic involves the use of the **FOR UPDATE** clause in a cursor.

Use of the **FOR UPDATE** Clause

The **FOR UPDATE** clause allows you to explicitly lock rows that you have selected in your cursor for processing. This prevents multiple users updating the same row or rows and prevents access to the rows until they are committed or released when the cursor is closed. When you declare a cursor that will be referenced in the **CURRENT OF** clause of an **UPDATE** or **DELETE** statement, you must use the **FOR UPDATE** clause to acquire exclusive row locks.

The **SELECT...FOR UPDATE** statement identifies the rows that will be updated or deleted, and then locks them. The **SELECT...FOR UPDATE** is used when you want to base an update on the existing values in a row. You must make sure another user does not change the row before the update.

The optional keyword **NOWAIT** tells Oracle not to wait if another user has locked the requested rows. Use of the **NOWAIT** clause allows control to be returned immediately to your program so that it can do other work before again trying to acquire the lock. Oracle waits (forever) until the rows are available if you omit the **NOWAIT** keyword.

All rows are locked when you open the cursor, not as they are fetched. The rows are unlocked when you commit or roll back the transaction. So, you cannot fetch from a **FOR UPDATE** cursor after a commit.

A workaround for the problem with fetching from a **FOR UPDATE** cursor after a commit is to not use the **FOR UPDATE** and **CURRENT OF** clauses. Instead, use the pseudocolumn **ROWID** to mimic the **CURRENT OF** clause. Simply select the **ROWID** of each row into a **UROWID** variable. Then, use the **ROWID** to identify the current row during subsequent updates and deletes.

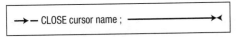

Figure 12.5 Syntax for the **CLOSE** command.

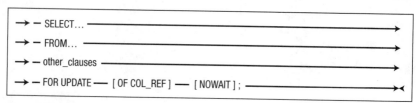

Figure 12.6 Syntax of the **FOR UPDATE** clause.

The **FOR UPDATE** clause is always the last statement in the **SELECT** statement, even after an **ORDER BY**. The **FOR UPDATE** clause cannot be used in a **SELECT** with a **GROUP BY** (therefore it can't be used with aggregation functions) The general format for a **FOR UPDATE** clause is shown in Figure 12.6.

Reference to any column in a table row will cause that row to be locked. Access to the rows that have been locked will be denied until the transaction completes. Remember that the rows are locked when the cursor is **OPENED**, not when the rows are **FETCHED**.

An example use of the **FOR UPDATE** clause is shown in Listing 12.2.

Listing 12.2   Example use of the FOR UPDATE clause.

```
AULTDB1:DECLARE
  2    owner          VARCHAR2(64);
  3    tab_name       VARCHAR2(64);
  4    total_bytes    NUMBER;
  5  CURSOR get_bytes IS
  6    SELECT owner,segment_name,megbytes
  7    FROM tab_extent
  8    WHERE owner ='SCOTT'
  9    FOR UPDATE;
 10  BEGIN
 11    OPEN get_bytes;          <-- Rows are locked here
 12    LOOP
 13      FETCH get_bytes INTO owner,tab_name,total_bytes;
 14      EXIT WHEN get_bytes%NOTFOUND;
 15      dbms_output.put_line('Table: '||owner||'.'||tab_name||'
has '||
 16         TO_CHAR(total_bytes)||' bytes.');
 17    END LOOP;
 18    CLOSE get_bytes;               <-- Rows are released here
 19* END;
AULTDB1: /


Table: SCOTT.ACCOUNT has 10240 bytes.
Table: SCOTT.BONUS has 10240 bytes.
Table: SCOTT.CHAIN1 has 522240 bytes.
```

```
Table: SCOTT.DEPARTMENTS has 10240 bytes.
Table: SCOTT.DEPT has 20480 bytes.
Table: SCOTT.DEPT2 has 10240 bytes.
...
Table: SCOTT.SAL has 20480 bytes.
Table: SCOTT.SALGRADE has 10240 bytes.
Table: SCOTT.SCOTT_OBJECTS has 1955840 bytes.
Table: SCOTT.SERVICE has 10240 bytes.
Table: SCOTT.TEST_NULL has 10240 bytes.
Table: SCOTT.TEST_TEMP has 93808640 bytes.

PL/SQL procedure successfully completed.
```

The companion to the **FOR UPDATE** command is the **WHERE CURRENT OF** clause, which is used with the **UPDATE** and **DELETE** commands to process all locked rows held in the current **FOR UPDATE** cursor.

Use of the **WHERE CURRENT OF** Clause

The **WHERE CURRENT OF** clause allows you to reference the current row from an explicit cursor. This means that the current row will be affected by an operation using a **WHERE CURRENT OF** without use of the **ROWID**. The **WHERE CURRENT OF** clause can be used only on rows that are locked using the **FOR UPDATE** clause of an explicit cursor. The syntax for the **WHERE CURRENT OF** clause is shown in Figure 12.7.

An example use of the **WHERE CURRENT OF** clause is shown in Listing 12.3.

Listing 12.3   Example use of the **WHERE CURRENT OF** clause.

```
AULTDB1: DECLARE
  2      owner              VARCHAR2(64);
  3      tab_name           VARCHAR2(64);
  4      total_bytes        NUMBER;
  5      CURSOR get_bytes IS
  6        SELECT owner,segment_name,megbytes
  7        FROM tab_extent
  8        WHERE owner ='SCOTT'
  9        FOR UPDATE;
 10   BEGIN
 11     OPEN get_bytes;
 12      LOOP
 13        FETCH get_bytes INTO owner,tab_name,total_bytes;
 14        EXIT WHEN get_bytes%NOTFOUND;
 15        dbms_output.put_line('Table: '||owner||'.'||tab_name||'
has '||
 16           TO_CHAR(total_bytes)||' bytes.');
```

```
17       UPDATE tab_extent
18        SET megbytes = megbytes/(1024*1024)
19        WHERE CURRENT OF get_bytes;
20        dbms_output.put_line('Table: '||owner||'.'||tab_name||'
has '||
21          TO_CHAR(total_bytes/(1024*1024))||' megabytes.');
22     END LOOP;
23     CLOSE get_bytes;
24* END;
AULTDB1:/
```

```
Table: SCOTT.ACCOUNT has 10240 bytes.
Table: SCOTT.ACCOUNT has .009765625 megabytes.
Table: SCOTT.BONUS has 10240 bytes.
Table: SCOTT.BONUS has .009765625 megabytes.
Table: SCOTT.CHAIN1 has 522240 bytes.
Table: SCOTT.CHAIN1 has .498046875 megabytes.
Table: SCOTT.DEPARTMENTS has 10240 bytes.
Table: SCOTT.DEPARTMENTS has .009765625 megabytes.
Table: SCOTT.DEPT has 20480 bytes.
Table: SCOTT.DEPT has .01953125 megabytes.
Table: SCOTT.DEPT2 has 10240 bytes.
Table: SCOTT.DEPT2 has .009765625 megabytes.
...
Table: SCOTT.SCOTT_OBJECTS has 1955840 bytes.
Table: SCOTT.SCOTT_OBJECTS has 1.865234375 megabytes.
Table: SCOTT.SERVICE has 10240 bytes.
Table: SCOTT.SERVICE has .009765625 megabytes.
Table: SCOTT.TEST_NULL has 10240 bytes.
Table: SCOTT.TEST_NULL has .009765625 megabytes.
Table: SCOTT.TEST_TEMP has 93808640 bytes.
Table: SCOTT.TEST_TEMP has 89.462890625 megabytes.
```

```
PL/SQL procedure successfully completed.
```

The example in Listing 12.3 updates the rows in the cursor *get_bytes* to set the value of total table bytes to megabytes as the table column name indicates. The table *tab_extent* is a table created by a CTAS (create table as select) from the **DBA_EXTENTS** view.

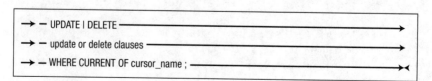

Figure 12.7   Syntax of the **WHERE CURRENT OF** clause.

Using Subqueries in Explicit Cursors

Explicit cursors can utilize subqueries just as normal **SELECT** statements use them. Subqueries can be used in the **WHERE** and **FROM** clauses of a cursor definition. As you may recall, a subquery is a regular query that is usually enclosed in quotes that appears in a second **SELECT** statement. Listing 12.4 shows an example use of a subquery in a cursor.

Listing 12.4   Example use of a subquery.

```
AULTDB1: DECLARE
 1    owner VARCHAR2(64);
 2    tab_name VARCHAR2(64);
 3    total_bytes NUMBER;
 4   CURSOR get_bytes IS
 5     SELECT a.owner,a.segment_name,b.megbytes
 6     FROM tab_extent a,(
 7                  SELECT owner, segment_name,
 8                       SUM(megbytes/(1024*1024)) megbytes
 9                  FROM tab_extent GROUP BY owner, segment_name) b
10     WHERE a.owner='SCOTT' AND
11           a.owner=b.owner AND
12           a.segment_name=b.segment_name;
13   BEGIN
14    OPEN get_bytes;
15    LOOP
16     FETCH get_bytes INTO owner,tab_name,total_bytes;
17     EXIT WHEN get_bytes%NOTFOUND;
18     dbms_output.put_line('Table: '||owner||'.'||tab_name||' has
'||
19      to_char(total_bytes)||' megabytes.');
21    END LOOP;
22* END;
AULTDB1: /

Table: SCOTT.ACCOUNT has .009765625 megabytes.
Table: SCOTT.BONUS has .009765625 megabytes.
Table: SCOTT.CHAIN1 has .498046875 megabytes.
Table: SCOTT.DEPARTMENTS has .009765625 megabytes.
Table: SCOTT.DEPT has .01953125 megabytes.
Table: SCOTT.DEPT2 has .009765625 megabytes.
...
Table: SCOTT.SALGRADE has .009765625 megabytes.
Table: SCOTT.SCOTT_OBJECTS has 1.865234375 megabytes.
Table: SCOTT.SERVICE has .009765625 megabytes.
Table: SCOTT.TEST_NULL has .009765625 megabytes.
Table: SCOTT.TEST_TEMP has 89.462890625 megabytes.

PL/SQL procedure successfully completed.
```

Notice the use of the aliases to relate query and subquery; these are required when the subquery verses main query **WHERE** clause refers to any other table column in the main query. Both subqueries and correlated subqueries are allowed in cursors.

A Review of Cursor **FOR** Loops

We covered cursor **FOR** loops in Chapter 10, but we briefly review the topic here in the chapter on explicit cursors.

A special form of the **FOR** loop is the cursor **FOR** loop. A cursor loop has the following format:

```
FOR rec_id IN cursor_id LOOP
---- processing ----
END LOOP;
```

One advantage of the cursor **FOR** loop is that no **OPEN, FETCH**, or **CLOSE** commands are required for cursor control, which is handled by the loop logic.

The *rec_id* must be a suitably defined record structure or properly typed variable to hold what is returned from the cursor. The *cursor_id* is the name of the cursor. The effect of issuing this type of command is to open and parse, then fetch rows from the cursor until no more records are found, at which time the cursor loop ends. An example cursor **FOR** loop is shown in Listing 12.5.

Listing 12.5   Example cursor **FOR** loop.

```
DECLARE
    endpoint analysis.result1%TYPE;
    CURSOR endpoint IS
        SELECT reagent1,reagent2,reagent3,analysis_name, units
        FROM results_table WHERE test_num = 1;
BEGIN
    FOR el_rec IN endpoint LOOP
        /* calculate analysis result and store the results */
        result := el_rec.reagent2 / (el_rec.reagent1 +
            el_rec.reagent3);
        INSERT INTO analysis VALUES (
            result1, el_rec.analysis_name, el_rec.units);
    END LOOP;
    COMMIT;
END;
```

In this example, the cursor *endpoint* is used to define the implicit record *el_rec*. When the loop is executed, the results that have the *test_num* value of 1 will be cycled through and each set of retrieved values inserted into the record *e1_rec* and processed.

When the cursor **FOR** loop is executed, the *cursor_id* that is used cannot belong to an explicit cursor name already opened by an **OPEN** statement or another *cursor_id* declared in an enclosing cursor **FOR** loop. The cursor is used to create an implicitly defined record. Before each iteration of the **FOR** loop, the PL/SQL engine fetches one set of values into the implicitly declared record. The record is defined only inside the loop. You cannot refer to the implicit record's fields outside the cursor **FOR** loop.

The set of statements inside the loop is executed once for each row that satisfies the statement associated with the cursor. When you leave the loop, the cursor is closed automatically—even if an **EXIT** or **GOTO** statement is used to leave the loop prematurely or an exception is raised inside the loop.

Practice Questions

Question 1

> Which of the following is not a usual step in the processing of an explicit cursor?
>
> ○ a. **CLOSE** the cursor.
>
> ○ b. **OPEN** the cursor.
>
> ○ c. Check if the first record of the result set has been processed.
>
> ○ d. Check if the last record of the result set has been processed.

The correct answer is c. Usually, you don't check if the first record has been processed because proper checking, if the last record has been processed, will catch both conditions. The other answers are all part of the normal processing of explicit cursors and thus are incorrect answers.

Question 2

> In which explicit cursor-processing step is the active record set determined?
>
> ○ a. During the **FETCH**
>
> ○ b. When you check for the first record
>
> ○ c. When you check for the last record
>
> ○ d. During the **OPEN**

The correct answer is d. The active set is determined when the cursor is opened. Answer a is incorrect because the **FETCH** retrieves one row from the active set and places it into the program variable set or record. Answer b is incorrect because you don't normally check for the first record. Answer c is incorrect because if you are checking for the last record, obviously the active set has already been determined.

Question 3

Evaluate this program fragment:

```
1   DECLARE
2    CURSOR get_bytes IS
3      SELECT owner,segment_name,megbytes
4      FROM tab_extent
5      WHERE owner ='SCOTT'
6      WHERE CURRENT OF get_bytes;
```

What line will generate an error?

- a. **CURSOR** get_bytes IS
- b. **SELECT** owner,segment_name,megbytes
- c. **DECLARE**
- d. **WHERE CURRENT OF** get_bytes;

The correct answer is d. The **WHERE CURRENT OF** clause is not applicable to **SELECT** statements. Answers a through c are syntactically correct and thus are incorrect answers.

Question 4

Evaluate the following program fragment:

```
BEGIN
    FOR per_rec IN per_cursor LOOP
        /* calculate salaries and store the results
        */
        new_sal := per_rec.sal * raise;
        UPDATE personel SET sal = new_sal
        WHERE empno=per_rec.empno;
    END LOOP;
    CLOSE per_rec;
    COMMIT;
END;
```

Which line will generate an error?

○ a. FOR per_rec IN per_cursor LOOP

○ b. CLOSE per_rec;

○ c. new_sal := per_rec.sal * raise;

○ d. END LOOP;

The correct answer is b. A cursor used in a cursor **FOR** loop doesn't have to be explicitly closed; the **CLOSE** command will generate an error. The rest of the lines are syntactically correct and thus are not the error-generating code.

Question 5

Evaluate this code fragment:

```
1  DECLARE
...
5    CURSOR get_bytes IS
6      SELECT owner,segment_name,megbytes
7      FROM tab_extent
8      WHERE owner ='SCOTT';
9  BEGIN
10   OPEN get_bytes;
11    LOOP
12      FETCH get_bytes INTO
     owner,tab_name,total_bytes;
13      EXIT WHEN get_bytes%NOTFOUND;
14        TO_CHAR(total_bytes)||' bytes.');
15      UPDATE tab_extent
16        SET megbytes = megbytes/(1024*1024)
17        WHERE CURRENT OF get_bytes;
18        TO_CHAR(total_bytes/(1024*1024))||'
     megabytes.');
29    END LOOP;
20    CLOSE get_bytes;
21* END;
```

Why will there be an error generated?

- ○ a. You can't **CLOSE** the cursor in this program as it will generate an error.
- ○ b. You don't need to explicitly **OPEN** the cursor because it has a **WHERE CURRENT OF** clause.
- ○ c. The **CURSOR** statement is missing a clause.
- ○ d. The **EXIT** command should be before the **FETCH**, not after it.

The correct answer is c. The **CURSOR** is missing a **FOR UPDATE** clause. Answer a is incorrect because CLOSEing explicitly OPEN cursors when you are finished with them is good programming practice. Answer b is incorrect because you must explicitly **OPEN** the cursor in this type of use. Answer d is incorrect because you must place the **EXIT** using a **NOTFOUND** after the **FETCH** if proper processing is to be accomplished.

Question 6

> Which of the following is not a **CURSOR** variable?
>
> ○ a. **%EMPTY**
>
> ○ b. **%FOUND**
>
> ○ c. **%NOTFOUND**
>
> ○ d. **%ROWCOUNT**

The correct answer is a. There is no **%EMPTY CURSOR** variable. The rest of the answers are proper **CURSOR** variables.

Question 7

> Which statement regarding explicit **CURSOR**s is true?
>
> ○ a. Explicit cursors can **SELECT** only a single row at a time.
>
> ○ b. Explicit cursors can **FETCH** only a single row at a time.
>
> ○ c. Explicit cursors must always be explicitly **CLOSE**d.
>
> ○ d. An explicit **CURSOR** is **OPEN** as soon as it is referenced in a **FETCH** statement.

The correct answer is b. A **CURSOR** can select more than one row into a active set but can **FETCH** only one row at a time for processing. Answer a is incorrect because an explicit **CURSOR** is used to **SELECT** multiple rows into the active set for processing. Answer c is incorrect because if you exit a PL/SQL routine without closing an explicit **CURSOR**, it will be automatically closed; however, explicitly **CLOSE**ing any **OPEN CURSOR** before exiting a PL/SQL routine or block is considered good practice. Answer d is incorrect because unless a cursor **FOR** loop is used, an explicit **CURSOR** is not automatically opened.

Question 8

> Which **CURSOR** variable would allow you to determine whether a **CURSOR** has been opened?
>
> O a. **%EXPLICIT_OPEN**
>
> O b. **%READY**
>
> O c. **%FOUND**
>
> O d. **%ISOPEN**

The correct answer is d. The **%ISOPEN CURSOR** variable will be **TRUE** if the **CURSOR** is open. Answers a and b are incorrect because there are no **%EXPLICIT_OPEN** or **%READY CURSOR** variables. Answer c is incorrect because **%FOUND** is valid only after a **FETCH**, and a **CURSOR** can be **OPEN** without having been fetched from yet.

Question 9

> How are implicit **CURSOR**s controlled?
>
> O a. The user process must issue commands to control them.
>
> O b. They are controlled internally by the server process.
>
> O c. The **RUNCUR** process is detached at cursor declaration to handle implicit cursors.
>
> O d. The **PMON** process wakes up to handle implicit cursor control.

The correct response is b. Implicit cursors are handled by the server process. Answer a is incorrect because you cannot issue **OPEN, FETCH,** or **CLOSE** commands against implicit cursors. Answer c is incorrect because there is no **RUNCUR** process associated with Oracle. Answer d is incorrect because this is not one of the functions of the **PMON** process.

. . . .

Question 10

What is the purpose of the **NOWAIT** clause?

○ a. If a table row referenced by a **FOR UPDATE** is already locked, a **NOWAIT** will return control to the program.

○ b. **NOWAIT** forces an implicit **CURSOR** closed if it encounters a row lock.

○ c. It allows processing in a **WHERE CURRENT OF** process, even if locked rows are present.

○ d. It causes a program to wait indefinitely if it encounters a locked row during a cursor **OPEN**.

The correct answer is a. The **NOWAIT** clause is added to a **SELECT FOR UPDATE**–type cursor to return control to the calling program in case any of the referenced rows are locked. Otherwise, the program would wait indefinitely for the lock to be released. Answer b is incorrect because **NOWAIT** is used with **EXPLICIT** rather than **IMPLICIT** cursors. Answer c is incorrect because it returns control to the program if rows are locked, but it doesn't return any rows, so a **WHERE CURRENT OF** statement (**UPDATE** or **DELETE**) couldn't process. Answer d is incorrect because this is the condition it is designed to prevent, not cause.

Need To Know More?

 Feuerstein, Steven. *Oracle PL/SQL Programming.* O'Reilly & Associates, 1995. ISBN 1-56592-335-9. This book is considered one of the seminal references on PL/SQL. Although the advanced edition of this book is also a must have for any serious PL/SQL developer, as far as study for the OCP-DBA exam, this earlier edition is probably the better choice.

 Oracle Corporation. *Oracle8i Server SQL Reference Manual, Release 3(8.1.7).* September, 2000, Redwood City, California. Part No. A85397-01. This is the source book for all Oracle SQL for Version 8i. This book can be found on the Web, at the time of writing, at **http://technet.oracle.com**. This site has free membership and has all current versions of Oracle documentation available online in Acrobat format (PDF files).

 Oracle Corporation. *PL/SQL Users Guide and Reference Release 8.1,* December 1999. Part No. A77069-01. This is the source book for PL/SQL. This book can be found on the Web, at the time of writing, at **http://technet.oracle.com**. This site has free membership and has all current versions of Oracle documentation available online in Acrobat format (PDF files).

 Oracle Corporation. *Oracle University, Introduction to Oracle: SQL and PL/SQL, Student Guide Volume 2,* Redwood City, California, Part No. M08945. This is the manual that the test is derived from—what better place to get information?

Handling Errors in PL/SQL (Exception Handling)

Terms you'll need to understand:

✓ EXCEPTION

✓ RAISE

✓ Pre-defined exception

✓ User defined exception

✓ PRAGMA

✓ Exception handler

✓ Propagation of exceptions

✓ WHEN OTHERS

✓ SQLCODE

✓ SQLERRM

Techniques you'll need to master:

✓ When and how to use exceptions

✓ Writing exception handlers

✓ How to trap for pre-defined exceptions

✓ How to create and trap for user defined exceptions

✓ The use of the **PRAGMA** precompiler directive with exceptions

✓ How exceptions are propagated from subprograms

✓ The use of **WHEN OTHERS** exceptions

✓ Use of **SQLCODE** and **SQLERRM** to report errors

Any reasonable programming language must contain methodology for the graceful handling of error conditions. In PL/SQL, error handling is accomplished through the use of exceptions. An *exception* is an error condition. Oracle PL/SQL provides several pre-defined exceptions and the capacity for the programmer and user to define their own based on any Oracle error. Oracle defines an exception as an identifier in PL/SQL raised by an error condition during the execution of a block that terminates its main body of actions in that block. An Oracle processing block automatically terminates when an exception is raised; it is up the programmer to write *exception handlers* that tell Oracle what to do next.

In Oracle there are two methods of raising an exception. Oracle will automatically raise an exception when an error occurs, or a process can deliberately raise an exception using the **RAISE** statement within a block.

Exceptions

Oracle exceptions fall into three major categories: predefined and non-predefined Oracle exceptions, and user defined exceptions. Predefined and non-predefined exceptions are implicitly raised by Oracle. User defined exceptions must be raised by application logic.

A predefined exception is one of approximately 20 errors that have been found to occur most often in PL/SQL code. Non-predefined exceptions are raised by any other standard Oracle server error. If you know that a particular error may be caused within a particular piece of PL/SQL code, you should define a pragma to handle that error gracefully.

Note: PRAGMA known also as a psuedoinstruction, is the keyword that signifies a compiler directive. A compiler directive is not processed when the PL/SQL block is executed. The directive tells the compiler to interpret the exception name as the associated error number.

A user defined exception is usually defined for a particular type of processing error, such as non-Oracle error raising conditions that nonetheless must be reported or handled.

The general format for declaring an exception is shown in Figure 13.1.

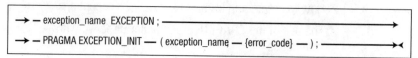

Figure 13.1   Syntax for exception declaration and association.

There are essentially three steps to non-predefined exceptions processing, these are declare, associate, and reference. Figure 13.1 shows the syntax for the exception declaration and association steps, the final step, reference of the exception, is accomplished in the exception handling area of the PL/SQL program.

Once a non-predefined exception is declared and associated to a PRAGMA, it is handled identically as would a defined exception. An exception handler is detailed in the exception handling part of the PL/SQL program. The general syntax for an exception handler is shown in Figure 13.2.

The general guidelines for exception handlers:

➤ You begin the exception-handling section of the block with the keyword EXCEPTION

➤ You can define several exception handlers in the same exception handler

➤ Only one exception is handled before the block is exited

➤ It is a good practice to always define a WHEN OTHERS exception in all exception handlers

➤ You can only have one WHEN OTHERS exception

➤ Exceptions cannot appear in assignment statements or SQL statements

A simple exception handler is shown in Listing 13.1.

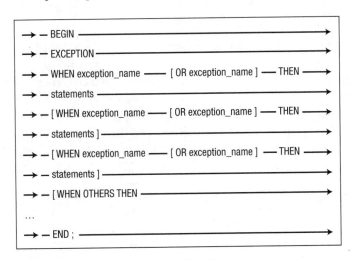

Figure 13.2 Syntax for an exception hHandler.

Listing 13.1   Example exception handler.

```
BEGIN
  stat_name := 'recursive calls';
      OPEN get_stat(stat_name);
      FETCH get_stat INTO temp_name, r_calls;
      CLOSE get_stat;
EXCEPTION
    WHEN NO_DATA_FOUND THEN
      CLOSE get_stat;
    WHEN OTHERS THEN
      CLOSE get_stat;
END;
```

Let's examine the types of exceptions in more detail.

Pre-Defined Exceptions

Oracle Pre-defined exceptions are shown in Table 13.1. Almost all of the errors you can expect to have happen in a PL/SQL program have been pre-defined for you by Oracle.

As you can se,e the pre-defined exceptions allow for many processing related errors to be automatically trapped. When an exception is raised, there are two functions that should be used to report the error number and/or the error code back to the user or to an error trapping table. The error functions are SQLCODE and SQLERRM.

SQLCODE returns the numeric value for the error code, it can be assigned to a numeric variable. SQLERRM returns character data containing the message associated with the error number. Between the two functions you can report the entire Oracle error back to the user. The SQLCODE values can range from 0 (No exception encountered) or 1 (user-defined exception raised) or 100 (NO_DATA_FOUND) to the actual numeric error code as a negative integer. The SQLCODE and SQLERRM functions are especially useful in the case of the WHEN OTHERS exception.

The WHEN OTHERS exception is a special exception used as a catch-all for any other Oracle error not already defined. Every exception handler should have a WHEN OTHERS that uses the SQLCODE and SQLERRM functions to trap and report non-predefined exceptions when they occur. Listing 13.2 shows an example of an exception handler using the WHEN OTHERS exception.

Table 13.1   List of predefined Oracle exceptions

Exception	Error Number	Description
ACCESS_INTO_NULL	ORA-06530	Attempted to assign values to the attributes of an unitialized object
COLLECTION_IS_NULL	ORA-06531	Attempted to apply collection methods other than **EXISTS** to an unitialized nested table or array
CURSOR_ALREADY_OPEN	ORA-06511	Attempted to open an already open cursor
DUP_VAL_ON_INDEX	ORA-00001	Attempted to insert a duplicate value
INVALID_CURSOR	ORA-01001	Illegal Cursor operation occurred
INVALID_NUMBER	ORA-01722	Conversion of character string to number failed
LOGIN_DENIED	ORA-01017	Attempted to login to Oracle with an invalid username or password
NO_DATA_FOUND	ORA-01403	Single row **SELECT** returned no data
NOT_LOGGED_ON	ORA-01012	The PL/SQL program issued a call to the database without being logged on
OTHERS	N/A	Any other non-predefined error
PROGRAM_ERROR	ORA-06501	The PL/SQL program encountered an internal program
ROWTYPE_MISMATCH	ORA-06504	The PL/SQL cursor variable and host cursor variable involved in an assignment have incompatible types
STORAGE_ERROR	ORA-06500	Raised when PL/SQL runs out of memory or a memory corruption is found
SUBSCRIPT_BEYOND_COUNT	ORA-06533	An attempt was made to access a nested table or **VARRAY** element using an index number larger than the number of elements in the collection
SUBSCRIPT_OUTSIDE_LIMIT	ORA-06532	An attempt was made to access a nested table or **VARRAY** element using an index that is outside the legal range of values
TIMEOUT_ON_RESOURCE	ORA-00051	A timeout occurred while Oracle was waiting for a resource
TOO_MANY_ROWS	ORA-01422	A single row **SELECT** (implicit cursor) returned more than a single row
VALUE_ERROR	ORA-06502	This is raised when an arithmetic conversion, truncation, or size-constraint error occurred
ZERO_DIVIDE	ORA-01476	An attempt was made to divide by zero

Listing 13.2 Raise_application_error procedure.

```
EXCEPTION
  WHEN OTHERS THEN
      raise_application_error(-20002,'Error in analyze:
'||to_char(sqlcode)||' on '||tab_name,TRUE);
      IF dbms_sql.is_open(cur) THEN
        dbms_sql.close_cursor(cur);
      END IF;
END;
```

Listing 13.2 also shows the use of the raise_application_error procedure used to communicate a predefined exception interactively by returning a nonstandard error code and error message. With RAISE_APPLICATION_ERROR you can report errors to your application and avoid returning unhandled exceptions. The format for its use is:

```
>-- RAISE_APPLICATION_ERROR (error_number, text [TRUE|FALSE]);----
-->< 
```

The error_number is a value from -20000 to -20999; the text returned is surrounded by single quotes and can be up to 2048 bytes long. If the optional **TRUE** value is reported then the error is added to the existing error stack, if **FALSE** is returned (the default) it replaces the error stack with its error message and text.

The **RAISE_APPLICATION_ERROR** can be used in both the executable section and the exception section of a PL/SQL program.

User-Defined Exceptions

Using the first part of the syntax defined in Figure 13.1 a user can define a user defined exception. Once an exception has been declared, it can then be activated using the **RAISE** command with the exceptions name as the argument. Processing is then transferred to the exception handler section of the PL/SQL program where the user should have defined a **WHEN** clause to handle it. An example use of a user defined exception is shown in Listing 13.3.

Listing 13.3 Example user defined exception.

```
DECLARE
  e_invalid_access_code EXCEPTION;
BEGIN
  UPDATE access_list
    SET username = user
    WHERE access_code = &access_code;
IF SQL%NOTFOUND THEN
    RAISE e_invalid_access_code
```

```
END IF;
COMMIT;
EXCEPTION
  WHEN e_invalid_access_code THEN
    RAISE_APPLICATION_ERROR(-20001,'Invalid code entered, access
denied');
END;
```

In the example in Listing 13.3, the exception e_invalid_access_code is declared. Notice how the exception is started with an "e_"; this is a good naming convention to follow to allow quick recognition of exceptions in your PL/SQL code. If a user enters an invalid access code (one not found in the access_list table) then the exception is raised and the exception handler uses the RAISE_APPLICATION_ERROR procedure to report the exception back to the user environment. This method of exception handling, where the exception is not handled internally but is passed back out into the calling environment, is called propagation. How propagated errors should be handled is shown in Table 13.2.

It is a good practice to handle exceptions at the lowest possible level in the program; this means in the block where it is raised or in the nearest block where it is applicable to be handled. If an exception is not handled within the PL/SQL block where it is raised, it will be propagated out through the nested block structure until it is either handled by an exception handler or forces the program to exit with an unhandled exception error. If you get an unhandled exception, all non-committed data is rolled back. If propagation of unhandled exception occurs, you must have an **WHEN OTHERS** exception to handle the propagated exception. This **WHEN OTHERS** exception is required because scooping rules state that a specific exception must be handled in the block where it is raised. When an exception is handled in a block, control is given to the first executable statement after the blocks **END** statement.

Remember, if PL/SQL cannot find a handler for a raised exception, it returns an *unhandled exception* error to the host environment, which determines the

Table 13.2 Error propagation methods	
Environment	**Method**
SQL*Plus	Displays error number and message to screen
Procedure Builder	Displays error number and message to screen
Oracle Developer Forms	Uses a trigger to access the error code and text using ERROR_CODE and ERROR_TEXT packaged functions
Precompiler Application	Uses the SQLCA data structure to access the exception number
PL/SQL Block	Traps the exception in an exception handling routine

outcome. For example, in the Oracle Precompilers environment, any database changes made by a failed SQL statement or PL/SQL block are rolled back.

Unhandled exceptions can also affect subprograms. If you exit a subprogram successfully, PL/SQL assigns values to **OUT** parameters. However, if you exit with an unhandled exception, PL/SQL does not assign values to **OUT** parameters (unless they are **NOCOPY** parameters). If a subprogram in a stored procedure fails with an unhandled exception, subprogram database is not rolled.

You should avoid unhandled exceptions by coding an **WHEN OTHERS** handler at the top level of every stored PL/SQL program.

Practice Questions

Question 1

Which of the following is not a usual step in the processing of a user defined exception?

- ○ a. declare the exception
- ○ b. OPEN the exception
- ○ c. RAISE the exception
- ○ d. Use RAISE_APPLICATION_ERROR procedure to report the error codes.

The correct answer is b. You do not OPEN an exception. OPEN is only used with CURSORs. Answers a, c and d are all valis steps in processing a user defined exception.

Question 2

What is the purpose of the WHEN OTHERS exception handler?

- ○ a. Allows processing of user defined exceptions
- ○ b. Allows processing of unclosed cursors
- ○ c. Allows handling of non-specified exceptions
- ○ d. Forces an exception when users other than the calling user attempt access

The correct answer is c. The WHEN OTHERS exception is used to handle non-specified exceptions. Answer a is incorrect since user-defined exceptions are usually handled by a specific exception statement by the creator of the PL/SQL routine. Answer b is incorrect because unclosed cursors are automatically closed when control passes out of a PL/SQL block. Answer d is incorrect since there is no exception that handles this; user access is controlled by grants and privileges.

Question 3

Evaluate this program fragment:

```
DECLARE
   e_too_many_records  EXCEPTION;
   renter_rec          apt_renters%ROWTYPE;
   CURSOR get_renters IS
    SELECT * FROM apt_renters;
   cntr                NUMBER:
BEGIN
   cntr:=0
   FOR renter_rec IN get_renters LOOP
   cntr:=cntr+1;
    IF cntr>10 THEN RAISE e_too_many_records;
    DBMS_OUTPUT.PUT_LINE('Too many renters in
     '||renter_rec.apt_address);
    END IF;
   END LOOP;
EXCEPTION
WHEN e_too_many_renters THEN
   RAISE_APPLICATION_ERROR(-20010,'Too many renters
     in '||
       renter_rec.apt_address);
END;
```

What line will generate an error?

○ a. e_too_many_records EXCEPTION;

○ b. DBMS_OUTPUT.PUT_LINE(
     'Too many renters in 'llrenter_rec.apt_address);

○ c. Cntr:=cntr+1;

○ d. WHEN e_too_many_renters THEN

The correct answer is d. The exception name is e_too_many_records, not e_too_many_renters. The other lines are syntactically correct.

Question 4

What are the purposes of the SQLCODE and SQLERRM functions?

  ○ a. Load a user defined error code and text into an exception handler

  ○ b. Register the error codes and text with a user defined exception server

  ○ c. Retrieve the error code and error message for use in an exception handler

  ○ d. Invoke the SQLCoder interface to debug the program for a specific SQL error

The correct answer is c. The SQLCODE and SQLERRM functions retrieve the error code and error message for use in exception handling. Answer a is incorrect since this is the function of the RAISE_APPLICATION_ERROR package. Answer b is incorrect since there is no such thing as a user-defined exception server. Answer d is incorrect since there is no Oracle product called SQLCoder for debugging.

Question 5

How are exceptions activated in a PL/SQL program? (Choose all correct answers)

  ○ a. Only through explicit calls to RAISE_APPLICATION_ERROR

  ○ b. Only implicitly by Oracle as errors occur

  ○ c. An Oracle error occurs and an exception is implicitly activated

  ○ d. A programmer calls the RAISE command to explicitly activate a user defined exception

The correct answers are c and d. Exceptions can either be activated implicitly by Oracle as errors occur or implicitly in the case of user defined exceptions using the **RAISE** command. Answer a is incorrect since while you can raise an exception using the **RAISE_APPLICATION_ERROR** it is not the only way. Answer b is incorrect, since Oracle does raise implicit exceptions as errors happen, it is not the only method.

364 Chapter 13

Question 6

> Which of the following is not an exception type?
>
> ○ a. The Oracle id10t error exception
>
> ○ b. Predefined Oracle Server error exception
>
> ○ c. Non-predefined Oracle server error exception
>
> ○ d. User-defined error exception

The correct answer is a. There is no Oracle id10t ERROR EXCEPTION. The rest of the answers are proper types of exceptions.

Question 7

> What is the major difference between an Oracle defined exception and a user defined exception?
>
> ○ a. User defined exceptions are implicitly raised while Oracle defined exceptions are explicitly raised.
>
> ○ b. User defined exceptions are explicitly raised while Oracle defined exceptions are implicitly raised
>
> ○ c. User defined exceptions are always propagated to the user environment while Oracle defined exceptions are handled internally
>
> ○ d. Oracle defined exceptions are always propagated to the user environment while User defined exceptions must be handled internally.

The correct answer is b. A predefined exception is implicitly raised by Oracle while the programmer must raise a user defined exception. Answer a is incorrect since it states just the opposite of b. Answers c and d are incorrect since both types of exceptions can either be allowed to propagate out to the user environment or can be handled internally.

Question 8

What is the purpose of the Boolean TRUE value passed into the **RAISE_APPLICATION_ERROR** procedure?

- ○ a. This is the default, the error will displace all the errors in the stack
- ○ b. This tells the procedure that the error is a true error and must be handled implicitly
- ○ c. This places the error on the existing stack
- ○ d. You can't pass TRUE or FALSE to RAISE_APPLICATION_ERROR

The correct answer is c. Passing a TRUE places the error on the existing stack. Answer a is incorrect since this describes passing a FALSE. Answer b is just a fabrication. Answer d is incorrect since you can pass TRUE or FALSE to the RAISE_APPLICATION_ERROR procedure.

Question 9

Which statement is true about the **RAISE_APPLICATION_ERROR** procedure?

- ○ a. It must be used only in the PL/SQL execution area.
- ○ b. It can be used in the PL/SQL execution area and in the exception handling section.
- ○ c. It must be used in the exception handling section.
- ○ d. It must be used only with a exception that has been declared.

The correct response is b. The **RAISE_APPLICATION_ERROR** procedure can be called in both the executable and exception handling areas. Answer a is incorrect since it can be called in both. Answer c is incorrect since it can be called in both. Answer d is incorrect since you can call it with out a defined exception being raised.

Need To Know More?

Oracle Corporation. *Oracle8i Server SQL Reference Manual, Release 3(8.1.7)*. September, 2000, Redwood City, California. Part No. A85397-01. This is the source book for all Oracle SQL for version 8i. This book can be found on the Web, at the time of writing, at **http://technet.oracle.com**. This site has free membership and has all current versions of Oracle documentation available online in Acrobat format (PDF files).

PL/SQL Users Guide and Reference Release 8.1, Oracle Corporation, December 1999. Part No. A77069-01. This is the source book for PL/SQL. This book can be found on the Web, at the time of writing, at **http://technet.oracle.com**. This site has free membership and has all current versions of Oracle documentation available online in Acrobat format (PDF files).

Oracle Corporation. Oracle University, *Introduction to Oracle: SQL and PL/SQL, Student Guide Volume 2*, Redwood City, California, Part No. M08945. This is the manual that the test is derived from, what better place to get information?

Sample Test

Question 1

Which two characters require the **ESCAPE** option to be used as literals?

- ☑ a. _
- ○ b. $
- ○ c. /
- ☑ d. %

Question 2

You attempt to create a view with this command:

```
CREATE VIEW parts_view
AS SELECT id_number, description, sum(quantity)
FROM inventory
WHERE id_number = 1234
GROUP BY id_number;
```

Which clause causes an error?

- ○ a. **CREATE VIEW parts_view**
- ○ b. **AS SELECT id_number, description, sum(quantity)**
- ○ c. **FROM inventory**
- ○ d. **WHERE id_number = 1234**
- ☑ e. **GROUP BY id_number;**

Question 3

What is one of the purposes of a column constraint?

- ○ a. Enforce relationships between tables.
- ○ b. Ensure that a column value is numeric rather than character.
- ○ c. Enforce entity rules.
- ◉ d. Enforce business rules.

Question 4

Table 14.1 Instance chart for table INVENTORY.

Column Name:	ID_NUMBER	DESCRIPTION	MANUFACTURER_ID	QUANTITY	PRICE
Key Type:	PK		FK		
Nulls/ Unique:	NN, U	NN	NN		
FK Table:			MANUFACTURER		
FK Column:			ID_NUMBER		
Data Type:	NUM	VARCHAR2	VARCHAR2	NUM	NUM
Length:	9	26	25	9	8,2

Based on Table 14.1, evaluate this **UPDATE** statement:

```
UPDATE inventory
SET description = 'Sold Out'
WHERE id_number = 'A12345'
AND quantity = 0;
```

Which clause will cause an error?

- ○ a. **UPDATE inventory**
- ○ b. **SET description = 'Sold Out'**
- ○ c. **WHERE id_number = 'A12345'**
- ○ d. **AND quantity = 0;**
- ◉ e. None of the above

Question 5

The PL/SQL executable section contains which type of statements?

- ☑ a. PL/SQL and SQL statements to manipulate data in the database
- ○ b. The procedure or function name and input/output variable definitions
- ○ c. The definition of program variables, constants, exceptions, and cursors
- ○ d. Statements to deal with error handling

Question 6

What is the purpose of the **IN** operator?

- ○ a. Compare two similar values.
- ○ b. Perform an equality comparison.
- ○ c. Evaluate a range of values.
- ☑ d. Restrict results to a specified list of values.

Question 7

Evaluate this command:

```
ALTER TABLE customer
DISABLE CONSTRAINT pk_customer CASCADE;
```

Which task would this command accomplish?

- ○ a. Delete only the primary key values.
- ☑ b. Disable all dependent integrity constraints.
- ○ c. Disable only the primary key constraint.
- ○ d. Alter all dependent integrity constraint values.

Question 8

When can an index be placed on a view?

- ○ a. When you only **SELECT** from the view
- ○ b. When you only **DELETE** from the view
- ○ c. When there is a **WITH CHECK OPTION** used to create the view
- ✓ d. When you can **UPDATE** using the view
- ○ e. Never

Question 9

You query the database with this command:

```
SELECT manufacturer_desc
FROM manufacturer
WHERE manufacturer_id LIKE '%F\%B\%I\_%' ESCAPE '\'
/
```

For which character pattern will the **LIKE** operator be searching?

- ✓ a. **F%B%I_**
- ○ b. **FBI_**
- ○ c. **F\%B\%I%_**
- ○ d. **F\B\I_**

Question 10

In the executable section of a PL/SQL block, you include this statement:

```
Product.max_inventory1 := 30;
```

Which task will this accomplish?

- ○ a. A composite variable will be assigned a value.
- ○ b. A constant will be assigned a value.
- ○ c. An index identifier will be assigned a value.
- ✓ d. A field/column in a record will be assigned a value.

Question 11

Table 14.2	Instance chart for table INVENTORY.				
Column Name:	ID_NUMBER	DESCRIPTION	MANUFACTURER_ID	QUANTITY	PRICE
Key Type:	PK		FK		
Nulls/ Unique:	NN, U	NN	NN		
FK Table:			MANUFACTURER		
FK Column:			ID_NUMBER		
Data Type:	NUM	VARCHAR2	VARCHAR2	NUM	NUM
Length:	9	26	25	9	8,2

Using Table 14.2, evaluate the following query:

```
SELECT TO_CHAR(price, '$099999.99')
FROM inventory;
```

How is the price value 0.50 displayed?

○ a. .50

○ b. $.50

○ c. $000000.50

◉ d. $0.50

Question 12

Evaluate this function created with SQL*Plus:

```
CREATE OR REPLACE FUNCTION raise_price
    (start_value IN NUMBER)
RETURN number
IS
BEGIN
    RETURN (start_value * 1.75);
END lower_price;
```

Why will this function cause an error?

O a. A clause is missing.

◉ b. The **END** clause is incorrect.

O c. A keyword is missing.

O d. The parameter mode should not be specified.

O e. The **CREATE OR REPLACE** statement is invalid.

Question 13

What is the purpose of the **USER_** set of data dictionary views?

O a. List all objects that the user has owns.

O b. List all objects, of the specific type, that the user has been granted rights on.

O c. List all objects, of the specific type, in the database.

O d. List all dynamic data, of the specific type, about the database.

Question 14

You have entered a three-line command in the command buffer of a SQL*Plus session. You press the Enter key twice. At the SQL prompt, you enter the following command followed by a carriage return (the Enter key):

```
DEL
```

What is the state of the buffer?

- ☑ a. The buffer is cleared of all lines.
- ○ b. The buffer is holding the command **DEL**.
- ○ c. The buffer is holding the first two lines of the original text.
- ○ d. The buffer is holding the last two lines of the original text.

Question 15

Table 14.3   Contents of the INVENTORY table.

ID_NUMBER	DESCRIPTION	MANUFACTURER_ID	QUANTITY	PRICE	ORDER_DATE
36025	Spike 1 in	acme0525	234	2.45	12-May-97
36027	Nail 3/8	smith0626	134	0.25	15-Oct-97
36023	Chain	Jones0426	245	8.25	20-Jun-97
36028	Canvas	packy0122	1245	2.21	26-Oct-97
43081	Rubber Sheets	rubberrus0804	334	28.31	02-Feb-98

Using Table 14.3, evaluate this command:

```
SELECT id_number
FROM inventory
WHERE price IN (0.25, 2.21);
```

Which value would be displayed?

- ○ a. 36025
- ○ b. 36023
- ○ c. 43081
- ☑ d. 36028

Question 16

> When processing a **CURSOR** what step comes first?
>
> ○ a. **CLOSE**.
>
> ○ b. Definition.
>
> ○ c. Check for last row.
>
> ○ d. **FETCH**.
>
> ◉ e. **OPEN**.

Question 17

> Evaluate this statement:
>
> ```
> SELECT a.isotope, b.gamma_energy
> FROM chart_n a, g_energy b
> WHERE a.isotope ='IODINE'
> AND a.isotope = b.isotope
> AND a.mass_no='131'
> ```
>
> Which type of join is shown?
>
> ◉ a. Equijoin
>
> ○ b. Nonequijoin
>
> ○ c. Self-join
>
> ○ d. Outer join

Question 18

> Which is not a benefit of using a **CURSOR FOR LOOP**?
>
> ◉ a. It must be explicitly opened and closed.
>
> ○ b. It is implicitly opened and closed.
>
> ○ c. Fetches are automatic.
>
> ○ d. You don't need to do a last value check.

Question 19

When will a PL/SQL block not compile? [Choose two]

- ☐ a. When an implicit cursor retrieves only one row
- ☑ b. When an implicit cursor retrieves more than one row
- ☐ c. When the data types within a **SELECT** statement are inconsistent
- ☑ d. When an embedded **SELECT** statement is missing a required clause

Question 20

What is the purpose of the SQL*Plus command **GET**?

- ○ a. Get the contents of a previously saved operating system file into the buffer.
- ○ b. Get a printer assignment.
- ○ c. Get the contents of the buffer for editing.
- ○ d. Return a storage location for the buffer contents.

Question 21

What is the purpose of a referential integrity constraint?

- ○ a. Enforce business rules.
- ○ b. Ensure that entities are internally consistent.
- ○ c. Validate data entries of a specified type.
- ○ d. Enforce the rule that a child foreign key must have a valid parent primary key.

Question 22

> Which two operators cannot be used in an outer join condition? [Choose two]
>
> ☐ a. =
>
> ☑ b. **IN**
>
> ☐ c. **AND**
>
> ☑ d. **OR**

Question 23

> Which of the following is executed automatically?
>
> ○ a. Anonymous PL/SQL block
>
> ○ b. Function
>
> ○ c. Procedure
>
> ○ d. Trigger

Question 24

> What is the default length of a **CHAR** column?
>
> ○ a. 38
>
> ○ b. 255
>
> ○ c. 4000
>
> ○ d. 1

Question 25

> Which of the following activities would take place in the production phase of the system development cycle?
>
> ○ a. Interview users.
>
> ○ b. Develop ERDs.
>
> ○ c. Perform normal routine maintenance.
>
> ○ d. Code all program modules.
>
> ○ e. Test the system for user acceptance.

Question 26

Which of the following would contain the list of tables from which to retrieve data?

- ○ a. **SELECT** list
- ○ b. **ORDER BY** clause
- ○ c. **FROM** clause
- ○ d. **GROUP BY** clause

Question 27

What function would you use to convert a numeric value into a **VARCHAR2**?

- ○ a. **TO_CHAR**
- ○ b. **TO_NUM**
- ○ c. **TO_DATE**
- ○ d. **TO_VARCHAR**

Question 28

Which section of a PL/SQL routine contains functions for error trapping?

- ○ a. Declarative
- ○ b. Definition
- ○ c. Exception
- ○ d. Executable

Question 29

You query the database with this command:

```
SELECT
CONCAT(LOWER(SUBSTR(description,10)),
LENGTH(product_name)) "Product ID"
FROM inventory;
```

Which function is evaluated second?

○ a. **CONCAT()**

○ b. **LENGTH()**

○ c. **LOWER()**

Question 30

You query the database with this command:

```
SELECT
    isotope, group_id,mass_no,
    DISTINCT(atomic_weight)
FROM chart_n;
```

What values are displayed?

○ a. Distinct combinations of **isotope**, **group_id**, **mass_no**, and **atomic_weight**.

○ b. **isotope** and distinct combinations of **group_id**, **mass_no**, and **atomic_weight**.

○ c. **isotope**, **group_id**, **mass_no**, and distinct values of **atomic_weight**.

○ d. No values will be displayed because the statement will fail.

Question 31

For which of the following would you use the **ALTER TABLE...DROP** option? [Choose all that apply]

❑ a. Add a column to the table.

❑ b. Drop a table constraint.

❑ c. Drop a table column.

❑ d. Increase the precision of a numeric column.

Question 32

Evaluate this command:

```
SELECT group_id, isotope, AVG(atomic_weight)
FROM char_n
WHERE AVG(atomic_weight) > 89.00
GROUP BY group_id, isotope
ORDER BY AVG(atomic_weight);
```

Which clause will cause an error?

○ a. **SELECT group_id, isotope, AVG(atomic_weight)**

○ b. **WHERE AVG(atomic_weight) > 89.00**

○ c. **GROUP BY group_id, isotope**

○ d. **ORDER BY AVG(atomic_weight);**

Question 33

Which type of PL/SQL statement would you use to increase the price values by 10 percent for items with more than 2,000 in stock and by 20 percent for items with fewer than 500 in stock?

○ a. An **IF...THEN...ELSE** statement

○ b. A simple **INSERT** loop

○ c. A simple **UPDATE** statement

○ d. A **WHILE** loop

Question 34

You query the database with this command:

```
SELECT id_number, (quantity - 100 / 0.15 - 35 + 20)
FROM inventory;
```

Which expression is evaluated first?

○ a. **quantity - 100**

○ b. **0.15 - 35**

○ c. **35 + 20**

○ d. **100 / 0.15**

Question 35

Table 14.4 Table calibrations.			
Column Name:	INSTRUMENT_ID	EFFICIENCY	CAL_DATE
Key Type:	PK		
Nulls/Unique:	NN, U		
FK Table:			
FK Column:			
Data Type:	NUM	NUM	DATE
Length:			

In light of Table 14.4, you attempt to query the database with this command:

```
SELECT NVL(100/efficiency, 'none')
FROM calibrations;
```

What would you have to do to make the query function properly (assuming there are **NULL** values in the efficiency column)?

○ a. Nothing, it will function as is.

○ b. Replace the **NVL** function call with a properly structured **DECODE**.

○ c. Remove the **NVL** function.

○ d. Wrap the **NVL** call in a **TO_CHAR** function.

Question 36

What is the purpose of the PL/SQL **FETCH** command?

○ a. To define a cursor to be used later

○ b. To retrieve values from the active set into local variables

○ c. To call the rows identified by a cursor query into the active set

○ d. To release the memory used by the cursor

Question 37

Table 14.5   Contents of the INVENTORY table.

ID_NUMBER	DESCRIPTION	MANUFACTURER_ID	QUANTITY	PRICE	ORDER_DATE
36025	Spike 1 in	acme0525	234	2.45	12-May-99
36027	Nail 3/8	smith0626	134	0.25	15-Oct-99
36023	Chain	Jones0426	245	8.25	20-Jun-99
36028	Canvas	packy0122	1245	2.21	26-Oct-99
43081	Rubber Sheets	rubberrus0804	334	28.31	02-Feb-00

After reviewing Table 14.5, and assuming that the 'RR' value is the default date format, evaluate this command:

```
DELETE FROM inventory
WHERE
order_date>TO_DATE('11.30.1999',
                'MM.DD.YYYY');
```

Which of the listed **ID_NUMBER** values would be deleted?

○ a. 43081.

○ b. 36023.

○ c. 36027.

○ d. None would be deleted because the statement will fail.

Question 38

Which privilege can be granted only on a **DIRECTORY**?

○ a. **ALTER**

○ b. **DELETE**

○ c. **READ**

○ d. **INSERT**

Question 39

Evaluate this procedure:

```
CREATE OR REPLACE FUNCTION found_isotope
   (v_energy_line IN BOOLEAN,
    v_proper_ratio IN BOOLEAN)
RETURN NUMBER
IS
Ret_val NUMBER;
BEGIN
   IF (v_energy_line AND v_proper_ratio)
   THEN
        ret_val:=1;
   ELSIF NOT (v_energy_line AND v_proper_ratio)
   THEN
        ret_val:=2;
   ELSIF (v_energy_line AND v_proper_ratio) IS NULL
   THEN
        rct_val:=-1;
   END IF;
   RETURN ret_val;
END;
```

If **v_energy_line** equals **TRUE**, and **v_proper_ratio** equals **NULL**, which value is assigned to **ret_val**?

○ a. 1

○ b. 2

○ c. −1

○ d. None of the above

Question 40

In a **SELECT** statement, which character is used to pass in a value at runtime?

○ a. \

○ b. %

○ c. &

○ d. _ (underscore)

Question 41

Evaluate this command:

```
SELECT i.isotope, g.calibration
FROM chart_n i, gamma_calibrations g
WHERE i.energy = g.energy;
```

What type of join is the command?

○ a. Equijoin.

○ b. Nonequijoin.

○ c. Self-join.

○ d. The statement is not a join query.

Question 42

What is the purpose of the **SUBSTR** string function?

○ a. To insert a capital letter for each new word in the string

○ b. To return a specified substring from the string

○ c. To return the number of characters in the string

○ d. To substitute a non-null string for any null values returned

Question 43

What will the following operation return? [Choose two]

```
SELECT TO_DATE('01-jan-00') - TO_DATE('01-dec-99')
FROM dual;
```

❑ a. 31 if the **NLS_DATE_FORMAT** is set to 'DD-mon-RR'.

❑ b. A **VARCHAR2** value.

❑ c. An error; you can't do this with dates.

❑ d. −36494 if the **NLS_DATE_FORMAT** is set to 'dd-mon-yy'.

Question 44

You query the database with this command:

```
SELECT atomic_weight
FROM chart_n
WHERE (atomic_weight BETWEEN 1 AND 50
OR atomic_weight IN (25, 70, 95))
AND atomic_weight BETWEEN (25 AND 75)
```

Which of the following values could the statement retrieve?

○ a. 51

○ b. 95

○ c. 30

○ d. 75

Question 45

In the executable section of a PL/SQL block, you include these statements:

```
Isotope_record.isotope := 'XENON';
Isotope_record.group := 'NOBLE GAS';
```

Which task will be accomplished?

○ a. A record field will be assigned a character string value.

○ b. A record field will be created based on the **isotope** table.

○ c. A constant will be initialized.

○ d. A constant will be created.

Question 46

Which of the following best describes a relationship?

○ a. A thing of significance

○ b. A distinct characteristic of a thing of significance

○ c. A named association between two things of significance

○ d. A description of the way that data flows

Question 47

Which statement is true about the **TRUNCATE TABLE** command?

○ a. It disables constraints in the target table.

○ b. It removes the target table from the database.

○ c. It can reset the high-water mark for a table.

○ d. Data removed is recoverable via the **ROLLBACK** command.

Question 48

Which of the following is a use of the **TO_NUMBER** function?

○ a. Convert a **VARCHAR2** value into a **DATE** value.

○ b. Convert a **DATE** value into a **VARCHAR2** value using a specified format.

○ c. Convert a **VARCHAR2** value into a **NUMBER** value.

○ d. Convert a specified **VARCHAR2** value into a **CHAR** value.

Question 49

Evaluate this command:

```
CREATE TABLE purchase_items
    (id_number         NUMBER(9),
     description       VARCHAR2(25))
AS
SELECT id_number, description
FROM inventory
WHERE quantity < 10;
```

Why will this statement cause an error?

○ a. A clause is missing.

○ b. A keyword is missing.

○ c. The **WHERE** clause cannot be used when you're creating a table.

○ d. The data types in the new table must not be defined.

Question 50

What is a characteristic of only PL/SQL?

○ a. Accepts input of variables

○ b. Allows shutdown of the database

○ c. Allows use of exception-handling routines based on error numbers

○ d. None of the above

Question 51

Table 14.6   Contents of the INVENTORY table.

ID_NUMBER	DESCRIPTION	MANUFACTURER_ID	QUANTITY	PRICE	ORDER_DATE
36025	Spike 1 in	acme0525	234	2.45	12-May-97
36027	Nail 3/8	smith0626	134	0.25	15-Oct-97
36023	Chain	Jones0426	245	8.25	20-Jun-97
36028	Chain	packy0122	1245	2.21	26-Oct-97
43081	Rubber Sheets	rubberrus0804	334	28.31	02-Feb-98

Examine Table 14.6. Which value is displayed if you query the database
with the following command?

```
SELECT COUNT(DISTINCT(description))
FROM inventory;
```

○ a. 8.

○ b. 1.

○ c. 4.

○ d. **COUNT** returns an error if it is not run against a primary key.

Question 52

Evaluate this command:

```
CREATE FORCE VIEW isotope_groups
AS SELECT element, group_id, count(*) isotopes
FROM chart_n
WHERE atomic_weight>50
GROUP BY element,group_id
ORDER BY atomic_weight;
```

Which clause will cause an error?

○ a. **AS SELECT isotope, group_id**

○ b. **FROM chart_n**

○ c. **WHERE atomic_weight>50**

○ d. **ORDER BY atomic_weight;**

Question 53

You write a **SELECT** statement with two join conditions. What is the maximum number of tables you have joined together without generating a Cartesian product?

○ a. 0

○ b. 4

○ c. 2

○ d. 3

Question 54

Which of the following is a purpose of the user-defined constraint?

○ a. To enforce not-null restrictions

○ b. To enforce referential integrity

○ c. To enforce business rules

○ d. To take action based on insertions, updates, or deletions in the base table

Question 55

Which character can be used in a table name if the name is not placed inside double quotes?

○ a. %

○ b. *

○ c. #

○ d. @

Question 56

Which command would you use to remove all the rows from the **isotope** table and not allow rollback?

○ a. **DROP TABLE isotope;**

○ b. **DELETE isotope;**

○ c. **TRUNCATE TABLE isotope;**

○ d. There is no way to remove all rows and not allow rollback.

Question 57

Table 14.7   Instance chart for table INVENTORY.

Column Name:	ID_NUMBER	DESCRIPTION	MANUFACTURER_ID	QUANTITY	PRICE
Key Type:	PK		FK		
Nulls/ Unique:	NN, U	NN	NN		
FK Table:			MANUFACTURER		
FK Column:			ID_NUMBER		
Data Type:	NUM	VARCHAR2	VARCHAR2	NUM	NUM
Length:	9	26	25	9	8,2

Table 14.8   Contents of the INVENTORY table.

ID_ NUMBER	DESCRIPTION	MANUFACTURER_ID	QUANTITY	PRICE	ORDER_ DATE
36025	Spike 1 in	acme0525	234	2.45	12-May-97
36027	Nail 3/8	smith0626	134	0.25	15-Oct-97
36023	Chain	Jones0426	245	8.25	20-Jun-97
36028	Canvas	packy0122	1245	2.21	26-Oct-97
43081	Rubber Sheets	rubberrus0804	334	28.31	02-Feb-98

Use Tables 14.7 and 14.8 to evaluate this command:

```
INSERT INTO inventory (id_number,
                       manufacturer_id)
VALUES (56023,'beth104ss');
```

Which type of constraint will be violated?

○ a. Check

○ b. Not null

○ c. Primary key

○ d. Foreign key

Question 58

What is the advantage of using the **%TYPE** attribute to declare a PL/SQL type?

○ a. The name of an unused column in the underlying table may change.

○ b. The data types or data type sizes of the underlying table columns may change by runtime.

○ c. The **%TYPE** attribute forces the data type of the underlying database table column to be what you specify.

○ d. All column constraints are applied to the variables declared using **%TYPE**.

Question 59

Which statement would you use to query the database for the quantity and description of each item that was ordered before June 1, 1999 and whose price is less than 0.25 or greater than 10.00?

○ a.

```
SELECT quantity, description FROM inventory
    WHERE price BETWEEN 0.25 and 10.00 OR
    order_date < '01-jun-1999';
```

○ b.

```
SELECT quantity, description FROM inventory
    WHERE ( price < 0.25 OR price > 10.00) AND
    order_date<'01-jun-1999';
```

○ c.

```
SELECT quantity, description FROM inventory
    WHERE price < 0.25 OR
    price > 10.00 AND
    order_date > '01-jun-1999';
```

○ d.

```
SELECT quantity, description FROM inventory
    WHERE price IN (0.25, 10.00) OR
    order_date < '01-jun-1999';
```

Question 60

Evaluate this code fragment:

```
 1   DECLARE
...
 5     CURSOR get_bytes IS
 6       SELECT owner,segment_name,megbytes
 7       FROM tab_extent
WHERE owner ='SCOTT'
FOR UPDATE;
 9   BEGIN
10    OPEN get_bytes;
11     LOOP
12       FETCH get_bytes INTO
     owner,tab_name,total_bytes;
13       EXIT WHEN get_bytes%NOTFOUND;
14         TO_CHAR(total_bytes)||' bytes.');
15       UPDATE tab_extent
16        SET megbytes = megbytes/(1024*1024)
17        WHERE CURRENT OF cursor;
18         TO_CHAR(total_bytes/(1024*1024))||'
     megabytes.');
29     END LOOP;
20     CLOSE get_bytes;
21*  END;
```

Why will this code generate an error?

○ a. You can't **CLOSE** the cursor in this program because it will generate an error.

○ b. You don't need to explicitly **OPEN** the cursor because it has a **WHERE CURRENT OF** clause.

○ c. The **CURSOR** statement is missing a clause.

○ d. The **UPDATE** statement is incorrect in format.

Answer Key

1. a, d	21. d	41. a
2. e	22. b, d	42. b
3. b	23. d	43. a, d
4. c	24. d	44. c
5. a	25. c	45. a
6. d	26. c	46. c
7. b	27. a	47. c
8. e	28. c	48. c
9. a	29. c	49. d
10. d	30. d	50. c
11. c	31. b, c	51. c
12. b	32. b	52. d
13. a	33. a	53. d
14. c	34. d	54. c
15. d	35. a	55. c
16. b	36. b	56. c
17. a	37. a	57. b
18. a	38. c	58. b
19. c, d	39. b	59. b
20. a	40. c	60. d

Question 1

The correct answers are a and d. The underscore (_) is used as a single-character wildcard, and the percent sign (%) is used as a multicharacter wildcard; both must be escaped to be used as literals in a **LIKE** clause. The dollar sign ($), answer b, and the forward slash (/), answer c, can be used as literals, so they do not have to be escaped.

Question 2

The correct answer is e. The **GROUP BY** clause will cause an error because it doesn't include the **DESCRIPTION** column. All of the other lines are syntactically correct, so all the other answers are incorrect.

Question 3

The correct answer is b. Column constraints are used to ensure that a column is not NULL or that it fits into a range of values. Answer a is incorrect because referential constraints are used to ensure data integrity between tables. Answer c is incorrect because there is no such thing as an entity constraint (as far as I know) to enforce entity rules. Finally, answer d is incorrect because user-defined constraints are used to enforce business rules and have nothing to do with data validation rules.

Question 4

The correct answer is c. The **WHERE** clause will cause an error. After examining the exhibit, you should notice that the **ID_NUMBER** column is a **NUMBER** data-type column. Attempting to compare this with 'A12345' would result in an error because the letter "A" cannot be implicitly converted to a number. The other lines have the correct syntax, so answers a, b, and d are incorrect. Answer e ("none of the above") is incorrect because answer c is correct.

Question 5

The correct answer is a. This answer comes directly from the definition of the executable section. Answer b is the definition of the header section; the executable section never contains the definitions for variables, nor does it provide the name of the procedure. Answer c is incorrect because this is the function of the declarative section of a PL/SQL program. Answer d is incorrect because this is the definition of the exception section of a PL/SQL block and not the executable section.

Question 6

The correct answer is d. The **IN** operator is used to compare a value or expression to a list of values. Answer a is incorrect because the **LIKE** operator is used to compare a wildcard search value against a column or expression that contains or yields similar values. Answer b is incorrect because the equal sign (=) is used to show equality, as in an equijoin, not to check a list of values. Answer c is incorrect because **BETWEEN** is used to compare a value or expression to a range of values, not to a list of values.

Question 7

The correct answer is b. The command disables the primary key constraint and cascades this to disable all dependent constraints. Answer a is incorrect because no data is deleted by this statement. Answer c is incorrect because this command disables the primary key and all dependent constraints. Answer d is incorrect because, once again, no values are altered; only constraints are altered.

Question 8

The correct answer is e. You cannot index a view. Whether you **SELECT, DE-LETE,** or **UPDATE** a view, index creation is not allowed, even with a **WITH CHECK OPTION** clause.

Question 9

The correct answer is a. The backslashes are used to escape the percent signs and the underscore, thus allowing them to be treated as literals. Answer b is incorrect because it doesn't include the percent signs (%) that have been escaped. Answer c is incorrect because the backslashes (\) would be ignored. Answer d is incorrect because the backslashes would be ignored and the percent signs (%) would be shown instead.

Question 10

The correct answer is d. The format of the declaration shows that you're dealing with a record because dot notation indicates that a record type is being used. Answer a is incorrect because the statement does not contain a composite variable. Answer b is incorrect because nowhere do you see the keyword **CONSTANT** in the declaration. Answer c is incorrect because you are not dealing with an index identifier.

Question 11

The correct answer is c, $000000.50. The leading $ and zero in the format statement tell Oracle to format the number such that if the leading numbers before the decimal are all zero, show a zero for each format character to the left of the decimal. (Because there is no answer that says, "The query will fail," you don't really need an exhibit to answer this question. You can safely assume that the **PRICE** column is numeric.) Answer a is incorrect because no leading zero or dollar sign is displayed. Answer b is incorrect because no leading zeros to the left of the decimal are displayed. Answer d is incorrect because this answer would be generated by the format $0.99, not the one shown.

Question 12

The correct answer is b. The **END** clause specifies a function name of **lower_price**, but the **CREATE OR REPLACE** command specifies it to be **raise_price**. All the other lines are syntactically correct, so all the other answers are incorrect.

Question 13

The correct answer is a. The purpose of the **USER_** set of data dictionary views is to list all objects, of the specific type, that the user has created. Answer b is incorrect because this describes the **ALL_** views and not the **USER_** views. Answer c is incorrect because this describes the **DBA_** views. Answer d is incorrect because this describes the **V$** views.

Question 14

The correct answer is c. The buffer is holding the first three lines of the original text. Entering the **DEL** (delete) command in SQL*Plus removes the current line (in this case, the last line) from the buffer. Because you had three lines in the buffer, if you remove one, you have two left. Answer a is incorrect because you deleted only one line, not all lines. Answer b is incorrect because the editing commands and **DEL** are not placed in the buffer. Answer d is incorrect because you deleted only the current line, thus leaving the first two lines still in the buffer.

Question 15

The correct answer is d. The key to evaluating the **SELECT** statement is to look at the **IN** clause. The command will return a value only if the price is either 0.25 or 2.21. Records 36027 and 36028 both meet these criteria, but the only record listed is 36028 (answer d). None of the other answers has a price value that is in the list of values specified in the **IN** clause.

Question 16

The correct answer is b, definition. The first step in a cursors processing lifetime is when it is defined. The proper order for cursor processing is:

Definition

OPEN

FETCH

Check for last row

CLOSE

Question 17

The correct answer is a. An equijoin occurs when an equality condition is used to join a table to one or more other tables. Notice that two tables are joined using an equal condition, making this an equijoin. Answer b is incorrect because the statement is an equijoin, not a nonequijoin. Answer c is incorrect because the statement is an equijoin of two tables, not a self-join of one table to itself. Answer d is incorrect because the outer join symbol (+) has not been used.

Question 18

The correct answer is a. A CURSOR used in a CURSOR FOR LOOP is implicitly opened and closed so statement a is incorrect. All of the other answers are benefits of a cursor for loop so they are not the correct answer.

Question 19

The correct answers are c and d. An error in the **SELECT** statement format for a cursor will result in a syntax error, prohibiting the build of the PL/SQL block. Answer a is incorrect because retrieving only one row is the correct behavior for an implicit cursor; thus, it wouldn't raise an exception or prohibit a block from being built internally. Answer b is incorrect because returning multiple rows to an implicit cursor will raise an exception when the block is executed, but it won't cause a compilation error.

Question 20

The correct answer is a. The purpose of the SQL*Plus **GET** command is to get the contents of a previously saved operating system file into the buffer. Answer b is incorrect because getting a printer assignment is the purpose of the **SPOOL** command. Answer c is incorrect because getting the contents of the buffer for editing is the purpose of the **LIST** command. Answer d is incorrect because returning a storage location for the buffer contents is not a function of any SQL*Plus command.

Question 21

The correct answer is d. Answer d—enforce the rule that a child foreign key must have a valid parent primary key—is actually the definition of a referential integrity constraint. Answer a is incorrect because a user-defined constraint is used to enforce business rules. Answer b is incorrect because entity constraints don't exist. Answer c is incorrect because a column constraint is used to validate data entry.

Question 22

The correct answers are b and d. The **IN** operator and the **OR** operator cannot be used in an outer join. Answer a is incorrect because an equal sign (=) can be used in an outer join. Answer c is incorrect because an **AND** operator can also be used in an outer join.

Question 23

The correct answer is d. Triggers are associated with tables and are automatically fired on specified actions against the table. Answer a is incorrect because an anonymous PL/SQL block must be called into the command buffer and executed; it is not executed automatically. Answer b is incorrect because functions must be implicitly called by a user, procedure, trigger, or other function, so they are not executed automatically. Answer c is incorrect because a user, procedure, trigger, or other function must implicitly call procedures, so they are not executed automatically.

Question 24

The correct answer is d. The default length of a **CHAR** column is 1.

Question 25

The correct answer is c. In the production stage, only normal maintenance functions are performed. Answer a is incorrect because users are interviewed in the strategy and analysis phase. Answer b is incorrect because ERDs (entity relationship diagrams) are developed in the build and document phase. Answer d is incorrect because all program modules are coded in the build and document phase. Answer e is incorrect because testing the system for user acceptance is part of the transition phase.

Question 26

The correct answer is c. The **FROM** clause contains the list of tables from which to select data. Answer a is incorrect because a **SELECT** clause contains a list of items to retrieve from a table. Answer b is incorrect because an **ORDER BY** clause contains a list of columns or expressions used to determine sort order for the result set. Answer d is incorrect because the **GROUP BY** clause contains a specified column list to group the returned data.

Question 27

The correct answer is a. The **TO_CHAR** function is the only function used to convert a numeric data item into a **VARCHAR2** format. Answer b is incorrect because the **TO_NUM** function is used to convert a **VARCHAR2** into a **NUMBER**, not the other way around. Answer c is incorrect because **TO_DATE** is used to convert a **CHAR, VARCHAR2,** or **NUMBER** into a **DATE** value. Answer d is incorrect because **TO_VARCHAR** is not a valid Oracle8 function.

Question 28

The correct answer is c. The exception section is used specifically to trap errors. Answer a is incorrect because the declarative section of a PL/SQL routine is used to define variables, cursors, and exceptions. Answer b is incorrect because the definition section specifies the PL/SQL object type, its name, and the input and/or output variables. Answer d is incorrect because the executable section contains the procedural logic and performs the processing for the PL/SQL object; although it may **RAISE** exceptions, it doesn't process them.

Question 29

The correct answer is c. The **LOWER()** function is evaluated second. The statement inside the parentheses is evaluated first. In this case, we have nested parentheses, so the inner and then the outer parenthetical functions will be executed, in that order. Answer a is incorrect because **CONCAT()** is outside the parentheses. Answer b is incorrect because **LENGTH()** is also outside the parentheses.

Question 30

The correct answer is d. No values will be displayed because the statement is syntactically incorrect and will fail. A **DISTINCT** operator cannot be used in this manner. Answers a, b, and c are incorrect due to the **DISTINCT** operator's improper placement, which will cause the entire statement to fail.

Question 31

The correct answers are b and c. The **DROP** option of the **ALTER TABLE** command is used only when dropping a constraint or a column. Answer a is incorrect because adding a column to the table must be done with an **ADD** clause. Answer d is incorrect because increasing the precision of a numeric column is done with the **MODIFY** clause.

Question 32

The correct answer is b. You cannot use a grouping function such as **AVG** in a **WHERE** clause. The rest of the clauses are syntactically correct and thus are incorrect.

Question 33

The correct answer is a. In this question, you are asked to perform conditional tests and take action based on the results of the test. The only PL/SQL structure capable of this is the **IF...THEN...ELSE** statement. Answer b is incorrect because a simple **INSERT** loop wouldn't use a condition complex enough to handle the conditions specified. Answer c is incorrect because a simple **UPDATE** statement couldn't do a conditional update as specified. Answer d is incorrect because a **WHILE** loop wouldn't properly handle the update specified.

Question 34

The correct answer is d because multiplication (*) and division (/) are evaluated first in the hierarchy of operations. The other two operators shown (+ and -) are below division in the hierarchy of operations.

Question 35

The correct answer is a. The character string 'None' can be substituted for a NULL value using the NVL function, therefore nothing has to be done. Answer b is incorrect even though we could use a DECODE to check for the NULL value and then replace the NULL with the 'None' the question asks for what we have to do, which is nothing. Answer c is incorrect because we want the NULL to be replaced with a 'None' when it occurs. Answer d is incorrect because converting a NULL value in an expression to an actual value is the purpose of the NVL function.

Question 36

The correct answer is b. The FETCH command retrieves values returned by the cursor from the active set into the local variables. Answer a is incorrect because defining a cursor to be used later is the function of the CURSOR command. Answer c is incorrect because calling the rows identified by a cursor query into the active set is the function of the OPEN command. Answer d is incorrect because releasing memory used by the cursor is the function of the CLOSE command.

Question 37

The correct answer is a. Of the values available in the table, only 43081 is in the answer set, so it is the correct answer. Its order_date is the only one greater than 30 Nov. 1999. Answers b and c are incorrect because they don't meet the selection criteria. Answer d is incorrect because the value in answer a would be deleted.

Question 38

The correct answer is c. The only allowed grant on a DIRECTORY is READ. Answers a, b, and d are incorrect because these privileges cannot be granted on a DIRECTORY.

Question 39

The correct answer is b. A combination of **NULL** and **TRUE** or of **NULL** and **FALSE** will result in a **FALSE** (a value of 2 in our function); a combination of **TRUE** and **TRUE** will result in a **TRUE**; and a combination of **FALSE** and **FALSE** will result in a **FALSE**. A combination of **TRUE** and **FALSE** also results in a **FALSE**. Answer a is incorrect because both conditions would have to be **TRUE** for the result to be **TRUE** (corresponding to 1 in our function). Answer c is incorrect because both conditions would have to be **NULL** for the answer to be −1, which corresponds to a **NULL** value. Answer d is incorrect because answer b is correct.

Question 40

The correct answer is c. The ampersand character (&), either by itself or with a second ampersand, denotes substitution at runtime. Answer a is incorrect because the backslash (\) is used to escape the percent (%) and underscore (_) characters, unless something else is specified with the **ESCAPE** keyword. Answer b is incorrect because the percent sign (%) is the multicharacter wildcard. Answer d is incorrect because the underscore (_) is used as the single-character wildcard.

Question 41

The correct answer is a. Because the **SELECT** statement is using an equality test (using an equal sign), this is an equijoin operation. Answer b is incorrect because this is not a not-equal (!=, <>) type of join. Answer c is incorrect because a self-join is a table joined to itself, and this statement has two tables being joined. Answer d is incorrect because answer a is correct.

Question 42

The correct answer is b. The entire purpose of the **SUBSTR** function is to return a substring from a character value. Answer a is incorrect because inserting a capital letter for each new word in the string is the purpose of the **INITCAP** function. Answer c is incorrect because returning the number of characters in the string is the purpose of the **LENGTH** function. Answer d is incorrect because substituting a non-null string for any null values returned is the purpose of the **NVL** function.

Question 43

The correct answers are a and d. When two dates are subtracted, you receive a numeric value that corresponds to the number of days between the dates—either positive if the first date is greater than the second, or negative if the first date is less than the second. Depending on the value of the **NLS_DATE_ FORMAT**, the 00 will be either 1900 (default of dd-mon-yy) or 2000 (if set to dd-mon-rr), so both 31 and −36494 could result. Answer b is incorrect because date arithmetic returns a date or a number, not a **VARCHAR2** value. Answer c is incorrect because answers a and d are correct.

Question 44

The correct answer is c, 30. Answer a (51) is excluded by the **BETWEEN 1 AND 50 OR atomic_weight IN (25, 70, 95)** clause. Answer b (95) is excluded by the **AND atomic_weight BETWEEN (25 AND 75)** clause. Answer d (75) is excluded by the **atomic_weight (BETWEEN 1 AND 50) OR atomic_weight IN (25, 70, 95)** clause.

Question 45

The correct answer is a. A record field will be assigned a character string value. Answer b is incorrect because you aren't using a **%ROWTYPE**, which is used to create a record based on a complete table row. Answers c and d are incorrect because you aren't using the keyword **CONSTANT**.

Question 46

The correct answer is c. A relationship is a named association between two items of significance; this is the definition of a relationship. Answer a is incorrect because it describes an entity. Answer b is incorrect because it describes an attribute. Answer d is incorrect because it describes a data flow diagram.

Question 47

The correct answer is c. The **TRUNCATE TABLE** command can reset the highwater mark for a table if the **REUSE STORAGE** clause is not used. Answer a is incorrect because **TRUNCATE** doesn't disable constraints and can't be used with active constraints in place. Answer b is incorrect because **TRUNCATE** removes data, not tables. Answer d is incorrect because **TRUNCATE** is a DDL statement and can't be rolled back with a **ROLLBACK** command.

Question 48

The correct answer is c. Converting a **VARCHAR2** value into a **NUMBER** value is a use of the **TO_NUMBER** function. Answer a is incorrect because this describes the **TO_DATE** function. Answer b is incorrect because this describes the **TO_CHAR** function. Answer d is incorrect because this is an implicit conversion and doesn't require a function.

Question 49

The correct answer is d. The data types in the new table must not be defined. Answers a and b are incorrect because the statements outside of the column definitions are syntactically correct. Answer c is incorrect because a **WHERE** clause can be used in a **CREATE TABLE** subselect.

Question 50

The correct answer is c. Only PL/SQL allows the use of exception handling routines based on error numbers. Answer a is incorrect because SQL allows input of variables, but no exception processing based on error numbers. Answer b is incorrect because PL/SQL cannot be used to shut down the database. Answer d is incorrect because answer c is correct.

Question 51

The correct answer is c. Four rows in the table are returned by the query. Answer a is incorrect because there aren't eight rows in the table. Answer b is incorrect because there is more than one row in the table with a unique description. Answer d is incorrect because you can count on any column in a table.

Question 52

The correct answer is d because you cannot use **ORDER BY** in a view. Answers a, b, and c are incorrect because they are syntactically correct.

Question 53

The correct answer is d. You can determine the minimum number of joins based on the formula $n-1$, where n is the number of tables to be joined. Therefore, with two join conditions, the maximum number of tables that could be joined is three.

Answer a is incorrect because a zero-table join is not possible. Answer b is incorrect because a four-table join would require three join conditions. Answer c is incorrect because, although you could use two join conditions to join two tables, the question specifically asks for the maximum number that could be joined without causing a Cartesian product.

Question 54

The correct answer is c. User-defined constraints are used to enforce business rules. Answer a is incorrect because enforcing not-null restrictions is the purpose of a column constraint. Answer b is incorrect because enforcing referential integrity is the purpose of a referential integrity constraint. Answer d is incorrect because taking action based on insertions, updates, or deletions in the base table is the purpose of a trigger.

Question 55

The correct answer is c because the only character that can be used is the pound sign (#). Answer a is incorrect because the percent sign (%) is a restricted character used for multicharacter wildcards. Answer b is incorrect because the asterisk (*) is used to denote multiplication and thus is a reserved character. Answer d is incorrect because the at sign (@) is used as a special character in SQL*Plus and thus is a reserved character.

Question 56

The correct answer is c. The **TRUNCATE** command removes all of the rows from a table. Because it is a DDL command, it does implicit commits, thus not allowing rollback operations. Answer a is incorrect because the **DROP** command would remove the entire table. Answer b is incorrect because the **DE-LETE** command, which can delete rows, allows rollback because it is not a DDL command. Answer d is incorrect because answer b is correct.

Question 57

The correct answer is b. The not-null constraint will be violated. Notice that the **DESCRIPTION** column is missing from the **INSERT** statement. **DESCRIPTION** has a not-null constraint, so you must include it in any **INSERT** activity on the table. Answer a is incorrect because none of the table items show a **CHECK** constraint as being assigned. Answer c is incorrect because the primary key is being inserted. Answer d is incorrect because a value for the foreign key column

MANUFACTURER_ID is specified; also, because the exhibits don't show that the value exists in the **MANUFACTURER** table, you have to assume that it does.

Question 58

The correct answer is b. The **%TYPE** declaration allows flexibility in that it automatically allows an increase or decrease in the size columns in a table or allows changes in the size or data type of a column. Answer a is incorrect because you don't care about unused columns. Answer c is incorrect because nothing except an **ALTER TABLE** command will force a change in a table column. Answer d is incorrect because constraints are never applied to variables.

Question 59

The correct answer is b. Answer a is incorrect because this statement uses a **BETWEEN**, and thus doesn't check for inequality (greater or less than). Answer c is incorrect because after **order_date** it uses the greater-than operator (>) and not the less-than operator (<), as would be required to find a date before the specified value. Answer d is incorrect because it limits the values to only those that are 0.25 or 10.00, not a range of values.

Question 60

The correct answer is d. The UPDATE CLAUSE is incorrect in that the WHERE CURRENT OF references the CURSOR cursor instead of get_bytes. Answer a is incorrect since with an explicit CURSOR not in a FOR CURSOR LOOP you should CLOSE it as a good programming practice. Answer b is incorrect since the only time you don't have to OPEN an explicit CURSOR is when it is used in a CURSOR FOR LOOP. Answer c is incorrect since the CURSOR definition statement is complete.

Glossary

ACCEPT
A SQL*Plus command that enables a SQL program to prompt a user for a variable at runtime and accept an input.

ALTER
A DDL (Data Definition Language) command that is used to change database objects.

analysis
In the system development process, the step in which the users' needs are gathered and analyzed to produce documentation used to design a program system. (This step is usually paired with the strategy step.)

ANALYZE
A command used to gather statistics, or remove them, from an index, table, or cluster.

archive log
An archive copy of the redo log. The archive log is used to recover to an earlier point in time or to roll forward from a backup to the present time.

attribute
A detail concerning a thing of significance (entity). For example, a Person entity may have the attributes of name, address, and date of birth.

audit trail
In Oracle, a defined set of actions that are specified to be audited with system audit tools. For example, you can audit connections to the database.

BFILE
A new data type that is actually a pointer to an external binary file that uses a previously defined **DIRECTORY** entry.

BLOB
A new data type that is an internally stored binary large object. A **BLOB** can be stored inline with other data if it is smaller than 4,000 bytes. If a **BLOB** is larger than 4,000 bytes, it must be stored in a special **LOB**-storage data structure.

buffer

In Oracle, a memory area used to hold data, redo information, or rollback information. Usually, you specify the buffers by using the **DB_BLOCK_BUFFERS, DB_ BLOCK_SIZE,** and **LOG_ BUFFER** initialization parameters.

cache

A memory area that is self-managing and is used to hold information about objects, locks, and latches. The caches are usually contained in the shared pool area of the SGA (System Global Area). A cache's size is based on internal algorithms that control how the shared pool memory is allocated.

cardinality

A term used in relational analysis to show how two objects relate. For example, "A person may have zero or one nose" shows a cardinality of zero or one. "A person may have zero, one, or many children" shows a cardinality of zero to many. A "A person has one or many cells" shows a cardinality of one or many. In reference to indexes, cardinality shows how many rows in the indexed table relate back to the index value. A low cardinality index, such as a person's sex (M or F), should be placed in a bitmapped index if it must be indexed. A high cardinality value, such as a person's Social Security number or employee ID, should be placed in a standard B-tree index.

CHUNK

The unit of storage for a **LOB** data type when it is placed in a **LOB** storage area.

CLOB

A character large object data type. The **CLOB** has the same restrictions as does a **BLOB**. (See *BLOB*.) A **LOB** is limited to a maximum of 4GB or the size limit for your operating system files.

collection

A UDT (User-Defined Type) that is either a nested table or a **VARRAY**.

column

Part of a table's row. A column will have been mapped from an attribute in an entity. Columns have data types, and they may have constraints mapped against them.

COMMIT

A transaction control statement, a **COMMIT** marks a transaction as completed successfully and causes data to be written first to the redo logs and then, after the DBWR process writes, to the disk. A COM-MIT isn't complete until it receives word from the disk subsystem that the redo-log write is complete. Committed data cannot be rolled back with the **ROLLBACK** command but must be removed with other DML (Data Manipulation Language) commands.

CONNECT

A Server Manager (SVRMGRL), SQL*Worksheet, or SQL*Plus command that enables a user to connect to the local database or to a remote database.

control file

The Oracle file that contains information on all database files and maintains System Change Number (SCN) records for each file. The control file must be present and current for the database to start up properly. Control files may be mirrored; mirrored copies are automatically updated by Oracle as needed. The control file helps you maintain system concurrency and consistency by providing a means of synchronizing all database files.

conventional path load
The most-used form of the SQL*Loader database load. A conventional path load uses DML (Data Manipulation Language) statements to load data from flat operating system files into Oracle tables.

CREATE
A DDL (Data Definition Language) command used to create database objects.

CURSOR
An explicit named memory area or an implicit memory area used to contain the context of a SQL DML statement during processing.

DANGLING
In a child object table, a record whose parent record has been deleted is said to be **DANGLING**. You must use the **IS DANGLING** clause to handle dangling records.

data dictionary
A collection of C structs, tables, and views that contain all of the database metadata (information about the database's data). The data dictionary is used to store information used by

all database processes to find out about database data structures.

DCL (Data Control Language)
A classification of SQL commands used to specify grants and privileges in an Oracle database.

DDL (Data Definition Language)
A classification of SQL commands that are used to create or manipulate database structures. Examples are the **CREATE, ALTER,** and **DROP** commands.

DELETE
A DML (Data Manipulation Language) command used to remove data from the database tables by rows (generally speaking).

DESCRIBE
A SQL*Plus or Server Manager command that is used to retrieve information on the database structure. Packages, procedures, functions, and tables (including those in clusters) can be described.

DIRECTORY
An internal database object that acts as a pointer to an external operating system directory where **LOB** files are stored.

direct path load
In SQL*Loader, a direct path load disables all triggers, constraints, and indexes, and loads data directly into the table by building and then inserting database blocks. It does not use DML (Data Manipulation Language) commands. There are conventional path loads and direct path loads in SQL*Loader.

discarded record
A record that SQL*Loader rejects for loading; the rejection is based on internal rules for data validation and conversion.

DML (Data Manipulation Language)
A classification of SQL commands that are used to manipulate database structures. Examples are **INSERT, UPDATE, DELETE,** and **SELECT.**

DROP
A DDL (Data Definition Language) command used to remove database objects.

Dynamic SQL
SQL used to build SQL. Essentially, queries are issued against data dictionary tables using embedded literal strings to build a set of commands. Usually, dynamic SQL is used to automate a long series of virtually identical commands acting on similar types of database objects. An example would be creating a script that uses the **DBA_TRIGGERS** table and a single SQL statement to disable or enable all triggers for a set of database tables.

entity
In relational modeling, a thing of significance. Examples of entities are Person, Car, and Expense. Entities are singular in nature and are mapped to tables. Tables contain multiple instances of entities.

equijoin
A statement using equality comparisons to join two or more tables.

ERD (entity relationship diagram)
A pictorial representation—using a standard symbol set and methodology (such as Chen or Yourdon)—of a relational database.

explicit cursor
A cursor defined with the **CURSOR** command in a PL/SQL program. The user or programmer is responsible for controlling an explicit cursor via the **OPEN, FETCH,** and **CLOSE** commands.

extended ROWID
A new 10-byte format **ROWID** used in Oracle8.

external function
An externally stored function, usually written in C for Oracle8, contained in a shared library, such as a DLL (dynamic link library), and referenced through a PL/SQL call or an internally stored **LIBRARY** object.

external procedure
An externally stored procedure, usually written in C for Oracle8, contained in a shared library, such as a DLL (dynamic link library), and referenced through a PL/SQL call or an internally stored **LIBRARY** object.

foreign key
A value or set of values mapped from a primary or parent table into a dependent or child table and used to enforce referential integrity. A foreign key must either be **NULL** or exist as a primary or unique key in a parent table.

function

One of several structures, either an implicit function that is provided as a part of the SQL language or an explicit function is one that is created by the user using PL/SQL. A function must return a value and must be named. As part of the SQL standard, a function cannot change a database's or package's state but can act only on external variables and values.

GET

A SQL*Plus command that loads SQL or PL/SQL commands from an external operating system file into the SQL*Plus command buffer.

GLOBAL TEMPORARY TABLE

A physical table used as a temporary storage location. The table is built in the temporary tablespace of the owner and holds transient data. Data is either removed at then end of the users transaction or at the end of the users session.

implicit cursor

A cursor defined by the server process when a SQL DML statement is processed that is not defined into an explicit cursor. The server process controls the implicit cursor area.

index

A structure that enhances data retrieval by providing rapid access to frequently queried column values. Indexes can be either B-tree structured or bitmapped. The two general types of index are unique and nonunique. A unique index forces all values entered into its source column to be unique. A nonunique index allows for repetitive and null values to be entered into its source column. Generally speaking, a column with high cardinality should be indexed using a B-tree index (the standard, default type of index), whereas a column with low cardinality should be indexed using a bitmapped index. An index can be either for a single column or on multiple columns. A multiple-column index is known as a concatenated index.

index-by table

Also known as a PL/SQL table; a memory structure used to hold a scaler value or a variable structure (**RECORD**) array.

index-only table

An index-only table (IOT) stores all data in a B-tree format. The table itself is the index in an IOT. Data in an IOT can be stored either inline or in an offline storage table. Higher efficiency is achieved when all the table data can be stored inline in the IOT itself.

INITIAL

A storage parameter that sets the size of the **INITIAL** extent allocated to a table, index, rollback segment, or cluster. The size is set in bytes (no suffix), kilobytes (K suffix), or megabytes (M suffix).

INITRANS

A storage parameter that reserves space in the block header for the transaction records associated with a table's blocks.

INSERT

A DML (Data Manipulation Language) command that places new records into a table.

INSTEAD OF trigger

In Oracle8, a form of trigger is allowed, known as the INSTEAD OF trigger. An INSTEAD OF trigger is placed on a view instead of on a table; this trigger is used to tell Oracle what base tables to modify rather than have Oracle attempt to operate against the view.

LIBRARY

An internal PL/SQL structure that acts as a pointer to an external shared (DLL) library of C++ or Java routines.

Locally managed tablespace

A tablespace whose extents are managed via a bitmap contained in the tablespace itself rather than by the UET$ and FET$ data dictionary tables.

LOGGING

A keyword used to tell Oracle that actions taken against a table, cluster, object, or objects in a specified tablespace should be logged to redo logs to allow for recovery of those actions.

MAP method

A special type of UDT method used to map a set of type attributes into a single value to allow comparisons between TYPE values. To perform this mapping of TYPE values, you can use either a MAP or an ORDER method, but not both. An ORDER method must be called for every two objects being compared, whereas a MAP method is called once per object. In general, when you're sorting a set of objects, the number of times an ORDER method would be called is more than the number of times a MAP method would be called.

MAXEXTENTS

Sets the maximum number of extents an object can grow into. The MAXEXTENTS value can be altered up to a virtually unlimited value; however, the maximum number of extents allowed should still be based on block size to prevent chaining of the reference blocks.

MAXTRANS

A companion to the INITRANS storage parameter, MAXTRANS sets the maximum number of transactions that can access a block concurrently.

NCLOB

A national character LOB used for storing multibyte characters. Its size limit is the same as for other LOB datatypes—4GB or the maximum size allowed for your operating system, whichever is smaller.

nested table

A form of UDT (User-Defined Type) that must utilize a storage table to be used. A nested table allows an unrestricted number of rows, based on its base type, to be stored in a single row's column. (Actually, a pointer to the nested table is stored.) Along with VARRAY, a nested table forms objects known as collections.

NEXT

Storage parameter that specifies the size of the **NEXT** extent allocated to a table, index, rollback segment, or cluster. The size is set in bytes (no suffix), kilobytes (K suffix), or megabytes (M suffix). The **NEXT** parameter is used with the **PCTINCREASE** parameter to determine the size of all extents after the **INITIAL** and **NEXT** extents.

NOLOGGING

A keyword used to tell Oracle that actions taken against a table, cluster, object, or objects in a specified tablespace should not be logged to redo logs. Using this keyword prevents the recovery of those actions.

object auditing

The specification of auditing options that pertain to database objects rather than to database operations.

object identifier

In Oracle8 and Oracle8i, each object (table, cluster, and so on) has a 16-byte object identifier. This object identifier (OID) is guaranteed to be globally unique across all databases in your environment. It is a 16-byte, base-64 number that allows for a ridiculously high number of objects to be identified. (In the peta-region of countability—a petillion?—the maximum is 2**128.)

object view

A special form of view that is based on a type that exactly mirrors the structure of a base relational form table. An object view is used to provide object identifiers (OIDs) to

standard relational tables so that they can be used in **REF** type relationships with object tables.

Optimal Flexible Architecture (OFA)

A standard, developed by internal Oracle Corporation experts, that tells how to optimally configure an Oracle database.

ORAPWD

The Oracle Password Manager utility, which is used to create and maintain the external password file. The external password file is used to tell the Oracle Enterprise Manager (OEM) and Server Manager who is authorized to perform DBA functions against a specific database.

ORDER method

A special type of UDT (User-Defined Type) method used to map a set of type attributes into a single value to allow comparisons between **TYPE** values. To perform this mapping of **TYPE** values, you can use either a **MAP** or an **ORDER** method, but not both. An **ORDER** method must be called for every two objects being compared, whereas a **MAP** method is called once per object. In general, when you're sorting a set of objects, the number of times an **ORDER** method would be called is more than the number of times a **MAP** method would be called.

OSDBA

A role that is assigned to users who are authorized to create and maintain Oracle databases. If a user is given the **OSDBA** role, he is also given an entry in the external password file.

OSOPER

A role that is assigned to users who are authorized to maintain Oracle databases. If a user is given the OSOPER role, she is also given an entry in the external password file.

outer join

A type of join in which data not meeting the join criteria (that is, the join value is NULL) is also returned by the query. An outer join is signified by using the plus sign inside parentheses (+) to indicate the outer join column for the table deficient in data.

package

A stored PL/SQL construct made of related procedures, functions, exceptions, and other PL/SQL constructs. Packages are called into memory when any package object is referred to. Packages are created or dropped as a unit.

partition

A physical subdivision of a table or index into subsections based on a predefined range or ranges of a list of columns.

partition key

The list of columns used to partition a table.

PCTFREE

Used by Oracle to determine the amount of space reserved for future updates in an Oracle block to rows that already exist in the block. A PCTFREE value that's too low can result in row-migration for frequently updated tables; a value that's too high requires more storage space.

PCTINCREASE

After INITIAL and NEXT, determines the percentage that each subsequent extent grows over the previously allocated extent.

PCTUSED

Determines when a block is placed back on the free block list. When used space in a block drops below PCTUSED, the block can be used for subsequent new row insertion.

permanent tablespace

A tablespace that holds permanent data structures such as tables, indexes, and clusters. By default, all tablespaces are permanent unless they are created specifically as temporary tablespaces or are altered to be temporary tablespaces.

PGA (process global area)

Represents the memory area allocated to each process that accesses an Oracle database.

PL/SQL table

(see index-by table)

primary key

In a relational database, the unique identifier for a table. A primary key must be unique and not null. A primary key can be either natural (derived from a column or columns in the database) or artificial (drawn from a sequence).

privilege auditing

Auditing of what privileges are granted, by whom they're granted, and to whom they're granted.

procedures

Stored PL/SQL objects that may, but aren't required to, return a value. Procedures are allowed to change database or package states. Procedures can be placed into packages.

production

The final stage of the system development cycle. The production stage consists of normal maintenance and of backup and recovery operations in a developed system.

profiles

Sets of resource allocations that can be assigned to a user. These resources are used to limit idle time, connect time, memory, and CPU usage.

PROMPT

A SQL*Plus command used to pass a string out of a SQL script to the executing user. The **PROMPT** command can be used with the **ACCEPT** command to prompt for values needed by the script.

RECORD

A user named memory area used to hold multiple variable values inside the PL/SQL memory area during execution of a PL/SQL program.

RECOVER

A command used in Server Manager to explicitly perform database recovery operations.

REF

Short for **REFERENCE**. A pointer from a child object to a parent object; this pointer usually consists of the parent object's OID.

referential integrity

The process by which a relational database maintains record relationships between parent and child tables via primary key and foreign key values.

rejected records

In SQL*Loader, records that don't meet load criteria for the table being loaded; rejections occur due to value, data type, or other restrictions.

relationship

A named association between two things of significance. For example, if a wheeled vehicle has one or many wheels, *has* is the relationship. If an employee works for one or more employer, *works for* is the relationship.

resources

The database and system resources that are controlled by the use of profiles.

reverse key index

An index in which incoming key values have their bytes reversed in order. This reversal of bytes forces a random distribution of the key values throughout the index, preventing hot-blocks from being formed. A reverse key index can be used only for single-row lookups or full-index scans. A reverse key index cannot be used in an index range scan.

ROLLBACK

A DML (Data Manipulation Language) command used to undo database changes that have not been committed.

rollback segment

A database object that contains records used to undo database transactions. Whenever a parameter in the database refers to **UNDO**, it is actually referring to rollback segments.

SAVE

A SQL*Plus command used to store command-buffer contents in an external operating system file.

SCOPED REF

A **REF** whose range of values is limited to the OIDs contained in the defined **SCOPE** object table.

SELECT

A DML (Data Manipulation Language) command used to retrieve values from the database.

SELF

A keyword used to tell Oracle that you are referring to the current value of a UDT (User-Defined Type). Known as selfish nomenclature. All TYPEs are self-aware.

Server Manager line mode

Server Manager has a GUI mode and a line mode. In line mode, all commands are entered at the command line.

SET

A SQL*Plus command used to change the values of SQL*Plus environment parameters such as line width and page length.

SGA (system global area)

Consists of the database buffers, shared pool, and queue areas that are globally accessible by all database processes. The SGA is used to speed Oracle processing by caching data and structure information in memory.

SHOW

A SQL*Plus command used to show the value of a variable that's set with the **SET** command.

SHUTDOWN

A Server Manager command used to shut down the database. **SHUTDOWN** has three modes: **NORMAL, IMMEDIATE,** and **ABORT. NORMAL** prohibits new connections, waits for all users to log off, and then shuts down. **IMMEDIATE** prohibits new connections, backs out uncommitted transactions, and then logs users off and shuts down. **ABORT** shuts down right now and not gracefully.

SPOOL

A SQL*Plus command used to send SQL*Plus output to either a printer or a file.

SQL buffer

A memory area used to store the last SQL command. The SQL buffer can store only the last command executed, unless the buffer is loaded with the **GET** command. A SQL*Plus command such as **SET, DESCRIBE,** or **SPOOL** is not placed in the SQL buffer.

STARTUP

A Server Manager command used to start up the database. A database can be started in one of several modes: **MOUNT, NOMOUNT, OPEN, EXCLUSIVE,** or **PARALLEL.**

statement auditing
Audits statement actions such as
INSERT, **UPDATE**, and **DELETE**.

STORAGE
A clause that Oracle uses to determine current and future settings for an object's extents. If a **STORAGE** clause isn't specified, the object's storage characteristics are taken from the tablespace's default storage clause.

strategy
In the system development cycle, the step in which the overall methodology for the rest of the development effort is mapped out. (This step is usually paired with the analysis step.)

SYSDBA
See *OSDBA*.

SYSOPER
See *OSOPER*.

table
The structure used to store data in an Oracle database. Entities map to tables in relational databases.

tablespace
The unit of logical storage in Oracle. All tables, clusters, and indexes are stored in tablespaces. Tablespaces are composed of physical data files.

temporary tablespace
This type of tablespace is not allowed to contain any permanent structures, such as tables, clusters, or indexes; instead, it holds temporary segments only.

transition
In the system development cycle, the step in which users test the applica-

tion, and support of the application moves from development to production personnel.

TRUNCATE
A DDL (Data Definition Language) command used to remove all rows from a table. Because it is a DDL command, it cannot be rolled back.

TRUNCATE (functions)
There are both string and date functions called **TRUNCATE**; both are used to shorten the external representations of internal data.

TYPE
May be referred to as a User-Defined Type (UDT). This is a user-defined internal storage structure that may include data types, other UDTs, and methods that act upon the specified attributes and types.

UDT (user-defined type)
See *TYPE*.

UGA (user global area)
Used to store user-specific variables and stacks. Only applicable if Oracle is running in multi-threaded server (MTS), otherwise it is part of the SGA.

UID (unique identifier)
Uniquely identifies a row in a table and usually maps to the natural primary key value. Each entity must have a unique identifier to qualify as an entry in a relational table.

UPDATE
A DML (Data Manipulation Language) command that allows data inside tables to be changed.

variable

A user-defined or process-defined storage area used to hold a value that will probably be different each time a script or procedure is executed.

VARRAY

A form of UDT (User-Defined Type) used to store multiple occurrences of the base type inline with the other data in a row. A **VARRAY** is used when the number of occurrences is small, and you know it won't exceed a specified maximum value. Along with nested tables, **VARRAY** makes up the collections type of objects in Oracle8.

view

A preset **SELECT** statement used against one or more tables. The view is stored in the database and has no physical representation. A view is also known as a virtual table.

virtual table

See *view*.

Index